The Macmillans

Also by Richard Davenport-Hines

Dudley Docker
Sex, Death and Punishment

The Macmillans

RICHARD DAVENPORT-HINES

HEINEMANN : LONDON

For
Jonathan Smith

William Heinemann Ltd
Michelin House, 81 Fulham Road, London SW3 6RB
LONDON   MELBOURNE   AUCKLAND

First published 1992
Copyright © Richard Davenport-Hines 1992

A CIP catalogue record for this book
is held by the British Library
ISBN 0 434 17502 1

Typeset by Hewer Text Composition Services, Edinburgh

Printed in Great Britain
by Mackays of Chatham PLC,
Chatham, Kent

Contents

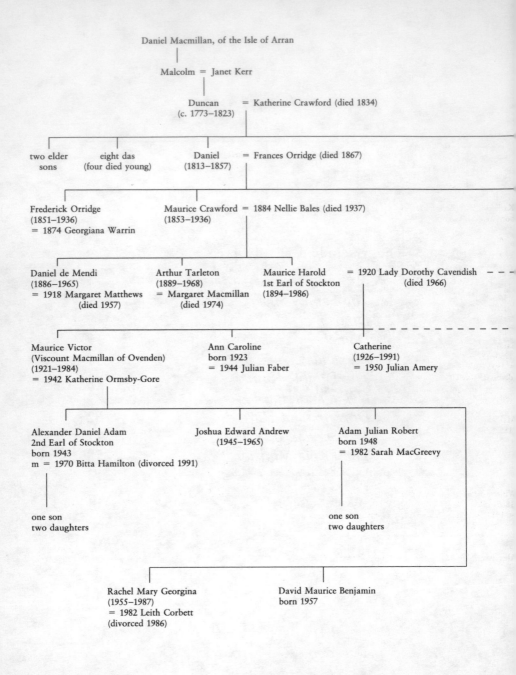

Daniel Macmillan, of the Isle of Arran

Malcolm = Janet Kerr

Duncan = Katherine Crawford (died 1834)
(c. 1773–1823)

two elder sons — eight das (four died young) — Daniel (1813–1857) = Frances Orridge (died 1867)

Frederick Orridge (1851–1936) = 1874 Georgiana Warrin — Maurice Crawford (1853–1936) = 1884 Nellie Bales (died 1937)

Daniel de Mendi (1886–1965) = 1918 Margaret Matthews (died 1957)

Arthur Tarleton (1889–1968) = Margaret Macmillan (died 1974)

Maurice Harold 1st Earl of Stockton (1894–1986) = 1920 Lady Dorothy Cavendish (died 1966)

Maurice Victor (Viscount Macmillan of Ovenden) (1921–1984) = 1942 Katherine Ormsby-Gore

Ann Caroline born 1923 = 1944 Julian Faber

Catherine (1926–1991) = 1950 Julian Amery

Alexander Daniel Adam 2nd Earl of Stockton born 1943 m = 1970 Bitta Hamilton (divorced 1991)

Joshua Edward Andrew (1945–1965)

Adam Julian Robert born 1948 = 1982 Sarah MacGreevy

one son two daughters

one son two daughters

Rachel Mary Georgina (1955–1987) = 1982 Leith Corbett (divorced 1986)

David Maurice Benjamin born 1957

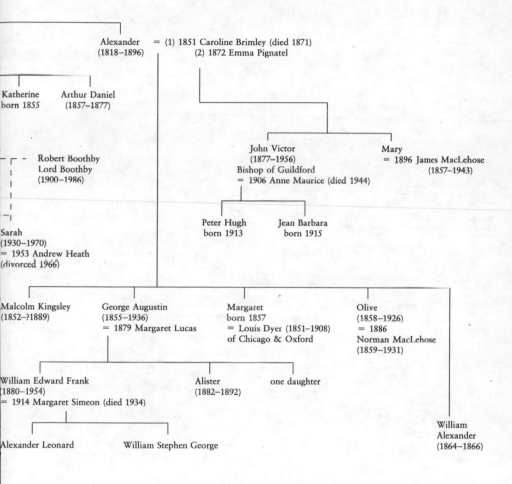

Alexander   = (1) 1851 Caroline Brimley (died 1871)
(1818–1896)   (2) 1872 Emma Pignatel

Katherine   Arthur Daniel
born 1855   (1857–1877)

Robert Boothby   John Victor   Mary
Lord Boothby   (1877–1956)   = 1896 James MacLehose
(1900–1986)   Bishop of Guildford   (1857–1943)
                  = 1906 Anne Maurice (died 1944)

Sarah   Peter Hugh   Jean Barbara
(1930–1970)   born 1913   born 1915
= 1953 Andrew Heath
(divorced 1966)

Malcolm Kingsley   George Augustin   Margaret   Olive
(1852–?1889)   (1855–1936)   born 1857   (1858–1926)
               = 1879 Margaret Lucas   = Louis Dyer (1851–1908)   =1886
                                 of Chicago & Oxford   Norman MacLehose
                                                      (1859–1931)

William Edward Frank   Alister   one daughter
(1880–1954)   (1882–1892)
= 1914 Margaret Simeon (died 1934)

                                                    William
                                                    Alexander
Alexander Leonard   William Stephen George   (1864–1866)

Preface

This is not an authorised family history. Shortly after it was commissioned by Heinemann, I wrote to the head of the Macmillan family, Alexander Stockton, telling him about the project and asking for his help. After an interval he replied discouraging the idea and added that he had seen my last book, which had looked at historical attitudes to homosexuality and venereal disease, and that he would not relish similar treatment himself. I did not trouble the family again until the book was nearing completion, when I wrote to several of its members asking for interviews. None of them replied immediately, though after an interval I received a letter from one of Harold and Dorothy Macmillan's granddaughters: she declined to meet me with a stylishness worthy of her grandfather. I also sent Lord Stockton a copy of most of the completed manuscript, and received a short letter dictated by him and signed by his secretary making his antagonism to the book remarkably clear.

I have had access to many family papers which were sold to the British Library, but have not been able to consult archives which remain under the control of the family. As a matter of copyright law it was necessary for me to obtain permission to quote from all previously unpublished family correspondence, even if it was freely available in public archives. My letters to Alexander Stockton seeking such permission elicited no reply from him, and in the autumn of 1991 under legal advice I therefore removed direct quotations from unpublished

Macmillan letters (dating as far back as the 1840s). The chief casualties were quotations from the large Macmillan archives at the British Library, but readers are also deprived of some direct quotations from the political papers of Baldwin, Butler, Eden, Gladstone and Kilmuir, from ecclesiastical papers at Lambeth Palace Library and even a Foreign Office file at the Public Record Office. This mutilation of the book although disappointing is not extensive.

The publishing house of Macmillan gave permission for brief quotations from Harold Macmillan's autobiography and war diaries, and from Alistair Horne's biography of him; but the effect of a letter which I received in December 1991 from solicitors representing the Macmillan family and the trustees of the Macmillan Trusts was to cancel this permission. I was told in this lawyer's letter that permission was withheld for the publication by me of any material, published or otherwise, where the copyright was owned by members of the Macmillan family, their estates or trustees. The scarcity in my text of direct quotations from Harold Macmillan's books reflects this interdiction: nevertheless a few quotes, such as those in Crown Copyright, survive. The Macmillans' lawyer's letter has also obliged me to remove other items, such as extracts from letters to Quentin Crewe, printed in his memoirs, which I had been given permission to use by his literary representatives.

Despite these difficulties I have had the benefit of permission to quote briefly from the following books published by Macmillan: Lovat Dickson's *The House of Words*; Leon Edel's *Letters of Henry James*, volumes 2 and 3; Sir Rupert Hart-Davis's *Sir Hugh Walpole*; Charles Morgan's *The House of Macmillan*; Simon Nowell-Smith's *Letters to Macmillan*; and Lord Skidelsky's *John Maynard Keynes*. Similarly I have been able to quote briefly from two Sidgwick & Jackson books: Lord Boyd-Carpenter's *Way of Life* and Cecil King's *With Malice Toward None*.

The passages of this book which refer to the political career of Harold Macmillan are not written in the manner of conventional political biography, and are not meant to be read as such. Those who want an authoritative narrative chronology of his life should refer to the two volumes of official biography written by Alistair Horne. No British prime minister had been so literary minded since Disraeli, and I have written about him with the techniques more often used by literary biographers. I have looked in detail at the formative influences of his life and at those moments of stress in which he showed his true character, but I have made no effort at comprehensive coverage of all his public life. Alexander Stockton, in a letter to me, condemned these techniques as psycho-history – a mistaken epithet, I think, for there is little if any jargon in the book and no psychoanalytical propaganda.

The idea for this book was conceived by Kate Jones, with whom I shared an office when we were both employed by the publishing house of Macmillan in the late 1980s. My job (once John Morley's job, as I liked to remember) was to read and report on manuscripts submitted for publication in Macmillan's general list. It was enthralling work, with moments of hilarity (reading the memoirs of a male nurse entitled *Oops, I dropped the lamp*), absurdity (as when one editor brought back from the Frankfurt book fair the memoirs of an elderly Israeli woman who ran a sphincter gymnasium) and skulduggery (detecting the forged memoirs of a Byzantine princess). My editor at Heinemann, Tom Weldon, who has been marvellous in his encouragement, introductions and advice, was one of many friends made during my working days at Little Essex Street.

My wife read an early draft of this book, offered many robustly sensible comments, persuaded me to eliminate several tasteless or misanthropic passages and with her usual generosity subsidised my life during the two years in which the book was in preparation.

It is a pleasure to acknowledge the help of the staff of the incomparable London Library, particularly that of the deputy librarian, Michael Higgins, who has done much to benefit my work during the preparation of this book. I must also thank

John Grigg, its former chairman. Though Mr Grigg is absolved from responsibility for the interpretations in this book, its later chapters are profoundly influenced by his matchless political commentaries over the last thirty-five years; I am also indebted to him for a fruitful discussion of Harold Macmillan's political career, and for providing me with notes of his own. My friend Christopher Phipps has given me innumerable references, teased me until I abandoned my more meretricious ideas and was generous in offering ideas of his own.

I have decided not to give a list of those whom I have interviewed during the research of this book. Several of those people who have given me the most valuable help did so on the basis of non-attribution. Others to whom I have spoken may be pained by what I have written, and will find no pleasure in seeing their help acknowledged.

Quotations from the Avon papers deposited at Birmingham University Library are by kind permission of the Avon trustees; for use of the Butler papers I am grateful to the Master and Fellows of Trinity College, Cambridge. For permission to quote from copyright material I am also grateful to Mrs Susan Crosland; the Earl of Derby; Maureen, Marchioness of Dufferin and Ava; Times Newspapers Ltd; and the Earl of Woolton.

Quotations from R.F.V. Heuston's *Lives of the Lord Chancellors 1940–1970* (1987) and from Cecil Lang and Edgar Shannon's *Letters of Alfred, Lord Tennyson*, volume 2 (1987) are by permission of Oxford University Press. I thank Weidenfeld & Nicolson as publishers, and Sir Robert Rhodes James, Keith Kyle, Sir Evelyn Shuckbrugh and Mark Amory as authors or editors, for permission to quote from *Anthony Eden, Suez, Descent to Suez* and *The Letters of Evelyn Waugh*. Similarly I thank Hutchinson for permission to quote from Sir George Mallaby's *From My Level* and from Lord Swinton's *Sixty Years of Power*. I am grateful to Hodder and Stoughton and Sir Robert Rhodes James for permission to quote from *Bob Boothby*. I thank the Random Century Group for permission to quote from *Caves of Ice* and *Ancestral Voices*, both by James Lees-Milne and published by Chatto & Windus. David Higham Associates have permitted me to quote from James Lees-Milne's *Midway on the Waves* (Faber) and Aitken & Stone have permitted me to quote from Quentin Crewe's *Well, I Forget the Rest* (Hutchinson). I apologise if I have inadvertently infringed the rights of any other copyright owner.

Kensington
December 1991

CHAPTER 1

The Family Silver

The old age of certain old men is
like the childhood of immortality

Goncourt journal, 12 June 1861

On 13 November 1984 a decrepit man of ninety rose to make
his maiden speech in the House of Lords: his audience was
spell-bound, although all the odds were against it. He tottered
by his bench, for it was hard for him to stand for long without
the support of his stick; his voice was piping, and quavered
with age; he had to speak from memory, for he was too close
to blindness to read notes. Yet he spoke for over half an hour
and captivated the House. The chamber was crowded, peers
craned forward to catch his words, and when he sat down
he was greeted by something near to a spontaneous ovation.
What was more startling, the content as well as the manner
of his speech reverberated through the country. Among the
chattering classes they talked of little else.

The speaker was the newly created Earl of Stockton. Sixty
years had passed since his maiden speech in the House of
Commons. Then he had been a spry young man called Captain
Harold Macmillan, disenchanted by the policies of the Conservative government which he had been elected to support.
Increasingly, as he recalled to the Lords, he had been regarded
with 'distaste and even dislike by the leaders of my party',
creating an awkwardness with which he was able to deal only
by eventually 'becoming the leader of the party myself'. The

style of his speech was consummate: much of it comprised a meticulous survey of the dilemmas of British economic policy in the 1920s, replete with tantalising reminiscence, impish analogies between economists and nursery maids, mischievous asides and well-timed flourishes. But what of the content? Was there sincerity behind the rhetoric? Some moments stood out, as when he rehearsed the prescriptive differences between neo-Keynesian expansionists and their monetarist opponents. The latter, who were favoured by the current Prime Minister, Margaret Thatcher, were, he said dismissively, 'new economists that have come into being – and nobody knows where they come from; they say that some come from America, and some from Tibet'. But to find his preferred economic strategy, he said,

> let us look somewhere else – at the country of my dear mother, the United States. Ah, that is a very different thing. I rejoice at what Reagan is doing. He has broken all the rules, and all the economists are furious. He has a completely unbalanced budget. . . . But what has happened? . . . Five million new jobs . . . it is a miracle.

For his peroration he turned to the coalmining strike which was raging in Britain, sundering communities with unprecedented viciousness: an industrial dispute so bitter that Margaret Thatcher likened the miners to traitors: 'the enemy within'. 'Although at my age I cannot interfere or do anything about it, it breaks my heart to see what is happening in our country today,' Stockton lamented.

> A terrible strike is being carried on by the best men in the world. They beat the Kaiser's army and they beat Hitler's army. They never gave in. The strike is pointless and endless. . . . I can only describe as wicked the hatred that has been introduced and which is to be found among different types of people. . . . If some of the dreadful, wicked systems which have crept into our lives are replaced, if we abandon cynicism, criticism and hatred for each other, and if we take up the great theme which St Paul gave to us . . . then I foresee the young men and women from every home in England setting out

with confidence on a new phase along the long road which
we call Man's pilgrimage here on earth.

This was his most decisive intervention in the House of
Lords, but he spoke several times again. He was for example
roused to speak against a bill to extend Sunday shop-trading.
'We are sacrificing a very old tradition,' he warned. 'We are
making another move in the gradual secularisation of our
people and in abandoning the old principles which made our
forebears great and kept them powerful.' He complained that
the Conservatives were no longer inspired by the principles of
Shaftesbury, Disraeli and Churchill, that 'all the worst elements'
of Victorian laisser-faire liberalism had 'infiltrated my old party
like some kind of disease'. He thought it was 'a great error' to
abandon 'the paternalist elements and traditions of the Tory
Party': it was because the British people 'trusted those whom
they regarded as their natural leaders to help them, support them
and protect them that we have had the great authority in the past
in our country'. He feared too that small shopkeepers would
take selfish advantage of any relaxation in Sunday trading laws.
'They will be just the kind of people who will try to exploit
the weak and often transient population who are the kind of
people likely to become shop assistants.' The situation would be
especially parlous 'north of the Trent', where under conditions
of high unemployment people 'are more easily exploited'.

In private he was sometimes harsher about Thatcherism.
'That woman is not just going to ruin the country, she's going
to ruin us,' he was quoted by Lord Annan as saying. On
other occasions he privately described Thatcher as 'a brilliant
tyrant surrounded by mediocrities', and criticised the Tory
grandees in her earlier Cabinets for permitting 'a great national
party to become reduced to a suburban rump'. The party had
been hijacked from landowners and handed over to estate
agents: passing from the Etonians to the Estonians, he would
say, in a jibe at the East European roots of Thatcherites like
Nigel Lawson and Leon Brittan. The reception of his public
performances varied. Some were moved by the effort which

the old man in his frailty put in to them. Some gloried in the resurgence of patrician Conservatism which his speeches seemed to promise. Margaret Thatcher's father had been just the sort of hard, grasping shopkeeper whom Stockton warned would exploit Sunday trading with contempt for his employees. Asked by a Macmillan publishing editor at the time of Thatcher's second general election victory in 1983 for his assessment of her as Prime Minister, he thought for a moment, then muttered with withering scorn, 'So common'. His speeches appealed to the snobbish instincts of his party and to the pretensions of those people who would like to have been brought up in a household with a nursery. His mellow style and aristocratic pantomime evoked for some memories of a mellower time, when governments emphasised continuities and unity rather than confrontation.

Many observers were dismissive of the old man's stunts. 'Stockton speeches, after all, are essentially the same speech,' the *Spectator* grumbled a year before his death.

> There is the sweep of history bit (things were better when I was in charge), the snobbish jokes about nannies, nursemaids etc, the passage about the importance of governments spending lots of money on everything, the moving appeal of an old and frail man and the curiously dull peroration about the new dawn of the Microchip, the whole dramatised by some beautiful stage business with his stick and his deafness.

One member of the Thatcher Cabinet, Norman Tebbit, disparaged Macmillan's 'corporatist' policies by comparing them to Nazi doctrines: 'there wasn't much difference between what he and the National Socialists were saying, if you take away the violence and anti-semitism.' The fairest assessment, perhaps surprisingly, came from Lord Hailsham, who as Lord Chancellor heard all Stockton's later orations: 'His speeches in the House of Lords, carefully rehearsed in advance and perforce delivered without a note, because he had largely lost the power of vision, were brilliant, indiscreet, replete with false analogies and *non sequiturs* and universally and rightly admired and applauded.'

What did his oratorical revival mean? How much of these speeches were the sham of a man whom Lord Bruce-Gardyne, in 1985, dubbed 'our greatest living Thespian'? His references to his mother, and his wish for a special relationship with her native United States, were all too sincere; but when the old man decried cynicism and invoked the authority of St Paul, many people felt sceptical. In fact his Christianity was fundamental and heartfelt; but too many remembered him too well as a crafty, stealthy opportunist in politics, more than ordinarily ruthless where his own interests were concerned, a man whose apparent cynicism as Prime Minister contributed to the secularisation of the age. Others found his glorification of British coalminers as 'the best men in the world', or his protective attitude to shopworkers, sentimental or self-serving. Ultimately the glorification of splendid underdogs is glorification of the splendid system which made and keeps them as underdogs. 'What thoughtful rich people call the problem of poverty,' wrote Tawney, 'thoughtful poor people call the problem of riches.' Stockton was a compassionate man, but as Frank Longford remembered him saying, 'When it comes to throwing in my lot with your wild men of the left, I must remember that I am a very rich man.'

Among the Thatcherite zealotry he was loathed as a wicked inflationist: he was cheated by death of savouring the irony that inflation in Britain after ten years of Thatcher's premiership was higher than in any year of his premiership, and he himself never underestimated the perils of improvidence. 'Many of the nicest fellows I've known in my life', he told millions watching on the first night of the televising of House of Lords debates, 'made a similar confusion between current and capital expenditure. But I am bound to tell your Lordships that they often ended up in rather seedy boarding-houses.'

As part of his belief in the Middle Way he had long propounded that there were some natural monopolies which ought to be run as public services, and that there were some industries which could never raise the money necessary for capital investment except by government subventions. His feelings about this led him to coin one of his most famous phrases in a speech of November 1985 at a dinner of the Tory Reform Group. The country was 'practically bankrupt', he warned, living delusively on North Sea oil revenues and the selling of national assets. The Thatcher government's privatisation of public enterprises like British Airways and British Telecom was, he said, like 'selling off the family silver' to pay the butler's wages. 'First of all the Georgian silver goes, and then all that nice furniture that used to be in the saloon. Then the Canalettos go.' Cynics might protest that Stockton had never owned a Canaletto in his life; but he had said two years earlier that the qualities of an artist were essential in politics, and there was an artistry about his images of a government dispersing national assets, unthinking of the economic results and uncaring of the social consequences.

How does one resolve the contradictions of this old man with his talent for emotive speechifying?

Some biographers summarise their subjects as complex people with three or four different characters each striving against the other. Those writing about Harold Macmillan have sometimes resorted to such clichés. But he was one man, with a single personality, indivisible and whole. The witty and wily speaker in the House of Lords, who seemed to embody the self-confidence and aristocratic dominance of an earlier age, was in fact a bourgeois literary intellectual who had spent the years of his greatest power in a state of ruthless fright. He was a man who painfully mistrusted his own powers and had developed an elaborate and even brilliant tangle of pretences to hide this mistrust from others. The pattern of his life was set by the intimidation, rejection and humiliation which he suffered as a child and younger man.

The intimidation was maternal. His mother was peremptory and demanding and left him with a lifelong sense of alarm; she died in 1937, when he was forty-three, but he never escaped the nervous fears with which his childhood imbued him. The rejection was political. He was elected to parliament when still young, as he thought with great talents and high prospects;

but for two decades he languished on the backbenches, his opinions dismissed as crankish, his manners derided as fussy and priggish, his speeches greeted with yawns. Though he tried to identify himself with Churchill's opposition to Chamberlain in the 1930s, his promotion by Churchill was initially slow and begrudging; never accepted by the Churchillians as one of their number, he was rejected even by the people who ought to have counted as his political friends. But worse than maternal intimidation or political rejection was his domestic humiliation. In 1920 he married a duke's daughter, but the grand world in which she moved treated him as a joke. He adulated her, in an idealised way; in return she cuckolded him, conducting for almost forty years an intrigue with one of his political colleagues.

This intimidation, rejection and humiliation built up in him a huge charge of resentment. When finally, in 1942, he was given his first experiences of power it was as Minister Resident in North Africa, and for several years he lived abroad. When he returned from the Mediterranean in 1945, he was like the Count of Monte Cristo in the novel of Alexandre Dumas: a man returning with a burning sense that he had been deeply and repeatedly wronged, implacable in his resentment, full of suppressed hostility and shocking ruthlessness, determined to prove invincible, but too subtle a man for quick or brutal revenges. 'Wait and hope' was the moral of the Dumas story, in which the hero adopts a phoney aristocratic style, favours all sorts of theatrical mystifications and with scarifying single-mindedness waits for his opportunities to take control and play at God. In British politics Harold Macmillan was the Count of Monte Cristo.

This book, then, is an attempt to portray his career in the light of his family life; but it also celebrates an unusual, fascinating dynasty which influenced British literature and politics to an extent which no other family can approach. Coming from a peasant world of crushing ignorance and remorseless poverty, two Macmillan brothers founded one of the greatest

publishing houses in Victorian London: a business which their
descendants still controlled in the 1990s, although in a sense the
business controlled their lives too. The Macmillans were always
publishers, their menfolk centred their lives around books and
their sons were brought up with dedication to the business. As
a little boy Harold's great-grandson Daniel, born in 1974 and
since his death styled Viscount Macmillan of Ovenden, was
taken round the publishing office in Little Essex Street and
introduced to several of the editors. With perfect manners
he shook their hands and said, 'Thank you for all you are
doing.' The Macmillans were defined by the family's publishing
business, and by the expectation that they would run it. The fact
that by the 1970s the real power of administration had shifted to
salaried executives was, like that moment in 1990 when for the
first time a chairman was appointed from outside the family,
painful for some of those concerned.

For two centuries the lives of the Macmillans have been like
a prism of national life, reflecting all the great social changes,
all the literary fashions and business vicissitudes of their times.
Generation after generation have shown the development of
family character and the resolution of family conflicts. Indeed
the history of the Macmillans – eighteenth-century peasants,
nineteenth-century tradesmen, Edwardian men of property,
noblemen approaching the millennium – encompasses the history of class, and parental attitudes, and modes of power, in
modern Britain. Yet above all this is a book about emotions,
for the tensions and disarray of their private lives often seemed
a magnification of those of other families. The Macmillans
were tireless, ambitious, intelligent, vehement and audacious;
but also wayward, depressive, introspective and guilt-ridden. It
was fitting that in his last great public speech the old statesman
spoke of 'the family silver': his sense of family was greater than
most men's, his pride in his ancestors was stronger, the intrusion
of domestic pressures on his public career more obtrusive. The
history of the Macmillan family is far more than a family
story.

CHAPTER 2

Duncan

I want to be on the mainland,
and go on with existence. This
is a waste of life.

Dr Samuel Johnson,
on the isle of Col

The Macmillans were Scottish. Originally settled on a gaunt and exposed peninsula on the coast of Argyllshire, they migrated in the eighteenth century to the isle of Arran a few miles across the water. The island had been given by King James IV of Scotland in 1503 to his cousin Sir James Hamilton, who was created Earl of Arran. Ownership of the island passed from generation to generation of the Hamilton family, which received a dukedom in 1643. The apogee of the island's prosperity was in the mid-seventeenth century, during the supremacy of Anne, Duchess of Hamilton, but by the time of the Macmillans' migration her benefactions were only a golden memory. Later generations of Hamiltons lived at their palace in Lanarkshire and governed their Arran property through a land agent installed in their castle at Brodick. Their intermittent gifts of churches, school-houses or primitive medical treatment – on one occasion even a picnic pavilion for visiting scientists – relieved their general attitude of lordly neglect. The tenth Duke was the proudest magnifico in Scotland, and once declared that the grandest sight on the Day of Judgment would be to see all the ten dukes of Hamilton resurrected and gathered together. His son (described by Lord

Brougham and Vaux as 'Very Duke of Very Duke') married the daughter of the ruling Grand Duke of Baden, and, as a cousin by marriage of Emperor Napoleon III of France, married his daughter to the Prince of Monaco. The Hamiltons latterly lived in regal splendour on the Continent and gave little attention to Arran, which passed to other hands on the death of the dissolute twelfth Duke in 1895.

Arran lies in the mouth of the Firth of Clyde and is part of the Western Hebrides. Although the largest island in Buteshire, at no point is its length greater than twenty miles nor its greatest breadth more than eleven. Its name signifies a land of mountains, and among many that are tall and picturesque, Goat Fell (the hill of the winds) stands highest at about 3,000 feet. Flanked by deep, dark corries which only the bright morning sun could penetrate, the mountains of Arran have lochs in their higher points and foaming waterfalls plunge from the granite mountain-sides, which are traversed by streams rich with trout.

Arran's people had some claim to be counted as Highland-ers. The Highlands with their distinctive traditions are usually defined as that part of Scotland north-west of a line from Dumbarton to Stonehaven but sometimes including the islands of the Inner and Outer Hebrides together with the county of Bute. Not every Highlander would grant that the people of Arran fully shared their culture; but the island was part of Buteshire, on the extremity of the Hebrides, and there were strong similarities between Highland ways and the habits of Arran's inhabitants. In the eighteenth century Highland tra-ditions were still preserved and protected by their bards and pipers. In the absence of books, bards constituted the library and concentrated the learning of Highlanders. They were living chronicles of past events, men who followed the clans into battle, where they eulogised the fame resulting from a brave death as well as preserving the disgrace of a cowardly retreat. The piper, in his turn, sounded mournful laments for the dead on high-toned bagpipes. The effect of bards and pipers alike was to connect the past with the present, to show that the hero, the honoured chief or respected parent, although no longer present to his friends, could not die in their memory, still survived in fame and might sympathise with those whom he had left behind. Although Highland Scots were much preoccupied with death, their burial rituals and mourning ceremonies were free from tormenting fears. Death was seen as merely passing from one state of existence to another. An army of ghosts was believed to hover around those who mourned for them. This belief in ghosts strengthened the attachment between the living and the dead, because the deceased were not only preserved in memory but present to the senses. Many of these beliefs survived on Arran too. The hills of the island were covered with heaps of stones, known as cairns, left to commemorate the dead. As long as memory endured, a traveller would not pass a cairn without adding a new stone to the heap. For a long time there was a saying among suppliant Highlanders beseeching a favour, which translated from Gaelic was 'I will add a stone to your cairn,' meaning 'When you are dead I will do every honour to your memory.'

Honesty and fair dealing were enforced by custom more than law. 'To be modest as well as brave, to be contented with the few things which nature requires, to act and to suffer without complaining, to be as much ashamed of doing anything insolent or ungenerous to others, as of bearing it when done to ourselves, and to die with pleasure to avenge affronts offered to their clan or their country; these they rank their highest accomplishments,' wrote Sir John Hamilton-Dalrymple-Mackgill. Sexual morality was enforced by strict social conventions. Young unmarried women never wore head dress, instead tying their hair with bandages or a scarf. 'This continued until marriage, or till they attained a certain age; but if a young woman lost her virtue and character, then she was obliged to wear a cap, and never afterwards to appear with her hair uncovered, in the dress of virgin innocence,' one observer reported in 1822.

Accustomed to traverse huge tracts of country, daily contemplating the most diversified scenery, surrounded everywhere by wild and magnificent objects, by mountains, lakes and forests, the Highlanders were influenced by the wild sublimity of their surroundings. When tempests howled over the heath, and the elements were mixed in dire uproar, Highlanders retreated to their caves or huts, there to sit in brooding melancholy.

At the time of the Macmillans' migration, the people of Arran, as of the West Highlands generally, were in a wretched condition. The staples in their diet were potatoes and oats. In summer this was supplemented by milk products taken from a runtish breed of cattle that could survive on the poorest herbage. Animals were slaughtered to provide winter food, and, when the dried goat-meat was all eaten, spring was a season of privation. There were few animals in the forests and heaths: only otters, wild cats, shrew mice, rabbits and bats. Stags were almost extinct by the 1770s, and together with woodcocks and other sporting birds were reintroduced to the island by the dukes of Hamilton only in the mid-nineteenth century. The rivers abounded with fish, but their use was restricted in the early nineteenth century to providing a source of a few weeks' amusement for visiting sportsmen.

During the Macmillans' settlement there, the people of Arran were Gaelic speakers. They endured poverty, mortification and distress. Much of summer was spent in collecting peat for fuel, or in building and repairing their homes; before and after the harvest they burned fern to make kelp, and some men fished for herring. In winter they made their herring-nets, while the women spun linen and woollen yarn. From February to May, weather permitting, they laboured on the soil. There were regular epidemics of smallpox and measles, but the principal fatal disease was pleurisy. In the eighteenth century the dukes of Hamilton paid for a surgeon to tour the island each spring and autumn to bleed the people as a supposed preventive against pleurisy. On the arrival of the surgeon, the inhabitants would assemble in the open air, extend their arms and be bled over a hole specially dug in the ground. These bleeding sessions were one of the few points of interest in the monotony of Arran life. Except for New Year's Day, marriage celebrations and two or three fairs, there were no amusements for the people. 'No wonder is there then at their depression of spirits,' commented an observant eighteenth-century English visitor, Thomas Pennant. The menfolk of Arran he found 'strong, tall and well-made'; their lives, although 'sober, religious and industrious', he felt passed in miserable deprivation. 'A deep dejection appears in general through the countenance of all: no time can be spared for amusement of any kind; the whole being given for procuring the means of paying their rent; of laying in their fuel, or getting a scanty pittance of meat and clothing.'

Arran was portioned out among numerous small tenants. One of these was the earliest of our Macmillans, named Daniel, who lived in the mid-eighteenth century at North Sannox. This was a desolate spot in the northern and most mountainous region of Arran, near Glen Sannox, described by the Victorian naturalist David Landsborough as 'one of the grandest glens Scotland can boast'. 'It is the sublime of magnitude, and simplicity, and obscurity, and silence. . . . perpetual twilight appears to reign here, even at midday; a gloomy and grey atmosphere uniting into one visible sort of obscurity.' Sannox in Gaelic meant the Glen of the Valiant Warriors, and nearby was a ruined hill fort and a jagged mountain called the Hound's Tooth. Visiting Sannox in 1772 Thomas Pennant passed 'through woods of birch, small, weather-beaten and blasted', and after reaching the settlement at Sannox heard 'a sermon preached beneath a tent formed of sails, on the beach; the congregation numerous, devout and attentive, seated along the shore, forming a group picturesque and edifying' – Macmillans perhaps among them.

Daniel's only son Malcolm was born on the banks of Lochranza, one of the finest sea-lochs in Scotland; its name probably derived from Gaelic phrases meaning the loch of the pirates or loch of the Sea Champions. Lochranza was a place of overwhelming but solitary beauty, gaunt with few trees, surrounded by granite peaks raggedly scarred down their sides by winter torrents. Pennant had first set foot on Arran at this very spot, Lochranza, on Midsummer Day of 1772. He thought the place 'magnificent': the bay and small village were 'environed with a theatre of mountains', with the serrated crags of Grianan-Athol looming in the background. The ruins of a fortress of red grit-stone stood on a shingle promontory in the bay, its floors 'strewed with the shells of limpets, the hard fare of the poor people who continually take refuge here'. A shark over twenty-seven feet long had been harpooned in the bay, and Pennant went to admire it. The Commissioners of Forfeited Estates, who administered the extensive Scottish lands which had been confiscated from rebels after the Jacobite rising of 1745, had tried to develop a commercial shark fishery, Pennant recorded; 'but the person they confided in, most shamefully abused their goodness; so at present it is only attempted by private adventurers'. A generation later the locality was celebrated by Sir Walter Scott in his poem 'Lord of the Isles':

> On fair Lochranza streamed the early day;
> There wreaths of cottage-smoke are upward curl'd;
> From the lone hamlet, which her inland bay
> And circling mountaineers sever from the world;
> And there the fisherman his sail unfurl'd,
> The goat-herd drove his kids to steep Ben-ghoil;
> Before the hut the dame her spindle twirl'd,
> Courting the sun-beam, as she plied her toil –
> For wake where'er he may, man wakes to care and toil.

To James Bryce in the 1850s the place had 'a singularly picturesque and unique aspect; the stranger will say he has never seen such a hamlet and bay before' – though he warned visitors that even in summer 'fearful squalls' made the bay a dangerous place to sail. Bryce's contemporary Lord Teignmouth similarly testified to the 'gloomy grandeur' of Lochranza. The spirit of the place almost entered into the souls of the Macmillans.

Malcolm Macmillan of Lochranza married his neighbour

Janet Kerr. After the birth of the seventh of their ten children
they moved a few miles south from Lochranza to Upper Corrie,
a house on the brow of a hill overlooking the Firth of Clyde.
On fine days it commanded a clear view of the Ayrshire coast.
Looming over Corrie was the hill of Am Binnein, and further
inland the majestic, gloomy, snow-bound bulk of Goat Fell
inhabited only by eagles and ptarmigans. Pennant dined at
Corrie on his visit, recording the 'small house' as 'belonging
to a gentleman of Ayrshire, who visits the place for the benefit
of goats whey'. Corrie's surroundings were barren: mountainous masses of moor-stone behind, while the nearby shoreline
comprised mill-stone and red grit-stone. The climate was 'very
severe', Pennant added, 'for besides the violence of winds, the
cold is very rigorous; and snow lay here in the valleys for thirteen
weeks of the last year'.

An unusual form of land tenure prevailed on Arran. Each
farm was held by several small tenants, who were bound by
their leases jointly and individually to pay rent to the owner.
The tenants lived on the farm in little cottages clustered together,
so that each farm was its own petty settlement. Both pasture
and moorland were open to all possessors, although the tenants
annually divided the arable land by lot. There was little incentive
to improve the property, because the leases for each farm ran
for only nineteen years: the tenants feared that if the lands were
in a desirable state when the lease expired, a neighbour would
get hold of it, by offering to the Duke of Hamilton's agent a
higher price than the person who spent his life and substance
enriching the farm. This induced the tenants to leave their land
in its original state.

Malcolm Macmillan worked on a farm by Corrie called the
Cock. The land was poor, but he prospered in a limited way,
becoming the local tacksman, a sort of 'chief peasant' who
purveyed corn-food and peat fuel to the small cotters in the
neighbourhood. When peasants came to buy their meal from
the tacksman, Malcolm would, in cases of need, increase the
measure, or else would draw home peats from the hill for poor

people who had no horses; but it annoyed him if any notice or thanks for his kindness were given.

As befitted a tacksman, Malcolm was also an elder of the Church of Scotland, stern, conservative and duty-bound in his ways. His two eldest sons served on board the King's cutter in the Preventive service, while his sixth son, Duncan, married Katherine Crawford, the daughter of one of his father's fellow elders, William Crawford, who occupied a small farm near the Cock. In course of time Duncan took over the farm at Corrie. There he lived the life of a crofter, keeping a few cows pastured on the burgh moor, and cultivating some acres of the town's land. It was a miserable patch that he miserably cultivated. The croft was small and its soil was poor: Duncan could not prosper on the land. At other times he worked as a carter, bringing coal from local mines to the little harbour at Irvine.

The lives of the Macmillans were transformed by the arrival on Arran in 1800 of James Haldane, who with his elder brother Robert had founded the first Congregationalist church in Scotland in 1799. Robert Haldane had been a fashionable duelling naval officer until 'he was aroused from the sleep of spiritual death by the excitement of the French Revolution', to quote his biographer. Seized by the desire to ameliorate human suffering, he dedicated himself to God while praying on a mountain top, and together with his brother became a lay preacher travelling districts left pagan by the laziness of the clergy. From 1797 onwards they made evangelical tours all over Scotland, preaching wherever and whenever they could. Arriving in a place, they handed out tracts to give notice that missionaries had arrived, and then walked through the streets, to the accompaniment of a drum, horn or bell, announcing the time of their sermon. James Haldane's preaching tour of Arran in 1800 had a lasting impact on the island. Indeed Alexander Macmillan, writing as a successful publisher in middle age, attributed the family's later prosperity to the effects of the Haldanes 'on the moral, spiritual and intellectual condition' of his parents, Duncan and Katherine.

Exposing the subterfuges and deceits of the human heart, James Haldane warned the sinners of Arran to flee from the wrath to come, and enjoined all his audiences to glory in God as their Lord and Master. Memories of his meetings were still vivid on the island in the 1860s, when Alexander Macmillan heard them recalled by 'a dear old Aunt'. Haldane, who preached in every village, was shocked by the feudal atavism of the inhabitants. On one occasion he was in a church where the parishioners hesitated to approach the table to receive the sacrament. Suddenly he heard the crack of sticks and looking round, he saw one hit the bald head of a man behind him. The ruling elders of the church were driving the congregation forward to the table, in much the same manner as they would pen their cattle. The Gaelic population of Arran submitted to such rough discipline without protest.

Malcolm Macmillan, as an elder of the local church, was hostile to the revivalists, but his son Duncan became a devout follower of the Haldanes, and after the brothers in 1808 adopted Baptist sentiments he joined the Baptist congregation at Irvine. Christianity was central to the life of the family. A stern but humorous man, Duncan conducted family worship in Gaelic, reading the Gaelic Bible aloud and praying extempore in the old language of Arran. 'I have the deepest reverence for him,' his son Daniel wrote in 1833. 'He was a hard-working man, a most devout man, and . . . cared for nothing but his family, that is, did not care what toil he endured for their sakes.'

Until the Arran revivals the peasantry there were 'turbulent, superstitious and otherwise degraded', believing in ghosts and witchcraft, so Alexander recalled. It was widely believed that evil spirits had haunted the island before the coming of the gospel in the shape of the Haldanes. Superstition had been a pervasive influence on the minds of the peasantry. Trust in ghosts, dreams, charms, omens, auguries, incantations and second sight were rife. Every incident of daily life – a baptism, a death, the illness of a cow, the churning of milk, the making of a journey – each was associated with a mysterious sign which foretold it, or some strange rite which caused or hindered it. In ancient times, the minds of the Highlanders were guided by their notion that honour or disgrace communicated to a whole family or district. After the preaching of James Haldane, these old attitudes existed side by side with the most austere Christian beliefs. Traditional poetry and tales kept their consciences alive: but so too did sharper fears of the Day of Judgment and the threat of hell-fire. These two mentalities were held with tenacity in the same mind, unconscious of incongruity. Life on Arran after the visitations of the Haldanes was governed by a mixture of piety and credulity, the crofters practising variously a devout superstition or superstitious devoutness.

At nearby Kintyre James Haldane ejected from one of his meetings a heckling old woman who demanded that the preacher speak in Gaelic. 'That woman rules the town magistrates, and all of us,' he was told later by one of the congregation. 'She knows the history of us all as far back as our grandfathers at least. In most families something wrong has happened; if any offend her, she publishes over the town whatever bad thing has been done by one of their progenitors.' The influence of generation upon generation, the interaction of past with present, were forces in the daily lives of the people of Arran. The reputations of one's ancestors, for good or ill, were part of one's conscious existence. Clannishness persisted in the Macmillans long after they had left Arran. 'I claim to have the true Clan feeling,' Alexander Macmillan wrote in 1861, 'and rejoice in it as one of the witnesses and helps which the Father of All has given us toward realising better the common brotherhood in the Brother of all.' Family history had been the keystone of their island world, and it continued so in their mainland experience. One member of the family after another was taught that an honourable, well-spent life entailed a blessing on descendants, while a curse would descend on the successors of the wicked, oppressive or worthless. A rich but complicated inheritance was unravelling.

CHAPTER 3

Daniel

Then did I seek to rise
Out of the prison of my mean estate;
And with such jewels as the exploring mind
Brings from the caves of knowledge, buy my ransom
From those twin gaolers of the daring heart –
Low birth and iron fortune.

Edward Bulwer Lytton

You will see so much of me
come out in the children.

Daniel Macmillan, 1857

Daniel Macmillan, the founder of the publishing firm, was the tenth child and third son (out of four sons and eight daughters) of Duncan Macmillan and his wife Katherine Crawford. He was born on 13 September 1813 at the family croft at Upper Corrie, where in his earliest years he had to endure both physical hardship and family distress. Within a year of his birth the four young sisters who had been born between him and his elder brother William died in an epidemic which swept the house. His parents had found it impossible to prosper on the little plot at Upper Corrie, and the place was perhaps made odious to them by memories of their dead daughters. For whatever reason, when Daniel was three, his parents left Arran and settled in the small coastal town of Irvine across the Firth of Clyde in Ayrshire. There Duncan Macmillan tried to make a living as a farmer until his death in 1823 at the age of about fifty.

Although as an adult Daniel was associated with some of the most progressive movements of Victorian Britain, he was a child of feudalism. It was in the primitive life at Upper Corrie that he began, and his family's experiences there shaped the meaning of his life. His parents had been born on Arran at a time when its conditions were feudal, its crofters for most purposes living like serfs in the fief of the Dukes of Hamilton. Though ancestral customs and domestic feelings had begun to change in the decade before his birth, he was born into a little enclosed community that was essentially medieval. The life at Upper Corrie had more in common with the lives of the Druids, whose stone relics were dotted across the island, than with the age of steampower or representative democracy. The Arran of his birth was one based on 'Feudalism and Preservation of the Game', to take a phrase from one of Daniel's favourite authors, Thomas Carlyle.

From the outset Daniel's mother Katherine was the strongest influence on him. She focused special attention on him after the catastrophe in which her four daughters had died: her tenderness and attention gave him perpetual strength, and left him with enduring gratitude. 'I know her as well as ever a son knew a parent, and my persuasion is that she is the most perfect lady in all Scotland,' he wrote when he was nineteen.

> With so little knowledge derived from books, with so very little intercourse with the higher ranks of society, with so little care or thought on what is most pleasing in external conduct, was there ever a lady who, so instinctively, so naturally, did what was right, acted with so much propriety in all cases? She has such high and noble notions that no one ever heard her say, or knew her do, a mean thing, no one could ever venture to say an impudent thing to her, or talk scandal in her presence. If anyone did so once, it was never repeated; some quietly spoken but most bitter and biting saying put an end to such garbage.

The child and widow of peasants, condemned to a lifetime of child-bearing and drudgery, she was a woman of fine instincts, whose ambition for her sons started the family on its ascendancy. 'There is nobody like mother in the whole world,' Daniel enthused. 'What a beautiful forehead she has! What an eye! What a face, take it all in all! A noble temple for her noble soul!' After her death aged sixty-three in August 1834 Daniel lost any wish to live in Scotland again. His adulation of her persisted throughout his life, and on his deathbed he was still thinking of his mother.

She was a devout woman who lived each day in the conscious presence of God: her religious beliefs were fundamental to her. In her home God was a true household God. She often repeated to her children her memories of the Haldanes' great revivalist meetings on Arran: indeed the most exciting of them, at which the congregants had erupted into a paroxysm of panting, trembling and convulsions, had occurred in 1812, only a year before Daniel's birth. Katherine Macmillan imbued her sons and daughters not only with her faith, but with a fierce, almost desperate need to distinguish right from wrong. She instilled in her children the habit of self-reproach for lapses from the good way, what Christians would call a moral conscience, what Matthew Arnold called 'the inward judge' and what Freudians describe as a punitive super-ego. The Haldanes' Society for Promoting the Gospel at Home, which worked to make Christianity a daily presence and living reality in the domestic lives of Scots in outlying districts, had a lasting influence on families like the Macmillans. A favourite text of the brothers was 'Except ye repent, ye shall all likewise perish.' James Haldane considered 'Christian life as a warfare', so he wrote, 'a constant struggle between the flesh and the Spirit'. The Haldanes depicted life as a contending battle of good and evil, but spread a message of social improvement. Their precepts were impressed by Katherine Macmillan on the daily and external lives of her children and inculcated into their inner consciences. The Macmillans were brought up to feel that they had enough of the diabolic in them to require a lifelong fight to be good. The effects of this outlook persisted for generations in the family.

Shortly before his marriage in 1850, Daniel described his earliest childhood memories to his fiancée. They were a mixture of the mundane and of the spiritually elevated, of family love and of crushing domestic loss. 'I remember watching the cows to keep them from the corn. I remember wandering alone and thinking of the infinite, of space and time, of heaven and hell, good and evil, of angels and of devils.' He remembered too the birth of his younger brother Alexander in 1818, when Daniel was aged five; the bonding that tied them so closely as adults in business together began early. 'I used to lie at the bottom of a very large cradle and rock him and myself to sleep,' Daniel wrote to his fiancée. 'I remember innumerable conversations with mother, and I remember my father's illness and death and funeral. It made so great an impression on me that up to the time I was twenty I could not speak of my father without the tear starting in my eye.'

After Duncan Macmillan's death, some of his paternal responsibilities for Daniel and the younger children were assumed by the eldest son Malcolm, who paid for their education and 'struggled to make us fear God, and do the will of God', as Daniel told his fiancée years later. Formerly a working carpenter, Malcolm had managed to learn Latin and Greek, and some Hebrew. Finding that he could write and teach the English language in addition to his native Gaelic, he left carpentry and together with his brother William kept a school at Irvine. Then he became the minister of a Baptist church. But although Daniel was a bookish and intelligent child, of obviously uncommon gifts, there was not enough money to complete his education, and in 1824, when he was aged ten, he was apprenticed to a local bookseller and binder, Maxwell Dick. Daniel's wage began at one shilling and sixpence a week in the first year, with a rise of one shilling a week for each of the remaining six years of the apprenticeship.

Daniel was so satisfactory an apprentice that in 1829, when he was only sixteen, he was trusted with care of the business while his master visited London. His employer he later described as 'a queer, queer man' and his wife as 'a wee daft, and told me all her love affairs before I was twelve'. On one occasion, when his employer unjustly blamed him for some fault in the shop, his retorts were so vehement that the man hit him: whereupon the youth threw a book at the man's head and vanished out of the door to Arran. The pair were soon reconciled, and Daniel served his apprenticeship to its end in 1831. By that date his brother Malcolm was the minister of a Baptist congregation at Stirling, and he arranged for the youth to take a job there. This proved a mistake. 'I had not enough to do and felt the place dull,' as Daniel later wrote. 'I wished to go to Glasgow or Edinburgh, or some large town, where there would be more room and better chances of rising. My brother was anxious that I should remain with him. I did not wish to oppose him, but yet the thing worried me. I felt "cribbed, cabined and confined". The result was a most violent brain fever.' This physical and nervous crisis at the age of seventeen or eighteen was the beginning of a decade of unhappiness and augured a lifetime of illness.

After his recovery, he took a job at Glasgow with a bookseller called Atkinson, a man of progressive political beliefs whose shop was a meeting place for a Glaswegian literary coterie; but here too Daniel's nerves and health defeated him. 'I hoped for a partnership in the business,' he wrote twenty years later.

I was always at work at seven, and never or hardly ever away before nine. It was often ten, eleven and twelve before I got away. . . . I used to read all the weekly, monthly and quarterly periodicals of any mark – a queer mass of rubbish to lie lumbering in any one's brain, but, as it seemed to me valuable for the purpose of business, very often it was three or four o'clock of a morning before I got to bed. The upshot, as was natural, was the most wretched health. It appeared to everyone that I was dying.

The overwork and anxiety were aggravated by his loneliness at being for the first time away from home, lodging in a small room for which the weekly rent was an exorbitant six shillings, and by the painful introspection usual in an intelligent but self-pitying adolescent. Daniel came from another world, centuries remote from the steaming, weaving and delving of Clydeside: the smells, smoke, noise and squalor of industrial Scotland put an extra strain on the boy, estranging him from his neighbours and surroundings. 'I feel as if I were dying,' he wrote in his journal just before Christmas 1832 at the age of nineteen. 'I have no one to sympathise with me; no one to mitigate my suffering; no comfort but what my paltry salary can procure. If I were rich, how many would be kind to me, ask what I needed, and anticipate my wants. But why do I shed tears? I cannot help them.' Finally in June 1833 his mother fetched him from Glasgow (refusing to go home without him) and he left Atkinson's shop.

Already, at this early date, Daniel had contracted tuberculosis, a disease which overshadowed the rest of his life and had a deep influence on his family. Its diagnosis was a prediction of early death. Known by various names and euphemisms – consumption, phthisis, decline, wasting disease, delicacy of the lungs, graveyard cough – tuberculosis was a debilitating and lethal disease. Lassitude, poor appetite, flatulence, emaciation, irritability, night sweats, facial pallor, wan eyes, vulnerability to colds, harsh coughing, spitting of foul sputum and coughing of blood were among the most notorious of its symptoms. John Keats, who had died of tuberculosis in 1821, described 'the weariness, the fever and the fret' vividly in his 'Ode to a Nightingale':

> Here, where men sit and hear each other groan;
> Where palsy shakes a few, sad, last grey hairs,
> Where youth grows pale, spectre-thin and dies;

> Where but to think is to be full of sorrow,
> And leaden-ey'd despairs.

The incubation period of tuberculosis was long but indiscernible, it was mostly diagnosed after the bacillus had begun destroying tissue, its progression was usually chronic rather than acute, and it exhibited no palpable climacteric. Tuberculosis might suddenly advance and kill within weeks, or arrest, or reappear after months or years, or spontaneously vanish. This cruel process of infection, activation and reinfection mystified physicians, and indeed the tubercle bacillus was not identified by scientists until more than twenty years after Daniel's death. The disease was a fearful, insidious killer, debilitating in its course. It was contagious (especially in overcrowded housing, such as Daniel's childhood home), although in mid-nineteenth-century Britain medical specialists were prone to list hereditary taints or moral degeneracy as causative agents. In fact Daniel is likely to have caught the disease as a boy from one of his siblings whom it killed; he probably later transmitted it to his wife and indirectly, through her, to his youngest son, Arthur. Among the symptoms which he reported were burning fevers in his hands and feet, lassitude, bad colds and weak, painful breathing.

Henceforth he was not only almost permanently unwell, and sometimes grievously sick, but he lived in expectation of imminent death. He was driven to make something good of what was likely to be a poignantly short life; but, more than that, his family's religious precepts had convinced him that what was left of his life must be a fight against evil if he was to find salvation in heaven rather than damnation in hell. 'The doctor looked very grave to-day,' he confided to his journal in June 1833 shortly after his diagnosis.

> This is a bad cough. I don't like this blood-spitting. I don't like this weakness in my limbs. . . . Of course I must die; and if I die with my sins unpardoned, I shall sink lower than the grave. At least, the Bible says so; Bunyan and other theological writers say so; and I hear it from Sabbath to Sabbath. . . . my conscience . . . says so too. Since this is

true, and acknowledged by saint and sage, by preacher and by poet, it would be as well to be prepared for Death – who, by coming in the rear of all our pleasure, and wealth, and fame, befools them exceedingly. But death is not all, *after death the judgement*. A serious matter that.

In his remaining years he grew progressively sicker. Under sentence of death, Daniel lived always with death in mind. 'Of all men I have known personally he was the one who lived most constantly and consciously eye to eye with death,' wrote his friend and biographer Tom Hughes. Death and its imminence guided the whole of Daniel's adult life, a life which in turn became an inspiration and seemed a living reality for his brother, his sons, his nephews and grandchildren. 'When all things are uncertain and confused, when I can neither look steadily at myself nor at society without agony, it does cheer me up to look back at my father's death-bed,' he told one of his brothers. 'Then my heart had no fear, my mind no doubt, no sceptical confusions; then this life did appear a God-appointed pilgrimage, through which God was leading us for our own good and His Glory.' The imminence of death intensified his religious passion. People who knew they were dying were ardent about the After Life, yearning to be rid of their old, sick, sinful bodies and to reach the purifying glories of heaven, he wrote to his dearest friend and fellow tubercular patient George Wilson in 1856.

The decay and inner putrefaction of his body profoundly influenced his thought. He was convinced 'that people's souls were not inside them – in stomach, heart and brain – but hanging or hovering around them', thus giving expression to their face or action to their limbs. This fancy was doubtless inspired by the Scottish superstition that a huddle of ghosts hovered around the living who mourned them, or that ghosts lingered around those of their descendants who venerated them. There was a tendency in this period to talk of spiritual health in the language of physical health: a man might speak of his soul as a mass of putrefying sores, or preachers were likened to unskilled doctors, prescribing the same pill and draught for every complaint. Influenced by his morbid condition, Daniel (and others of his family) were prone to metaphors of sickness. 'We – all mankind – have led and do lead disobedient lives, diseased lives,' he lamented to a nephew in 1855. 'We feel the evil nature within us struggling for predominance. We feel the higher nature, the true Christ-given constitution, warring against . . . the world, the flesh, and the devil.'

He could often deny the hopelessness of his condition, or reconcile himself and others to his fate, by thinking that his illness was a God-given opportunity for self-improvement. 'The burthen of suffering seems a tombstone hung around us: while in reality it is only the weight necessary to keep down the diver while he is collecting pearls,' he wrote in 1841 to George Wilson. 'It is only through suffering that we can be made perfect: and in hard struggles we acquire spiritual strength, and spiritual riches.' This invalid creed – the life and testimony of a dying man, a man dying painfully and bravely, by inches, over the course of twenty years – became the creed of the Macmillans, and in great measure remained so until the 1930s.

But all this lay in the future. After his diagnosis, he had first to recuperate, and then to try bolder strokes to give meaning and value to his life. After his mother had taken him from Glasgow, Daniel went to stay on Arran with an uncle, who was for fifty years Independent minister at Glen Sannox. 'I know all the people for miles round,' Daniel wrote. 'The people are most simple. It is very pleasant to call on them and listen to their stories. They always seem glad to see me. They think I am dying, and do all they can to cheer me. They are most thoughtful and kind and tender-hearted, and all without pretence.'

After convalescing on Arran, Daniel in September 1833 took a ship from Leith which bore him south to London. He trudged round the offices of publishers like Longmans in search of a job that would be the beginning of a career in metropolitan publishing. Almost everywhere he met rejection. 'It is an easy thing to depress me,' he reported to his brother William. 'I felt dreadfully depressed. Tears relieved me. Prayers relieved me. Prayer seemed to me a more real thing than ever.' He was offered one job in magazine publishing which would have involved working through the weekend until five or six on Sunday morning. 'This would not do for me at all,' he decided. 'I might learn a great deal about business, but my health, moral and physical, must suffer.' He spent time stumbling through the streets in tears.

> My mind was in the most restless state. . . . Old sins kept stalking before me. I was miserable. I walked about the streets, yet I saw no face that I cared about, scarcely noticed those who pressed on me. The strangeness of everything increased my misery. I prayed. I tried to pray. I thought. I tried to think, my mind was a strange whirlpool. I could look at nothing. I could only weep, and try to pray. I do hope that these things will leave some powerful and permanent impression on my mind and heart.

Although it was the mode for religious young men to castigate themselves for 'old sins' in cloudy language, if one actual indiscretion had been proved against them, the penalty would have been ostracism from most religious communities.

Eventually he accepted a job at £30 a year as shopman to a Cambridge bookseller. Once settled in the university town, he joined a local Baptist congregation and was roused to a frenzy of self-improvement. He set himself methodically to widen his culture and knowledge, both to improve himself as a man and to qualify himself for success in business. He devoured authors such as Milton, Voltaire, Gibbon and Virgil, paraphrasing or criticising their works in his notebooks. Another favourite was Walter Savage Landor, whose profuse, disputatious dialogues between ill-matched or incongruous historical figures, entitled *Imaginary Conversations*, were a lively introduction for an eager, ill-educated youth to the interplay between ideas and action. The dialogue form favoured by Landor was one calculated to show the world as composed of opposites, to show men's impulses as antagonistic and their actions warring with their reasoning. It was a form which matched Daniel's own mood of inner conflict.

He was a man who found his heroes in books. Literature helped him in every crisis of his life. Sick and prematurely tired, he found comfort and inspiration in the writings of the seventeenth-century divine Jeremy Taylor, particularly in *Holy Living and Holy Dying*, the magnificently sonorous advice on making a good life and preparing for a good death which had brought such comfort to another tubercular patient, John Keats, on his deathbed. If one feared God one need have no other fear, he learnt; intense love would annihilate death.

Another critical influence was Thomas Carlyle, whose *Sartor Resartus* published in the 1830s became 'a necessity of life' to him. Carlyle was a potent inspirer of high purposes, often absurd in his extremism, but full of zeal, endurance and courage. Partly the attraction of Carlyle was his understanding of the isolation of city life which so oppressed Daniel ('A feeble unit in the middle of a threatening Infinitude', runs a passage in *Sartor*, 'in the midst of their crowded streets and assemblages, I walked solitary'). Daniel responded to Carlyle's sense of the brevity and mystery of human life, to those passages in *Sartor* which described how humans 'haste stormfully across the astonished earth'. It is unclear how Daniel, who was so generous in his dealings with others, reconciled himself to Carlyle's cruel derision of his contemporaries and their perplexities; but he may have sensed that Carlyle's exaggerated reverence for brute force was that of a man who feared his own weakness.

Daniel's thirst for life through literature brought turmoil too. 'Byron, David Hume, Gibbon, Paley, Sterne, Fielding, Swift, and innumerable novels, plays and theological productions have unhinged my mind,' he wrote at this period of his life. 'My reading has been altogether without order. Whatever came first to hand was greedily devoured. The result is a horrid chaos of the most undigested and contradictory notions.' He adulated Shelley ('*Prometheus Unbound* is a noble utterance of his most noble nature') but felt 'indignant contempt' for the 'hollowness' of Byron's published letters. 'He seems never to have loved anyone. No one seems ever to have loved him heartily. . . . To me the never-ceasing witticisms, the everlasting tittering and smirking, is most loathsome.' This hostility to Byron was shared by his brother Alexander, who in course of time set out to ruin the poet's reputation.

Daniel had precise views on literature. 'I, who am a simple person and without learning – and don't pretend to any – judge as I find, and don't feel at all influenced by the authorities or the majority,' he wrote in 1856. For Wordsworth his admiration was unbounded, writing that the poet's 'hearty love for human worth in all its humblest forms, his deep insight enabling him to see it through the most rugged covering, and to despise the opposite, however much it might be decked and gilded, prove that he was a strong massive Englishman'. Of Tennyson he wrote: 'There is gigantic strength; all the more evidently strong because of its calmness and grace, and most wonderful harmony. His clear insight and manly sense is always noble and dignified.' More generally, so he wrote to George Brimley, the librarian of Trinity, in 1855, 'Every poem worth the name is itself a glimpse of the elements of true blessedness – it is self-forgetful, free, orderly and harmonious – complete, too, in itself, what we call perfect, and yet pointing to something higher than itself.' Poetry, like other artistic forms, 'may be used for degrading purposes, to strengthen the devil and the beast in each man rather than to subdue and expel them. The power is not the less a God-given one. The power is good though it is used for a bad, a frivolous, or selfish purpose.'

In 1837 he left Cambridge, and took work with the firm of Seeley in Fleet Street, London, by whom he was employed until 1843. His initial annual salary was £60, and he lodged with his younger brother Alexander in dingy boarding-houses in places like Hoxton. He was ill, poor and depressed, filled with inexhaustible longings and blank misgivings. Part of a prayer which he entered in his journal at this time betrays his state of mind. 'Though I am pressed under a load of debt, and have sometimes to struggle with hunger, O Lord, preserve me in my integrity. May I never stoop to anything mean. May my morality be stern, dignified and upright. O Lord God, if it please Thee, release me from my present difficulties. While they last may they give strength and steadfastness to my principles. Keep me from cant and carelessness, haughtiness and sycophancy.'

Daniel and Alexander saw the world as a crowding mass of antitheses. Their experience was of peace and strife, joy and grief. Life for them was perpetual wrestling with evil and clinging to good. Human existence was a battle between constructive and destructive impulses: the brothers were so strident about behaving constructively, so insistent on self-betterment, because they felt so sharply the potential for destructive behaviour in themselves. Like multitudes of other nineteenth-century Britons, they had learnt from Christian teachings as well from their own self-scrutiny that love and hate are inseparable from one another, that these two extreme emotions are given form and definition by their mutual antagonism. Daniel could be his own worst enemy. He was a man wrestling with inner demons. Whenever his prospects were improving, his hopes raised and his fears abated, demons would dart out at him, putting to flight everything good in his life and filling him with trepidation: so Daniel confessed to George Wilson in 1843 when under the stress of trying to buy his first shop in Cambridge. 'Your namesake the Prophet was in a Den of Lions,' Wilson replied to Daniel on another occasion. 'Yours is a trial of an opposite kind, for the den and the lions are in you.'

One of Daniel's correspondents was the Rev. John Llewelyn Davies, then a young Christian Socialist, later an influential Broad Churchman and Macmillan author. To Davies he wrote that his Calvinistic education had taught him to treat hardships as '"the chastening of the Lord" . . . even when envy and anger rose in me, I looked upon *that* as teaching me humility, as telling me that it was only the grace of God which kept me from being violent and dishonest'. He was always 'sure that such faith as I saw from my earliest days would be one of the powerfulest means of enabling the poor to bear and to conquer poverty; from becoming mere haughty and rebellious radicals, or sneaking sycophants. Yet I think poverty a real evil; and pray for its extinction daily. . . . I see no chance of the destruction of that and the deeper evils of which it is the sign, except in the coming of the kingdom, and the doing of the will of God.'

Floundering and uncertain, ambitious yet diffident, talented but poor and unadmired, Daniel had seven dreary and anxious years in London before finding the self-confidence and approval that he craved. In the autumn of 1840 he read *Guesses at Truth by Two Brothers*, written by two Sussex clergy, Augustus Hare and his brother Julius, Archdeacon of Lewes. Dedicated to their friend Wordsworth, the book was a collection of maxims and Christian reflection which, although too long for modern tastes and occasionally sententious, was written with intelligence and glee. They were keen to be read by 'acute but half-taught men' who relished philosophical speculation and wanted to live better lives with the help of Christian revelation. The Hares personified the link between Coleridge's beliefs – his praise of the imagination and of individuality, his romantic glorification of the universal, the permeating spirituality of his approach to life – and the Broad Churchmen, a group of erudite, reform-minded clergy whose influence was greater outside than inside the Church of England. Daniel urged on the Hares the need for a 'guidebook' to morality and religion directed at young men working in London as clerks. 'Hundreds of them are continually coming here, fresh from the country, with warm, pure, genial hearts, which soon become, one can scarcely say what,' he told the Hares with unfeigned anguish. 'Many of them get on in the world, as it is called, and keep clear of the grosser and more disgusting forms of vice; but their "enlightened selfishness" leads them to look on all pretension to higher motives as mere hypocrisy.' Daniel believed, like so many men of his time, that secular life and religious beliefs were indivisible, that no one could be a good Christian who was not a good citizen, above all that the essence of Christianity lay less in doctrine than in a Christian character. His first letter to the Hares was followed by others recounting how London's shopmen, clerks, artisans and porters craved forthright advice on their beliefs. His attendance at religious, Chartist and socialist meetings had convinced him of the miserable absence of spiritual guidance to meet the needs of the time. His answer was for Hare and similar-minded Christians like F.D. Maurice to write regular catchy letters to working men's newspapers describing the opinions and designs of churchmen on subjects of popular interest. The Hares and Maurice were not convinced by this proposal, but were attracted by its author's vehement sincerity and transcendent wish to do good in the world.

City life had always excited and disturbed him, and his desire to protect other young men from what he had endured was to have a persistent if sometimes obscure influence on what the family firm later published. Nineteenth-century urban life seemed to him a pandemonium of dangerous extremes which it became part of his life's work to subdue. 'To think of those who are enduring pain, and those who are enjoying pleasure: of the villains, and the saints: the active and the indolent: the virtuous and the vicious: the pious and the profane: the prodigiously rich and the miserably poor: the noble and the mean, who inhabit or infest that marvellous and mighty place, improving or injuring its morals, saving or destroying its souls,' he had written to his brother during his first visit to London in 1833. 'It is awful beyond description. I can hardly bear it.' It was for such young men working in the City that in 1840 he was instrumental in persuading Carlyle to give a series of lectures on literature, although Daniel himself was working so hard at the time that he could attend only one on Dante and Shakespeare. Lord Brougham and Vaux had founded the Society for the Diffusion of Useful Knowledge in 1827 to make high-minded literate works available at a cheap price, but its productions were sometimes too abstruse, on other occasions superficial and disconnected. The *Penny Encyclopedia* had more success in sustaining the interest of working men, but was written with a bias towards mechanical science. Daniel responded to these trends and learnt from the false starts: as early as 1843 he was trying to excite enthusiasm for the compilation of a short but comprehensive encyclopedia for 'commonplace people'. Edifying books for young self-improving men became a Macmillan speciality. Education was for him not merely a means to inner self-enrichment, worldly prosperity or political empowerment, but a protection against sinful corruption and a means to spiritual redemption. He equated books with the progress with which all free peoples shone. In his attitude he resembled George Cassell, the temperance lecturer who became a London publisher. 'Educate the working men and women, and you have a remedy for the crying evils of the country,' Cassell exclaimed at one temperance meeting. 'Give the people mental food and they will not thirst after the abominable drink which is poisoning them.' In 1850 Cassell launched *The Working Man's Friend and Family Instructor*, a penny weekly magazine to improve the minds of artisans and instruct their families; in format it resembled the *Reader's Digest* of today, and within a year Cassell was claiming a circulation of 100,000 copies.

A turning point of Daniel's life was his visit to Archdeacon Hare's house at Hurstmonceaux in 1842. With his usual impetuosity, he developed an immediate and profound admiration for this clergyman, who had known such of his heroes as Thomas Arnold, Landor and Carlyle. The Archdeacon owned what Daniel the bookseller judged as perhaps 'the best private library in England', and the rooms of his house were filled with books. 'The rugged almost uncouth presence of the master of the house pervaded everything,' his nephew Augustus Hare later wrote, recalling 'the eagerness with which he called for sympathy over every public event of passing interest, his uncontrolled vehemence where he detected any wrong or oppression, his triumphant welcome of any chivalrous or disinterested action, his bursts of unspeakable tenderness, the hopeless unpunctuality of everything'. This was the man who now became Daniel's mentor: who in course of time introduced him to some of the great churchmen and social reformers of the epoch, including F.D. Maurice, A.P. Stanley, Richard Chenevix Trench (a poetic disciple of Coleridge who became Archbishop of Dublin in 1863), Bishop Colenso and Charles Kingsley. Years later, in 1888, Alexander Macmillan told Lord Coleridge that Hare had been 'paternally kind' to Daniel, and indeed the bookish clergyman did assume the role of a protective and admiring father to the tubercular young Scot.

Personal change is always wearisome. It requires emotional adaptation and mental exertion which would have been particularly taxing for an overworked, under-appreciated tubercular man like Daniel. It is almost impossible for anyone to change the direction of their life without affectionate support from other people, and Daniel at this time was lonely and felt unloved. The first move could not have been more profound, symbolically or practically. He repudiated the dissenting religion of his parents, and conformed to the orthodox religion of his new found father-figure Hare. Under Hare's influence, and that of Maurice's *The Kingdom of Christ*, Daniel in 1842 seceded from the Baptist community and joined the Church of England. 'Dissent and Dissenting systems have been for a long time very hateful to me, so extremely repulsive that I kept them out of my mind as much as possible,' he explained to the minister from whose congregation he resigned. His nature had so 'revolted from the thing, that it really injured my health, physical and spiritual.'

While initially keeping his job with Seeley, in 1843 Daniel borrowed money to lease a shop in the City of London. He installed his younger brother Alexander as manager, and commenced business as a bookseller. Later in the same year he took over a small bookselling business in Cambridge, near Trinity and St John's colleges, opposite the gates of the Senate House (the building is still identifiable as the premises of the Bowes & Bowes bookshop, bearing the surname of Daniel's nephew Robert Bowes, but owned since 1953 by the multiple retailers W.H. Smith). In this course he had not only moral encouragement but financial support from Archdeacon Hare, who lent him £500 at 4 per cent interest and urged his Cambridge friends to give their patronage to his ambitious and intelligent protégé. Hare's support and recommendations were crucial to the success of the Macmillans. As Daniel wrote to the Archdeacon in 1853, 'When I see so many blessings showered down on my brother and myself and those who are dearest to us, I am reminded that God has sent them to us in great measure through you.'

The brothers, following Hare's advice, next sold the London shop so as to concentrate on their more important business in Cambridge. They left the City with regret because the London premises had provided such a fine chance of meeting 'young Scotch ministers, young Dissenting missionaries, and young men about to leave England for the colonies – who were every now and then calling on us when they were in London'. The most distinguished of these pioneers was the missionary and explorer David Livingstone, who visited the shop when a medical student. For Daniel books were not just articles of trade to be sold at a profit. He loved books as 'friends', to quote Tom Hughes, 'whom it was a joy as well as a duty to introduce to as wide a circle as possible'. The duty was a Christian one. In Daniel's own words, 'We booksellers, if we are faithful to our task, are trying to destroy, and are helping to destroy, all kinds of confusion, and are aiding our great Taskmaster to reduce the world to order, and beauty, and harmony. . . . As truly as God is, we are His ministers, and help to minister to the well-being of the spirits of men.' (With sensible Scottish caution, he added, 'at the same time it is our duty to manage our affairs wisely, keep our minds easy, and not trade beyond our means'.) To another correspondent in 1842 he wrote that it was in books that 'one finds the only true communion of saints'. Some items he would not stock in the Cambridge shop, where undergraduates might call. 'I never had patience enough to seek for truth in common sewers', he told Archdeacon Hare in 1844. Neither as bookseller nor as publisher would he or his brother encourage novels which might confuse the reader's notions of good and bad, or produce a blurred and blotted vision of life.

His position as a bookseller was difficult. Aside from the anxiety of his tuberculosis, he was short of capital. He and Alexander had borrowed a total of £750, which soon proved insufficient. University towns like Oxford and Cambridge had a tradition of shopkeepers giving long credit to their customers – often young gentlemen who took pride in running up debts – land this weighed heavily on a new firm, short of money itself, like Macmillan's bookshop. Daniel expected his customers to pay bills within a year, but they did not always do so; the strain of keeping the business afloat in the early years was severe.

Nevertheless it was a good moment for a man of his outlook to open a bookshop in Cambridge. Britain was in religious, social and economic ferment. 'The Anti-Corn Law agitation was stirring the nation to its depths, and the triumph of the middle-class was all but assured,' so Tom Hughes wrote. 'Behind and beneath it, the great movement of the working-class was already making itself felt, in Chartism, and half-blind associations in one and another direction.' Literacy was coming to be seen as a cause, a consequence, a guarantor and even the measure of progress. The number of children at school had doubled between 1820 and 1834, and by the late 1850s it was estimated that all but about 5 per cent of children were attending school. The increasing investment by the state and by individuals in educating children culminated in the Education Act of 1870, which provided for the schooling of all children up to the age of thirteen, with remission of fees for poor parents. As a result the illiteracy level officially fell below 1 per cent by 1913. This apparent triumph of nominal national literacy was in truth rather compromised: official figures were dubious in some respects, and begged important questions about the nature of the education given to the poor.

Nevertheless an unprecedented demand for reading materials accompanied this proliferating literacy. Increasing numbers of people sought knowledge, and turned to books for it. As readers bought more books, larger production runs reduced prices, and cheaper books drew a still wider readership. The average price of a book fell by 40 per cent in the quarter century after 1828. The impact of the written word as a new mass product was as profound and pervasive upon Victorian minds and homes as a century later television was to prove – although the progress of literacy was gradual, and its consequences were sometimes contrary to the meliorists' hopes. One result for example was the proliferation of broadsheets and magazines like the *Terrific Register*, with their gory accounts of child murder, cannibalism, disembowelling, torture and immolation, a genre which provided the nineteenth-century equivalent of video nasties. Similarly the new working-class preoccupation with studying national horse-racing form, the perpetual, pitiful hopes of betting coups and squandering family resources, were sustained by the poisonous mushrooming of turf newspapers, which in turn were made possible only by the new literacy. It disheartened men like Daniel that broadsheets about murders were the most popular literature in the early days of ascending literacy rates, but they were consoled that some readers progressed from penny dreadfuls to shilling editions of Shakespeare. A penny which was only enough to buy a 250-word broadsheet in the 1840s paid for a fifty-page songbook or a 7,000-word serial by the 1860s, and a 20,000-word novella in the 1880s or an unabridged classic in the 1890s. Daniel was at first a puny figure in these momentous changes; but he was determined to play his part, and to treat that part as a high vocation. It had been in Cambridge, twelve years earlier, that he had formed his high ideal of a bookseller's calling, and to Cambridge he returned to test how far that early dream could be realised.

In 1845 Macmillan bought the business of one of the best established older Cambridge booksellers at a cost of £6,000. They doubled their retailing power, but the cost of the purchase forced Daniel and Alexander to take other partners, who provided the cash buut had no experience of bookselling. Under the conditions of this new partnership, the profits were divided into equal thirds; in the event of the death of either of the working partners, his interest ceased and passed to the surviving partners. After his marriage in 1850, particularly after the birth of his children and with his increasingly poor health, this provision became a terrible worry to Daniel. In the event, and fortunately for the interests of his children, this potentially ruinous arrangement ceased a few months before his death. For a long time before then it had been, in his own phrase, 'like a carrion crow gnawing at his heart'; once the threat of it had been driven off, he died. The menace to his family had helped keep him alive. In other ways the sleeping partners, with their preference for steady returns rather than diversification and with their dislike of Daniel's ambitious ideas, exasperated him.

Daniel had many benefactors, as he reported to F.D. Maurice in 1845. Many of his customers recommended their friends to patronise his shop, and they passed the recommendation to yet others, so that the scope of his clientèle was always increasing; yet he often felt disheartened, and overwhelmed with work, and grieved that he had been presumptuous in setting up for himself rather than working for others. He consoled himself in hoping that his promotion of good books had moral utility, for all moral regeneration, he was sure, began with education, and in Cambridge he was selling books to the future educators of the nation.

His health was so bad that he contemplated emigration to Australia for his health in 1849. 'I often have great hope,' he recorded in his journal in 1853. 'But then comes sudden weakness, utter prostration of strength, pain in the back and chest, difficulty of breathing, and numerous symptoms which can hardly be named . . . One craves above all things to be brave and gentle and loving, and really to live a life of Faith.' His brothers, sisters and nephews all succumbed through the years to tuberculosis or diseased lungs, and he maintained a long, loving correspondence with his oldest Scottish friend George Wilson, who was also dying of the disease. 'I have only been kept alive by issues, blisters, setons, till my whole chest is a series of scars got in the battle of life,' he wrote in 1852. 'I have been kept alive by having been able to take ease and rest, and get pure air, and the kind of food which consumptive people need.' Yet he concluded, with Christian resignation, 'I can say from the heart, thank God for my afflictions.'

'All I can hope for', he wrote in September 1855, 'is a constant stand-up fight with death,' but he did not fight alone. Family and friends not only nursed and encouraged him, but took a keen interest in the merits of the different cures available. The intelligence and forbearance with which he approached his suffering turned at least one physician whom he consulted into a friend. This was Dr James Tetley, who had qualified in medicine at Edinburgh and was Physician at the Torquay Hospital for Consumptives and its related Institution for Reduced Gentlewomen with Affected Chests. It was characteristic of Daniel that he admired and respected Tetley because the latter had a well-stocked and eclectic library.

One of Daniel's customers at this time described him as:

> tall, but with a frame already somewhat wasted; pale face, aquiline nose, a large mouth with full lips, dark lustrous eyes with long lashes. He looked like one whom God loved, I mean one who might pass away from us while yet young. He was fond of talking, especially on books, and soon groups of men would gather round him in the shop and listen to criticisms full of humour and knowledge on books and authors ... There was a little snuggery in the top of the house, in which in the evenings many of us first learnt to appreciate little-known Scotch songs and ballads.

After a crisis in his health in 1844, Daniel was less able to work in the Cambridge shop, and from 1848 onwards spent long periods trying to recuperate his strength at coastal resorts like Torquay or Cromer. He had long hankered after trying his success as a publisher. After the doubling of the

Macmillan retailing business in 1845 this became viable. The advantages of the firm's position in the heart of Cambridge were strong. 'Here was a mine, hitherto almost unworked, of the best book-producing power of the nation, especially for educational works,' as Tom Hughes wrote: 'in every generation of undergraduates were men specially fitted for writing or editing them.' Daniel accordingly turned to publishing with his usual mixture of zeal and caution.

He was not the only bookseller to enter publishing. His contemporary George Routledge, who originally had a bookshop off Leicester Square, had begun publishing in 1843, but, unlike Macmillan, made his reputation as a publisher of cheap books. Nor was Daniel the only earnest, self-improving working-class man of his generation to found a great publishing house. George Cassell, originally a carpenter and itinerant temperance speaker, became a magazine publisher in 1848, and devoted his business to aiding the self-improvement of the poor. The three men were of the same generation: Routledge a year older than Daniel, and Cassell four years younger. This was the generation which provided the commercial vanguard for mass literacy.

The first book that Macmillan published was a short educational treatise entitled *The Philosophy of Training*. Its author, A.R. Craig, had formerly been classics master at Glasgow Normal Seminary and now taught in Islington. Like Daniel, he saw education as 'one of the great moral engines that Providence has put into the hands of man for ameliorating and elevating the condition of all ranks of society', without which 'the moral renovation and perfection of the species' was impossible. Craig argued the case for teacher-training: it was a fallacy to suppose that the young men who had graduated with the highest honours from Oxford and Cambridge would make the best teachers or understand the 'eccentric freaks of light-hearted children'. It required more exact training to excel at teaching, as he argued with many elegantly phrased but rather laborious examples. This worthy but now almost unreadable volume was the first of thousands of such books that appeared under the Macmillan imprint. It resonated with the high-mindedness which Daniel saw it as his calling to serve.

Daniel wished to publish books that would help men to resist whims and caprices. Of all the novels that he published, *Tom Brown's Schooldays*, by Tom Hughes, was most quintessential of him. This famous story of the eponymous hero's school career at Rugby under the headmastership of Thomas Arnold is a didactic tale against sin, vice, idleness and cruelty. Yet, whereas Arnold himself was an oppressively sombre man, *Tom Brown's Schooldays* for all its moralising is a hopeful and not a dark book. Hughes himself was a working barrister, a plain and jolly man, with a real though narrow talent. To an ideal extent the book was a collaboration between its author and its publisher. When denouncing to F.D. Maurice the frivolous, ignorant, idle and selfish behaviour which was demoralising Britain, and insisting on the need for truth, vigour and beauty in daily life, Daniel had extolled Arnold as a man whose beautiful example would uplift the nation. The idea of a novel in praise of Arnold's beliefs delighted him. Hughes consulted Daniel repeatedly about his text before its completion: Daniel in turn excised the words 'damn' and 'infernal' throughout, and turned 'beastly' drunk into 'inhumanly'. The book was an immediate success. It sold 11,000 copies in the seven months after publication in 1857, bringing its author royalties of £1,250 in that period alone. Daniel's purpose in publishing it, and that of Hughes in writing it, was to do good. Their object was to condemn 'too much over-civilisation, and the deceitfulness of riches', to encourage the proper valuing of a good man for his own sake. Tom's father discouraged class exclusiveness: 'the village boys were full as manly and honest and certainly purer than those in a higher rank'. The book's message was Christian to its roots and reflected Daniel's own sense of himself as ensnared in a battle between extremes of good and bad. Arnold had identified the task of schooling as the making of good, obedient future citizens. 'If he'll only turn out a brave, helpful, truth-telling Englishman, and a gentleman, and a Christian, that's all I want,' Tom's father thinks to himself. 'It makes you feel on the side of all the good and all the bad too,' Tom reflects after taking the sacrament at his Confirmation. 'Only there's some great, dark, strong power, which is crushing you and everybody else. That's what Christ conquered, and we've got to fight.' Muscular Christians, for whom *Tom Brown's Schooldays* was a text, deplored scepticism as a morally reckless attitude for which the only antidote was energetic manliness: Hughes himself went 'mad' on seeing the sybaritic luxuries of Paris and wanted 'to smash some of the mirrors on the boulevards and to punch the heads of some of the little coxcombs who sit sipping and smoking all along the Café fronts'.

Every age needs its heroes, but the Victorians knew this more immediately than we do. John Lothrop Motley's magnificent three-volume history of *The Rise of the Dutch Republic*, which rediscovered for modern readers the heroic qualities of William of Orange in resisting the Spanish military occupation of the Low Countries, sold 17,000 copies in English in the first year of its publication in 1856. Carlyle wrote *Heroes and Hero-Worship*, Charles Kingsley wrote *The Heroes* and Macmillan published Charlotte Yonge's history of heroism, *The Book of Golden Deeds*. This need for objects of admiration had many roots: the need to idealise father-figures; the need to exaggerate other people's virtues and power in order to compensate for one's own weakness or lack of worth; the need in unsettled times for saviours. Daniel's hero was the Broad Churchman and founder of so-called Christian Socialism, the Rev. Frederick Denison Maurice, who was also Archdeacon Hare's brother-in-law. A letter of 1844 from Maurice to Daniel shows the high opinion and confidence which this obscure young Scot inspired. 'We are threatened', Maurice wrote,

> with Atheism. Everywhere I seem to perceive this peril. The battle within, the battle without is against this. . . . The upper classes become, as may happen, sleekly devout for the sake of good order, avowedly believing that one must make the best of the world without God; the middle classes try what may be

done by keeping themselves warm in dissent and agitation to kill the sense of hollowness; the poor, who must have realities of some kind, and understanding from their betters that all but houses and lands are abstractions, must make a grasp at them or else destroy them.

In these views Daniel and F.D. Maurice were united.

The more that Maurice's views were assailed, the more staunch became Daniel's support for them. Criticism of them, so he wrote, was 'spiced with lots of slang and cant, and spite and malignity, and is making a very great fuss, of course, among the religious world'. When in 1853 the Macmillan brothers published Maurice's *Theological Essays* people 'shuddered at the very look of the book', Alexander recalled in 1884, 'and Daniel and I were warned by friends, who were attached to us, that we were doing vast harm to religion – and to ourselves! – in publishing such a book'. In its most controversial section Maurice argued that belief in eternal punishment for sins was superstitious, and that the word 'eternity' did not mean indefinite duration. In consequence Maurice was dismissed as Professor of Ecclesiastical History at King's College, London because the college principal believed that his theological malpractices would jeopardise future benefactions to the college. Maurice's dismissal excited ferment across the nation: a ferment in which the Macmillans were prominent, publishing Maurice's rejoinder to his critics and entering keenly into his defence. For men who had been reared by their mother to believe in a God of wrath who punished sinners with eternal torment in hell –

> nursed in the drear nightfold
> of your fatalist creed . . .
> of a hell without help, without end

as Tennyson wrote – this required a convulsive change of belief.

Another Christian reformer whom Daniel befriended was Charles Kingsley, the Hampshire clergyman who was for a time Professor of Modern History at Cambridge. Like Daniel he was a man of immense enthusiasms and profound contradictions. Constantly fighting against black despair, he was often too restless to sit at table through a meal and was frequently reduced to nervous and physical collapse by overwork. His incessant need to reiterate his dogmatic beliefs was a defence against the crushing doubts which assailed him, a ploy to deny the weakness which he felt in himself. The historian J.R. Green, who met Kingsley at Macmillan, described how 'he marched up and down the room like a restless animal, shouting out about the living God'. Stopford Brooke, a friend of Alexander Macmillan, similarly described meeting Kingsley at a garden party: 'A keen, keen face like a sword, and a body thinned out to a lathe, a quick, rushing walk, and deep-set eyes, and a long-lipped mouth'. Highly sexed, Kingsley would forgive himself for the joys of orgasm only by regarding intercourse as sacramental, as he told his wife, treating 'our marriage bed' as 'our altar'. He felt himself defiled, dirtying whatever he touched; a dominating theme of his best books is the cleansing of filth. Kingsley's first work published by Macmillan was *Cheap Clothes and Nasty* (1850), a pamphlet denouncing the vile working conditions of London tailors for spreading 'degradation, pestilence, heathendom, and despair'. Kingsley described how 'young tailors, fresh from the country, are decoyed by the sweaters' wives into their miserable dens, under extravagent promises of employment, to find themselves deceived, imprisoned, and starved, often unable to make their escape for months – perhaps years; and then only fleeing from one dungeon to another as abominable'. Shops selling the products of this 'evil' were cursed by God, and their customers were 'partakers of their sins'; but Kingsley proposed a remedy. 'No man who calls himself a Christian – no man who calls himself a man – shall ever disgrace himself' by buying clothes from such a shop. *Cheap Clothes and Nasty* had considerable impact. Copies were read at the smartest London clubs, and fashionable young men took their custom away from Mayfair tailors who relied on sweated labour, instead patronising those tailors named by Kingsley as treating their staff decently. Later generations have condemned the Victorians as exploitative and hypocritical, but this incident shows an active conscience and fine scruples unknown in later generations. It is hard to imagine young men at the Turf club in the 1990s reading pamphlets on East London working conditions, still less forsaking their tailor because he treated his staff badly. The Victorian conscience was real, and could be admirable.

Kingsley's ardour was raised by the ravages of cholera at Bermondsey. His passionate sermons on the evils of bad drains and polluted water were published by Macmillan, although his great novel on working-class co-operation and the lethal cess-pit of London slums, *Alton Locke*, was published by a more established house. Nevertheless, Kingsley sometimes stayed at Daniel's London house and other novels by him were published by Macmillan. Daniel wrote in 1852 that he had been gladdened by 'the fiery zeal of Mr. Kingsley ruffling the dead calm of the comfortable and respectable classes'. Finally in 1854 Kingsley gave his new novel, *Westward Ho!*, to Macmillan in return for an advance of £40. Its publication in 1855 not only earned £400 for Kingsley, but immeasurably raised the prestige of the Macmillans as publishers. This rattling account of Elizabethan heroes fighting the Spanish had stirring resonances for the British at a time when they were warring with Russia in the Crimea. It was 'a most ruthless, blood thirsty book', its author boasted, 'just what the times want, I think'; he dedicated it to Sir James Brooke, who had conquered Sarawak on the north-west coast of Borneo and was installed as its Rajah in 1842. The Malays whom he subjugated were 'enemies of Christ' according to Kingsley, 'beasts, all the more dangerous because [they] have a semi-human cunning' whom he hated 'with a perfect hatred' and wanted to 'beat ... as small as dust before the wind'. Critical reaction to *Westward Ho!* was mixed, with George Eliot judging that Kingsley 'sees, feels and paints vividly, but he theorises illogically and moralises absurdly'.

But, important though Daniel's work and friendships were, the greatest changes in his life were in the private sphere. In

1850 he married Frances Orridge, daughter of a Cambridge chemist who enjoyed sufficient local standing to serve as a magistrate. He had admired her for some time, but his ill health and the precarious state of his business had prevented him from proposing marriage earlier. Their first child Frederick Orridge was born in 1851; their next, Maurice Crawford, named after his godfather F.D. Maurice, in 1853; their third Katherine in 1855; and their youngest, Arthur Daniel, in 1857. Domesticity was a joy to Daniel. His mentor Hare, in *Guesses at Truth*, the book that so changed Daniel's life, had written, 'To Adam Paradise was home. To the good among his descendants home is Paradise.' This represented Daniel's view. He was a home-loving Victorian, for whom marriage provided sensual delights purified and minted by religion and for whom the affections of family life were a deep solace. When his beloved brother Alexander married in 1851, Daniel wrote to him on honeymoon, 'you know nothing yet of the deep blessedness which month after month of quiet and constant intercourse and love will give you. The honeymoon is nothing compared with the months that follow.' Daniel did not mean a sexual reference with these phrases, but they carried a sexual under-meaning.

Their love of domesticity was mixed with their love of literature. For Daniel, Alexander and their wives, literature was not only the stuff of their business lives but one of the closest bonds in the family circle. In many of their most intimate and happy moments at home they were reading. Literature provided some of the most precious memories of the Macmillans. They were of essence a *bookish* family, which found transcendent meaning in books. 'Mr Tennyson is linked in the minds of myself, my wife and sister-in-law who lives with us by bonds deeper than as a writer of noble poetry,' Alexander wrote to Mrs Tennyson a few years after Daniel's death. His brother, 'who was my partner in all ways, for eighteen years of most blessed intercourse', had introduced him to Tennyson's poetry. From 1842, when the first two-volume edition was published, there had been no book except the Bible 'so often in our hands, or whose words have been so often on our lips. Each successive publication was hailed with a fresh joy and conned and discussed and read and re-read together till every sentence was familiar to us. Our most earnest aspirations after any nobleness in life or thought got its best expression oftenest I believe in the words of these books.' They had both known 'for at least two years before he went, that any day almost might be the last'. Knowing this to be the case, Tennyson's sequence on the death of his beloved friend Arthur Hallam, *In Memoriam* (1850), proved irresistibly poignant to them. It became 'the constant companions of our fireside, or of any pleasure outing we had': so much so that Daniel's youngest child seems to have been named Arthur in memory of Hallam. In sharing this experience with the Tennysons, Alexander was revealing to them what was richest in the Macmillan family circle and what, after God, was most meaningful in their inner lives.

But as they knew when they read and reread *In Memoriam*, Daniel was hastening to the grave. In May 1857 he had an attack of pleurisy just a week before his last child Arthur was born. He was able to rejoice at the child – 'A jolly little fellow, who looks very wild' – and made all the arrangements for the christening, which he must have suspected that he would never see. Tom Hughes was godfather to the boy, who inherited Daniel's weak health, and despite a voyage to India intended to restore his strength, died at the age of nineteen in 1877. After this bout of pleurisy in the early summer of 1857, Daniel's health steadily declined, and soon he could swallow neither food nor drink without being racked by violent coughing. On Midsummer Day he got up for the last time, and sat for some hours on a sofa in his dressing-room in sunshine. He could speak with difficulty only at intervals. His children were allowed to play silently in the room, and at one moment he gasped, 'Oh, I should like to see my children have a beautiful home, to speak gently to each other, and to help in every way to spread the kingdom of God.' Looking at his second son Maurice, he told his wife, 'he will be very like me, and very like me in character, and be the same comfort to you that I was to my mother'. A few friends and associates came for leave-taking. To his confidential clerk he managed to say, 'I am sure you will do right. I am sorry to leave you, but I think I shall come floating among you all. We have talked over everything in life before this.'

He survived for a few days longer, watched by his wife and his brother Alexander. He spoke of dreams of bathing at Arran, of his mother singing 'I'm weary of hunting and fain would lie down', of her death and their imminent meeting in heaven. Looking through the window at the blue sky above St Mary's church, he said, 'How beautiful to float up there! I am so tired, tired! O God, sure to deliver!' Finally and feebly he spoke to his wife again. 'Goodbye, kiss me, why don't you speak to me? You will see so much of me come out in the children, dear. It will be a great comfort to you; but you will see the impetuosity.' A few hours later, on 27 June 1857, Daniel died. 'These things sicken & puzzle one; & force one, in order to avoid despair, to believe absolutely that God is Love,' Kingsley wrote to Alexander in commiseration on the news of Daniel's death. 'There is no other escape.'

From his earliest years Daniel Macmillan was intent on self-discipline. He condemned himself for impetuosity and excessive vehemence, although others regarded him as amiable and even playful. He clung to notions of religion and rectitude in a life beset by uncertainty and temptation. He was enthusiastic, fretful and always scarred by the loneliness of his youth. Consumed from an early age by a longing for intercourse with the best minds, he had the wonderful fortune to achieve his ambition. Whereas most people of his class and background were 'condemned', in Matthew Hale White's phrase, 'to almost total absence from themselves', to unremitting work and struggle in which the roar of the world was never lulled to rest, to endure a life without peace for introspection, Daniel escaped this doom. By filling his life with books, he had calm, enriching days in which to renew himself and find wider meaning. Publishing was for him not a mercenary trick, or a sullen craft, but a life-enhancing calling for the greater glory of God.

He was not serene in his conscience or in his exercise of virtue. For all of his love of calm and truth, Daniel was a warrior fighting not only his own ill-health and his own inner demons, but also a hand-to-hand fighter in the spiritual battlefield around him. 'So many wars are going on unceasingly in all parts of the earth,' as Hare had written in *Guesses at Truth*: 'the war waged by the mind of man against the powers of Nature in the fulfilment of his mission to subdue them – the war of Light against Darkness, of Truth against Ignorance and Error – the War of Good against Evil, in all its numerous forms, political, social and personal.' Here Daniel was a combatant too.

Although an invalid, his life and ideas touched many people and had an enduring influence on the family he left behind. Daniel's devotion to his brother, the unanimity with which they worked, moved many of their contemporaries and speaks of deeply affectionate and united natures. 'My dear Friends,' Kingsley began a letter of 1853 to Daniel and Alexander, 'For in answering one, I answer both, never being able to tell either your writing or your thoughts apart.' This kinship promoted a family solidarity and contributed to forming a family heritage, which is one of the chief themes of this book.

CHAPTER 4

Alexander

He was one of those who cannot *but* be in earnest. . . . From of old, a thousand thoughts . . . had been in this man: What am I? What *is* this unfathomable Thing I live in, which men name Universe? What is Life; what is Death? What am I to believe? What am I to do?

Thomas Carlyle,
Heroes and Hero-Worship

A life lived in earnest does not die; it goes on for ever.

Edward Thring, 1887

Alexander Macmillan was in earnest, a man very much of his era, for earnestness was one of the ruling traits of the Victorian age. The earnest strove to know the causes of things and to master the great principles which governed existence. Earnestness meant searching for the truth of human destiny, both in life and after life; it required at best a scrupulous searching of one's own motives and actions, at worst it resulted in an irritability of conscience that paralysed or poisoned everything one might do. Life for the earnest Victorian was not a pilgrimage of pleasure, but a scene of toil and appointed work. Every thought and action was subordinated to the individual's sense of right and wrong. The earnest dedicated themselves to strive for grand purposes, to wrestle with evil, to extirpate what was bad but elevate all that was good. These were the exacting tasks which Alexander set himself.

He was born on 3 October 1818 at Irvine in Ayrshire, where his parents had moved after the death of their four daughters on Arran. He was five years younger than Daniel, to whom from early childhood he was devoted. Their separation when he was about five or six was always a regret to him and, coming shortly after his father's death, was a double loss; his adult devotion to Daniel was an attempt to recover from this early and undeserved wrench. One of their tightest bonds, as boys and men, was their adulation of their mother, who in their memory became an almost immaculate being.

Alexander's education, like Daniel's, was paid for by their eldest brother, Malcolm. As a boy and in later life Alexander was inspired by the example of James Connel, the master of the Commercial Department at Irvine Academy, a self-educated man who had originally been a hand-loom weaver but raised himself by self-education and wrote a book on *Differential Calculus*. 'How great is the influence unseen and unnoted at the time', Alexander wrote in celebration of Connel many decades later, that one man 'intent on doing his work simply, unselfishly, manfully, may have on the future' of another man's life. Connel was one of several substitute father-figures who were adopted by Daniel and Alexander as good models to be emulated. When Alexander in middle age held up Connel as exemplary – 'a perfect gentleman, courteous, high-toned, simple, really noble, and with what a keen intellect!' – he was also describing the sort of man whom he had tried to be. The memory of his brother Malcolm, and of Connel, gave him unremitting sympathy for the loneliness and frustration of poor men struggling to widen their vision and experience; a sympathy which took material form, years later, in 1855, when he helped to found the Cambridge Working Men's College for those who wished for a broader education than was offered at Mechanical Institutes.

In other ways Connel's example and ambitions were a perpetual influence on Alexander. Connel, like so many self-improving working men of his era, was a keen botanist. In their study of wildlife such men strove to touch the universal, to find a chink in the hard and narrow lives which they were condemned to live so that they could gaze and be uplifted. Daniel and Alexander, too, sought the universal. Their spiritual lives were quests for the absolute, their working lives as publishers of edifying or educational books a quotidian expression of that quest. As Alexander told the Rev. Fenton Hort in 1859, knowledge was concerned with the infinite and with absolutes. It was central to this outlook that Alexander, years later, delighted to publish books like *The Depths of the Sea*, by Sir Wyville Thomson, which reported on pioneering explorations of the North Atlantic, proving that many types of marine life still existed which had hitherto been known only in a fossil state. He took comparable pride in handling the books and articles of Sir William Thomson, the Glaswegian who was perhaps the best-known Victorian scientist and as Lord Kelvin became known as the Lord of British Science.

Little is known about Alexander's early life, although there is a story that the boy proved so gifted a pupil that, at the age of sixteen, he was briefly headmaster of a little school in Irvine. Later, like Daniel, he moved to Glasgow as assistant to a bookseller, but this arrangement did not last long. His employer was a fractious man of excessive piety who, discovering a light novel in the pocket of Alexander's overcoat, pulled it out, tore it to pieces and flung it in a fire. Alexander left immediately, and in return for assisting the master of the junior class at Irvine Academy was given a grounding in classics. His brother William, headmaster of a school by Shewalton colliery near Irvine, then fell ill, and Alexander ran the school for three months in his absence. He was afterwards an assistant teacher at a commercial school in Glasgow, but then toyed with the idea of becoming either a pharmacist or a sailor. To this end he worked for a time as an assistant in a chemist's shop in Glasgow, and later, in 1836, sailed before the mast to America. 'This adventure, which was doubtless prompted by discontent or rebellion against his straitened circumstances, was never repeated and seldom referred to,' according to his biographer Charles Graves. In later life he regarded it as 'foolish'.

For less than a living wage he was in 1838–9 usher of a colliery school at Paisley, supervising 130 rough colliery children, many of them Irish and all of them poor. He was rescued from this unhappy paupery in 1839 when a vacancy arose at the office of Daniel's employers in London, Messrs Seeley. Alexander was recommended for the job by Daniel, and arrived in London on his twenty-first birthday in 1839.

Like Daniel he took from their mother a love of books; and, although less well read than Daniel, the variety of his early jobs had given a wider grounding in life. His endurance of miserable grind as a colliery schoolmaster especially proved a valuable experience when he became an educational publisher. On starting work at Seeley's in London, he set out to educate himself by mastering the prose classics of English literature. His youthful enthusiasms for Burns, Carlyle, Coleridge, Shakespeare, Shelley, Tennyson and Wordsworth never faded.

Earnest men glorified work as a means to serve God. Work was the way to attain supreme virtue: the outer action that led to the inner good. Idleness was akin to a state of perpetual despair. Alexander's gospel of work owed much to the writings of Thomas Carlyle, whom he admired as a seer. He recognised his kinship with Carlyle's Scottish earnestness and vehemence, and as a Cambridge bookseller offered his undergraduate customers such Carlylean injunctions as: 'Only find work to do and your doubts will disappear like the mists of morning'; 'Do something that you know to be useful and you will see your way clear through every difficulty'; 'Keep yourself busy with your commonplace duties and your faith will be established'; 'The noble life is fighting the world, the flesh and the devil by constant employment in what your conscience tells you ought to be done.' Alexander felt an unbreakable affinity with his fellow Scots, preferably those of heavy diligence and outlook, surrounding himself with them in his office, so that by 1861 Dante Gabriel Rossetti was jokingly referring to 'MacMillan's Macademy of stones'.

He was devoted to the ballad poetry of Scotland, and loved to sing 'Annie Laurie' or 'The Bonny House of Airlie'. George Fox's *Journal* made a deep impression in his younger days. Fox was the seventeenth-century itinerant preacher whose followers combined – not in a new sect or new Church – but in the Society of Friends, the Quakers. Fox believed that he had come into personal contact with God: that God was not above the sky or at the end of a logical syllogism, but a living spiritual presence revealed within the soul. Fox's emphasis on the development of individual inner potential, his view of Christ as an inward teacher, struck deep resonances in Alexander. The *Journal*'s record of Fox's transcendent experience, his exalted sense of the infinite preciousness of every person of whatever class or type, had an affinity with Alexander's deepest beliefs. It was consistent with his liking for Fox's ideas that Alexander disliked the Haldanes' Revival meetings, which had transformed the religious life of his family on Arran, because they rested on the idea that 'the work of the Spirit of God is exceptional, monstrous, what is called miraculous, instead of being what I believe the Bible assuredly teaches us it is, orderly, universal, permanent'. Nor could the poor, obscure young Scot miss the further appeal of the *Journal*: it is a simple, sincere history of the persecution that had to be endured in order to keep faith, written by a man of little education and obscure antecedents struggling against the world's contempt.

After the deterioration in Daniel's health in 1848, Alexander was often left solely in charge of their business for months at a time. When Daniel was away in Torquay, Alexander wrote daily to his brother describing not only the state of business, but gossiping about customers who had visited the shop. He reported too on the progress of Daniel's children, who were separated from their father and stayed in Cambridge. He was fascinated by the university and regaled Daniel with the latest news about prizes won or fellowships awarded. The university magazines were scrutinised by him, and he sought out those contributors whose ideas impressed him. No books were accepted for publication by Alexander without the approval of Daniel, and on some occasions Mrs Daniel was consulted. The work was long, the responsibilities were heavy and his health suffered. He described himself to Daniel in 1855 as 'a man with chronic dyspepsia . . . whose acrid stomach is always getting into his brain and clouding his heart'. (It is possible that his life was saved by his dyspepsia: tuberculosis is contracted by swallowing germs, and some late-twentieth-century researchers suggest that stomach acid kills the germ.)

Daniel's death in 1857, wrote a Cambridge friend, Dr Sebastian Evans, developed 'a hitherto latent strength of will in his brother', whose life became fired with 'the spirit of a kindly religious fanatic, who felt he had a sacred mission laid upon him'. Evans believed that there were few people of Alexander's generation 'to whom the Church of England as a national institution owes a deeper debt of gratitude'. Alexander followed all the theological controversies of his day and became convinced that if the Church was to retain its hold upon the people, an intellectual renaissance was needed. The best chance of this, he decided, was offered by the works of the Broad Churchman F.D. Maurice ('He is a grand man, and must endure like other prophets. The good people of the next age will build his tomb'). His *Kingdom of Christ* (1837) attempted to show that there was a portion of divine truth in the claims of each sect: that differences in ritual and doctrinal practice should be mediated, rather than refuted. From the late 1850s Alexander was one of the most enthusiastic exponents of Maurice's beliefs (although he was bored by sports other than croquet, and despised the athleticism at some schools). 'No work in our day is half so important as this of vindicating the reality of God's revelation of Himself to man,' Alexander assured Maurice in 1859. 'It is never long out of my mind how best to help you in the work which I think has evidently been given to you to do in this age, and I am filled with shame when I feel how little I have been able to do.'

As a Broad Churchman, Alexander deplored, as he wrote to Frederick Temple, afterwards Archbishop of Canterbury, the 'imbecile panic and fury' with which the Victorians surrounded questions of religious conscience. Not an instinctively tolerant man himself, he advocated religious toleration and the free play of theological speculation: he loathed the tirades and misrepresentation that accompanied sectarian fervour. 'This undiscriminating howl against all but stereotyped utterance, against all living thought and speech, has dangers on all sides, and should be steadily exposed,' he informed another like-minded churchman, Dean Stanley, in 1861. His special position was widely recognised. 'Among the Stanley and Kingsley set', wrote the historian J.R. Green in 1862, 'Macmillan is the "pet publisher" of the day.'

The high-minded circles in which he moved, the friends and authors whom he consulted, lived in a hubbub of contention, scouring pamphlets and tracts that Matthew Arnold called 'hot dizzy trash'. They argued about heaven and hell, about eternal damnation, about the power of moral choice, about whether humankind was descended from apes, about every ethical issue raised by new theories of political economy or new mass move-ments for the empowerment of the populace. Alexander was an agency but perhaps also a victim of this unsettlement. His beliefs and assumptions were constantly challenged. It was not surprising that Alexander worried about the insecurity of religious faith as the reading public was bombarded with new ideas, reams of statistics, historical revisions, scientific advances, ethical convulsions. As Alexander wrote to Charles Kingsley in 1859, Britain was 'sorely perplexed at the terrible breaking up of old landmarks on all sides'. He craved for certitude, was dismayed by what was vague or anomalous, felt assailed by the heresy and strife around him. 'A large and intelligent class of Engglishmen is fast drifting away from the old moorings and steerings too, and don't appear either to have or to care to possess any in their stead,' he told Sebastian Evans in 1859. 'A kind of hopeless, aimless philosophy – somewhat of the Topsy order – is all that remains.' He revolted against agnosticism as implying that human being were mere 'toys of circumstance' just as he held fast to the belief that ultimate truths in religion, ethics, political economy, science and aesthetics *did* exist, or could be discovered and asserted with enough honest mental effort. The realisation in the last fifteen or twenty years of his life that this had not happened depressed him.

Alexander felt ardently committed to 'the well-being of the class from which I sprung and to which in feeling and sympathy I still belong – the working class'. His wish for it to enjoy more political power was one of his deepest conscious feelings. 'Met Macmillan, the Cambridge publisher, whose language [was] very democratic,' recorded the Conservative politician Lord Stanley in 1864. 'He would talk of nothing but the elevation of the working-class, by which he means giving them votes.' Though Stanley doubted that the middle class, which had held supreme electoral power since 1832, would voluntarily relinquish it to the poor, Alexander 'felt sure they would fraternise with the working men' and extend suffrage to them. 'Such language is worth noting,' Stanley wrote, though he was relieved that such beliefs were not yet 'general among the literary class'. In the event the publisher proved more prescient than the politician. In 1867 the government headed by Stanley's own father, Lord Derby, extended adult male suffrage: 938,000 voters were added to an electorate in England and Wales of 1,057,000, giving the working class an electoral majority in towns for the first time.

In the cause of democracy, and in loyalty to his origins, Alexander worked to edify the poor and to enlarge their outlook. Thus, in 1861, he read aloud to a working men's society Christina Rossetti's bizarrely innovative poem, 'Goblin Market'. 'They seemed at first to wonder if I was making fun of them; by degrees they got as still as death, and when I finished there was a tremendous burst of applause.' To some people readings of

'Goblin Market' may seem a specious way of bringing social and political reform, but others will admire it as a brave and imaginative stroke. It was in the same spirit that Alexander in 1864 decided to publish cheap scholarly texts of Shakespeare's plays under the general title of Globe editions: the series was soon expanded to include authors like Burns, Defoe, Goldsmith, Pope and Spenser. The Globe texts were carefully edited and strongly bound, but their price of three shilling kept them within the reach of literate artisans. 'I have had to work, and work hard, for my bread all my life, and I have a great sympathy for all those who are in a like case,' he wrote to a Birmingham workman in 1862. 'I perhaps know more about working men and working struggle than many who are now in the midst of it. . . . Common love and help, everything done that can knit to class, the highest with the lowest – that is true, human and divine work.'

Alexander never forgot his early poverty, and, although he was as strict about efficiency as any successful Victorian employer, his egalitarianism was sincere. It had been as recently as the 1820s that the British had begun to speak and write about a class system: it was in that same decade that people began to think of themselves as middle-class or working-class. The issue of class was confused by many rhetorical complexities: in practice class identity was oscillating and equivocal. It was clear though that class distinction was intended to enforce social dispersion or separation; it set limits between people. Alexander was fortunate to stand outside all this. The contemporaries whom he trusted, and whose acceptance he wanted, were little interested in class demarcations; if they believed in the superiority of one class mentality over another, it was not that of the middle class over the working class, but of the 'industrious classes' over the rest. Alexander was the personification of industriousness. He felt neither embarrassed nor threatened by treating people equally; he felt no inhibition at recognising the common humanity of masters and men, and it was from this inhibition that so much of the spirit of class exclusiveness derived. 'I really care intensely

for the simple human being and his individual worth,' he wrote
in 1870 without a trace of humbug. On one occasion he was
driven into London by his coachman for a meeting and came
back to his horse and carriage in company with Gladstone.
In the coachman's own account, ' "Mr Gladstone," my master
said, "This is my friend S—". He did not say, "This is my
servant, or my coachman, he said "This is my friend S—",
and Mr Gladstone shook hands with me.' It was this sort of
touch which showed him at his best. His egalitarianism drew a
similar response in others. He was accepted everywhere as a man
of talent. He was seldom rebuffed by the class exclusiveness of
others; his broad Scottish accent was no social hindrance in the
years of his prosperity; and it was only in the next generation
of his family that the icy touch of class consciousness began to
chill and shrink their outlook.

His instincts were deeply protective. In 1840 he compiled a
little book entitled *The Genius of Shelley* which was published
anonymously.This opened with a sketch of Shelley's life, and
was followed by a selection of his poems. The governing principle of the selection, so Alexander avowed, was to protect the
young from 'any risk in reading the strange, crude and even
false opinions' that could be found in Shelley's works. This
expurgation went to the core of Alexander's beliefs. Passionate
in his love of good writing, he was even more passionate in his
love of God and his idealisation of domestic harmony: his life
was given shape by his determination to protect both God and
the family from mockery or attack. Shelley was a man who
defied authority, whose children were taken from him because
of his religious free-thinking and who was ostracised because
of the free-loving that was reputed to occur at his house at
Marlow. 'An entire generation was robbed of the pleasure of
reading Shelley because Tory criticism was in the ascendant,and
he was a "Republican" and an "Atheist",' as Alfred Austin, a
Macmillan author, lamented to Alexander in 1881: Shelley's
burlesque on the attempt of King George IV to divorce his
wife, written in 1820 under the title *Oedipus Tyrannus, or*

Swellfoot the Tyrant, was for example not published until 1876 because of threatened prosecution by the Society for the Suppression of Vice. Filth festers worst in the minds of censors – as Whitman said, 'the dirtiest book in all the world is the expurgated book' – yet it would be a cruel misunderstanding of Alexander to present him as just another bowdlerising meddler who wanted to proscribe other people's pleasures or interdict their thoughts for dirty reasons of his own. He wanted to censor what was irreverent or unsettling – in particular to protect young people from what he thought was the spiritual and personal catastrophe of religious unbelief – but he also longed to share what he found elevating and soul-enhancing in Shelley, particularly those passages which, like the botany of his old schoolmaster Connel, offered glimpses of the eternal or universal. Alexander's life was a long and not despicable struggle to prove 'how vital goodness is, and how impotent badness', to use a phrase from a letter of 1865 in which he commented on the murder of Abraham Lincoln.

Alexander, like Daniel, wished to publish edifying books. In 1859, for example, he quoted a couplet of Heine's with the comment that it summarised 'the utter destruction of all hope and fear' that characterised too much modern literature. So many authors, he felt, wrote.

> As if the Lord in Heaven had perished,
> And down below the Devil were dead.

A rejection letter which he sent to a young Scottish poet around the same time is typical of his outlook. 'I have read the greater part of your manuscript very carefully, and found what seemed to me a vein of palpable poetic feeling of considerable merit in its kind,' he wrote.

> The kind, however, I confess does not seem to me desirable to be cultivated. Boccaccio regretted his own work in later years, and I don't think without reason. That Italy is the thralled place she is, is owing in no small degree to her indulgence in that luscious enfeebling vein of literature. A young Scotch

poet should I think strive to make himself and others as pure
and strong and fit to do God's work in the world as he can.
We have enough to drag us down without our being sung
down in strength and purity.

Alexander initially distrusted his own judgment of novels,
and in the years immediately after Daniel's death sent several
submitted manuscripts for the opinion of an austere young
clergyman whom he had befriended as a Cambridge undergraduate, Fenton Hort ('the deadliest of literary sins', he told
Alexander, was 'fine writing').

His attitude to publishing novels was much affected by the
reception given to one of the earliest novels fostered and published by the house of Macmillan after Daniel's death. This was
Out of the Depths, written by a young clergyman, Henry Jebb,
who as an undergraduate at Cambridge had been a visitor to the
Macmillans' shop. His novel depicting the career of a prostitute
– her seduction, prosperity, misery, repentance and finally her
social and spiritual rehabilitation – was not the first Victorian
novel to figure prostitution (Mrs Gaskell had touched on the
subject in *Mary Barton* (1848) and in *Ruth* five years later), but
it was unique on Macmillan's list, and had special importance
to future editorial judgments by Alexander and his sons. On
receiving the manuscript Alexander consulted Mrs Tom Hughes
and Lady Goderich, wife of a politician of Christian Socialist
sympathies who a few years later brought in the Contagious
Diseases Acts to control venereally infected prostitutes; both
women recommended publication. Alexander then satisfied
himself that Jebb was a clean-natured, high-minded man whose
knowledge of prostitution had been imparted by a dissolute
young lord who had wrecked his health and encumbered his
estates by fast living.

Jebb's narrator was a domestic servant whose ruin was begun
by reading trashy novels. 'Books were my only companions,
and the loftiest characters there were my only intimates,' she
confessed. 'Thus I despised my class, and God, to punish me,
suffered me to fall far below the meanest of those I thought

scorn of.' She began her downfall by chasing after a 'man of higher station. . . unknowing of the dangers and perplexities to which it was sure to lead'; her ambition of 'becoming a lady' was simply 'sinful'. She allows herself to be seduced by an Oxford undergraduate, and after his death is lost in 'a hurricane of godless excitement'. As the kept woman of a dissipated peer, she becomes 'besotted in selfishness, living for the present hour'; after being abandoned by her lord, her 'hideous life' turns into a 'delirious rout' of 'hollow dreadful merriment'. Eventually she is befriended by a muscular Christian, returns to Christ but is snubbed and ostracised as she struggles to regain respectability. After many mortifications she finally escapes 'from the bondage of the Evil One', becomes a village schoolteacher, is reconciled to her family and is on the brink of marrying a widower farmer, only to die, apparently of tuberculosis.

Alexander went painstakingly over the text at proof stage, insisting that many phrases be sanitised, and notably insisting that a long passage, describing how the reformed woman suffered an attempted rape when her shopkeeper employer 'discovered something of my previous history', be shorn of all details and reduced to a sentence. Even his most mundane letters about the book were not copied into the firm's ordinary letter-books, but were entered in his Secret letter-book; ostensibly this was partly because Jebb wished to preserve his anonymity, but it was unique in a century of publishing by the firm, and suggests that Alexander had a furtive interest in Jebb's themes which he could not share with anyone. Fantasies about the rescue of prostitutes, so common among the Victorian middle classes, famously exemplified by Gladstone's nocturnal outings among London streetwalkers, were a way of reconciling the conflicting pressures of sexual desire and guilt. Stories like Jebb's satisfied men's impulse to degrade sexual objects – women – but also restored women to the immaculate ideal which Alexander, for one, identified with his revered mother.

Proudly in 1859 he sent out complimentary copies and praised the book's brilliant force. But in June, after its publication, he and the anonymous author were covered with obloquy. A letter from Daniel's oldest friend and fellow consumptive, Wilson, denounced it; so did reviewers. Jebb was agonised by the response and vowed never to write again. Alexander, like a good publisher, tried to console him: the supreme objection of the good folk who had attacked the book was that if people were free to discuss such subjects *publicly*, then both sides of the question would be discussed and moral libertarians would be allowed a voice. Then Alexander was thrown into a paroxysm of distress when Charles Kingsley rebuked him for publishing the novel: he reacted as a guilty man, caught out. It agonised him to realise that men whom he admired thought he had done harm when he was trying to do good, Alexander replied before offering to remedy the ill he had done. He deleted it from Macmillan's list, withdrew it from display in his shop and exerted himself to keep it from readers whom it might corrupt. He had however received so many letters praising its literary merits and moral utility that he was reluctant to suppress it, but behaving like an obedient son to Kingsley he asked for a definite opinion on whether the book should be withdrawn. He promised that he would not have published *Out of the Depths* if had received Kingsley's remonstrance earlier, even though others had recommended it.

This experience left Alexander more squeamish than ever and set a tradition for caution about such matters within the firm. Macmillan's prudery became notorious among authors. Tennyson half-expected him to reject his poem 'Lucretius' for publication in 1868. Anne Gilchrist, who wrote a biography of William Blake in the 1860s, recognised that it would be hopeless to try to treat properly Blake's *Visions of the Daughters of Albion*. This rich and wonderful poem included a passage which depicted Christian demands for chastity and eulogies of sexual self-denial as hopeless delusions which ignored the universal realities of fantasy and masturbation:

The moment of desire! the moment of desire! The virgin
That pines for man shall awaken her womb to enormous
   joys
In the secret shadows of her chamber: the youth shut
   up from
The lustful joy shall forget to generate and create an
   amorous image
In the shadows of his curtains and in the folds of his silent
   pillow.
Are not these the places of religion, the rewards of
   continence,
The self enjoyings of self denial? why dost thou seek
   religion?
Is it because acts are not lovely that thou seekest solitude
Where the horrible darkness is impressed with reflections of
   desire?

Mrs Gilchrist quoted the poem extensively but excised these lines, informing her readers that 'formidable moral questions' were raised in Blake's allegory, 'questions on which he had his own views, and gave fearless and glowing expression to them. . . but we will not enter on them here'. Privately she recognised that given the qualms of her publisher it would be 'useless to attempt to handle this side of Blake's writings', as she told William Rossetti in 1862. 'It was no use to put in what I was perfectly certain Macmillan (who reads all the Proofs) would take out'. She therefore reduced the section 'to a very shadow condition indeed – but left enough, I trust, for the cause of truth'.

She also warned Swinburne, who was contemplating some dealings with Alexander, 'that Mr Macmillan is far more inexorable against any shade of heterodoxy in morals than in religion – and that in fact, poor flustered propriety would have to be most tenderly and indulgently dealt with'. Alexander's susceptibilities were the subject of discreet apologies by his staff. Mowbray Morris of *Macmillan's Magazine*, warning Thomas Hardy in 1886 against treating sexual themes in a novel contemplated for serialisation, wrote that his readers were 'pious Scottish souls who take offence wondrous easily': Hardy will have known that Morris meant one pious Scottish soul in particular.

Alexander more than ever saw himself as a guardian of 'good society' after he had become the head of a family. In 1851 he married Caroline, daughter of Augustine Gutteridge Brimley, a member of a Cambridge family which enjoyed some academic and literary distinction. His wife's brother George had been for several years Alexander's closest friend; librarian of Trinity College, Cambridge, George Brimley was a literary critic who was broken by illness and died young. Their sister Harriet married a Cambridge headmaster named William Johnson: among their five sons, George William Johnson was principal clerk of the Colonial Office until 1917, and wrote books on such varied subjects as Cambridge, Christian Socialism and sexual morality; Brimley Johnson, who founded his own small publishing business (which issued the first works of G.K. Chesterton), was a prolific biographer and editor, particularly of women writers such as Jane Austen or George Eliot; while William Ernest Johnson was a Cambridge mathematician whose work on logic, though criticised by Bertrand Russell, had a strong influence on Keynes's *Treatise on Probability*. The latter's son Stephen Johnson became Professor of Classics at Newcastle at the age of thirty-four, but died prematurely in 1936.

Alexander and Caroline Macmillan's eldest child, born in December 1852, was named Malcolm Kingsley, one of the godparents being Charles Kingsley. Their next son, George Augustine, was born in August 1855; daughters Margaret in 1857 and Olive in 1858; their third son, and fifth child, William Alexander, was born in February 1864. He was idolised by his parents, and his death in June 1866 of gastric fever, apparently aggravated by the family weakness of bad lungs, left them distraught. The family governess, Louisa Cassell, suffered equally in the child's loss, and the parents drew close to her as a result; by their influence she later became Lady Superintendent of the Working Women's College in Bloomsbury (of which Alexander was for twelve years treasurer from 1875). After

Daniel's death in 1857, his widow Frances and her children came to live with Alexander and Caroline, and he professed to regard his three nephews and niece 'as my own children'. Frances inherited her husband's partnership in the business and took a close interest in its progress. 'In giving us sisters, God gave us the best of earthly moral anti-septics; that affinity, in its habitual, intimate, domestic, desensualised intercourse of affection, presenting us with the ideal of love in sexual separation,' so the Hares had written in *Guesses at Truth*, and Alexander felt something similar for his sister-in-law. After ailing for some time, she died in January 1867, ten years after her husband, to the distress of the extended family. The death aged nineteen of Arthur Macmillan, the boy born as his father Daniel lay on his death-bed, was also a great grief to the survivors. However, the little cousins grew up together and as adults three of the next generation, George, Frederick and Maurice, worked together as publishers, sometimes even sharing the same room, eventually all dying within three months of one another in 1936.

Alexander rejoiced in the comforts of home, which like many rich Victorians he saw as a refuge from the bustle of life, a sanctuary from violence and ugliness, a secure and inviolable base in times of disorder and danger. 'To him the family was a God-given institution to relieve the isolation of the individual – the feeling expressed in Matthew Arnold's line "we mortal millions live alone"' – so wrote his biographer Charles Graves. Amid the stresses and insecurities of urbanisation and industrialisation – 'the huge demon of Mechanism', in Carlyle's phrase – his home was like a lair in which he could bind his wounds and recover his energy.

The joys of family life were captivating, and it was mean and discreditable of men not to revel in them to the utmost, Alexander wrote shortly after Christmas of 1858 in celebration of the seven young, joyous, zestful children who were gathered in his household and stood out in all the diversity of their characters. He thought ceaselessly of their futures and their well-being: he hoped everything in his life was devoted to helping them serve God's purpose. He rejoiced too that his sister-in-law Frances and his wife were the best women, with the exception of his mother, that he had known. Yet, as the son of feudal Highlanders, his view of family life embraced the dead as well as the living: there was a continuous strand connecting dead ancestors with the present. 'Family worship', he wrote, was 'a very wholesome practice'. Throughout his adult years Alexander savoured his memories of 'the old life we all had in the dear old Irvine home'. As he wrote to Daniel in 1855, 'it surely is a blessing that God has built us in families and knit us together by natural bonds which we cannot ignore, and not left us to our wayward wills to settle for themselves whom they should love'. He disliked sending his sons and nephews away to boarding school – 'how hard it is', he wrote in 1872, 'to break up the home circle when you want to get your boy taught as a boy should be taught' – perhaps because he remembered the wrenching loss and grief in his own childhood when poverty and deprivation forced his beloved, protective Daniel, still a child at ten years old, to be sent from home to live with a cranky, unpredictable apprenticemaster. He and Daniel had been unusually close even at that age, and, though the pain of this first separation must have healed, its influence on his adult sentiments was permanent; he mentioned it with deep feeling to Tennyson's wife nearly forty years later.

Alexander's feelings about family life are shown in a little book, *The Child in the Midst*, which he wrote and published after Willie's death. His aim was to extract a Christian message from domestic catastrophe: he wanted to console himself in his fearful grief that the child's loss had a wider, less personal meaning. His wording shows his idealisation of Willie – a child born to him in prosperous middle age, a toddler whose bubbling humour reflected the love and physical comforts amid which he was reared, a boy whose contentment appeased Alexander's gnawing memories of the deprivations that he had endured as a child. But as he strove to commemorate and celebrate Willie's

life, his mind returned to its eternal preoccupation: the endless
struggle in himself and others between what he regarded as the
forces of good and evil, what later generations might describe as
the tension between one's impulses to love and hate. Like many
Victorians, his images of childhood were split into extremes
of idealisation and condemnation: for him a child was both
an innocent flower and potentially evil incarnate. Willie, he
wrote, was born 'with the snowdrop, with the crocus, with
the promise and hope of spring-time'. He brought 'joy and
love to a home which . . . had much of both' and 'added
human tenderness to the Divine message of joy and peace'.
By the age of three his step was 'firm and independent, his
speech articulate and wise, his clear ringing laugh an ever new
delight; the glory of his flaxen ringlets and sunny brow, the
open vision of the serene blue eye . . . were in the home a
treasure unspeakable'. Returning 'from the bustle and worry
of business in the city, to see the boy surrounded with his
sisters, and the household servants kneeling around him, and
listening to grave wise speech – prattle we call it – or to merry
laughter, mixed with the ineffable sweet serenity or the playful
sparkle of the intense blue eye, was in itself a well-spring of rest
and refreshment' to Alexander. But abruptly 'while summer was
still in its flowery prime, our Willie left us, and we . . . shall see
him on earth no more'.

In the years that followed Willie's death, Alexander often
meditated on the meaning of childhood. He likened life in the
Garden of Eden to childhood: a time of 'perfect innocent delight
and goodness . . . undisturbed by apprehension of possible evil'.
Yet there was no mention of a child in Eden. It was not until
humankind had left 'the joyous haven' and faced 'the terrible
problems, perplexities, labours, which after all these centuries
he is still fighting with' that the first child was seen: and that
child was Cain. For Alexander it was unforgettable that Cain
was not only the first murderer but also 'the first child that sat on
a mother's knee, on the knee of Eve, the mother of all living; that
it was he who woke the first chord of mother's love, the music

that has never since ceased to vibrate in and thrill and purify the heart of humanity through countless generations, which is the purest strand in every hope we have for its perfection'. The lesson that Alexander drew from this paradox was a gloomy one: everything that was purest, loveliest, most hopeful and idealised – the baby like Willie born in spring-time, as innocent as a flower – was liable to turn vicious and corrupt. We all had the mark of Cain: the best of us were capable of terrible crime.

Caroline Macmillan died in 1871, and in the following year, in the words of his son George, Alexander restored his 'shattered home by a singularly happy second marriage to Miss Emma Pignatel, a former schoolfellow of our governess and dear friend, Louisa Cassell'. Although after his only previous trip abroad, to France, Alexander had vowed that he would never leave Britain again, his new wife had a taste for travel, and soon coaxed him to Italy. His youngest son John Victor, who was born of this marriage in May 1877, was one of three of his children whose marriages perpetuated their father's friendships. In pleasing fulfilment of a family friendship traversing three generations, John Macmillan, by then a clergyman, in 1906 married F.D. Maurice's granddaughter. Previously Alexander's daughters Olive and Mary had both married sons of their father's friend James MacLehose. Many of their descendants were earnest folk (one became a charity worker in the slums of East London) or high achievers. Olive's grandson Murray was a diplomat who served as British Ambassador to Vietnam during some of the most critical passages of the war there in the 1960s, and in 1982 was created Lord MacLehose of Beoch after his retirement as Governor and Commander-in-Chief of the Crown colony of Hong Kong. Mary's great-grandson, Robert McCrum, is a novelist who enjoyed a brilliant reputation as an editorial director at Faber & Faber in the 1980s.

In 1863 Alexander transferred the headquarters of the business from Cambridge to London. He was reluctant to leave the little city which was so full of memories of his life with Daniel and the scene of his own intellectual vitalisation; but, for the publishing business to grow, he needed a metropolitan and not a provincial headquarters. The expansion of the business was steady and progressive: so too was the rise in his own reputation. He had opened an agency in India in 1860 and began another in the United States in 1870. To his delight he was publisher to Oxford University from 1863 until 1881: the honorary degree and membership of Balliol with which he was rewarded gave him much pleasure, though not as much as would have the knowledge that Daniel's grandson Harold would be elected as the university's Chancellor a century later.

By 1865 he was complaining that as a result of his heavy business responsibilities he was suffering from 'swimmings in the head, a sense of faintness, fits of distressing and . . . causeless anxiety, so that at times in the night I wake with a feeling as if everything were going to crack around and leave me sinking into horrid abysses'. To reduce the burden he took as his partner a gruff-mannered Glaswegian accountant with a wooden leg called George Lillie Craik, who proved 'good and wise and careful and kind', so Alexander wrote in 1873. 'I cannot tell you how much I have got to love that man. He is a daily comfort and guide to me.' Yet, even with Craik's help in the business, Alexander continued to overwork. 'He ought always to have a minimum of six hours' sleep; and on four days of the week, at least, he should go to bed like a good Christian baby, at 10 o'clock,' his physician advised in 1868.

During the 1850s and 1860s Alexander used to spend every Thursday night in London and to keep an open house for anyone who wished to have a meal, followed by discussions of literature or other subjects. These 'Tobacco Parliament' meetings, as they were called, were important to the directions in which Alexander developed his business, especially after the foundation of its magazine in 1859. Every year Alexander gave a dinner on All Fool's Day, either at his Tooting house or at the Garrick Club. His guests were as various as the poet Browning, the politician John Bryce, Dean Farrar (the author of that sickly, sadistic moral tale for children, *Eric, or Little by Little*) and the painter Millais. This annual party was an event in the literary calendar which authors could ill afford to ignore. 'Macmillan chooses this very suitable day to give a dinner to all his authors,' wrote Matthew Arnold on April Fool's Day 1870, 'and I am just starting for Streatham with a toothache, and the prospect of an endless dinner and a return to Harrow in the middle of the night in the east wind.' But Arnold went all the same.

A description of one of Alexander's receptions in 1879 was given by the American historian John Fiske, whose book *Cosmic Philosophy* had been published to acclaim by Macmillan. 'At 9 o'clock went to Macmillan's in Covent Garden,' Fiske wrote home.

> He used to live over his shop when he was young, and now has large parlours there, where he gives receptions in the 'Season'. It is more convenient than to have people go to his 'Castle' at Upper Tooting. It was truly a *stupendous* affair. I went quite uninvited, knowing that I would be welcome. There were at least 400 people there I should think. What did the bonny old boy do but *throw his arms about my neck* and hug me like a grizzly bear (!!!) and then step off a bit and hold me at arms'-length, and scan me from head to foot, and then exclaim with a broad grin, 'And was't na a naughta bay,' t wad coom aver all the way to Englund, and *wadna* wrait me a *lun* ta tell me that a was coomin?' I began to apologise . . . but the old fellow hit me an awful thump between my shoulder-blades and said, 'De'il take it, mon; I shall have ta forgie ye, for ye're sach a gude bay.' Then he introduced me to a lot of celebrities.

These included three of the most distinguished physicians in Victorian London, Sir James Crichton-Browne, Sir Lauder Brunton and Henry Maudsley. Praise of *Cosmic Philosophy* was being heaped on him when 'Macmillan came up and said: "Fiske, here's *Glaadstane* a-askin' ta be antradooced ta ye," and so I turned around and had a very pleasant chat with Gladstone, chiefly about Russia.'

A man's friends are as integral a part of himself as his

ancestors, his wife and children, his reputation or his body. He cannot be judged without knowing something of his friends or the quality of his friendships. Alexander's certainly were important to him. Among the most valued was the Rev. Stopford Brooke, a fashionable London preacher who seceded from the Church of England in 1880 to become a Unitarian. Brooke was a prolific writer whose *Primer of English Literature* sold half a million copies in the forty years after its publication in 1876. He was an expansive Irishman, whose talk was full of drollery and zany flights of imagination. Vehement in his opinions and rapacious for knowledge, his sermons *Theology in the English Poets* were a characteristic attempt to find the Christian meaning in literature which had an innate appeal to Alexander. An admirer of Kingsley, Brooke took a rhapsodic delight in the beauty of the natural world and was given a mystical sense of unity by the sights and sounds of running water: he believed in the existence of water sprites and held regular conversations with one who was 150 years old. Another beloved clergyman was Alfred Ainger, who first spoke to Alexander as an undergraduate visiting the Trinity Street shop and who described their friendship as 'one of the most valuable and valued of my life'. Alexander, wrote Ainger's biographer, provided 'a cheering hearth for talent, often obscure and unrecognised'. At the Macmillans' he 'was a loved and loving guest, one of the leaders of their society, yet perhaps most welcome when alone with them'. In the summer he often stayed for weeks at Tooting. At bedtime there, excited by reading Shakespeare, he would fascinate the Macmillans with moonshine antics, breaking forth into a shadowy dance, swift and graceful, which seemed part of the witching-hour. After ceasing his fantastic pirouettes he would resume his clerical dignity (he was a housemaster at Eton), and woe betide anyone who asked him to repeat them. Alexander hated gossip, but he delighted in Ainger's conversational style: verbal quips, puns and piquant wit.

The publication in 1859 of Darwin's *Origin of the Species* made Evolution a great word among earnest Victorians and

raised history almost to the importance of a religion. Alexander
was the publisher of several of the most eminent historians of
his day, such as the ferocious pedant E.A. Freeman and William
Stubbs, Bishop of Oxford, both of whom he numbered among
his friends. He was devoted to the Rev. John Richard Green,
whose *Short History of the English People* he published in 1874.
The genesis of this bestseller set the pattern of their friendship.
In 1869, just at the moment when he was preparing to write
a major history of medieval England, Green was discovered to
have tuberculosis. Knowing that his survival was precarious, he
resolved to write a book which, if he lived, would be an introduction to his future work, and which would ensure that, if he died,
his researches should not have been wasted. Daniel's sufferings
always remained so real to Alexander, and his memory so
venerated, that consumptives and their families were always
assured of kindness from the house of Macmillan. Alexander
advanced Green £350 to write the book, with further royalties
after publication; for five years, the sick author laboured to
finish his *Short History*. Disabled by illness and disheartened
by criticism, only Alexander Macmillan and Stopford Brooke
buoyed him up with their faith and optimism. The book was
a success, selling 35,000 copies in its first year; after 8,000
copies had been sold, Alexander sent for the contract in which
Green had assigned his copyright, destroyed it and substituted
a royalty agreement far more advantageous to Green and his
family. Alexander was always mindful of the need to revive
the invalid's spirits and ensured a steady income for Green
by appointing him as general editor of a series of historical
and literary primers. 'Hardly any enterprise we have ever been
engaged in has been more satisfactory to me personally, and
not less to other members of the firm, than your Primers,'
he wrote in 1877. 'Believe me, my dear Green, that you are
loved, and honoured, and trusted among us all in a very high
degree, and we count all that you do with and for us as
among our most precious work.' Later in the same year Green
lay ill in Florence, where, as Sir Leslie Stephen wrote, 'he

fortunately met with the Macmillans, who nursed him with their usual kindness'. Alexander was protective throughout Green's long and agonising tubercular decline: he attended the dying historian's last weeks of life in the South of France in 1883, showing a practical solicitude and gruff tenderness which Green's widow found unforgettable.

Alexander felt special affection for Charles Kingsley's younger brother Henry, whose first novel, *The Recollections of Geoffrey Hamlyn*, he published in 1859. This was an unevenly written tale of Devonshire emigrant pioneers in Australia, a rattling adventure story with moralising overtones – a mixture which Alexander particularly liked. He read the manuscript in draft and suggested some characteristic revisions: it seemed to him too gloomy, he advised his budding author, and should end on a merrier note, with happy marriages, teeming children and joyous mirth. Kingsley made his revisions accordingly. The chief villain of *Geoffrey Hamlyn* resembled in character its author, who was sometimes more adept in writing about villainies than virtues. He was a self-critical, self-destructive man who exasperated and hurt his family with his drinking, his debts and his bisexuality. 'His life and work trace the pathological edge of the muscular school, where its cult of virility merges into narcissistic depravity,' as John Sutherland has written. 'At its best his fiction has picaresque jollity, and devil-may-care verve.' Alexander was innocent of some of the erotic implications of Kingsley's plots; but he felt an affinity with the author's intensity, some sympathy for the conflict between Henry's high aspirations, low life and damaged personality. Kingsley 'lived his books, battled them out, and forced them into their living shapes', wrote one friend: Alexander's recognition of this creative struggle, and respect for the suffering that it represented, brought out his protective instincts. He heard with 'anxiety and pain' of Henry's domestic troubles, 'heartily and cheerfully' lending him several hundred pounds to clear his debts. Kingsley responded by decrying himself as 'a poor troublesome beggar' and by flattering his 'beloved Mac' with advice to stand for parliament. With whimsical or unorthodox friends like Stopford Brooke, Ainger or Henry Kingsley, the bonhomie of Alexander's circle was neither factitious nor drab.

The novelist Dinah Mulock Craik, a gorgon who was married to Alexander's business partner, complained in 1882 'about the worry, the loss, the actual torment that inaccurate, irregular, impecunious and extravagant authors are to that much enduring and necessarily silent class – their publishers'; but Alexander never forgot his debt to writers, or lost his wish to serve them. One of his devices for the prosperity of his authors and his business was *Macmillan's Magazine*, a shilling monthly which he launched in 1859 offering a mixture of essays and serialised fiction for family reading. It was intended to serve as a proving ground for younger authors like Matthew Arnold and as a means to involve more established writers like Tennyson with the house of Macmillan. He intended it to exclude the acrimony of party politics, spite and degrading ephemera, he told Lord Robert Montagu, and to attract readers without taking a derisive or trivial tone – unlike its main rival, the *Cornhill*, which was edited, a little racily, by Thackeray.

It was *Macmillan's Magazine* which confirmed his role as a pillar of the Victorian literary world. The 1850s were a critical decade in the history of British journalism. The Crimean War, which erupted between Britain, Turkey and Russia in 1854, created a thirst for news, and brought *The Times* to the apogee of its power. The newspaper tax was abolished in 1855, in which year the *Daily Telegraph* was launched as a penny paper and the *Saturday Review* began its success as an intellectual weekly newspaper. The public hungered for intellectual guidance, avid for new ideas on religious doctrine, Evolution, social reform, political progress. 'It was the age of science, new knowledge, searching criticism, followed by multiplied doubts and shaken beliefs,' according to John Morley, afterwards editor of *Macmillan's Magazine*. People wanted 'neat phrases, opinions in packets', to borrow a phrase of George Meredith; George Routledge, another bookseller turned publisher, made his fortune by issuing a series of one-shilling books entitled the Railway Library, which eventually ran to 1,060 volumes, material proof that the Victorians wished their information to be available, as Walter Bagehot wrote, just 'like sandwiches on a railway journey'. Weekly newspapers like the *Spectator* were revitalised, and new monthly reviews like the *Contemporary* and the *Nineteenth Century* were begun.

Alexander originally wished to call his magazine *The Round Table* in Tennyson's honour, and a visit by the poet and his wife to the Macmillans in Cambridge was followed by 'three glorious days with Tennyson' in October 1859. Proudly he reported to an old friend that the poet had proved 'in all ways genial, manly and pleasant. We talked and walked and smoked and chatted with the ladies, and altogether were as happy as we could be'. As a result of these meetings he was able to secure the first publication of Tennyson's new poem 'Sea Dreams' in the January 1860 issue of the magazine: a coup which gave him 'inexpressible delight', only equalled a quarter of a century later when Macmillan acquired all Tennyson's rights. Macmillan treated him generously – paying £300 for the right to publish his poem 'Lucretius' in the magazine in 1868 – and gave advice (which was gratefully received) on the most auspicious publication dates and the euphonious ring of certain lines.

The magazine's inaugural issue carried the first instalment of a serial novel entitled *Tom Brown at Oxford* by Tom Hughes. In this and subsequent episodes the undergraduate hero learnt the reprehensibility of selfish personal ambition, snobbery, insincerity, ostentation and fornication with pretty barmaids. Within months the great Victorian sages were contributing: Thomas Huxley, Herbert Spenser, F.D. Maurice and others. There were keenly argued pieces on European politics, of such quality that the Foreign Secretary, Lord John Russell, sent a copy of one to the Ambassador in Paris, Lord Cowley, who found it 'very interesting' in clarifying his thoughts. Within six months of the launch of the magazine it had a monthly sale of 15,000 copies, each of which he estimated had ten or twelve readers, 'a decided success' Alexander judged, although its rival, the *Cornhill*, had an initial sale in 1860 of 120,000. *Macmillan's Magazine* was about the first periodical of its kind to publish signed, rather than anonymous, articles: partly because Alexander wished to promote the names of contributors who were also writing books for him, and partly because he liked to think, in a revealing phrase, that the magazine was an 'open pulpit'. Those who mounted Macmillan's pulpit included many of the greatest Victorian savants together with such creative titans as Matthew Arnold, George Eliot, Charles Kingsley, George Meredith, Walter Pater, Christina Rossetti, Robert Louis Stevenson and Tennyson.

The most controversial article published in the magazine was 'The True Story of Lady Byron's Life' by Harriet Beecher Stowe in 1869. It caused uproar on two continents by publicising for the first time Lady Byron's accusation that the poet had enjoyed incestuous sexual relations with his half-sister Augusta Leigh. 'From the height which might have made him happy as the husband of a noble woman, he fell into the depths of a secret, adulterous intrigue with a blood relation, so near in consanguinity that discovery must have been utter ruin and expulsion from civilised society,' in Mrs Stowe's words. 'From henceforth, this damning, guilty secret became the ruling force of his life, holding him with a morbid fascination, yet filling him with remorse and anguish, and insane dread of detection.' She despised Byron as a 'man who skimmed over the deepest abysses with the lightest jests': Lady Byron by contrast was presented as 'a blessed being' more 'detached from earth' than 'an ordinary mortal' whose 'whole life had been passed in the most heroic self-abnegation and self-sacrifice'. According to Stowe, 'While speaking on this subject the pale ethereal face became luminous with a heavenly radiance; there was something so sublime in her belief in the victory of love over evil, that faith with her seemed to have become sight.'

Many Victorians concluded that Lady Byron was sincere

in her belief, but mistaken; others took the view of Vicary Gibbs that 'the loathsome charges' which she made 'secretly' against Byron and 'his estimable sister' were unbelievable: 'while their publication may be fairly traced to love of gain or notoriety, their origin may be charitably attributed to a diseased mind rather than to fiendish malice'. This was a dig at the author of the article and its publisher, who both protested strongly the moral probity of publication. Mrs Stowe's avowed reason for the article was to counteract the pernicious moral influence of cheap editions of Byron's poetry reaching the class of clerks which Macmillan books aimed to uplift and edify. Alexander too hoped that the article's portrayal of Byron would 'awaken a wholesome disgust that will repel the influence of his writings which his great genius renders dangerous'. The furore that surrounded publication worried him greatly, but he was convinced of the need to rebut the 'theory that genius is an excuse for any excess', and hoped that the article would 'destroy this damnable doctrine and bring home to the public mind and also to men of all sorts of genius that they have no more right to misuse their brains than a navvy has a right to misuse his muscles. Nothing seems more likely to further this end than to make it clear what sort of man Byron really was.' The vehemence with which Alexander defended Stowe's article, and the extent to which it brought him into collision with some of his closest advisers like Morley, suggest that the affair touched the heart of his beliefs.

A huge mass of the firm's letter-books survive. For years not only were almost all of them entered in his own handwriting, but they show that he read almost every manuscript that was submitted. He wrote long, meticulous criticisms even of manuscripts that were rejected. 'I have frequently sent back what I felt to be beautiful and touching in verse, simply because I knew it would not pay,' he explained in a rejection letter to a prospective author in 1862. 'That is my business, to calculate what will commercially pay. Unless it will there is no reason why it should be printed.' The list of books published by him reflected his opinions on religion and politics as well as his tastes in art and literature. Considering his upbringing in the severe simplicity of Scottish peasant life, he had a superb ability to recognise the merits in manuscripts on subjects about which he knew little and cared less. He intuitively knew what constituted literary excellence, although the workings of his intuition were mysterious even to himself. With such talents Alexander impressed Matthew Arnold in the 1860s as 'an extremely intelligent, active man', while George Eliot told him in 1874 that his publishing list was 'the most tempting I ever look at', not least because the books themselves were always 'in a costume that soothes the eyes with its soberness and good taste'.

Alexander had a sincere wish to share with children the joy which he had got from books. He did not want them to be excluded from the proliferating literacy of Victorian Britain. He wrote of a hypothetical reader of *Alice in Wonderland* called 'Little Miss Nell Puss, aged 6¾', and was in earnest to meet the needs of such readers, taking pains to publish novels like Charles Kingsley's *Water Babies* (1863). This was an immediate success, despite some parts of it being unreadably abstruse and others incomprehensibly muddled. It became one of the bestselling children's books of all time, and was adapted into a film as early as 1907. The story of a maltreated boy chimney sweep called Tom, it had (like Kingsley's earliest Macmillan work, *Cheap Clothes and Nasty*) an avowed philanthropic aim of stopping abuses of the poor by employers. It had such impact that the Chimney Sweep Regulation Act was enacted within a year of its publication; but it is rampant with sexual imagery, a parable about masturbation in which a dirty little boy resists temptation, is cleansed and grows up pure to marry; a parable heavy, too, with overtones of death, judgment, heaven and hell.

The 1860s were a momentous decade in Alexander's business and social life. 'On the whole life is very pleasant to me, moving as I do freely and with acceptance among the best in the land,' Alexander wrote with pardonable pride to his friend James MacLehose in 1864. 'I was at a club the other night, where were Tennyson, Browning, Anthony Trollope, Lord Houghton, Lord Stanley, Tom Taylor, FitzJames Stephen . . . with all of whom I had a pleasant gossip, and a very long talk with Lord Stanley. I thought how much better worthy of such company dear Daniel would have been.' Alexander's personal and business life remained devoted to Daniel's memory. 'May I never disgrace that noble and sweet memory,' he had written to MacLehose in 1859. To another friend in 1870 he described Daniel as 'the noblest and best of brothers'.

The first-known intervention of the Macmillan family in party politics occurred after Alexander met the blind Cambridge don Henry Fawcett in the 1860s. 'Macmillan was often in our rooms, trying rather fruitlessly to stimulate Fawcett's interest in the writings of Carlyle, Maurice and Kingsley,' as Sir Leslie Stephen later recalled. 'At Macmillan's we occasionally met men of some literary eminence, whom we respected with juvenile simplicity.' Fawcett was persuaded to contribute to *Macmillan's Magazine* before contracting with Alexander to write a popular textbook entitled *Manual of Political Economy*. He owed his election to a Cambridge professorship to the success of the book; and, when in 1863 the sitting MP for Cambridge retired, Alexander, who had hitherto taken no part in politics, went to Fawcett and begged him to contest the constituency as a Radical. Fawcett agreed. 'If I am anybody's candidate,' he said at the time, 'I am Macmillan's candidate.' After a hard fight, Fawcett was defeated; but at Macmillan's instigation he had received his political blooding and had proved that a blind man could take to the hustings. Later, in 1868, Millicent Fawcett, his 'charming and clever little wife' in Alexander's phrase, publicly inaugurated her campaign for women's colleges at Cambridge with an article in *Macmillan's Magazine* which its proprietor had encouraged. Despite welcoming Mrs Daniel's publishing advice and encouraging Mrs Fawcett's educational projects, he was suspicious of the cause of 'women's rights', fearing 'that their *rights* will prove *wrongs*, to themselves first, and afterwards to their bairns'. His adulation of his mother made him idealise women but regard them as separate from the fraternity of men. Brotherhood had been one of the best feelings of his life, and women were excluded from it.

Other progressive Victorian politicians published by Macmillan included Sir George Otto Trevelyan, John Bryce and Sir Roundell Palmer. Alexander enjoyed a closer intimacy with the Liberal statesman John Morley, who briefly edited *Macmillan's Magazine* in the 1880s. For almost half a century Morley read manuscripts for Macmillan, advising on their potential for publication: Alexander described him in 1869 as 'the bravest, clearest headed fellow I know', and Morley later rejoiced to celebrate him as his 'earliest and his greatest benefactor'. Morley was a vain and fretful nag: George Meredith said that he always sounded like an old maid reprimanding an errand boy, while other contemporaries felt scorched by the white heat of his gloomy earnestness. Morley felt threatened by 'the most awful influx the world ever saw of furious provocations to unbridled sensuality and riotous animalism', to quote his abusive review of Swinburne's *Poems and Ballads* which had much to do with the withdrawal of the first edition of that book. This recoil from sensuality permeated his judgments as a publisher's reader, and he had other moments of ill-judgment, as when he dismissed the essays of Henry James as lacking 'charm, delicacy, finesse', or called the poetry of Yeats an 'absolute nullity'; yet overall he proved one of the great publishers' readers.

Alexander detested the cynicism of Disraeli, whose political influence he judged as demoralising; but his Liberalism was tempered by Scottish pride, so that he admired the Tory Lord Aberdeen, coalition Prime Minister during the Crimean War, for his conspicuous nobility and talent (which few others had noticed). He was supremely a Gladstonian Liberal who was proud of publishing the Grand Old Man's Homeric translations. The two men breakfasted together through the years, and in 1877 Gladstone dined with the Macmillans to meet J.R. Green (Alexander characteristically forewarned Gladstone that they would eat early so as not to weary the other guest, who was tubercular). In 1875, when he thought journalists were being especially 'insolent' to Gladstone, he asked John Bright to write in his magazine in defence of 'a great and good man to whom his country owes so much'. Five years later, addressing Gladstone directly, he wrote that 'millions . . . look on you as their leader in high and noble, national and human endeavour'; and by the 1880s he was wont to end his letters to Gladstone with a phrase emphasising his steadfast personal loyalty to his party leader. The two men, although they were not intimate friends, recognised a similarity in their most ardent beliefs. A typical subject of correspondence between them was *Ecce Homo*. Originally published by Macmillan in 1865, this anonymous book (its author, Sir John Seeley, succeeded Kingsley as Professor of Modern History at Cambridge), sought to show the life, work and teaching of Christ in a simple way, without theological doubts or casuistry, in the manner of a historical biographer recounting the facts of his subject's career. It provoked huge controversy, Lord Shaftesbury denouncing it at a public meeting as 'the most pestilential book ever vomited from the jaws of Hell'. Alexander himself had felt 'overwhelmed with . . . shame at the poverty and feebleness of our Christian life' when reading *Ecce Homo* for the first time. Seeley's belief that true Christianity was characterised by a 'union of morals and politics' was crucial to the direction of the life work of both Alexander and Gladstone; so too was Seeley's conviction that the Christian Church was 'the Moral University of the World – not merely the greatest, but the only School of Virtue existing'.

As early as 1859 Alexander contemplated a series of small, five-shilling British biographies to catch the interest of boys and to cultivate reverence for the past. As he told the Rev. Edward Benson, afterwards Archbishop of Canterbury, whom he hoped to persuade to write a volume on the Duke of Wellington, 'the characteristic of so much of our modern writing is to depreciate the bygone people and time'. This sneering would 'do nothing but harm', he believed, 'and lead to shallowness and conceit'.

Mockery of any sort was anathema to earnest Victorians: if it led to levity in matters of morality, it was evil. Macmillan's English Men of Letters series was eventually launched in 1877 under the general editorship of Morley. Morley's aim – shared by both the Macmillan brothers in their time – was 'to make industrial England a sharer in the classic tradition of the lettered world', to improve the minds of the masses as part of a gradual process of political self-empowerment. Literary critics in the late twentieth century have criticised these intentions as patronising, or destructive of the culture and integrity of the poor; but their asperities have said more about the mentality of our own time than about the motives of men like Morley and the Macmillans. The latter saw ignorance, hardship and social inequity, and, with instincts that were supremely generous, they attacked these evils by trying to disseminate what had been enriching and invigorating in their own lives, literature.

Morley thought of Alexander as a Minister of Letters.

> He was sincerely interested in the drift and matter of good books in serious spheres. . . . He went about his work with active conscience and high standards. He had the blessing, both attractive and useful, of imagination, added to shrewd sense and zeal for the best workmanship. His eye for the various movements in his time of knowledge and thought, lit-erary, scientific, and religious, showed extraordinarily acute insight. He knew his world: it comprised the most enlightened of our divers social strata, and he gathered a body of men around him with many vigorous talents, with his own strict exaction in way of competency, and his own honourable sense of public responsibility.

J.R. Green, receiving some comments on one of his manuscripts, wrote appreciatively that Alexander's letter was 'very keen and good, just because it expresses the thoughts of an average clever reader. That is just the sort of criticism it is so difficult to get, and yet which in the long-run settles . . . the fate of a book.'

In 1868 Alexander rejected the first novel of Thomas Hardy, entitled *The Poor Man and the Lady*. The care and detail with which he penned the rejection letter to Hardy not only show his usual massive conscientiousness; they also recognise Hardy's talent, and offer some of his own credo as a publisher. 'Your picture of character among Londoners, and especially the upper classes, are sharp, clear, incisive, and in many respects true, but they are wholly dark – not a ray of light visible to relieve the darkness, and therefore exaggerated and untrue in their result. Their frivolity, heartlessness, selfishness are great and terrible, but there are other sides. . . . it is inconceivable to me that any considerable number of human beings – God's creatures – should be so bad without going to utter wreck in a week.' As a result of this letter, publisher and prospective author met, but while recognising that the book 'might create a considerable curiosity if published', Alexander felt that he should not publish it. In 1870 Hardy's second novel, *Desperate Remedies*, was declined by Macmillan on grounds of excessive sensationalism; and Hardy wrongly understood them to reject *Under the Greenwood Tree* a few years later. In 1889 *Macmillan's Magazine* decided against serialisation of *Tess of the D'Urbervilles*. Despite these rejections Hardy felt befriended by Alexander and was for some time a regular visitor to the house at Tooting, the comforts of which he admired. A garden party held by the Macmillans inspired Hardy's account of a similar event, with lawn tennis for the young, dancing to the sounds of harps and violins, and supper by candlelight, in his novel *A Laodicean* (1881). Alexander in his solicitous way introduced Hardy to various 'distinguished and earnest men', to quote a favourite phrase of his. When Hardy fell ill, the Macmillans sent their family physician to advise. Hardy's pertinacity in submitting manuscripts which were repeatedly rejected suggests great respect for the publisher.

Alexander followed the events of the American Civil War closely. From the outset of hostilities he favoured the emancipationists: John Stuart Mill wrote to the American historian and diplomat John Lothrop Motley in 1862 drawing his attention to a series of articles published by Edward Dicey in *Macmillan's*

Magazine as 'likely to do much good in England'. Alexander's sympathies were not with friends like Henry Kingsley, who wrote to him, 'I don't care much what happens so long as the American Union goes to smash,' but with fellow Radicals like John Bright, who had written a few months earlier to Motley that the British 'ruling class, by a natural instinct, hates democratic and republican institutions, and it dreads the example of the United States upon its own permanency'. Their chief wish, therefore, was for the United States to be 'divided and enfeebled'. Hence the support for the slave-owning states that was given by the Tories, or noisily trumpeted by periodicals like *The Times* and *Saturday Review*.

In later life Alexander placed great hopes on American business. His admiration for the United States was increased by a tour there which he made in 1867, meeting such authors as Longfellow and Lowell. 'America! the land of life, of liberty, the hope of the world, inheritor of our greatness, our light, our freedom, alas! inheritor to too great a degree of our arrogance, money-worship and faithlessness to high calling,' he apostrophised. 'Of course, the Yankees have their faults, and when I see them I don't hesitate to tell them in very plain words what I think of their faults. But have we none like them? Where did they get their brag from? their love of money? their contempt of other people?' He blamed the vices of the Americans on their 'unnatural parents', the British. The lavish endowments of universities like Yale, Cornell, Boston or Chicago drew his particular admiration. 'You go nowhere where princely munificence, bestowed by plain citizens, does not meet you,' and characteristically he contrasted the superior powers of good over bad. 'The gigantic charities which spring up on all sides outweigh the scarcely less gigantic corruptions,' he rejoiced to his friend Trench, Archbishop of Dublin. He was delighted, on his journey of 1867, to meet prairie farmers 'who had read and understood Carlyle, Mill, Buckle, Ruskin, Lecky and authors of that class'. From this he concluded, 'Abuse democracy as you will, and there is much to dislike and laugh at in it, it is yet an enormous power for stirring up the human intellect.' The political powerlessness of the European poor, in contrast to the conditions which he attributed to American democracy, 'has a terribly depressing effect on the mind of that lower class, as witness the utter stupidity and brutishness of the English labourer'.

On settling in London he bought a rambling house on Streatham Lane – the 'pleasant old house out at Balham [of] my canny old publisher Alexander Macmillan', as Henry James described it. Surrounded by trees, it enjoyed an easy railway connection to central London. Alexander's house was on the north edge of Tooting Graveney common, and commanded a fine view over the picturesque pond and gypsy settlement. Both Tooting Graveney and the nearby common of Tooting Bec were soon afterwards adopted as open spaces, and kept a semi rural charm. The amenities of Alexander's new house included a croquet lawn and were so admired by Thomas Hardy that with snobbish inaccuracy he claimed the Macmillans as his neighbours. 'In its large, leisurely rooms, or in its spacious, old-world garden, there gathered together informally the men and women of note and the young promise of the day – authors, poets, painters, English and French,' wrote one regular visitor, Alfred Ainger. Alexander called his house Knapdale after the area of Argyllshire where the family had lived before emigrating to Arran. 'I grow more attached to the past, it is fuller of meanings and interest I hardly dreamed of in earlier years,' he wrote in 1860. He took 'delight' from 'the green fields of Tooting', so he wrote to the Rev. Hugh Macmillan in 1866, 'and yet, my dear Cousin, I will confess that I could weep with longing after Glen Sannox this very moment, and the great glen over to Lochranza is tender in my memory, like the dear lost friends with whom it is bound up'.

In his choice of the name Knapdale for the house Alexander revealed his yearning for the simplicities and certitude of the old Argyllshire peasant life, his weariness at the cosmopolitan controversies of nineteenth-century life which so many Macmillan books had fermented. Alexander was distracted from what he most wanted – mental security and equanimity – by the business he was in. He and Daniel had seen it as their calling to publish eternal verities and to advance learning; but Alexander found instead that the great intellectual and social movements which his firm had served had created more doubts than anything else: as in Arnold's poem, their life-work had promised 'a land of dreams, / So various, so beautiful, so new', but had ended with 'neither joy, nor love, nor light, / Nor certitude, nor peace, nor help for pain'. Alexander was not alone in feeling threatened and exhausted by the quantity and mediocrity of Victorian writings. George Eliot, for example, was gratified by an article on her novels by Morley in *Macmillan's Magazine* of 1866; 'and yet', she wrote, 'I sicken again with despondency under the sense that the most carefully written books lie, both outside and inside people's minds, deep undermost in a heap of trash'. A decade later Alexander's guest Frederick Harrison was lamenting that modern readers were swamped in 'the Slough of Despond of an illimitable and ever-swelling literature': verbiage which exemplified 'that rattle and restlessness of life which belongs to the industrial Maelstrom wherein we ever revolve'. Few readers can have felt as overwhelmed as Alexander, who delegated so little of the work within the firm, checking even proofs himself. (Correcting 500 pages of the official biography of F.D. Maurice in rough proof in 1879, he told Charles Kingsley's widow that it was the third time he had read through the book.)

Knapdale was a refuge from the hurly-burly, not only mechanical, but spiritual, social and political, of which his publishing house was both an agent and a reflection. His life there followed a regular pattern. On weekdays prayers were at eight or soon after, and breakfast at half-past, so that he could take an early train to work. Sunday was set apart. He wore a special Sunday garb, in the early days a brilliant scarlet coat and later on a brown velvet coat and cap, and his daughter remembered him as always bearing a happy and serene expression on Sundays. The family went in a body to church and after the usual long service of those days took a family walk before a meal together at the unusual hour of three. There would be guests for this meal: a prospective author, or clerks from the office, or an old friend like Ainger or Stopford Brooke. After lunch, which was a talkative affair, the afternoons were spent in the garden in summer, and in winter divided between the library (thick with pipe smoke), and the drawing-room, until the household gathered round the dining-room table for tea. Some part of Sunday evening in those early days was given to reading aloud – the Bible, or a sermon by Maurice or Kingsley, but most often poetry. Apart from the Bible, family favourites were Blake's illustrations to the Book of Job, Scott's novels, Charlotte Yonge's *Pupils of St John and Book of Golden Deeds*, Kingsley's *Hermits* and *Westward Ho!*, Dean Farrar's *Sketches after God* and Carlyle's *Past and Present* and *Heroes*. After the arrival of Louise Cassell as governess in 1864 music was added. All the family sang hymns, but Alexander in particular sang to her accompaniment such tunes as 'He shall feed his flock' or 'Oh rest in the Lord'. He lacked musical training, and there were faults in his singing, but there was character too; he was very attentive to the words, and his singing of Scottish songs gave pleasure at Knapdale. 'Those Sundays in the early days at Tooting were certainly most bright and happy days,' his daughter wrote afterwards. The happiness was of a quiet kind, which consolidated the ties of family and friendship.

He remained at Knapdale until 1888, when he took a more fashionable house at 21 Portland Place, on the edges of Mayfair, giving Knapdale to the Diocese of Rochester as a home for its suffragan bishop (it was in fact let, until sold by the bishopric in 1905). He also bought a country house near Hindhead, called Bramshott Chase, standing in countryside which, as he wrote to Gladstone in 1886, redolent of his birth-place in his beloved Scotland. It was at Bramshott that he was eventually buried, his grave marked by a Highland cross.

The intensity of Alexander's earnest pursuits caught up with him in the 1880s. He tired easily and became more hidebound. Afflicted with rheumatism, he delegated increasing amounts of work after 1883. This was unpopular with authors accustomed to dealing with him personally. 'The management seems to be falling off, now that Mr Macmillan is no longer on the spot,' Lewis Carroll complained in his diary in 1889. 'I fear the firm is going down, and I may have to find another publisher.'

The old man's life deteriorated after the loss of his eldest son Malcolm, who vanished while visiting Greece in 1889, as described in the next chapter. He was broken by this catastrophe. He wept as he told the details of the story to his friend Sebastian Evans, and then lay back in his chair sighing wearily, 'I keep on wondering what Daniel thinks of it all,' an appeal to Evans (who was an atheist) to confirm his belief in an afterlife. Alexander never recovered from his grief and was tormented by the cruel uncertainty which surrounded Malcolm's fate. Tired and dispirited, he withdrew increasingly from business and finally died at his house in Portland Place in January 1896.

Alexander's character was a discordant medley of magnanimity, sympathy, generosity, industry, shrewdness and antipathies. He was often in the thrall of contradictory feelings whose nature he never understood; inwardly he suffered from more discrepancies than most. In early life, particularly, his distrust in the possibility of happiness amounted almost to morbidity; yet his belief in progress was fervent. Like Daniel he was impetuous, forcible in his opinions, but affectionate and shiningly free from personal or professional jealousy. His three leading traits were his devotion to his family, his belief in his friends and his trust in his helpers: he was a loyal, generous and affectionate man, who went to great pains to keep his amities in good repair. A phrase of his in a letter to Gladstone about *Ecce Homo* – 'distinguished and earnest men' – evokes his ideal. This is what he strove to be, what he wished future Macmillan menfolk to be.

CHAPTER 5

The Double Family

A father is *such* a *near* relation,
you are a *piece* of him in fact.

Queen Victoria,
letter of 6 February 1844

Duty to a son is a paramount duty.

Benjamin Robert Haydon,
journal of 24 December 1844

The next generation of Macmillans were reared in a double family. From the day of Daniel's death his widow and children lived with Alexander and his wife and children in a special domesticity and with a concentrated family feeling that lasted out their lives. Alfred Ainger, who visited the Macmillans when they were still living above their shop in Cambridge, was impressed by 'the absolute unity in affection and purpose of this two-fold family'. The household had its own mentality and ways: earnest, godly, full of family traditions, venerating Daniel's memory but above all asserting and carrying out all his sacred, mighty principles. They were reared in an atmosphere of duty and prayer. 'I speculate and wonder at the variety of humanity possible in a small double family,' Alexander wrote in 1870. 'They all know that they are the children of what the world calls *humble* parents, and I pray daily that I and they may pray to be humble and helpful, and carry on the world's work as in the sight of the Lord of Man.'

It is doubtful that the children were indulged. The Victorians could be harsh parents, particularly when they wanted to inculcate good lessons. Augustus Hare, who was reared in the house of the Macmillans' mentor Julius Hare and his wife Esther, was taught self-denial and the denial of Self by means which seem little less than torture. 'I had a favourite cat called Selma, which I adored, and which followed me about . . . wherever I went,' Hare recalled in adulthood. 'Aunt Esther saw this, and at once insisted that the cat must be given up to her. I wept over it in agonies of grief: but Aunt Esther insisted.' The adults who ruled over him were 'relentless in saying that I must be taught to give up my own way and pleasure to others'. Other refinements of cruelty were practised on the boy, ostensibly for his benefit. His dinners were long confined to roast mutton and rice pudding; but then suddenly 'the most delicious puddings were talked of − *dilated* on − until I became, not greedy, but exceedingly curious about them'. Finally the great moment for a moral lesson arrived. Delectable desserts were put before him, but were then snatched away as he moved to eat them, and he was ordered to carry them to some poor villager. This was the way in which the best of Victorians, in their conscientious wish to do good, blindly and inadvertently hurt people, oblivious to the pain they were causing or of the patterns of distress that they were perpetuating. There was a general atmosphere of merriness and affection in the Macmillan home when the 'double family' was young, but under the surface there was the usual story of moral lessons harshly applied, particularly because Alexander (as he wrote in *The Child in the Midst* after Willie's death) was always looking to see the mark of Cain on children as they grew older.

The Macmillan children grew up in the publishing business. Authors were invited to Knapdale and would talk or walk with the young Macmillans. At the age of six, Alexander's youngest son John was receiving correspondence from the formidable historian of medievalism, E.A. Freeman. Unable to decide upon the best of eight possible titles for a book in 1875, C.L. Dodgson (the author as Lewis Carroll of *Alice in Wonderland*) sent a list of them to Alexander enquiring, 'Would your family circle kindly resolve themselves into a committee of taste, and give me their opinions, collectively if unanimous – otherwise, individually.' Whether Alexander consulted the family is unclear, but Dodgson, who admired Alexander's pubescent nieces and went with Malcolm and George to a theatrical comedy about fairies in 1873, was just one of the authors with whom the children were intimate from their early years. They learnt not to be unduly impressed by reputations. 'We had the *Punch* people . . . to dinner a little while ago,' Malcolm wrote to his cousin Robert Bowes in 1869. 'They really didn't say anything very brilliant.' The memory of childhood meals with Tennyson and Kingsley impressed Malcolm more.

Alexander admired Archibald MacLaren, proprietor of the Gymnasium at Oxford and adviser to the military schools at Aldershot and Woolwich, whom he first met when holidaying on the Isle of Wight. MacLaren had devised a new system of physical education based on German schemes, the sort of manly exercise that muscular Christians thought so admirable, and two articles by him on the subject were published in *Macmillan's Magazine* in 1862. 'He is my special friend, and a man of very noble nature, fine natural gifts of head and heart – not omitting the body,' Alexander wrote in 1869. MacLaren together with his wife Gertrude (the daughter of the printer to Oxford University Press) opened a preparatory school near Oxford called Summerfields, in which she undertook the teaching and he kept the boys fit. The school accordingly had the unoriginal but appropriate motto *Mens sana in corpore sano*. Alexander sent his younger son George, and his nephews Arthur and Maurice, as the first pupils there (together with two sons of a future editor of *Punch*) in 1864. His decision inaugurated a long connection between the Macmillan family and the school. He came to admire the proprietress hugely: '*she* is the scholar and maker of scholars' who was responsible for 'my Geordie' gaining the senior scholarship into Eton in 1868. Gertrude

MacLaren's regime at Summerfields was conventional, exacting and strict, but was not without compensatory moments of individual tenderness. She herself was a woman of strength and dignity who was steadfast in her Christianity. Offered some beef tea and port wine moments before she died in 1896, she replied, 'Please let me go to Him whom I love and do not keep me back.'

Alexander's relations with his eldest son Malcolm were troubled, and ended with what seemed the great tragedy of his life. Tennyson had sent his sons to be educated at Marlborough, and when Alexander came to select a boarding school he thought he could do no better than Britain's greatest living poet. At the age of eleven, in 1864, Malcolm was sent to board at Marlborough. The school had been founded in 1843 to provide a first-class education at a low price for the sons of clergy, and was the earliest of the great Victorian boarding schools to imbibe the principles of Thomas Arnold's Rugby. In its early years it was notorious for bullying, and in the 1850s was the scene of several riots, in which the pupils destroyed property or attacked staff. Discipline was restored by the appointment as headmaster of a Rugby housemaster who had been already immortalised in *Tom Brown's Schooldays* for his solemn sincerity. Another boy who went to the same house at Marlborough as Malcolm, and in the same year, was Rowland Prothero, afterwards an author and government minister. His first two years in B House were so 'absolutely numbing' that he still felt 'dumb misery' when writing about them seventy years later. B House 'in its glaring newness struck even my childish eyes as almost criminally ugly', Prothero wrote in the 1930s. Living without privacy in the continuous pandemonium of boyhood, he was left with the 'paralysing feeling of being smothered in the grasp of a crowd from which I was powerless to free myself'. Malcolm and Prothero were akin in temperament, and their sufferings were similar. Malcolm left Marlborough prematurely, after a year, his pain too much for his father to ignore. The boy's education was completed at King's College School, but the breakdown of his career at Marlborough betokened a sensitivity with which Alexander found he could show little patience or sympathy. Alexander recognised Malcolm's curiosity about books, poetry, science and general knowledge as resembling his own devotion to learning, but he worried that the boy was so 'dreamy and wayward'.

It was perhaps to impose his discipline and to teach Malcolm that, like Augustus Hare, he must yield his wishes to others that Alexander refused to allow his eldest son to complete his education at Cambridge, working for the Moral Science tripos. In a long, sententious letter of 1870 Alexander withheld his consent. 'I am no longer a younger man, my life has been a long strain,' he wrote when he finally reached the crux of his objections. 'I sometimes feel very weary, and would gladly see you, whom I have always looked forward to as the one who will take my place in the business, getting into mood and shape for doing so.' A university education would not fit him for this. Malcolm instead was forced into the business, but never settled to its routine. In painful contrast to his hopes, Malcolm was sent to Cambridge in 1870, not as an undergraduate, but to train as a retailer in the Bowes bookshop. He was 'a queer, wayward boy', so Alexander wrote in 1873, 'with very much good in him and plenty of brains, only not always duly administered'. For years Malcolm had to persevere in work which gave him little satisfaction before receiving belated permission to go to Oxford in the late 1870s. The compulsion which Alexander exerted on Malcolm was in sharp contrast to the way he had treated the children when younger. Little children like Willie he idealised: older children he crushed with rebuke. In the words of his biographer Charles Graves, 'as his own children grew older there came a stage in which his vehement expressions of enthusiasm and aversion and his impatience of remarks of which he did not approve impaired for a while the ease of companionship, and in fear of saying the wrong thing, they often preferred to remain silent. Yet he did not understand and even resented the notion that anyone should be afraid of him.'

At Oxford Malcolm showed the family awareness of the tensions between gentleness and violence. 'Everybody goes in for "taste", and the natural man is tamed by the soothing harmonies of blue china, and sits with all his wild passions folded humbly under the wings of contentment,' Malcolm wrote soon after his matriculation at Oxford. 'Some of the most savage and dangerous specimens of our aristocracy have been known to come into this blessed region, from an atmosphere of betting shops, and in a month or less to be shedding tears of joy over an opal glass.' Malcolm was one of those who tried to quell his passions and soothe his feelings by cultivating a mild, studied aestheticism.

In 1879 Malcolm was involved in an accident which cast a long sadness over his life. Early in June he went boating on the River Isis with a Balliol undergraduate, Clarence Collier. At Sandford Lasher the boat capsized. 'I very nearly lost my own life to begin with and, still more impressive and unbalancing, was the witness of a frightful tragedy of a young and promising life snatched away from me,' Malcolm wrote a month later to his friend Cecil Standish. 'I was with the poor boy when he was swept over that fearful Lasher, as it boiled and roared, into the middle of Sandford pool, got breath on a raft and swimming hard to avoid the current, managed to reach the shore.' Clarence Collier was less lucky. Trapped in a mountainous eddy, his body was whirled round in it all night and recovered only with difficulty the following day. Collier was aged eighteen, the only child of a military family. At his funeral service at Balliol the voice of the Master, Benjamin Jowett, broke with grief as he read the service, and Malcolm for a moment found relief in 'the Anglican rite, with its few triumphant and consoling sentences', although the other paraphernalia of Victorian mourning – 'the hideous mummery of hearses and feathers and mutes' – revived his misery. Months later he was still burdened with guilt at his survival, trying to make sense of catastrophe. His feelings for Collier seemed, he told his brother-in-law Louis Dyer, 'like a beautiful bright dream, full of perfect sympathy and a constant soft rippling stream of happy intellectual communion and affectionate hope'.

The burden on Malcolm, as Alexander's eldest child, remained heavy. Having graduated from Balliol, he became a law student at the Inner Temple in 1884, but never practised as a barrister. He was a sensitive, cultivated man, with a freakish sense of humour: for years he would send Alfred Ainger postcards covered with conundrums and epigrams which were received with delight. His favourite prose writers were Balzac, Boccaccio, Daudet, Dickens, Mérimée, Montaigne, Richardson, Thackeray and Tolstoy: tastes more sceptical, more playful and more sensual than his father's. In 1885 he described himself as becoming 'the idealistic grandson of Zola' – a description that would have horrified his father. Malcolm adored the theatre and had a masterful knowledge not only of the Elizabethan dramatists but of modern playwrights like Ibsen. He visited Germany in 1883, mainly to study music, and succumbed to the commanding power of Wagner's operas. The following year he was in Italy, where he was 'introduced to the great Ibsen, who gives his little senate laws in a certain café at five o'clock. ... He regrets that he had not the opportunity of blowing up the ark with dynamite.' In 1886 he published anonymously a slim volume, somewhat mannered in style, entitled *Dagomet the Jester*, and increasingly he turned life aside with over-polished jests. Under the pretext of poor health he went abroad in 1887, ostensibly to study art and architecture. His letters during over two years of travel around the Mediterranean were exercises in artful mockery, funny in their way, but averting everything with a light quip in a way which failed to hide inner pain. He retreated into a love of paradox which nullified his father's progressive hopes. 'My Conservatism strengthens,' he wrote to his cousin Maurice from the Near East in 1889. 'I believe in great despotic powers, full of vitalities, ardours and fecundities, – not in little skilful, self-conscious, deprecating, jobbing nationalities, tripping along the bye-paths of Progress.' In his unhappiness and loneliness, he had become a high and perverse reactionary, affirming that the conservative Pope Leo XIII and Sultan Abdul Hamid the Terrible of Turkey were 'the only two forces that can save Europe'. The wicked perversity of this opinion suggests a mind reaching a painfully contorted extremity of its own: the truth, as the British Ambassador at Constantinople, Lord Dufferin, had recently reported, was that the Sultan with his 'diseased and almost maniacal nature', surrounded by 'corrupt intriguers', misled by 'dishonest parasites' and relying on the most extensive network of police spies in the world had pursued a policy of genocide against his Armenian subjects until 'the cruelty, imbecility and abuses of Turkish rule' stank to the heavens. It was grotesque for this ignorant, feeble, morbidly suspicious tyrant to be hailed by Malcolm as Europe's potential saviour.

A few months later Malcolm was gone. In July 1889, on the eve of his long-awaited return to England, he went with his friend, Arthur Hardinge, then secretary to the British Embassy

at Constantinople and afterwards Viceroy of India, to Mount Olympus, which they proposed to climb. Hardinge made a direct ascent to the highest peak, while Malcolm took a gentler incline to a lower peak. As he reached the steep slope of the main peak Hardinge saw his friend on the top of the lower peak, and waved. Malcolm was never seen again.

It had been a beautiful and happy day for Hardinge, whose incredulity changed to distraction as it became evident that Malcolm had vanished. Help was summoned, searches were undertaken, judicial enquiries were held. No trace of his body or belongings was found: the possibility of a fatal fall seemed impossible. In any case Mount Olympus was not dangerous to climb: 'pretty much like a Cumberland or Westmorland fell', to quote Hardinge's report, which was swiftly remitted to London. Malcolm's cousin Maurice Macmillan and brother-in-law Norman MacLehose hurried out to investigate and were at one time convinced that some fierce Albanian shepherds had robbed and murdered him. They hired Sir Edwin Pears, a lawyer in practice at Constantinople, to pull wires for them

– again in vain. The whole family felt their powerlessness miserably. George in September consulted the Foreign Office about publishing a letter in *The Times* publicising his brother's disappearance: 'public comment in England might rather stimulate the zeal of the Turkish Government to clear up so disgraceful an occurrence'. His suggestion was referred to Lord Salisbury, then combining the offices of Prime Minister and Foreign Secretary. 'I doubt the expediency,' he minuted on George's letter. 'Abuse in the press or in Parliament does not, as a matter of experience, stimulate the Sultan to do better. It only makes him draw closer to Russia.' Sir Thomas Sanderson, the permanent under secretary, duly advised against starting a press agitation, and George, always respectful of authority, complied. The Turks had done everything asked of them, Sanderson wrote to him: as Jack the Ripper's Whitechapel murders were drawing worldwide attention at the time the Turkish authorities 'might possibly reply, and with some effect, that startling crimes and mysterious disappearances occurred in other countries, which the police were unable in any way to trace. But they would be more likely simply to sulk.'

It is bad to outlive one's own son, but worse literally to lose him. It was excruciating for Alexander to be left ignorant of what had happened to Malcolm: the rest of the old man's life was left in the pall of this mystery. It is impossible, even now, to decide what happened, or where Malcolm went. The most obvious possibility – that he could not endure the prospect of returning to London next day to resume the uncongenial life which his father expected of him and therefore killed himself – is unconvincing. A dead man could not have removed his body and possessions so utterly. For the same reason an accidental death seems unlikely. Desperate for an explanation, the family alleged that Malcolm had been abducted or murdered by brigands, a misadventure not without precedent, for Lord Muncaster and his party had been held ransom by brigands at Marathon in 1870; but close investigation produced not one jot of evidence of this. Malcolm could have been done to death by Albanian shepherds, and his body hidden in the dense woods covering the lower stretches of Mount Olympus; but no one seems to have believed this very vigorously or for very long. There is an alternative solution which is no less improbable and no more provable: that the solitary beauty of Olympus overwhelmed Malcolm, that as he climbed to its peak he thought of the pagan gods living there in brutal, magnificent isolation according to legend and knew that he could not return to the grimy crowds of London; that he revolted from spending the rest of his days trying to bridle his contempt for the Macmillan creed of progressive, optimistic Christianity. He had been trying to turn his back on such things for years, and finally he resolved to do so literally: he turned and walked away. Almost three years of lonely travel in the more primitive corners of the Mediterranean had estranged him from his father's version of civilisation. It surely signifies something that Malcolm vanished on the very eve of returning to his family: perhaps he could not face them.

He would not have been the first educated Englishman to fend off disagreeable reality by vanishing abroad and going native: setting up in an oubliette somewhere in the Sultan of Turkey's empire, or in North Africa, with a girl or a succession of boys. He might not have lived well, or long, but at least he would have escaped the red plush curtains of Tooting respectability; have silenced the hubbub of incessant self-consciously high-minded conversation that must have sounded like a demon drumming in his ears. Malcolm was not the last Macmillan to feel oppressed by family expectations or inadequate to the demands of an unforgiving father; nor was he the last to take drastic measures to avoid ugly realities. His long Mediterranean tour had been, as much as anything, a retreat from the family; its termination seemed unbearable to him and was almost unendurable in its consequences for others.

Though Malcolm's defensiveness was not unique in the Macmillans' history, it was unique in his generation. Indeed from childhood he had always been set apart, at least in his father's estimation. He was often contrasted by Alexander to his next brother, George, usually to the latter's advantage. George was 'a capital boy in his own way, sorely given to chattering and larking, hates thinking and dreaming', wrote his father with relief after listing some of Malcolm's quiddities, 'but he will get on in the world'. George had an altogether more contented character and settled life. His school career was steady and successful: from Summerfields he was sent to Eton (at a time when it cost a parent £300 a year with board, lodging and clothes). When he left in 1874, he was set straight to work in his father's office. George Grove, then editor of *Macmillan's Magazine*, urged that the youth should study at Cambridge after Eton, but as George wrote grimly later, 'circumstances prevented me following his advice'.

The motives behind Alexander's decision were unattractively muddled. He wanted his sons to be educated as gentlemen. The idea that he, who had been born in peasant poverty, should send his son to Eton gratified him. It must have been pleasant to know that a boy with his plebeian blood was mixing on similar terms with the cadets of the aristocracy. But Alexander indulged his social ambitions only so far. The boast that he had a son at Eton – and boast he certainly did to his more trusted friends or more admired authors – was satisfaction enough. His disposal of George's life after Eton was more brutal: what had been good enough for Alexander would be good enough for George; the boy would have to work his way up. Alexander ignored the fact that George's education had scarcely fitted him to begin office work at the age of eighteen; that he was wrenching George, as he had Malcolm, apart from his friends and giving a turn to their lives which would separate them from their schoolfellows. Instead, with uncharacteristic crudity, he played to perfection the part of a self-made businessman and trampled underfoot the feelings of those closest to him.

George adapted better to this treatment than Malcolm, but it affected him nevertheless. As a child George had been a playful, spontaneous chatterbox, but his enforced training resulted in a decidedly different office manner. 'His commanding figure, his pale scholarly face, his stately walk and precise speech, his habit of sitting in a high-backed chair with his fingers pressed together and his gaze aloofly directed at the opposite wall, made him a little intimidating' to his staff and to younger authors, wrote Charles Morgan, whose books were published by Macmillan. Victorianism sat earnestly upon George long after the Queen herself was dead. Conscientious, austere and just in his dealings, he was adept at handling classicists, jurists, philosophers, theologians and their works of monumental scholarship; his dealings with them, and the rich intellectual interests which sustained him in his private life, compensated for the university education that he regretted missing.

Away from business he was a genial and hospitable man who was for years a member of a Sunday Walking Society founded by Sir Leslie Stephen and known as the Tramps. He was elected in 1898 to the Society of Dilettanti, which had been formed in 1741 as a private body of noblemen, scholars, collectors, painters and sculptors interested in public taste and the arts in Britain. Its membership was limited to fifty-four, including an official painter to the Society, a post held at different times by Reynolds, Lawrence and Sargent. George became secretary of the Society in 1911, serving jointly first with Lord Welby, formerly head of the Treasury, and later with Sir Cecil Harcourt-Smith, Keeper of Greek and Roman Antiquities at the British Museum. A magnificent three-quarter-length portrait of George, wearing the robe and bands of the Society, was the last oil-portrait undertaken by Sargent before his death in 1925.

George had a passionate love of music, particularly Greek and Italian music, which led to his appointment as honorary secretary of the Royal College of Music. For many years he was a member of the Bach Choir. He was also chairman of a specialist publishing house which produced many important books on music under a joint imprint with Macmillan. He found time for public benevolence: he was supporter of the Boys' Home set up in General Gordon's memory, and (ever mindful of the swathe of death which tuberculosis had cut through previous generations of the Macmillans) he was for years chairman of the Brompton Hospital for Consumption.

An enthusiasm for Greek studies was kindled in George by a visit which he made to Greece in 1877 in company with his future mentor the Irish Professor H.P. Mahaffy and two other young Dubliners, including Oscar Wilde. George and Wilde were the same age, twenty-two, and George reported to his parents from Italy, on the trip out, that Wilde was 'a very sensible, well-informed and charming man'. They maintained contact for years: in 1879 Wilde offered to translate Herodotus for publication by Macmillan, and in 1891 offered them his masterpiece *The Picture of Dorian Gray*, which they declined: for his part George tried to help get Wilde elected to the Savile club. But the main result of George's tour with Mahaffy was that in 1879 he took the initiative in founding the Hellenic Society to foster scholarly studies in Greek culture and antiquities. He was the society's honorary secretary for its first forty years, and then honorary treasurer from 1919 until 1934. In addition he was chosen as honorary secretary of the British School at Athens in 1886, becoming chairman of its managing committee in 1897. He wrote histories of both the Hellenic Society and the British School at Athens, and took interest in the *Journal of Hellenic Studies* and cognate scholarly journals. As a result of his enthusiasm Macmillan developed a publishing pre-eminence in archaeology, classical art, history and literature. His services to Hellenic scholarship were recognised by an honorary degree from Oxford in 1903 and by his election as an honorary fellow of Lincoln College, Oxford in 1911.

Two of the most distinguished authors on his list became intimate friends: Sir Arthur Evans, the Minoan archaeologist, and Sir James Frazer, author of *The Golden Bough*, who spoke in 1929 of George's 'sober enthusiasm, calm wisdom and sound good sense'. Evans was a nephew of Alexander Macmillan's friend Sebastian Evans: in 1900 George, as a hereditary friend of the family, launched a public appeal for funds to support the future exploration of the Knossos site. Ever zealous in promoting archaeological scholarship, George later agreed to publish the great work by Evans entitled *The Palace of Minos*, and to share profits if expenses were met.

George was devoted to his Yorkshire estate, Botton Hall near Danby. He bred pedigree stock there, and was an ardent horticulturalist. Friends and favoured Macmillan authors were sometimes invited to stay with him at his remote, ruggedly picturesque fastness. One such guest was Herbert Hensley Henson, the controversial Bishop of Durham, who left an account of his visit there in 1920. 'Macmillan took me for a walk before lunch,' wrote Henson. 'We went onto the moor above the house, and enjoyed the incomparable air, and rich prospect on every hand.' But George's visitors were usually high-minded and, where other people would enjoy the scenery, they felt impelled to hard thought too. 'As we looked down on his red-roofed homesteading enwreathed by shrubberies and gardens, so comfortably suggestive of prosperity, I reflected on what the spectacle implied and presupposed,' Henson internally sermonised. 'It illustrated the power and paradox of industrialism. . . . Like another Tarquinius Superbus, organised "Labour" is for striking off the tallest poppies on the field of society, and establishing a mean deadness of equality. What power has industrial society for defending itself against such a rebellion from within?'

In 1879 (the year in which he was admitted as a partner in the business) George married a Tooting neighbour, Margaret Helen, daughter of Joseph Lucas, by whom he had a daughter and two sons (one of whom, Alister, died in March 1892, at his school, shortly after his tenth birthday). Malcolm enjoyed the company of his nephews – the 'little boys are so extremely jolly that they rival their uncle in shrewd merriment', he wrote in 1886. George's surviving son William Edward Frank (1880–1954), known as Will, was educated at Eton and King's College, Cambridge before becoming a director of Macmillan in 1911. He fought in the Great War with the Scottish Rifles and was on the staff of the Intelligence Corps in France. Will followed his father's interest in both music and classical scholarship and was a keen natural historian; but he lacked strong literary intuitions, and sold his interest in the business to his cousins Dan and Harold after George's death. He married in 1914 Marjorie Simeon, daughter of an official at the House of Commons and granddaughter of a Victorian Cabinet minister, Hugh Childers. They had two sons, one of whom, known as Alastair, was mentally handicapped; and after Will's death the Botton Hall estate in Yorkshire was given by the family to Camphill, an organisation dedicated to challenging conventional treatment of mental disorders. Alastair became a treasured member of the community there, and was filmed talking about his life and cleaning the home of a member of the Camphill staff in a television programme entitled *Botton Is My Home* broadcast in 1990.

By the time the only son of Alexander's second marriage, John, was old enough to leave Eton his father was in his dotage, and the family had learnt from the mistakes which had delayed or prevented Malcolm and George from attending university. John was permitted to matriculate at Magdalen College, Oxford, from where he graduated with a first-class degree in modern history in 1899. Having been ordained as a priest, he was domestic chaplain and then chaplain to Randall Davidson, the Archbishop of Canterbury. An affectionate trust was established between the two men, with a hint of filial admiration on the part of John Macmillan. In 1916 he went to the Front as an army chaplain and was a protective companion for the primate when he toured the Western Front in May of that year ('Mac most helpful in every way, and as completely absorbed in the interest of it all as I am,' Davidson reported to his wife). Afterwards he was recalled by Davidson for special work with the National Mission for Repentance and Hope. He went out to work in Egypt and the Sudan in 1920, but Davidson wanted to keep him in his own diocese, and appointed him in 1921 as Archdeacon of Maidstone and Canon of Canterbury. In 1927 he was consecrated by Davidson as Suffragan Bishop of

Dover, charged with lifting diocesan work from the shoulders of the ageing and weary primate. He continued to fulfil this task for Davidson's successor, Cosmo Lang. The new Archbishop, who was a hard man to please, praised his 'invaluable Bishop of Dover' often and widely. John Macmillan was 'admirable', he told the Bishop of St Albans, 'a man of excellent judgement, good temper, tact and zeal'.

As John Macmillan assured Cosmo Lang in 1933, he was a man under holy orders who always obeyed the instructions of his superiors. The following year he was translated from his suffragan bishopric to become the second Bishop of Guildford. The diocese, which had been created as recently as 1927, covered a rich and increasingly populous area of Surrey. Not only did the new diocese lack common bonds or sense of unity, but its short life had been unusually disrupted. John Greig, the first Bishop, had developed, as Lord Ebbisham reported to Ramsay MacDonald, 'anaemia of the brain' resulting in 'frequent and serious lapses of memory'. The burden of running the diocese had thus fallen on the Canon of Guildford, Lionel Blackburne, and the Archdeacon, Cyril Golding-Bird. A rivalry worthy of Trollope's Barchester novels had developed between the two men: once it was known that Bishop Greig's retirement was imminent, each man exerted his influence to obtain appointment as the new bishop. Archdeacon Golding-Bird, who had a disconcerting resemblance in manner to Trollope's Archdeacon Grantley, enlisted the support of an equally vigorous character, a hard-nosed City merchant and treasurer of the Conservative Party who had been recently ennobled as Lord Ebbisham. Canon Blackburne's supporters were led by another Guildford magnate of more genuinely aristocratic antecedents, Lord Midleton. Neither clerical party could be conciliated with the other, and Cosmo Lang was convinced that an outsider was needed for this expanding new diocese 'to be pulled together, given confidence and a sense of a directing mind'. A strong man, who was also a gentleman, was needed to stand up to Ebbisham, Midleton and other opinionated plutocrats in the diocese.

The suggestion of John Macmillan was received cautiously in Downing Street. Stanley Baldwin 'had serious misgivings about sending to Guildford one who had suffered from something like nervous breakdowns, particularly in view of the circumstances in which Bishop Greig had to resign', the Prime Minister's patronage secretary informed Cosmo Lang. Downing Street agreed to the appointment only after receiving medical assurances that 'Bishop Macmillan should be able to discharge the duties of a diocesan bishop without further danger to his health.' Tragically this medical opinion proved false. The chief task facing the new Bishop was church-building, particularly the construction of a cathedral for the diocese; but great frustrations and petty jealousies beset him. 'Not only is there opposition from those who object to a Cathedral on principle,' wrote another Guildford landowner, Lord Onslow, who had offered a site for the cathedral, 'but the site is opposed by the Guildford tradesmen who think that the position of the pro-Cathedral in the High Street suits them better – & also by other charitable interests e.g. the Hospital who fear diversion of funds.' John Macmillan accepted that building a cathedral was essential for bringing unity to the diocese, but it was a hard task made more difficult by the character of Golding-Bird (who had previously been a colonial bishop and was never diffident in his dealings with anyone). The resultant strain more than once struck John Macmillan down into bouts of depressive anxiety such as had afflicted him in 1931.

As mentioned in Chapter 4, he had married a granddaughter of F.D. Maurice; the death of his wife in 1944, after almost forty years of marriage, was not only a personal tragedy but provoked a new crisis in his emotions. 'You probably have anticipated the grave results of the death of Mrs Macmillan upon the nervous system of the Bishop,' wrote John's confidant Canon Feilding Ottley to William Temple, Archbishop of Canterbury, in April 1944. Ottley warned the Archbishop that 'an unexpected spanner may be thrown into the machinery, which was in any case running with difficulty', by Golding-Bird's wish that the Archbishop should advise the Bishop to leave his diocese for several months of recuperation. 'I believe that Your Grace is aware that Diocesan relationships have been strained acutely in recent years: and if any suspicion were to be aroused in John's mind just now that Bishop Golding-Bird had approached Your Grace to advise a long leave of absence, I tremble to think of the consequences.'

In the event the grieving, broken-spirited Bishop was persuaded by family and physicians to go away to rest: first with his daughter Jean to a quiet Devon farmhouse, then to his sister Mary MacLehose in Scotland. His son Peter called on Archbishop Temple to discuss his father's predicament, and the solicitude with which both children treated their father was both tender and moving. Temple too showed true affection and sensitivity in his handling of a man whose dedication to the Church was so hampered by his nervous inheritance. The letters between Archbishop and Bishop make painful reading: Temple counselling full and complete rest; Macmillan fearing that a rest-cure would sink him in deeper introspection and asseverating that his greatest wish was with God's help to serve Christianity and strive to become worthier of his wife's memory. John Macmillan returned to Guildford later in the summer of 1944, feeling better but nevertheless riven by indecision and unsettled by Golding-Bird. On three occasions Golding-Bird had taken over the diocese when John had been too ill to work, and the latter castigated himself for ingratitude for wanting to be rid of him; yet, as he told Temple, they were incompatible as colleagues. The Bishop felt that he irritated the Archdeacon by his inability to take decisions, and was himself made miserable by Golding-Bird's peremptory manner and intractable opinions. He offered his resignation as bishop to Temple in a letter which reiterated his grief for his wife, and stressed his continuing need of the harmony and balance which she had given to his life.

This letter to Temple was followed by another from Canon Ottley, written at Jean Macmillan's instigation, urging that it would be mistaken to accept the Bishop's resignation. 'However deplorable it may seem, the real obstacle to his psychological recovery is Golding-Bird,' wrote Ottley: 'I have sometimes wondered if a Colonial Bishopric might be a solution to this complex situation.' In the event John Macmillan persevered as bishop until 1949 and lived until 1956. He was a man who for more than half a century served his Church with a passion, intensity and obedience which few men can muster for even the shortest task; with a more robust nervous system, he might have been one of the great ecclesiastics of his age. As it was this 'good and wise' man, as Cosmo Lang called him, gave great service to two Archbishops of Canterbury and endured his own lonely agony as he tried to serve his Church at Guildford. He suffered deeply, though he should be remembered for his successes as well as for his suffering; one of the lesser known of the Macmillans, he was an admirable man whose worst failing was that he would not spare himself.

Daniel's eldest son Frederick did not receive the privileges of an Eton education like George and John: instead he was sent as a boarder to a lesser school, Uppingham. From there he went immediately for training in retail bookselling by his cousin Robert Bowes at the Cambridge shop, and acquired a broad knowledge of printing from the University Press. He was then put to work for five years in the New York branch, during which period he met and married Georgiana Warrin from Long Island. He returned in 1876 to the London office, where he worked in all the departments in turn as well as working as a 'traveller', selling the Macmillan imprint to bookshop-keepers. He was, so Alexander wrote when Frederick was aged nineteen, 'a clever, well-behaved boy' who grew up into an eager, exuberant man. He enjoyed foxhunting and was gregarious in company. An attractive description of him has been left by Henry James, who referred 'the flourishing and convivial young Frederick, who has a pretty, dressy, worldly little American wife, and a very charming and hospitable house – also with a garden –

in St John's Wood'. James was often invited to this house, although after the flush of novelty had faded he was bored by some of the entertainments there: 'The genius of conversation in the great upper-middle class is not a dazzling muse; it is a plain-faced, portly matron, well covered up in warm, woollen garments and fond of an after-dinner nap.'

With his rosy face and twinkling eyes, Frederick was always preternaturally youthful in spirit: his final illness was brought on by his refusal, in his mid-eighties, to abandon his morning exercises in the bathroom until one morning he slipped and broke his thigh. It was characteristic of his organising powers and accessibility that he was four times president of the Publishers Association and a trustee or council member of other literary or bookselling bodies, for all of which he was knighted in 1909. Within the firm he specialised in literature, handling poetry and art books together with fiction. When the firm was turned into a limited company after Alexander's death in 1896, it was agreed that as the eldest of the double family he should be the first chairman. 'He was universally curious and quite free from priggery,' wrote a Macmillan author, J.C. Squire, 'a jolly, kindly, chuckling old gentleman who was the soul of honour and who loved Homer, Shakespeare, Pall Mall and a good cigar.' It typified his personal touch and clubland habits that it was he who masterminded Kipling's election as a member of the Beefsteak.

A similarly affectionate view of Frederick was left by another Macmillan author, Hugh Walpole, the novelist. The two men first met in 1914 at the house of Sibyl Colefax, the tuft-hunting hostess. Shortly afterwards young Walpole joined the Macmillan list. He had the habit of falling in love with married men in middle or late middle age, and soon became infatuated with Frederick. Relations between the two men were happy, intense but sexually innocent; Frederick's response to Walpole's affection showed that he had a large measure of his father Daniel's responsive, endearing nature. 'I love him dearly', Walpole confided to his diary in the early 1920s. 'I should like hugely to have been his son. We would have had a wonderful relation. He is the only human I know of in London of whom no one ever speaks a word of ill.' Walpole was an ideal author, whose manuscripts were always punctual and whose sales grew steadily (60,000 copies of the one-volume *Herries Chronicle* were sold before publication in 1939). Frederick proposed him for membership of the Athenaeum in 1922, and when praising *Harmer John* to its author in 1926 'spoke of it with tears in his eyes'. In turn Walpole commemorated Frederick as Sir Donald Winchester in his novel *John Cornelius*: 'the grandest old man I've ever known. He looks you straight in the eye and says what he thinks . . . Why, any time I'm a bit low I think to myself of Sir Donald, aged eighty, sitting there in his shining white collar and black stock and white pin, and his voice with just a bit of Scotch in it and his eye as clear and sharp as a bird's.'

Frederick's younger brother Maurice (Daniel's second son and Harold's father) joined the business in 1882 after a few years as a schoolmaster. He became a partner in the firm in 1883, and toured India and Australasia on their behalf in 1884–5. After cautious deliberation, the firm appointed an educational agent in India in 1893, and finally opened a branch at Bombay in 1901. Thereafter the Indian business, chiefly in educational books, expanded under Maurice's stewardship. Maurice's father Daniel had believed passionately in the powers of education to provide people with inner enrichment but also with the means to influence, or take control, of their own destinies. The wish to educate the ignorant had been a mainspring of Daniel's decision to become a publisher: so it was fitting that his son Maurice, venerating his father's memory, took responsibility for educational books in the next generation. Of his character and domestic life more will be told in the next chapter.

Frederick, George and Maurice were paragons of filial piety. After Alexander's death in 1896, John Morley encouraged George to collect his father's letters, and the latter spent more than a decade going through letter-books and old files, ordering the papers and arranging transcripts, latterly with the help of Arthur Tilney Bassett, who had sorted Gladstone's papers. Yet, despite the obvious continuities, there were difficulties after the chief power of decision had moved from Alexander to the three younger men of his family. 'I cannot help feeling that the firm has suffered much by losing the personal supervision of Mr Alexander Macmillan,' Lewis Carroll wrote tartly to Frederick in 1893, threatening to sever a connection of nearly thirty years unless better attention was paid to his wishes. Carroll was one of their more demanding authors, who, after he had sent his timepiece to a watch-mender, instructed his publisher to have it collected for him by 'a trusty and resolute messenger'.

Not only were Macmillan willing to serve as Carroll's errand boys, but at the instigation of Frederick in the 1890s they also served a greater cause dear to Carroll's heart. Book pricing and price control had been the subject of contention throughout the nineteenth century. Originally it was the custom for books to be sold below their advertised price: publishers competed to offer booksellers the best terms, and booksellers undersold one another. In 1829 major publishers settled a trade agreement which controlled book prices by cutting off supplies to retailers who sold at less than agreed prices. This arrangement collapsed in 1852, to the distress of publishers, who bemoaned the ruinous effect of underselling. Alexander inflicted on Gladstone at least one long jeremiad on the subject. In the 1870s and 1880s Lewis Carroll, already a Macmillan author, made unilateral efforts to fix the price of his books and to control discounts on them. It was partly as a result of Macmillan's identification with Carroll's initiative (and his bombardment of them with closely argued letters on the subject) that the firm emerged as leaders of a new effort to set regulations that authors, publishers and retailers were bound to uphold. A letter from Frederick Macmillan was published in the *Bookseller* in 1890 proposing that publishers should set the retail price of each book: a bookseller could only deviate from this price under pain of boycott from all publishers. 'It is rapidly becoming impossible for a bookseller, pure and simple, dealing in current literature to make a living profit out of the business,' Frederick declared. 'A well-stocked bookshop is a centre of mental culture, and any disorganisation of trade that renders the existence of such centres difficult or impossible is an injury to the community.' In order to advance the abolition of discounts to the public, Macmillan issued sixteen titles with a net price in 1890, rising to over a hundred such titles by 1894. Supplies were refused to retailers which ignored Macmillan's stipulated net price. Frederick's initiative was at first fiercely opposed but gained such momentum that it was enshrined in the Net Book Agreement of 1899. After *The Times* opened its Book Club in 1905, sometimes supplying discounted books to the 'carriage folk' who called at its premises in New Bond Street, a 'book war' broke out with the Publishers Association arrayed against *The Times*. After much sound and fury, the latter was vanquished.

Publishing was changing in many ways. When Daniel and Alexander went into business together, religious disputes were creating great passions and parties. But by the 1880s theology was no longer the focus of intense national interest, although a minor inaccuracy about the sixteenth-century Reformation of the English Church brought an outburst of ecclesiastical wrath upon the partners' heads in 1894. 'I have written to George Macmillan to say that really such things ought not to occur to a decent firm,' Bishop Mandell Creighton informed the Archbishop of Canterbury. 'Has some Romanist compositor interpolated a passage to suit his own views?' George mollified Creighton and other bishops, but such eruptions grew increasingly rare: the strongest currents of thought were secular. Under the triumvirate of the brother-cousins, Macmillan books became less identifiable with the heartiness of the previous generation's muscular Christianity.

There were other undercurrents of change. Daniel and

Alexander had been high-spirited men, who enjoyed facetious-ness and boisterous laughter – tastes discernible in some of the books which they published. Their sons were staider men, who brought few signs of joy to their working lives. They were affectionate, in the manner of their time, but less eager or impulsive than their fathers. Though the Victorians have been represented as rigid, stuffy and obsessed with the preservation of respectable outward forms, it was in the Edwardian and Georgian Britain of the twentieth century that stultification reached its nadir. The stiff composure of the members of the double family reflected a wider ossification of authority and outlook. Daniel and Alexander had mixed with men who were advanced thinkers and outspoken reformers: they believed in progress: they were Radical Liberals in politics. Their sons were altogether different. Malcolm, as we have seen, became in the 1880s a reactionary who liked to treat great issues as trivial games. Frederick by the mid-1890s believed that radicalism was disreputable, and he always disliked signs of the non-conformist religious conscience in politics. Maurice was a Liberal Unionist, who admired great Liberal states-men/Macmillan authors like Bryce and Morley but voted for Balfour's Conservative candidate in the general election of 1905. George remained a Liberal voter until the First World War: during the Irish crisis in the spring of 1914, when the threat of a British civil war seemed real, he wrote in both *The Times* and the Liberal *Westminster Gazette* in support of the suggestion by Sir Henry Newbolt, the poet and naval historian, that the threat might recede if the proposed Liberal government legislation to give Home Rule to Ireland only came into effect for Ulster a stipulated number of years after the other Irish provinces.

These changes in the family's politics signified many things. Partly they reflected the changes in the political parties that occurred in the late nineteenth century, particularly the split in the Liberal Party after Gladstone adopted the policy of Home Rule for Ireland in the 1880s. But the family's drift

The ruins of the crofter's cottage on Arran where the Macmillans began.

Daniel, the idealistic invalid who founded the family fortune.

Alexander, eminent
Victorian and
publishing patriarch.

Knapdale, the house at
Tooting where two
generations of
Macmillans lived.

Alfred, Lord Tennyson,
a Macmillan author
who was venerated by
the family.

Thomas Hardy, another
of the Macmillans'
monumental authors.
Some of his writings
were rejected by them as
too sensationalist.

Sir Frederick
Macmillan, 'a jolly,
kind, chuckling old
gentleman who was the
soul of honour and
loved a good cigar'.

Sargent's portrait of
George Macmillan,
'commanding, stately,
intimidating,
conscientious and just'.

Rudyard Kipling, a Macmillan author.
Harold pitied the way he was bullied by Mrs Kipling.

Dorothy and Harold Macmillan as a young married couple.

Dorothy with her three daughters,
Catherine (left), Carol (right) and baby Sarah.

Dorothy's cousins the Marquess and Marchioness of Salisbury. Bobbety came to detest Harold's political morality and Betty thought Dorothy's affair was unforgiveable.

John Maynard Keynes, who was attracted to Dan Macmillan, influenced Harold's political thinking and was published by the brothers.

Bob Boothby, the hard-
living political maverick
with whom Dorothy
was sexually obsessed.

Dorothy was 'the most
formidable thing in the
world – a possessive,
single-track woman',
said Boothby. 'At every
crucial moment she acts
instinctively and
overwhelmingly.'

rightwards also signified the shifting social allegiances of the
family. Though Daniel and Alexander had been radical in their
beliefs, they had also been socially ambitious for the family: their
sons were essentially conservative. Their schooling at Eton and
Marlborough and Uppingham had done its work: they might
be the grandsons of Scottish crofters, but a distinctive new
outlook had been instilled in them. In the petty worlds of their
boarding-houses they had learnt that it was not only a 'bad
show' to be conspicuous, but likely to bring physical retribution.
In the boarding-houses of their great schools survival had
depended upon respecting the conventions and on conforming
to group pressure; heterodox opinions, flamboyant behaviour,
assertive individuality drew the crushing weight of schoolboy
disapproval. A less crude but equally unrelenting coercion was
perpetuated in the adult world: although the boys of the double
family had been born above a shop in Cambridge and reared in
the suburbs at Tooting, their way of life was very different from
their parents'. It was their educational experience which made
this difference.

Frederick and George were both elected to the Athenaeum
club in 1894, Maurice a few years later. They were tenacious,
orderly, prudent men. Prematurely venerable, they were grandees of Victorian publishing who survived to be even more venerable grandees among twentieth-century publishers. Maurice
took the closest interest of the trio in the firm's finances, and its
solidity was a byword: 'the Macmillans are as safe as the Bank
of England', wrote one of their authors, the bestselling novelist
F. Marion Crawford. Their self-confidence was spectacular:
their books bore the stamp of their certainty in themselves.
The trio were 'fine bluff Christian gentlemen dispensing good
and making a satisfactory profit out of it', as one of their
employees, Lovat Dickson, recalled. It was peculiarly suitable
when they were asked to fulfil a last duty to one of the most
enduring of their authors, by helping to organise one of the
great public events of late Victorian England: the funeral, at
Westminster Abbey, in 1892, of Tennyson. The Macmillans

allocated tickets, and coped with the weight of letters that fell upon the poet's grieving family. The event itself commanded the presence of all the intellect of England, in all its force and variety. 'A more splendid spectacle I have never witnessed, for it combined every element of grandeur,' wrote one of the pall-bearers, the Marquess of Dufferin and Ava, who as a former Viceroy of India was not easily awed. 'No one who was present will ever forget the scene, which was unparalleled in its dignity and splendid significance.'

In their way the Macmillans were as dignified and monumental as Tennyson's funeral. They were always strong men, but the mixture of love and conflict which had characterised their boyhood in the double family was perpetuated in adult form at the office. They met together daily so that Frederick could read aloud the more important correspondence that had reached the office upon which each partner could offer his opinion. They came together again for luncheon, discussing business over their chops and whiskies, or while taking a glass of madeira with some cake. Inevitably such close dealings led to outbreaks of mutual irritation or fussy squabbling.

The shortcomings of the Macmillans became more evident after William Heinemann started his own publishing house in 1890. Heinemann's business was based on fiction, principally intended for subscription libraries, and ballasted by such series as *The Complete Works of Heinrich Heine*. It was Heinemann who destroyed the public taste for three-decker novels just around the date, in 1898, when Macmillan bought for £8,000 the publishing house of George Bentley, which specialised in such fiction. Heinemann's discovery or promotion of novelists such as H.G. Wells, Joseph Conrad, D.H. Lawrence, George Moore, John Galsworthy and Somerset Maugham; his acquisition of blockbusting American books like Stephen Crane's *The Red Badge of Courage*, Upton Sinclair's *The Jungle* and Jack London's *The Call of the Wild*; his popularisation of French novelists and Russian translations – all these profitable lines were in areas in which the brother-cousins were weak in the quarter-century before 1914. By contrast Macmillan's successes were first-class editions of established English authors like Matthew Arnold, Edward FitzGerald, Charles Kingsley, Rudyard Kipling, Charles Lamb, Walter Pater and Tennyson, or momentous, high-prestige books which were more widely consulted than read: five volumes of Sir Henry Craik's *English Prose Selections* (1892–6), six volumes of W.J. Courthope's *History of English Poetry* (1895–1909), Sir John Fortescue's *History of the British Army* in thirteen volumes (1899–1929), a *History of the English Church* in eight volumes (1899–1910) and several series of scientific and medical works. This was the area of the firm's prowess: in gigantic, authoritative editions, rather than in intuitive novelties.

Whereas Daniel and Alexander had been able to use their own judgment in appraising manuscripts in the early days of publishing, the scale of the business obliged Frederick and his partners to rely increasingly on readers for advice. Macmillan's readers reported in 1891 on 315 manuscripts (of which 293 were rejected), and the number of submissions steadily increased. These outsiders inevitably had areas of myopia; the longest serving of them, Morley, distrusted the perturbations raised by imaginative new writing, and another literary adviser who was personally beloved by the partners, Mowbray Morris (1848–1911), had an even more baneful effect.

An Etonian who left Oxford without taking his degree, Morris spent four years in South Australia as aide-de-camp to its Governor before joining the staff of *The Times*, where in 1877 he was appointed dramatic critic. The Macmillans recruited him as editor of their magazine and as a general literary adviser in 1885. He took his responsibilities gravely, yet approached them narrowly. A foe to slovenliness of style, he castigated contributors for slang or clichés, but in many literary matters his mind was closed. Under his editorship the magazine steadily lost its vivacity and appeal: in a desperate effort at survival, it was first reduced to the ranks of the sixpenny magazines and, when this had no avail on sales, was shut in 1907. In his spare time Morris wrote biographies of heroes of Stuart Scotland, Claverhouse and Montrose, and co-operated with the Duke of Beaufort in compiling the volume on fox-hunting in the Badminton Sports Library series: these extra-mural interests were a sign of his limitations. He had no interest in foreigners. 'France and Germany were as remote from his experience as the South Pole,' wrote his friend Charles Whibley. 'His noble insularity saw in America a land which no gentleman should visit.' As a member of the Travellers Club and a founder of the Beefsteak, Pall Mall was his spiritual home. Adorned with a top-hat of uniquely opulent sheen and unforgettably florid curves, from which he refused to be separated either in his club or at a dinner party, Morris wore braided coats and flawless cravats. By a hundred small divergences he marked his loathing of modern fashions and thoughts. The din and jargon of his own time were anathema to him. Modern appliances like the telephone were as vile to him as the pert vulgarity of modern literature. 'He was an extravagant version of the man about town, resuscitated from some earlier generation,' wrote his colleague at Macmillan, Stephen Gwynn, who inwardly regretted that 'this mixture of old-fashioned ways with a complete assurance that they embodied the last word of style went into his literary work'. Predictably Morris disliked modernism, realism and stylistic heterodoxy, typically dismissing the poetry of Yeats, which was first offered to Macmillan in 1900, as 'unreal, unhuman and insincere . . . nonsense'. It is hard to imagine a man with such mannerisms attracting Daniel or Alexander, still less being so thoroughly trusted in his judgments; but Frederick, George and Maurice loved the rituals of Pall Mall almost as dearly as Morris.

The blemishes traceable to Morris were erased under the influence of Charles Whibley, who succeeded him as the Macmillans' chief literary adviser. Whibley had been Paris correspondent of the *Pall Mall Gazette* in the 1890s and had a more cosmopolitan outlook than Morris (for many years too he cherished a cat that had belonged to Mallarmé). By combining the roles of man of letters and political pamphleteer he seemed a latterday version of Defoe or Johnson. The pungent High Tory opinions which he contributed to *Blackwood's Magazine* were born of his hatred of humbug and pretensions. He flogged out shams without mercy; he flailed prigs, hypocrites and liberals. He had so many *bêtes noires*, someone said, that being with him was like living in Haiti: scarcely a white in sight. His politics were the violent antithesis of Morley's, and would have been loathsome to Daniel and Alexander; it was significant of the family's new place in the world that they relied on the opinions of a man like Whibley. Yet his identification with the Macmillans was a great benefit to them, for unlike Morris he never allowed questions of aesthetic taste to be obscured by moral indignation or the pressure for social conformity. He was an early and generous friend to T.S. Eliot: he recognised too the brilliance of Yeats, who was at last signed up in 1916 and was followed by a succession of other Irish writers, notably Sean O'Casey. Although not a don, he kept a set of college rooms in Cambridge during the university terms. His two successive wives (of whom he excluded all mention from *Who's Who*) were left at his country house while he lived in Cambridge, where (despite being vexed by the presence of 'the Harpies of Newnham and Girton', as he told George Macmillan in 1921) he exhibited a formidable interest in male undergraduates. Whibley was a popular, witty companion, although young Lord Balniel resented it when, at a dinner in 1896, he 'got very fond of me about midnight and persisted in giving me little hugs'. For his juniors a dinner alone with him in his Cambridge rooms, accompanied by lashings of good wine and a long talk, were sometimes memorable experiences and sometimes better forgotten.

Whibley's molestations were doubtless unknown to the Macmillans, but other issues of sexuality, or fears of sexuality, did reach the family. The obscenity laws, which like so many features of British society were largely concerned with the enforcement of class distinction, were part of the context of their professional and personal lives. Prosecutions under Lord Campbell's Act of 1857, which governed obscenity laws until 1959, were directed against books which the authorities believed were suitable for a gentleman to read in foreign or dead languages in his own library, but were dangerous for the newly literate masses to enjoy in the English language. Thus the Society for the Suppression of Vice prevented the sale of cheap translations of Boccaccio and Rabelais by threatening publishers with prosecution: Zola's luckless English publisher was imprisoned after prosecutions inspired by the National Vigilance Association in 1888–9 (the prosecuting barrister was Asquith, the future Prime Minister). Prosecutions under Campbell's Act reflected the class-bound fear that libidinousness and indecency, especially indecencies imported from France, were menacing British social stability. There were signs in contemporary literature, so a Macmillan author, Coventry Patmore, warned in 1887, 'that the love of violent, foul and vicious excitements, which already taints all degrees of life in France and widely disgraces the governing classes in England, may soon assail our middle and upper ranks; and that the acrid fumes of lust, cruelty, horror, and the infra-natural may gradually poison and supersede the mild and wholesome interests of average English life, even among those classes which are at present least corrupted'. In practice the Macmillans were careful to conform to conventional morality while privately indignant at meddlesome zealotry. Thus in 1900, Frederick (in correspondence with the former Prime Minister and Macmillan author Lord Rosebery) urged that neither the police nor private individuals should be able to prosecute for obscenity without some safeguard against private mischief-making such as the Attorney-General's prior approval. He was indignant that reputable publishers might face the vexation and cost of defending their edition of a classic (whether ancient or modern, foreign or British) which some zealot had prosecuted as indecent.

The complexities of the Macmillans' position was shown in their dealings with H.G. Wells. He not only expected large advances, but fretted over the promotion of his books, and would call without appointment to urge some quirky sales ploy while threatening otherwise to place his future books elsewhere. It was therefore a grave decision in 1908 when Macmillan declined to publish his new novel *Ann Veronica*. Nowadays it seems one of Wells's weakest books – a priggish sentimentalisation of philandering – but at the time Frederick described it as 'very well written', with an 'entertaining' account of middle-class life. However, he told Wells, 'the plot develops on lines that would be exceedingly distasteful to the public which buys books published by our firm'. When the heroine 'offers herself' as mistress to a professor 'and almost forces herself into his arms, the story ceases to be amusing and is certainly not edifying'. Subsequently St Loe Strachey, editor of the *Spectator*, denounced *Ann Veronica*, fulminating that 'the muddy world of Mr Wells's imaginings . . . is a community of scuffling stoats and ferrets, unenlightened by a ray of duty or abnegation', provoking a clergyman headmaster called Herbert Bull to use the book as a pretext to raise funds for the prosecution of authors and publishers of 'moral poison'. This response was disliked by the Macmillan partners. They did not wish to deal in obscenities, as Frederick wrote to Maurice, but it would be equally intolerable for their literary judgments to be constrained by bigots like Bull and St Loe Strachey.'

The class-consciousness of these anxieties about indecent literature was explicit in the stir provoked by Wells's novel. In response to 'the new immorality' which *Ann Veronica* represented, the major circulating libraries (which controlled about two-thirds of shops selling new books in London alone) in 1909 introduced a complicated secret censorship of books which they handled. Some authors, like Edmund Gosse, were appalled at 'the reading class' in Britain resigning 'its literary judgment . . . to the good pleasure of a group of commercial gentlemen' and led an agitation against such presumptuous, mercenary censorship. At the same time a Macmillan writer, Maurice Hewlett, opposed the Society of Authors trying to negotiate with the circulating libraries to lift the censorship: it was 'not only undignified but almost indecent that representative writers should discuss these matters with tradesmen'. Such responses showed the narrow path which the Macmillan family had to tread. Old boys of Eton and Uppingham though they might be, they were also 'commercial gentlemen', and in peril of being treated as 'tradesmen' too. The idea that men might be accepted for themselves and their own achievements – which had enabled Alexander to move freely almost everywhere as a respected example of the 'industrious classes' – grew steadily more moribund during the course of the brother-cousins' lives.

Nevertheless they were generally respected and earned encomia that were thoroughly deserved. 'I believe Macmillans are almost the only firm nowadays who ever publish for glory without profit,' that astute literary observer Sir Edward Marsh wrote in 1922, though his opinion should be balanced with an equally veracious warning by Henry James a generation earlier. 'Don't nurse yourself in the fond illusion that he will give you a palpable sum of money,' he advised a friend who contemplated offering a book to Macmillan for publication: 'that is not the strong point of the good Macmillans.' Yet despite their canniness about money the three male survivors of the double family did, as their fathers would have wished, great and useful work. In a real sense their work was a blessing to them. Men who had inherited a coal business in Camberwell or a shoe factory in Leicester would have been condemned in all likelihood to dismal, illiberal lives; but Frederick, George and Maurice were blessed that it was a publishing firm that they inherited. It was their daily dealing in literature which saved them from becoming, as Cardinal Newman described the sons of Birmingham's self-made businessmen, uncouth imitations of polished ungodliness. Books were the saving of them as they had been for their fathers.

For over half a century these three men had worked together, and in 1936 they died together. First George died at his beloved house in Yorkshire on 3 March, aged eighty. At the end of the month, on 30 March, Maurice died, aged eighty-two, released after several years of illness and blindness. On the day of Maurice's funeral, his elder brother Frederick was admitted as a patient to the London Clinic, which was opposite his house in Devonshire Place. The clinical austerity of his new surroundings was a great contrast to the elaborate and cluttered Victorian ornamentation of his home. On the day after the old man's admission to the clinic, his nephew Harold called to see him. Frederick said how pleased he was that Harold had visited him, but could not understand how he had managed it, and worried how Harold would 'get back'. It was not a bad place, Frederick added, and some nice women had given him sips of champagne. After saying this, he began fretting again about how Harold would 'get back', until Harold at last realised that Frederick thought he had died and was in heaven. In this muddled state Frederick lingered until 1 June, when the eldest of Alexander's double family died at the age of eighty-five.

CHAPTER 6

Nellie and Harold

Nobody can misunderstand a boy like his own mother.

Norman Douglas, *South Wind*

It is the tragedy of childhood that its catastrophes are eternal.

Hugh Walpole, *Jeremy at Crale*

None of us can help the things life has done to us. They're done before you realise it, and once they're done they make you do other things until at last everything comes between you and what you'd like to be, and you've lost your true self for ever.

Eugene O'Neill, *Long Day's Journey into Night*

This book is a history of the Macmillan family. It is the story of an ambitious but sometimes wayward publishing dynasty which made a fortune and whose members turned to politics; but though it is a family chronicle, there is no doubt that the most famous of the Macmillans was Harold. His public career and private experiences were most important: it is his part in the family story which most obviously touches British history. The events of his life, and their sequel, will dominate the rest of this book, which now becomes not only an account of his place in history but an account of his place in his family.

In many ways the family's circumstances were indistinguishable from those of thousands of other upper-middle-class Londoners. They seemed all too conventional to most of the people who knew them. Yet each family has an inner history of its own, and that of the Macmillans was distinctive: it put its own unique pressure on its children, reared them in its own distinct traditions, gave them its own special outlook and sent them in directions of its own making. It was where Harold Macmillan came from.

It was a family originally bereft. Maurice Macmillan (1853–1936) was aged only four when his father Daniel died: the death of his mother when he was thirteen left him an orphan. His godfathers were Charles Kingsley and F.D. Maurice, after whom he was named, but from 1857 he was reared in the house of his uncle Alexander, who took the decision to send the boy to Uppingham for his schooling. This was an experience which had exceptional influence on Maurice.

Uppingham had been founded as a grammar school in 1584, and had remained swathed in the provincial obscurity of Rutland until the appointment as headmaster of the Rev. Edward Thring in 1853. Thring took charge of twenty-five boys and two masters, situated in mean premises, but over the course of thirty-four years he raised Uppingham to a leading position among English schools, with noble buildings, a fine chapel, a library, eleven boarding-houses and 320 boys. With no less earnestness, and with scarcely less personal magnetism than Thomas Arnold, Thring was more original in his educational methods, for Uppingham was the first of the great Victorian schools to have workshops, laboratories and a gymnasium for its pupils. His talents had been noticed by the Macmillans when he was scarcely free from adolescence. Writing to Thring in 1868, Alexander recalled how, more than twenty years earlier, 'my dear brother and I used to speculate on the line in which you were to become eminent, for you were among the first of Cambridge men whom his clear eye determined as fitted to do world work in one line or another'. Thring wrote copiously on the principles of education, and his books were published by Macmillan from an early date. His writings were characterised by an enthusiasm for the moral and religious purposes to be served in education, and by those flashes of grotesque fancy which Alexander found so attractive in friends like Ainger and Stopford Brooke. Although he could seldom be lured to London, he and Alexander corresponded through the years. The tone of their exchanges is conveyed by a letter sent after the Prussian defeat of the French in the war of 1870, an event which deeply disturbed Alexander. 'We may well mourn ourselves at the intense reluctance in England to do true work', wrote Thring, 'when we see as you say France plunged into a misery ... simply from their prolonged efforts to make self-indulgence the law of their world.' Their belief in work, simplicity and high purposes, with its accompanying horror of misery and self-indulgence, shaped Maurice's character.

The boy won a scholarship to Uppingham, where Thring pronounced his 'very high opinion of Maurice on all that makes a man'. His status as a favourite pupil was confirmed when he won a scholarship to Christ's College, Cambridge, and graduated with a first-class degree in classics in 1875. These successes delighted Thring, who confided to his diary that Maurice was 'a most deserving fellow, and has worked excellently'. The boy's singularity as a pupil is suggested by the fact that when he left Uppingham in 1871 he was presented with a marble clock with an inscription from the other members of his boarding-house: this was hardly an ordinary proceeding and surely marks some special meaning in his school life.

Initially Maurice kept clear of the family business. Thring had been an inspiration for the fatherless boy and the headmaster's ideals were also paternal ones. Thring and his father, Maurice knew, were united in their beliefs that the propagation of educational truth was a mission in the world, that the business of schooling was to train men for the service of God. It was under these influences that, after leaving Cambridge, he became classics master at St Paul's School in Kensington in 1877. Although he remained as upright and unselfish as Thring's model, Maurice seems to have lost his religious faith as an adult, and went to his prayers in the spirit of a man setting his children and servants a good example of discipline. His agnosticism perhaps made him more rather than less anxious to respect the proprieties of good society. This loss of faith may have contributed to his decision to abandon Christian schoolmastering for publishing, but there were financial pressures too: his life took a new direction when, at the age of thirty, he met an American widow, Nellie Hill.

The early life of Helen Artie Tarleton Belles (1856–1937), to give her original name in full, had surpassed even that of Maurice in its bereavements. Her father Joshua Tarleton Belles (1826–96) came from Kentucky and had been orphaned by the age of thirteen. In 1851 he graduated with his brother-in-law's help from the Indiana Medical College, and eventually settled in the little prairie town of Spencer, Indiana in 1864. He became one of the leading citizens of Spencer, a landlord and a Freemason as well as Government Examining Surgeon for almost twenty years. Originally a member of the Baptist Church, he was a dedicated temperance worker; there being no Baptist community in Spencer, he later became a strict Methodist. His life was however dogged by domestic sadness. In 1850 he had married Julia, daughter of Archibald and Laura Reid, who had been among the earlier settlers in Indianapolis after the state capital was first laid out in 1821, five years after Indiana was admitted to the Union. The newly married couple lived in a house at the corner of East and Louisiana streets in Indianopolis; but of their five children, only one, Harold Macmillan's mother Nellie, survived. This was a high mortality rate, even by the standards of nineteenth-century urban life; and it is probable that Dr Belles, returning from his medical duties, brought into his home infections which killed his children. Daniel Macmillan's parents had left Arran for mainland Scotland after their children had been decimated in an epidemic, and the Belles family too left Indianapolis for California after the death of their little daughter Emma in 1854. They returned to the mid-west a year later, and it was at Indianapolis in December 1862 that Julia Belles died.

Nellie was six at the time; although at least one of her siblings, Emma, had died before Nellie's birth in 1856, she had seen enough to know that life was uncertain, that brothers and sisters and mothers abruptly died, that the world was an incomprehensible, frightening place where uncontrollable catastrophes happened. Little is known of Nellie's childhood except that she remained caught in the shadows of death. In 1864 her father remarried. His wife Amanda Tull was the widowed daughter of Samuel and Amanda McCurdy, of Marion County, Indiana; but, of the four children born to this second marriage, only two reached maturity. Meanwhile she was educated in Spencer and at a finishing school at Indianapolis. It was there that she met John Bayliss Hill, a promising young painter who was a scion of the nearest that approached in Indiana to being a patrician family. They shared a love of music and were full of artistic ideals. In June 1874, when Nellie was eighteen, the couple were married at Spencer, the local newspaper reporting that they left 'on the 2 o'clock eastward bound train followed by the kind wishes of many friends'. But death was inexorable in its pursuit of Nellie. Five months later, in November 1874, Jack Hill died at his father's house in Indianapolis at the age of twenty-five. One can only suppose that Nellie was devastated.

The young widow remained in Indianapolis for a time, singing in the Methodist choir and living with Zerelda Wallace, the widow of another Methodist, David Wallace, a bloated alcoholic who had been a notably corrupt Governor of Indiana (seen at election-time by one of Jack Hill's family 'in high glee . . . at the gullibility of the people'). Her bereavements marked her for life, although in an attempt to palliate her loss she moved to Paris to study music and sculpture.

Both Indianapolis and Spencer had been unbroken wilderness until the 1820s. When Nellie was young there were many people in both places who had known the area as it was before Columbus landed on the shores of the new world, or the cavaliers of Cortez invaded the halls of the Montezumas. The people of southern Indiana lived a hard, insular existence: 'I assure you that Indiana is at the last or at least sixth circle of desolation,' as Ezra Pound wrote from the state in 1907. Its pioneer pride and traditions were strong, perhaps repellently so. Celebrating the growth of Spencer, one of its citizens wrote in the year of Nellie's marriage to Maurice Macmillan:

> Such a thing is only found in America, and is possible only with Americans. Cities like Chicago or Denver rise almost like magic within a few years. It is the peculiarity and pride of American civilisation that it advances so swiftly, that the dull and slow going mind of Europe is unable to follow or comprehend it. Accustomed to the stupidity and snail-like pace of the old world, the brilliancy of American enterprise is to the European as the whirl of a great city to an unsophisticated rustic. . . . That so soon after the first white man saw the country, he is surrounded with the comforts and luxuries of an advanced civilization, the descendant of the pioneer owes to the fact that he belongs to a superior and chosen people.

Nellie, with her musical tastes and her delicate, artistic husband, was not roused by such rhetoric. In fact, although she returned to Spencer several times before her father's death in 1896, she erased her origins as best she could. Jack Hill was never mentioned by her. After settling in London, her American accent was obliterated and she spoke in the purest English tones. She and her father had been left together in terrible circumstances in the early 1860s, and one may fancy that they were particularly close; but after his death her interest in her Indiana family diminished. In many ways she became more English than the English, and found safety in the most conventional English phrases and habits of thought. After the outbreak of war in 1914, for example, she patriotically sent to Indiana some letters on morale. 'All classes are brought together in a wonderful way,' she enthused. 'There are no such things as party politics and differences in religion, or class. All are Britons. Even the poorest is willing to give the best he has and the whole empire is giving its best.' Evidently Nellie was one of those people able to convince themselves of the truth of whatever it might be convenient to pretend.

In the late 1870s and early 1880s Nellie remained in Europe, where she met Maurice, who married her in 1884. The three sons born to this marriage were the only grandchildren of Daniel to bear the surname of Macmillan.

The eldest son Daniel de Mendi Macmillan (1886–1965) was named in memory of his venerated grandfather. Dan was brilliant from childhood: he was Newcastle scholar at Eton, a scholar of Balliol who took a first-class degree in classics. Both as a child and in manhood Harold was awed by Dan's academic prowess as well as envious of his powers and privileges. Nellie, who had a streak of parsimony, handed down Dan's old clothes and books for his youngest brother to use, and this left Harold with a surprisingly long resentment that he had been treated as second best. Opinions greatly differed on the respective aptitudes of the two men as publishers: some colleagues considered that Dan was a steadier influence on the business than Harold, while Harold's admirers judged that Dan was sometimes narrow-minded, or too dismissive of new ideas or new authors.

Maynard Keynes met Dan when they were both Eton boys, liked him, was attracted by him and admired his intellectual gifts; it was his feeling for Dan, who became a director of the family firm in 1911, which resulted in *The Economic Consequences of the Peace*, and Keynes's other great books, being published by Macmillan. On an early visit to the Macmillans' house in Sussex, Birch Grove, probably in 1913, Keynes outraged Nellie by appearing at breakfast in bedroom slippers, and this was not the only occasion when Dan's friends pained his parents. As a young man Dan shocked Nellie and Maurice by his almost desperate dissipation, drinking, chasing women and sitting up late to play poker for high stakes with young blades like Duff Cooper and Alan Lascelles, who both rose to eminence later, and Edward Horner and Patrick Shaw-Stewart, who were both cut down while fighting in 1917. Dan himself joined the King's Royal Rifle Corps after the outbreak of war in 1914, but was invalided from the Army in the following year, and worked at the Admiralty for the rest of the war. During the subsequent peace negotiations he attended the Versailles conference as a junior official, before resuming work as a publisher. His friend Keynes also attended the conference, as part of the Treasury delegation, and arranged with Daniel that his historic indictment of Versailles, *The Economic Consequences of the Peace*, was published by Macmillan. Daniel was chairman and managing director of Macmillan from 1936 (when the three survivors of the double family died) until 1963.

As a young man Dan was enchanting (in the opinion of Lytton Strachey) but often in wretched spirits. When in 1910 he visited Keynes in a state 'verging on melancholia', the latter described him to Duncan Grant as 'thinking himself an utterly worthless creature' with 'few intimate friends, practically no interest in life, and a bad liver. He ought to have a little work, plenty of exercise and troops of lovers.' In this depressed, isolated state of mind one can see the result of the emotional exactions which Nellie Macmillan levied on her sons, results which were a permanent influence on their characters. In late life Dan remained a reserved man 'whose temper', so Edith Sitwell told Pamela Hansford Johnson, usually 'needs a little sugar adding'.

The next son Arthur Tarleton Macmillan (1889–1968) was named after Maurice's youngest brother, who had died prematurely of tuberculosis. Arthur was an epileptic who was educated mainly at home (though with a spell at Summerfields), before admission to Balliol. He was called to the Bar and practised in Chancery from 1921. He lived in London all his life, and never felt at ease when out of reach of his favourite retreat, the Athenaeum club. He was a shy, modest man like his father, but his reserve masked neither his sensitivity nor the ardour of his feelings. Arthur shared his mother's love of music, but forfeited much of her regard by his marriage (which was childless, like that of his brother Dan, who married Margaret Matthews in 1918). He also dismayed Nellie when, as a young man, he became a high and devout Anglo-Catholic. In the 1930s, as Arthur told the Archbishop of Canterbury, Cosmo Lang, he became convinced that he was being called by Christ for a sacred vocation; but his wish to be ordained was frustrated by the circumstances of his marriage. Peggy, his wife, had been married previously. Her husband had separated from her, gone to Africa and after four years she had obtained a divorce in the Scottish courts on the grounds of desertion. Arthur's conscience as an Anglo-Catholic had been troubled by his wish to marry a divorcee, and with characteristic punctilio he consulted Arthur Winnington-Ingram, Bishop of London, and three other divines before marrying. Peggy and her first husband had promised each other before their marriage that if it failed either party would be free to obtain a divorce, and Arthur persuaded himself that this promise nullified the validity of the first marriage by implying lack of consent as understood by the Church. It was on the basis of the same argument that Arthur proposed in 1939 to Cosmo Lang that he could become a candidate for holy orders. After consulting other theologians, the Archbishop rejected Arthur's special pleading and declared that he could not ordain a man who had married a divorcee. Arthur, protesting his obedience to God and to his archbishop, felt mortified at this rejection.

It was partly as a result of his special position that Arthur devoted years of effort to composing his treatise entitled *What Is Christian Marriage?*, which examined ecclesiastical teachings and practice in relation to divorce law, and was published by his family's firm in 1944. In it he argued, among other points, for the formation of a discretionary ecclesiastical court on marriage law (which, if it had existed, might have eased the heartbreak of his own case). William Temple, who by then had succeeded Cosmo Lang as Archbishop of Canterbury, was so impressed on reading the proofs of the book that he was tempted to break his lifetime rule and contribute a preface. Unfortunately for Arthur, Temple consulted Sir Harry Vaisey, a judge in the Chancery Division where Arthur practised law. 'Macmillan is an able man, but rather "unknown", and I don't think it unfair to hint at a slight eccentricity of appearance and manner,' Vaisey reported sniffily; this was enough for the Archbishop to decide that it would be incautious to be identified with Arthur's book. The latter retired from legal work in 1946, and dedicated his retirement to the Church. His brothers' firm in 1961 published his abridged translation of a biography of Abbé Fernand Portal, the French priest whose friendship with Lord Halifax had resulted in their collaboration to bring reunion between the Church of England and the Church of Rome – an attempt culminating in the famous Conversations at Malines in the 1920s.

Like his elder brother Dan, Arthur disappointed Nellie. Both were intelligent and talented men, but they were conspicuously withdrawn, and both left the impression of being emotionally disabled in life. They led useful and respectable lives, as their father and grandfather would have wished, but they did not have the fortitude to achieve the acclaim that would satisfy their mother's ambitions. Perhaps they did not want to. In the moderation of their achievements they found both the foil for her interfering and their revenge. Macmillan & Company was a focus of family life, and devotion to the publishing business was one of the earlier lessons learnt at home. Arthur excluded himself from this by becoming a lawyer instead.

Nellie's hopes and ambitions eventually centred on the youngest of her three children, Harold. He was born on 10 February 1894 in the tall, thin house at 52 Cadogan Place, on the border of Knightsbridge with Belgravia. This was his parents' home for almost all of their married life, a home in which solid and expensive comfort was joined with a dread of worldly show and a pretence of the spartan ethic. As a small child Harold was largely confined to the nursery domain at the top of the house. Its distance from the kitchen in the basement seemed formidable to him, and perhaps too to the half-dozen luckless servants who had to carry everything, including food and coal, up six flights of stairs. His time was divided between the day nursery, which looked out over a garden square, and the night nursery at the back of the building, high above the mews called Cadogan Lane, which contained the stables of the Cadogan Place houses. Among Harold's earliest memories was the din of a blacksmith striking an anvil as he hammered shoes for the carriage horses in the mews. He never forgot the horsey smell of London in those days.

At the north end of Cadogan Place stood Chelsea House, the London mansion of Lord Cadogan, who owned much of Chelsea and was Viceroy of Ireland during Harold's nursery years. The splendours of Chelsea House awed the young Macmillans, for whom it was outclassed only by Buckingham Palace. On the steps outside the mansion the Macmillan children often saw a bewigged man in blue coat and knee-breeches, with a red velvet waistcoat, yellow stockings and silver-buckled shoes, a servant whom they believed was Lord Cadogan beholding his great properties. Another favourite sight on the children's walks with their governess was the Guards, a medley of red, white, black and gold, with their sabres and fine horses, on their way to or from drill in Hyde Park. These memories of grandeur were mixed with those of simpler pleasures, for example of visits to a kindly fishmonger in Sloane Street.

Maurice never wholly discarded Thring's outlook. Aloof by temperament and uncomplaining by habit, he was an absent parent who worked long hours, and would in spare moments retreat to the Athenaeum to immerse himself in newspapers. Occasionally he took Harold rowing on the Serpentine or bicycling in Battersea Park, and there were rare outings to Hampton Court or the zoo. He was most accessible on Sunday evenings when, adapting a tradition from the days when the double family lived together at Tooting, he would read aloud to his family, mostly poetry, Tennyson of course above all others, but also Shakespeare, Milton and Keats. Although Maurice was impassive, his sons usually knew his feelings from his demeanour and were as anxious as any boys to earn paternal approval; they were sure too of his devotion to them, although he was never demonstrative. He was a very controlled man, who used neither tobacco nor alcohol; in business he saw it as his task to curb the impulsiveness of the other partners – to repress that family trait of impetuosity which his father Daniel had so disliked in himself. This struggle to keep control was emulated by Harold, a nervous, uncertain man whose struggle for self-mastery in the period of his political apogee was sometimes no less than heroic. While Maurice effaced himself not only from Harold's life but from the household, Nellie by contrast was inescapable and commanding. Where Maurice was self-controlled, she was controlling; a woman, one may think, whom the shock of so many early bereavements had convinced that the world was an ominous, unpredictable place where she needed to control everything about her. She tried to protect herself against adversities, contradictions, doubts and chance by being supreme comptroller of her world. She ruled the house in Cadogan Place like Catherine II of Russia without any of the redeeming vices of that empress. Dowered with a daunting personality, like one of Saki's characters 'she became a power in the household, in a very short time the only power – a sort of Governor General and Mother Superior and Political Boss rolled into one'.

She was a great organiser outside her home too. She sat on women's committees, both philanthropic and social. For years she was one of the London School Board's visitors, regularly inspecting schools near Cadogan Place, from which she was wont to recruit promising pupils to become clerks in her husband's office. She was treasurer for almost forty years of the Victoria League, which was founded after the death of Queen Victoria in 1901 with the object of drawing the scattered citizens of the British Empire closer through links of personal sympathy. This was not Nellie's only tribute to the great Queen, for in 1897 she was one of the forces behind the Women's Dinner to commemorate the sixtieth anniversary of Victoria's accession. Nellie's choice of companions at her table at the dinner is all too revealing of the starchy, stilted, high-minded circles in which she moved. Nellie sat at one end of her table: Dame Emily Penrose, a redoubtable pioneer of women's higher education, at the other. Her other guests included Sir John Evans, a numismatist; Sir Robert Giffen, a statistician interested in bimetallism; Sir William Broadbent, a physician of learned tastes and resolute manner; Professor E.S. Beesly, translator of Comte and formerly editor of the *Positivist Review*; Margaret Llewelyn Davies, the tirelessly altruistic secretary of the drab but uplifting Women's Co-operative Guild; Sir Richard Claverhouse Jebb, author of a great commentary on Sophocles; and Sir Mountstuart Grant-Duff, politician and botanist, who was one of the most amiably boring raconteurs in London. The guests were notable for their industriousness and high purposes; but most people would judge them a staid set of companions. Grant-Duff left an appreciative account of the entertainment in his diary: the speeches, and even the jokes, leave an impression of exemplary dullness. Nellie's parties were designed less for pleasure than for edification: they drew recondite, high-minded worthies, speaking in resonant banalities, the dullest section of good society.

Nellie's social aspirations can be seen in her choice as Harold's godmother of Lady Arthur Russell. Lord Arthur Russell had been a Whig MP who shared with the historian Acton and Sir Mountstuart Grant-Duff the reputation of erudition in the House of Commons. He was too timid for any outward success as a politician, but had a love of conversation and a curiosity about all that was of interest in the spheres of philosophy, literature and politics. The Russells' house in Audley Square off Park Lane was consequently one of the most distinguished meeting-places in late Victorian London. There lingered on the combination of aristocratic Liberalism and intellectual distinction which had characterised the best Whig houses. Lady Arthur presided over decades of leisurely, informed conversation which

made her salon renowned; it was to the Russells' house that a
statesman like Lord Dufferin, when Viceroy of India, would
send long, informal letters when he wished to convey his opinions to a wider circle of influence than his official correspondence could reach. Vivacious, caustic and forthright, Lady Arthur
achieved the influence in political and literary society which
Nellie wanted, although some of the mannerisms of her coterie
seemed disagreeably wooden to the next generation, so lifeless
indeed as to mortify all true emotions and candid feelings.
Virginia Woolf as a young Edwardian woman was taken by her
pompous publisher half-brother George Duckworth to petrified
parties at Audley Square, and the memory of them remained
excruciating to her. 'A fear haunts me even now, as I drive past
Park Lane on top of a bus and think of Lady Arthur Russell,'
she wrote in 1926, 'I become out of love with everything.'
Nellie had a similar effect on people: she knocked the love
out of everything.

Nellie was one of those mothers who cannot accept that their
children are separate from themselves. She was intrusive and
persecuting even as she protested that her behaviour was in
their best interests. Her impact on them seemed threatening, for
she might abuse any confidences which they were rash enough to
make, or distort their meaning. Perhaps her girlhood in Spencer
had branded her with the fear that her children might die: her
anxiety was so high that she could not let them go. She was
more intimately engaged in her sons' education than normal;
indeed two of them were kept home from school for long periods
of their boyhood, ostensibly to protect their health. Arthur,
although fit enough to attend Summerfields, was thought too
epileptic to be trusted to Eton, and returned to Cadogan Place
for his education around the time that Harold went to Eton;
Harold was brought home from Eton not long after Arthur had
made his escape to Balliol. Ostensibly this educational durance
at home was a precaution against illness, but it is the trick of
mothers like Nellie to present intensely selfish and manipulative
acts as selfless sacrifices, in anyone's interest but their own. She

recurrently falsified the role that she was playing in family life. Seemingly she was impervious to her children's feelings and incapable of pursuing a course that ran counter to her own feelings.

Each of Nellie's three boys resented the way she tried to pierce their lives with her controlling curiosity. She found it hard to accept that they were autonomous of her, and intruded into their thoughts, friendships, pleasures and plans. Harold as her youngest child suffered most from her domination, although he was convinced that her intimidation was loving and his gratitude to her was lifelong. It was his mother's pushiness that brought him the outward successes of his life. Her early teaching of him as a boy, like her later meddling in his adult life, gave him both tenacity and fortitude – qualities which every biographer of him must recognise and admire. Nellie tried to imbue him with the confidence that he could surmount every adversity, would confound his opponents and rout the dunces whose conventional ideas stood as obstacles to his own reforming zeal. In the short term such pressure left him prey to self-doubt, as he fretted that he could not meet her expectations; but, once he had begun to succeed in the world, it gave him a ruthless power of his own. While other members of the family recognised that Harold would have been justified in resenting her behaviour, he persisted as an adult in denying his resentment and in stressing his devotion to her. No child cares to admit that its parent is at fault. It is painful to recognise that a mother is manipulating you to satisfy her own needs, and frightening to accept that you are in the grip of an arbitrary despot. Most children will try to interpret bad behaviour by a parent in a favourable way or will offer excuses to themselves for parental maltreatment. It would have been intolerable for Harold to admit his own ill-intent to Nellie or his resentment of her. His hostility was redirected at other objects: as his experiences hardened him in later life, he developed that trait of ruthlessness which was so widely disliked in his political dealings.

Harold had a frustrated childhood. Maternal care enables

an infant to be enriched rather than overwhelmed, but the sort of obtrusive and twisted care which Nellie offered was likely to leave a small child in fear of annihilation. Nellie was a persecutor, not a protector. Parents ideally should be both accessible and responsive. They need not only to respond to calls for support and protection, but to respond *helpfully*; yet Nellie's responses were often helpful only in her own eyes, and felt painful or intimidating to everyone else. A successful mother protects her child's sense of its Self: she celebrates its existence as a separate person and encourages its growth away from her into its own identity. Thus she helps it to feel that life is real and worth living. A True Self begins to have life, through the strength given to the infant's puny character by the mother's recognition of its wishes. This True Self has a spontaneity which connects with the events of the outer world.

But when childhood relations go wrong, as Harold's did with Nellie, a False Self is constructed in order to defend the child from maternal demands. For Nellie's children love was not given freely, but the semblance of love was given as a reward for compliance to her will. This childish compliance was the earliest stage of the False Self, a defensive mask assumed by emotionally isolated men and women who adapt or imitate or steal other people's styles or mannerisms. Someone hiding behind such a façade depends for reassurance that life is real on the responses of other people. For example a False Self may result in a child growing up to be an actor: perhaps the type of actor who can act professionally but lives as himself in private life; or the sadder category of actor who can only act and is lost when not in a role, being reassured by applause that he exists, the misfit who has trouble knowing or saying what he thinks and can only be coherent if his lines have been written by someone else. Other examples of individuals whose façade becomes a life force of its own are those politicians who only feel safe declaiming thunderous orotundities or in recycling meaningless clichés to public audiences, those public figures who come alive when addressing a mass of people but are dull to the point of deadliness with individuals, the vehement party speakers who become cardboard characters off the platform.

In the period of Harold's political apogee friends and commentators often likened him to an Edwardian 'actor–manager', but what they detected as his theatricality was actually the protective acting of the False Self. 'He is an actor, to a much greater extent than most politicians,' wrote John Boyd-Carpenter, who was a minister throughout the Macmillan government. 'Sometimes he is the great aristocrat; sometimes the cultured publisher; sometimes the Edwardian dandy.' Yet, as Boyd-Carpenter's description concluded, Harold combined with all this posing 'a powerful intellect and enormous power of work'. In Harold's case a tense, agitated state of mind was masked by the semblance of taut, controlled intellectuality, but his attempts to solve his personal problems by using his intellect resulted in the fussy, over-intellectualised lonely miseries of his youth and early middle age, the culmination of which is described in the next chapter.

Harold was the second British Prime Minister to have an American mother: Winston Churchill was the first. The contrasts between the backgrounds and characters of Jennie Jerome and Nellie Belles are instructive in understanding their sons. Lady Randolph Churchill's father Leonard Jerome was a New York speculator who made and lost several fortunes; a founder of the American Jockey Club and devotee of horse-racing, he was at one time the principal owner of the *New York Times*. His daughter came to Europe and married a duke's son at the age of twenty. She was a woman of rare beauty, wayward, vivacious, extravagant and specious. She lived in a sparkling, racketty set of people and radiated (in her son Winston's words) a 'supple, vital, gracious personality'. Her devotion to fashionable parties left her little time or energy for her children: Winston, as her elder son, received meagre affection or attention from her in his boyhood, and was saved from emotional starvation by his nanny, Mrs Everest. The love and play and cuddles which give a child a sense of its own value came to Winston Churchill from his nanny. Yet he showed no resentment of his mother's selfish fecklessness. He protected himself from realising the extent of her neglect by idealising her. 'She shone for me like the Evening Star,' he wrote. 'I loved her dearly – but at a distance.' As an adult he romanticised women, but included none of them in his inner circle of friends. Notoriously he had a propensity to fits of what he called 'the black dog' of depression, but he usually kept this at bay by an indomitable effort of will. Oddly, in view of early neglect of him, there was a great deal of truth in Lord Esher's remark to Winston after Jennie's death: 'her greatest reward in life was you'.

Nellie's background was more dour. She came from a small town in the mid-west, where her father was the local sawbones; her early education as a Methodist was a pervasive influence. In contrast to Lady Randolph Churchill's insouciant neglect of Winston as a child, Nellie gave her son all too much attention, often of painful intensity. Like Winston he idealised his mother, but not as an ethereal and remote beauty; instead she was someone more monumental and permanent, 'a rock-like, unshakeable support', as he wrote. Long after her death, he still felt her presence in the house at Birch Grove which she had built, and sensed her encouragement at moments of stress or doubt.

The Macmillans of Cadogan Place lived abstemiously, even priggishly, with their own restricted and almost heartless etiquette. Though Maurice encouraged his sons to debate among themselves, there were two topics of conversation which he deprecated: money, which he thought a vulgar subject, and food, which he was still enough of Thring's pupil to regard as wickedly epicurean. The Macmillans of course were not the only Edwardian family which judged that a conversation about food outraged the canons of good taste: it was a widespread rule among the upper-middle class. Led in gluttony by the example of King Edward VII, aristocrats and plutocrats might indulge in frantic over-eating, but for the professional classes such behaviour was dangerously near to acknowledging the insatiability of appetite or the loss of control which it might bring. 'Soup and fish explain half the emotions of life,' as the Rev. Sydney Smith had quipped earlier in the nineteenth century; but it was not the sort of self-explanation which the Macmillans wished to understand. The fact that families needed nourishing was, if not denied, at least made something almost shameful; sustenance was not to be celebrated. Harold's indifference to food was lifelong.

Family traditions were strong. Harold was first taken to Arran at the age of eight, and the family's visits to the island were like pilgrimages to a sacred place. As Cabinet Minister and Prime Minister he always displayed prominently in his room a photograph of the crofter's cottage where Daniel had been born; indeed the same photograph was used to open the induction course for recruits to the family publishing house in the 1980s. The old Arran belief that one's ancestors were part of one's conscious existence, that their character and achievements should shape one's ambitions and remain a living reality, persisted with the Macmillans long after their move to Tooting and their rise in the world. The dead were kept alive in memory and example. The spirit of Christian high-mindedness, the trust in democratic politics and the belief in material progress which the crofter Macmillans had learnt from the Haldanes were adapted by the family in their own way, but the lesson was perpetuated in Harold's childhood. As a boy he was given by his father a copy of Tom Hughes's biography of Daniel, and this book became a treasured possession. He read it repeatedly, and some sections of it encouraged his own secret hopes. The existence of Hughes's book made Daniel an inspirational influence on Harold's imagination, though Daniel, who in Hughes's words had lived 'constantly and consciously eye to eye with death', was a morbid choice of boyhood hero. It was the memory of Daniel's description of tramping round London in search of a job in 1833 that fired Harold, as a young MP, when he saw so many of his constituents trudging the streets in search of work in the 1920s. In 1931, as a successful publisher approaching middle age, he told George Moore how much he and the other partners still depended on what Daniel had done. It was not only in acts of veneration that Daniel kept his influence; his agonies about what was good or bad, his fight to love and not hate, remained a reality in Harold's formative years.

The Macmillans remained an uncommonly bookish family, and Harold himself recognised that he had learnt about life first from books and only later by living it. Literature gave the terms of reference for his life, although he used literature as much to evade some parts of his inner world as to understand other parts of the outer world. He took a boyish delight in the adventure stories of Conan Doyle, Henty and Rider Haggard, and became a devotee of the novels of Dickens and Scott at an early age. 'We had an enormous respect for learning – we lived in a world of books,' Harold declared in 1966. 'It was a simple life, and a very hard-working life because in my family we respected scholarship.'

As his brothers were somewhat older, and often away at school, Harold's childhood was solitary. His lessons were given to him by his mother in the morning, in the library of their house; she was drivingly ambitious for all her children, and he found her a formidable teacher, who demanded the highest quality of work and made him miserable with anxiety over his ineptitude at mental arithmetic. His mother insisted that French was spoken by the children downstairs, and employed French nursery-maids and a French governess; as a result Harold was fluent in the language from childhood, which a lifetime later he found an advantage when negotiating with General de Gaulle. Otherwise he was left in the care of Nanny Last, who provided the best security and affection in his little world. Like most nannies of her day she was engaged in a war of attrition with the cook, who would sometimes let Harold break the rules and sneak out of the house by a back door; like many nannies too she was a fierce patriot, with a dark distrust of French governesses. Nannies were powerful figures in the lives of families like the

Macmillans. Two generations later Ellen Stevens, known to her children as Diddy, was nanny to the family of Harold's nephew by marriage, the Duke of Devonshire. In 1965, after Harold's political retirement, he was put next to Diddy at a luncheon party to celebrate the coming of age of Devonshire's son, Peregrine (nicknamed 'Stoker'). 'Ex-nanny sitting next to ex-Prime Minister,' she said later in a tone which suggested that she saw herself as at least his equal. Such was the perceived power of nannies, and fortunately in Harold's case it was a power to the good. His life without Nanny Last would have been bleak. She remained with him for most of the rest of her life, acting as housekeeper to Dorothy and Harold Macmillan after their marriage in the 1920s. In old age his conversation often betrayed an obsession with nannies. When, for example, he went to Brussels in 1972 to attend the British signature of the treaty of accession to the European Community, he was overheard dilating on its future to the Belgian statesman Paul-Henri Spaak. 'It's not a question of the price of haddock,' he said; but when Spaak interrupted to say that he liked haddock and its importance should not be underrated, Harold rejoined, 'Yes, yes, but it does rather stay with one, as nanny used to say.'

Maurice had been one of the first Summerfields pupils of the founder of British gymnastics, MacLaren, and sent Harold to a weekly class at a gymnasium and dancing academy in Chelsea. Here he was expected to climb ropes, scramble over bars and juggle with Indian clubs, drills which he loathed. This experience exacerbated his long detestation of performing in public, which made speechifying an agony for him until extreme old age. He was a precocious little boy who had a sharp memory of public events. He remembered watching Queen Victoria's Jubilee procession in 1897 from a bookshop in the Haymarket, and was impressed by the tallest soldier in the British Army who marched in front. He remembered being in Hyde Park with his French governess when excited crowds swelled to celebrate the relief of the besieged British troops at Mafeking in 1900. The Queen's funeral procession in 1901 also impressed him.

Generations of writers have perpetuated the myth that British confidence and optimism were shattered only on that dreadful Tuesday night in August 1914 when the lights went out all over Europe. In fact the self-confidence of the nineteenth century was destroyed in its last moments, in the Black Week of December 1899, when the defeat of the British Army by Boer irregulars at Colenso and Magersfontein gave the British their first ugly premonition of public disasters. The Edwardians were overshadowed by apprehensions of catastrophe. Whatever privileges Harold's generation enjoyed in their youth, a sense of security was not one of them. Half a lifetime later he was often described as the last of the Edwardians without its being recalled that almost the governing characteristic of the Edwardian age was pessimism. It is hard to think of one important Edwardian optimist in the arts or public life. The Edwardians lived in dreadful anticipation: something was coming, destruction was palpably imminent. Esmé Wingfield-Stratford, in his great study of the *Victorian Aftermath 1901–14*, characterised it as 'An Age of Nerves', and Harold himself, in 1966, told the future Chancellor of the Exchequer Nigel Lawson that in his Edwardian boyhood, 'we lived in a certain sense of anxiety always. I have all my life had the feeling that something rather unpleasant would be likely to happen.' His relations with other people were a messy tangle of apprehensions; an ominous predestination seemed to hover over each new relationship which he formed. He felt threatened throughout his childhood, particularly by other people. Such perpetual expectation of mishaps develops if something unpleasant has happened, and recurred; in Harold's case it was Nellie's over-mothering, perhaps aggravated by Nellie's own feeling from childhood that life would go awry, that death or apparitions were waiting in ambush. He learnt from Nellie's treatment of him that people are hostile when they claim to be friendly, or that their behaviour can be hurtful or frightening when they claim it is loving; by a process of assimilation, he came to suppose that other individuals whom he met would harm him, that good things would turn out bad. Harold was oppressed by the fear that a malign power would get him in its clutches; he felt culpable and powerless. This pessimism (though typically Edwardian) was partly the result of Nellie's treatment of him, but also part of the family heritage: the gloomy grandeur of Lochranza and despondent introspection of the Corrie crofters cast a long shadow over the Macmillan family.

For a few years Harold attended a day school off Sloane Square before at the age of nine following his brothers to board at Summerfields in 1903. After a restrained farewell at Cadogan Place, he was taken with his trunk and box by a Macmillan clerk to Paddington Station, where he was met by a Summerfields master. The first night of exile at boarding school is scarifying for any child. Harold wept profusely during his first evening at Summerfields, but was consoled by another boy with words which he never forgot. The school dormitories where little boys learnt not to cry themselves to sleep were one of the forcing grounds of British public life. The children were taken from their families and left in an enclosed community at an age when their emotional dependence was deepest; in their longing for reassurance, they became acutely dependent on that community for succour. Each child had to learn to play the game if it was to survive; together they created a domain ruled by totem and taboo; and so began all the worst traits of the British boarding-school product. A fear of conspicuousness and obsession with outward conformity first emerged in the Macmillans in the earliest generation to be educated away from home – Maurice, George and the other boys of the double family whose manners, loyalties and social outlook were profoundly and permanently changed by their experiences at Uppingham and Eton. Donald Hankey, whose book *A Student at Arms* was cult reading at the time of the Great War, dismissed one of his contemporaries with the phrase 'fatally original', encapsulating that petty world in which originality was often fatal for the happiness of the boarding-school child. In fairness, Eton was a different case from Uppingham. 'You could think and love what you liked: only in external matters, in clothes, or in deportment, need you do as the others do,' recalled Sir Lawrence Jones, who was an Eton boy a few years before Harold.

The adult world in which Harold lived and worked was shaped by the British boarding-school ethos, with its arcane forms of deference, its ritualised conformity, its intellectual debasement, its fearful contempt of outsiders and its belief that injustice, or arbitrary misuse of power, was part of the nature of things and should be accepted without snivelling or complaint. The fact that Harold's fatalism was so widely admired during the Great War and was afterwards seen as a form of moral courage in his political life, shows how pervasive this outlook was. Boys of Harold's generation and experience grew up in the belief that, though life might be bad, it need not be desperate if one kept one's solidarity with the group. His first night at Summerfields was a lesson for life.

Harold never shook off the assumptions of this petty world, and never wanted to; in fact some of his school friendships, with boys like Harry Crookshank, were among the most nurturing experiences of his life. His most affectionate and enduring friendship in later years – with John Wyndham, who was young enough to be his son – in some ways resembled the exchange of service and protection between a senior boy and his fag. The peculiar intimacy of people with a private language and private jokes is hard for outsiders to breach: it is perhaps the most valuable coinage of boarding-school life: it characterised the friendship between Harold and Wyndham.

From Summerfields he was elected a King's Scholar at Eton in the election of 1906. Harold was third in this election, placed after E.W. Hamilton, a mathematician who became a stock-broker, and Julian Lambart, who became one of Harold's closest Eton friends and whose long career as a master at the school was eventually crowned by his appointment as Vice-Provost. Nicknamed 'the Widow' at Eton, Lambart was 'amiable, scholarly, all that there is of the most worthy but . . . lacking in red corpuscles', according to a fellow housemaster, George Lyttelton. In his bloodlessness Lambart had some resemblance to young Harold. In the Eton election of 1906 there were twenty successful candidates, of whom seven were killed in the First World War. Altogether there were seventy scholars in the school, enjoying endowments given by King Henry VI in the fifteenth century, and by Harold's time their existence differed significantly from that of the other pupils, known as Oppidans. The King's Scholars were Collegers, living in the school's oldest Tudor buildings, under the Master in College, while the other boys were dispersed round the town of Eton in boarding-houses headed by tutors. Collegers were brainy types who tended to become clergymen, scholars or pedagogues; the Oppidans were usually brawnier men who succeeded to landed estates, joined the armed forces or entered public life. 'College was thus an intellectual élite thrust into the heart of a social elite,' as the biographer of another King's Scholar, George Orwell, has written. 'The Collegers tended to look down on the Oppidans as aristocratic Philistines and athletic hearties, and the Oppidans looked down on the "Tugs" as being middle-class "Saps" (Etonian for swots) living in villas in Tooting.' In the case of Harold (one generation away from the house called Knapdale) they were nearer the mark than they knew.

Little is known of Harold's time at Eton, but he looks unconfident, pensive and wistful in surviving school photographs; in any case his career there had an abrupt and perplexing end. At his mother's instigation he had been treated as a delicate child at Summerfields, where he was sent to bed earlier than other children; once more she intervened in his schooling, under the pretext of protecting his health. Harold left Eton prematurely, in 1909, supposedly having been diagnosed as suffering from a weak heart. Some mystery surrounds his early departure from Eton, but the suggestion that he was expelled after some sexual familiarity with another boy is a less likely explanation of the shadow over the proceedings than the Eton authorities' resentment when a gifted pupil was unnecessarily removed by a meddlesome mother. It was a pity that Harold 'missed that last year which is so often the best for an Etonian and so perhaps did not greatly enjoy his time at Eton', wrote a later Provost, Lord Charteris of Amisfield, 'but what is quite certain is that he greatly enjoyed being an Old Etonian'.

Harold was sent to rest at Birch Grove, his family's small estate in Sussex, where he received special tuition for the Balliol entrance examinations. He had several tutors, including Bernard Swithinbank, who together with Maynard Keynes had been in love with Dan Macmillan at Eton, and Ronald Knox, who proved a critical influence on his life. Knox had recently graduated from Balliol after a scintillating academic career. He was an Anglo-Catholic destined a few years later to join the Church of Rome and eventually to die a monsignor. Knox decided that Harold needed spiritual guidance as well as tutoring, took him to an Anglo-Catholic mass and began discussing his religious beliefs with the boy. Nellie however retained all the prejudices of an American Methodist: she abominated Catholicism and 'Jesuitical' was one of the most pejorative words she knew. As soon as she discovered the tone of their religious conversations, she forbad Knox to continue with propaganda which might infect her son with 'Roman fever'; when Knox refused her interdiction in florid and self-righteous language, she dismissed him peremptorily. The enforced separation of the two young men was a bad blow to each of them. Knox regarded the rejection of his advances as one of the formative experiences of his life; for Harold the banishment of his closest friend, the man to whom he had given his trust most freely, was further evidence of his mother's power, confirmation of the abrupt and arbitrary way in which things went bad and affections proved a cheat. Happily the two men were able to renew their friendship when Harold won an exhibition to Oxford in 1912. Knox was by then chaplain at another college, and they came together again, with less passionate interest, yet with deep trust: as late as 1915 Harold was still agonising about whether to convert to Roman Catholicism. This early religious crisis was of lasting importance for him, and the two men remained friends for the rest of their lives. Indeed Knox went to stay for some days with Harold in Downing Street in 1957 when he knew that he was dying.

Harold remained a devout Anglo-Catholic who when Prime Minister took a more scrupulous interest in ecclesiastical affairs than any Prime Minister since Gladstone. He was Daniel's grandson to the end, claiming to confidential friends that Christianity underpinned his ideals and that it was only in the service of God that one could do good politically. Geoffrey Fisher, who was Archbishop of Canterbury when Harold became Prime Minister, found him 'a keen and very well-informed churchman' with a vexingly 'squirearchical view of the Church' and its appointments. When Fisher retired in 1961, Harold was specially conscientious about the choice of his successor.

Friendship should be the study of every biographer. The way a man relates to other people and chooses attachments is as eloquent of character as anything else. At every stage in his life he should be judged by the quality of his friendships. What was true of Daniel and Alexander stood for Harold too. Harold wrote in 1980 that it was in the friendships of youth that he found and kept feelings of real trust. His most intimate friends at Eton were fellow scholars, Julian Lambart, Harry Crookshank and Harry Willink.

Crookshank was Harold's closest friend. He lived all his life in Pont Street, just round the corner from Cadogan Place, and the two boys knew one another as children. They went to Summerfields together, and won their Eton scholarships at the same election. They were Oxford contemporaries, and served together in the same battalion of the Grenadiers. In 1915 the explosion of a German mine in front of Crookshank's trench resulted in his being buried under more than four feet of earth. He was able to breathe, but unable to move or call out, and was trapped for more than a day. Once he heard a search party standing over him, discussing whether to abandon looking for him, but he could not get them to hear him. Eventually he was dug out; such was his pretence of imperturbability that, after a day's recuperation at a dressing station, he rejoined his men in the trenches. Later in the war he was horribly injured in his genitals, his wounds preventing him from having any future sex life. In peacetime Crookshank was briefly a diplomat, before entering parliament as a Conservative MP in 1924 and being promoted through a succession of offices to Cabinet rank. 'He was a man of the utmost probity and uprightness of character, a bachelor before all bachelors, a sharp intellect, a brave soldier, an assiduous constituency member,' wrote R.A. Butler, although James Lees-Milne in 1947 found him 'jovial' but 'physically sinister'. To John Boyd-Carpenter Crookshank seemed 'a superb parliamentarian' who for many years deliberately made himself distinctive by always wearing a top-hat in the House of Commons: a piece of showmanship worthy of Harold Macmillan himself. As a political speaker he was suave, unflurried and mocking; his stinging tartness could infuriate political opponents. He was an accomplished linguist, a discriminating if fussy collector of *objets d'art* and an assiduous churchgoer ('hard work and luck under God's help may prevent me from crashing too badly', he confided to his diary on becoming Secretary for Mines in 1935).

Willink was a strange mixture of gregariousness, intellectual power, diffidence and vulnerability. As an undergraduate, he was (like Harold) a keen debater, and became immersed in religious affairs. During the war he served as a field gunner, and then, deciding against teaching at Eton, he read law at the Bar. He was a phenomenal success there, so that his earnings, mainly in the commercial court, exceeded £15,000 a year by 1939. He became a Conservative MP in 1940 and Minister of Health two years later; but he was so unsure of his abilities, and doubtful of his judicial capacity, that he foreclosed any possibility of either Cabinet office or promotion to the Bench as a judge by accepting the mastership of a Cambridge college. There Willink laid almost comic stress on the observance of precedence, protocol, outward form and exactitude in modes of address. 'When issues he found unpleasant or incomprehensible thrust their rude way through the generally smooth surface . . . he often reacted with the anger which is born of having expected too near an approach to well-ordered perfection,' wrote his college's librarian. 'It was part of his nature that, while he added jollity to a social occasion, and *gravitas* to a solemn one, he also, and less fortunately, heightened the tension in a troubled one.' Behind his integrity, distinction of mind, wit, gaiety, eloquence, poise and graciousness, 'there lay an emotional, self-critical and in many ways vulnerable person' who often wept at 'the joys and frustrations of life'. Willink's long friendship with Harold Macmillan was commemorated in the first honours list which the latter prepared as Prime Minister in 1957, in which Willink received a baronetcy. In the next few years his advice was sought by the Macmillan government on ways to muster academic opinion to contradict the propaganda of the Campaign for Nuclear Disarmament.

With his closest friends from Oxford days there was no break in understanding, although they sometimes met only at intervals through the years. Apart from Knox, Harold's most intimate Oxford friend was Humphrey Sumner, afterwards an expert on Russian history and Balkan culture who became Warden of All Souls College, Oxford. Sumner was the product of Victorian episcopal traditions, both his grandfather and great-grandfather having been bishops. Of all the Balliol scholars and exhibitioners of 1912, he and Harold were the only ones who survived the carnage of the Great War: indeed trench warfare permanently weakened Sumner's health and strained his nerves. In Oxford after the war he was nicknamed 'the Emperor'; as a master of intimidating silences, he could be formidable in his personal dealings. But, despite the austerity of his scholarship and the imperiousness of his teaching manner, Sumner was a good friend for Harold: delighting in natural beauty, knowledgeable about art, witty, apt in quotations, felicitous in literary allusions, endowed with a magnificent memory and an ordered store of knowledge.

At Oxford too Harold became more intimate with an Eton contemporary, Geoffrey Madan: selfish, misanthropic, fastidious and reactionary, Madan was a scholar of dilettante grace, and a devotee of French cooking, whose chief memorial is his witty and subversive *Notebooks* (posthumously published with a foreword by Harold). Madan was thrown off balance by his wartime experiences in Mesopotamia, which left him in his widow's words with 'an undercurrent of stress, which, running beneath a sense of privilege, made it hard for him to accept the terms of ordinary life'. After his death in 1947, the publisher John Murray wrote of his 'uncanny aloofness, as if he had stepped from the everywhere and the nowhere into here; as if, in his curious way, he was in time but not of it'; and indeed he was a man saved from a life of grotesque disappointment and loneliness by his wife's income (derived from the profits of a family armaments company) and the impersonally couched sympathy of his clubland friends.

Harold claimed that it was at Oxford that he forged a friendship with Bobbety Cranborne, heir of the great Cecil political dynasty, but this is a dubious assertion; certainly any mutual liking before 1914 evaporated later. By the time they were Cabinet colleagues in the 1950s (Cranborne having meanwhile succeeded as Marquess of Salisbury) they felt something approaching mutual contempt: Salisbury distrusted Macmillan as an opportunist (one of the Cecils' family jokes was about 'MCMs', or 'Middle-Class Monsters'), while Harold in 1970 told Kenneth Rose that earlier Cecils 'did nothing: they were like characters in Proust'; and that more recent generations were like 'cockneys', even if their table-talk resembled that of the Medicis. To Lord Woolton in 1955 he remarked unsympathetically that Bobbety Salisbury was a neurotic hypochondriac.

The impact of Oxford on Harold was immense. 'After the rather narrow life of an old-fashioned English home suddenly to come into Oxford in those days' was thrilling, Harold told

Nigel Lawson in 1966. Oxford was still a small town of old colleges, a place of 'extraordinary beauty' before Lord Nuffield despoiled it with his motorcars and factories. 'Suddenly to meet chaps from all over the world, Rhodes scholars, like Vincent Massey, with whom I made a great friendship which lasted all my life, and boys from all sorts of schools, and to enter into a much wider world, ranging from the reading men to the hunting men, I loved it.'

As an undergraduate he showed little youthful irreverence. He joined many political clubs, but concentrated his efforts on the Oxford Union, that undergraduate debating society which until the 1970s had a reputation as a cradle of British parliamentary orators. Harold was elected secretary of the Union in 1913 and junior treasurer in the following year. He put time and effort into preparing his speeches, which were shimmering performances: 'the most polished of the epigrammatists', as the Oxford magazine *Isis* called him. An early speech, in November 1912, on the principles of socialism 'was horribly logical and rambled badly', according to one of his audience; but he made his mark with a speech in March 1913 on public school education. A later effort, in May, supporting women's suffrage, was judged 'the best speech we have heard this year from a Freshman'. At the start of the new academic year, in October 1913, Harold opposed A.P. Herbert's motion calling for a general election. It was 'an exceedingly brilliant speech, witty, powerful and at moments eloquent', the *Oxford Magazine* reported. 'Mr Macmillan is not afraid of making the most of a melodramatic and grandiloquent style. But he should be very careful not to be over-attracted by words, and not to say anything he does not feel.'

Those who had heard Ronald Knox debating at the Union a few years earlier were struck by the similarities of Harold's debating style to those of his mentor. It is worth adding that the Oxford Union was not only an arena for precocious statesmanship, or a pit for ambitious young men to ape national figures. It also represented the quintessence of the False Self. Speakers like Harold struck poses of adult mastery to hide the turmoil of adolescence; their fluency of speech and oratorical flourishes were stylish denials of all the fears which worried them. Like Harold's Oxford contemporary H.G. Strauss (afterwards the Conservative politician Lord Conesford), who was described by *Isis* as 'the exponent of the sincerest form of affectation' in the Union, speakers there drew all the attention of others on to the surface of themselves because their inward reality was so unsettled. It was predictable that a youth with Harold's temperament should be drawn to the Oxford Union. Its officers and star speakers were already the personification of inauthenticity; the Oxford Union then as now was both refuge and showcase of False Selves.

Perhaps the most calamitous incidental effect of Harold's Oxford education – an effect by no means unique to him – was to keep him in a condition of petrified adolescence. As far as he was concerned, it was an all-male society which he left, understanding little of women, except what he could divine from the misleading example of Nellie. His ignorance and uncertainty about women were total. Nor was he unusual in this. A few years later, during the First World War, a dancer called Maude Allen sued for libel an MP who had accused her of lesbianism in an article headlined 'The Cult of the Clitoris'. The lawsuit drew huge publicity, and Lord Albemarle, visiting the Turf club at the height of the brouhaha, said bemusedly, 'I've never heard of this Greek chap Clitoris they are all talking of.' The anatomical ignorance of men like Albemarle was matched by deliberately cultivated and robustly enforced emotional foreclosures where women were concerned. The denial or distortion of sexual impulses at Oxford was phenomenal, deliberate and congenial – at least to men like Harold's favourite Balliol don, F.F. ('Sligger') Urquhart. (Harold planned to travel abroad in the summer of 1914 in a party led by Urquhart – 'a purring old doctored tomcat who gave lemonade-parties at which he stroked the knees of rugger blues', Harold's fellow publisher and Balliol man Rupert Hart-Davis called him – but the outbreak of war intervened.) 'What I value in Oxford is principally what may be called nervous intensity,' wrote Lord Hugh Cecil, who was MP for the University of Oxford during Harold's undergraduate years. 'It leads to nervous breakdown, and it leads to drunkenness and riotous evenings in the colleges. But the benefits far outweigh these disadvantages. It produces a certain sort of temperament which . . . is not to be obtained in any other way.' The nature of this temperament, which Lord Hugh Cecil so misprized, and the miseries which it brought on Harold, will emerge in later chapters.

Harold got a first in Honour Moderations early in June 1914, and was ready to proceed with a promising Oxford career. But then Mars in his shattering horror came. On the morning of Sunday 28 June, two members of the Young Bosnia independence group, Gavrilo Princips and Vaso Cubrilovic, murdered the heir to the Habsburg Empire at Sarajevo. Cubrilovic survived until 1990, but his world did not. Instead the fire of war blazed. Harold would later recall the evening of the assassination:

> I remember going to a ball for the coming out of a young lady who afterwards became a great friend – indeed my sister-in-law. It was . . . lovely: string band, smilax up the stairs, Mr Cassani's band . . . and of course all the swells came, in ribbons and medals and Garters. You couldn't really dance until after supper: the swells went away about midnight and then the young people got down to it. . . . I went into the street, because we used to wear boiled shirts and stiff collars, and if you were a great dancer – and I loved it – you brought two or three extra collars and when they got soaked through you got a new one out. I went into the street – they sold the papers all through the night then – and I heard a voice calling 'Murder of the Archduke', and I didn't take the slightest bit of notice, it conveyed absolutely nothing to us. Within three weeks I and all my friends were in the army or trying to get in, but that night it meant nothing.

Harold's story has an almost theatrical vividness: as in a scene from a play, a carefree rich young man stands on a London pavement, with the lights and sounds of a ball flooding out of the house behind him. He pauses for a moment to adjust his collar, and the moment is frozen in time forever: he hears the news that is going to destroy his world and ruin the next years of his life. The artistry of Harold's image betrays it. For there were no balls in any great London house on the night of 28 June: it was a Sunday, and such an entertainment would have been unthinkable. The event which most nearly approaches his description was held by Lady Salisbury on 9 July, almost a fortnight after the Archduke's assassination. Harold's imagination, his flair for personal theatre, had mastered his verisimilitude. He always had a fine literary imagination, which inspired others to further flights of creative genius. Alan Bennett's play *Forty Years On* (first produced in 1968) contains a pastiche of an old man's memories of the Edwardian swansong: after 'dutifully dancing to Mr Casani's band at Dorchester House', the author goes out into the evening of 3 August 1914 ignorant of the doom to which he and his friends were spinning: 'another ball had ended and life had not yielded up its secret. "This time," I always thought as I tied my tie. "Perhaps this time."'

Though Harold had no previous ambitions as a warrior, he soon enlisted as a second lieutenant in the King's Royal Rifle Corps, billeted in a lodging house at Southend, where his battalion drilled incessantly and was given simple training in musketry. He was rescued from this unglamorous soldiering by the intervention of his mother, who felt that neither Southend nor a rifle corps was suitable for her son; as a result of her exertions, he was gazetted to the Reserve Battalion of the Grenadier Guards in March 1915. The Grenadiers were a regiment of the highest social and military prestige, with unquenchable pride in itself. As Harold's contemporary and future Cabinet colleague Oliver Lyttelton wrote in 1962, 'I have seen many institutions in my life, universities, colleges, Government offices, joint-stock companies, colonial administrations, Cabinets, but the best human organization, the most efficient and the most closely knit of which I know is the Brigade of Guards.'

Once in France wrote almost daily to his mother, and sent few letters to anyone else except Knox. His literariness was incorrigible. He was a publisher's son and grandson even at the front. Beautiful language, and magnificent, arching, justifying ideas were his solace. Early during his first spell at the front in 1915 his travelling library included the Bible, the *Iliad*, St Augustine's *Confessions*, works by Homer and Shakespeare, poetry by Emily Brontë and Robert Browning, essays by Ruskin, burlesques by Meredith and a novel by Gorky. He was the third generation of his family to read Scott's Waverley novels, but the only one to do so in a field of carnage.

In the first full-scale battle in which he fought, at Loos in September 1915, he was shot through the hand and concussed, injuries which resulted in his being shipped back to England. Nellie arranged for him to be sent to a hospital near Cadogan Place, temporarily set up in the house of one of her friends; but Harold soon returned to the battlefront. In September of that year, during the Battle of the Somme, Harold was wounded in the knee by shrapnel and in the pelvis by machine-gun bullets: characteristically he had a copy of Aeschylus' play, *Prometheus*, in his pocket at the time. He lay for over twelve hours in no-man's-land, feigning death when Germans approached the shell-hole in which he had fallen; but a rescue party eventually found him. With a crowd of other casualties he was sent back to London, where he arrived at Victoria Station with a high temperature. An ambulance driver was bribed to take him to his parents' house, rather than to the country hospital to which he had been ordered; Nellie took him immediately to a hospital for the wounded run by two American women in Belgrave Square and called her husband's Athenaeum crony, the surgeon Sir William Bennett. Harold was found to have a poisonous abscess and to be on the verge of death. Bennett's operation saved him; but that in turn was only made possible by Nellie's ruthless promptitude.

Harold's first-hand experience of the fighting was mercifully brief. Unlike other officers who had to endure prolonged bouts of trench warfare, he faced only two spells at the Front, each of only a few months' duration; his wounds did not finally heal until 1920, so he was condemned to four years of gruelling pain (including several operations) and was unfit for further combat. His experiences had been vile, and unforgettable. Harold was only twenty when war was declared and twenty-four when the Armistice was agreed in 1918. He brooded more over the horrors of the war during his inaction of 1916–18 than if he had been in the trenches. Men of whatever age are not often confronted with death, still less with violent death, experienced daily on a massive scale. Neither Harold nor the other survivors of trench warfare whom he knew could forget the horror of their experiences. The loss of friends like Gilbert Talbot and Ivo Charteris affected him deeply. A list of his Eton or Oxford contemporaries becomes almost a necrology: he was haunted by the memory, for example, of a young officer, like himself no more than a boy, who came to see him just before going on an attack, and wept quietly, in the certainty that he would be killed, before going to his death. He felt guilty for having avoided this death and the deaths which took so many others.

Like his grandfather Daniel after the diagnosis of tuberculosis, Harold felt obliged to make good use of the life granted to him. He was inspired by witnessing the courage of others. He recognised that war was loathsome yet some of its dangers excited him, and he enjoyed the enforced intimacy with other men. It was during his time as an officer that he had his first insights into the lives of the poor: he gleaned much from his duties censoring the letters which his men sent home. The broken family lives and sordid domestic disintegration that were the inevitable sequel of war caught his imagination. In this and other ways his experiences in the trenches gave him a better understanding of the fears and aspirations of the poor than any member of his family for two generations. His insights were partial, and hopelessly hobbled by the assumptions of his class; but he came out of the war convinced that the men who had fought for Britain deserved well of their country: secure jobs, better pay, improved housing, more generous treatment of their diseases, better education for their children. He became distressed too by the arrogance with which earnest intellectuals (among whom he classed himself and his family) devalued or despised men who were not fluent in their cant or interested in apeing their pretensions.

His trench experiences accentuated his hereditary tendency to fatalism. Harold's generation, and those that followed, were dominated in mind and memory by the events of the Great War. He judged his contemporaries by whether they had been combatants, and distrusted those who had not. He felt a special sense of belonging to the Brigade of Guards. Its *esprit de corps* never left him, and in old age he would refer proudly to the twelve battalions that formed the Guards division in the Great War as the world's most formidable fighting body since the Macedonian phalanx.

The war disrupted his life despite giving it the possibility of extra meaning; but when peace came his problems were still unresolved. He was an exceedingly intelligent young idealist. His life was wonderfully enriched by a strong imagination which had developed along literary lines and gave his character unsuspected reserves of strength. Though his temperament was painfully nervous, though he was prey to nameless forebodings and always apprehensive of ambushes that fate might prepare for him, he was saved by an extra measure of fortitude and tenacity. His bookishness was a wonderful way of fending off the worst that happened and making it bearable. With the earnestness and self-control taken from the example of his grandfather and father, he kept going when others of his temperament might have collapsed. He was driven as others of his family felt driven, and felt threatened as they had felt threatened.

Daniel and Alexander had recognised that the world was often dangerous and corrupt: they took refuge in hard work, and protected themselves by becoming warriors for Christian ideals. The next generation of the family found its refuge in the personal reserve and social ossification of post-Victorian respectability. Harold had faced the additional catastrophe of a mother like Nellie: a catastrophe that was also the making of him. A childhood with this over-powering she-dragon blundering around was a discouraging introduction to reality. If *she* was typical of the outside world – if reality was as bad as that – he needed a protective façade. And so this wistful, nervous, harassed, brave little boy, who saw life so dreadfully, gradually evolved his defence: a False Self, the protective mask that eventually became one of the most distinctive political personalities of his century.

CHAPTER 7

Dorothy and Harold

There's nothing in the world so bad for some women as marriage, he thought; and politics; and having a Conservative husband.

Virginia Woolf, *Mrs Dalloway*

Our owne parents by their offences, indiscretion, and intemperance are our mortal enemies ... They cause our griefe many times, and put upon us hereditary diseases, inevitable infirmities: they torment us, and we are as ready to injure our posterity.

Robert Burton
'*The Anatomy of Melancholy*'

After the cataclysm of war Harold felt disinclined to resume his Oxford studies or join his father, uncles, cousins and brother in the family business. They suggested that he should start working in the firm shortly after the Armistice in November 1918, but he longed to escape from the curdling thickness of family life and to break with the frustrations of his drab invalid existence in England. Fresh air and new faces were what he needed. To this end he settled with his acquaintance George Lloyd, an ardent imperialist who had just been appointed Governor of Bombay at the early age of thirty-nine, to join him in India as an ADC. Unfortunately, as Harold's war wounds had not healed, the Army doctors judged that the risk of infection would be too high in India and he was refused a medical certificate.

At this point Nellie intervened. She was a friend of Lady Edward Cavendish, whose son the Duke of Devonshire had been Governor-General of Canada since 1916. With these two women as intermediaries it was arranged for Harold to join Devonshire's staff as an ADC, and he reached Government House at Ottawa in March 1919. The following ten months in Canada he ranked as among the happiest of his life. King Edward VIII, who as Prince of Wales visited Canada in 1919, thought that his host Devonshire, though in a 'hopelessly narrow groove', was 'a damned good fellow and has no side'. The other ADCs included Lord Haddington, Lord Minto and the pleasure-loving Lord Molyneux (afterwards last Earl of Sefton), to whom is attributed the disdainful description of the military evacuation at Dunkirk in 1940: '*Too* awful – the noise and *the people.*' With such colleagues the atmosphere at Government House under the Devonshires was like that of a blue-blooded house-party. The light work required of the ADCs scarcely disturbed the cheerful round of dances, fishing, boating, swimming and touring.

An American tour, culminating in a visit to New York, was *de rigueur* for Canadian governors-general and their staff. They always found New York a maelstrom of contending malice and vanities. New York was not 'a place I should care to return to', one of Devonshire's predecessors, Dufferin, had written. 'Individually the people are nice enough, and wonderfully kind and civil, but their jealousy and abuse of each other is stupendous. Every American lady seems ashamed of her best friend. Indeed one is made constantly to feel as though one was living in the Servants Hall.' Little changes; Harold, in 1919, found New York equally loud and vulgar.

Within a few months of arriving in Canada Harold had fallen in love for the only time in his life. The object of his excitement was the Devonshires' third daughter, Lady Dorothy Cavendish. Born in July 1900, she was six years his junior. Her education had been limited to the family schoolroom, or rather schoolrooms, for after 1908, when her father inherited the family dukedom and estates, she had a peripatetic child-hood, travelling in private trains between the various Cavendish houses: Chatsworth and Hardwick Hall in Derbyshire, Bolton

Abbey in Yorkshire, Compton Place at Eastbourne and Lismore Castle in southern Ireland. In contrast to Harold, she had an outdoors life which had little place for books and little interest in ideas. She was an earthy girl, keen on golfing and riding, and bursting with bucolic health. After a courtship of some nine months, Harold proposed and was accepted on Boxing Day of 1919. It is easier to see what attracted Harold to her than to understand why she responded to his overtures; but she was only eighteen when their flirtation began, and still inexperienced and imperceptive when they agreed to marry. Neither of them had much knowledge of the opposite sex, and they met under considerable constraints. Her early letters from Canada to her future mother-in-law show that she had glimmerings of her ignorance: Harold's glowingly happy letters home forewarned his mother that his bride was in many ways young and immature. Though some members of her family thought that Dorothy married early in order to escape from her mother's despotism, the truth surely is that she accepted Harold's proposal because she was flattered and excited by his obvious love, and did not know any better.

Harold's engagement was one of the transforming moments of his life. Marriage to Dorothy involved the Macmillans with the extraordinary family of Cavendish, and complicated the already complex family heritage. Harold's connection with this great ducal family brought him snubs and pain as well as pleasure and distinction; it was also a connection which he exploited when it suited him. As a young politician fighting for election or re-election in a marginal constituency he deployed his mother-in-law as a weapon: a duchess as guest of honour at a fund-raising event or local party rally was guaranteed to pull the crowds in. The Cavendish connection had other advantages for Harold. 'I have it either way; my grandfather was a crofter; my wife's father was a duke' – or so Lord Boyd-Carpenter quoted Harold as saying.

With Harold's marriage to Dorothy in 1920, the Cavendish family – their earthly glory, their eccentricities and their contacts – become part of the Macmillan story. Their fortune had been founded by that grasping Tudor adventuress known as Bess of Hardwick, whose son William was created Earl of Devonshire in 1618. His descendants were the greatest magnates in seventeenth-century Derbyshire, surviving civil war and rebellion without loss of fortune. The fourth Earl, who was raised to a dukedom in 1694, was described by Bishop Burnet as 'the finest and handsomest gentleman of his time; loves the ladies and plays; keeps a noble house and equipage; is tall, well made and of princely behaviour; of nice honour in everything but the paying of his tradesmen'. He was not the last of his family to chase after women, just as the third Duke was not the last of the family to be described (by Lord Waldegrave) as 'negligent in his dress'. The eighteenth century was the heyday of English dukes, and the fourth Duke of Devonshire, who was Prime Minister in 1756-7, enjoyed all the advantages of his rank. His son, the fifth Duke, was a gambler and drunkard who gave few signs of enjoying his dissipation: his distinguishing characteristic, according to Wraxall, was 'constitutional apathy', another family characteristic. The story of his household, in which he lived for years in a *ménage à trois* with his brilliant first wife Georgiana and his mistress Lady Elizabeth Foster, was, according to the gossip Charles Greville, 'amusing as a scandalous chronicle, an exhibition of vice in its most attractive form, full of grace, dignity and splendour, but I fancy full of misery and sorrow also'. At Chatsworth 'the most interesting things are invisible', Malcolm Macmillan wrote after a visit in 1885, and generations of Cavendishes at Chatsworth have pursued their complicated private lives all but invisibly.

The sixth Duke – bachelor, bibliophile, diplomat, connoisseur, diarist, high-spirited host and friend, guilt-ridden lecher, ranting born-again Christian – is the subject of a biography by that masterful observer of idiosyncratic Englishmen, James Lees-Milne. It was his cousin who developed the Cavendish estates after his succession in 1858, settling their fortunes on a sound basis for another century. He also maintained the Cavendish reputation for imperturbability. Woken in bed one night by a servant who came into his bedroom shouting 'The house is on fire', the Duke replied, 'Very well, go and help put it out – it's your business, not mine.'

His son, Spencer, eighth Duke of Devonshire was better known by the nickname 'Harty-Tarty', derived from the title of Marquess of Hartington which he bore until his succession in 1891. Harty-Tarty entered political life in his early twenties, held government office by the age of thirty, and on three occasions declined to take office as prime minister. Originally a leader of the Whig component of the Liberal Party, he separated from Gladstone over the question of Irish Home Rule in 1886, and from 1895 until 1903 sat as a Liberal Unionist in the Cabinets of the Conservative Prime Minister Lord Salisbury. He was a hero to those Whiggish Liberals who resisted Gladstone's Irish policy: Lord Stalbridge wrote to Lord Dufferin in 1887 of Hartington's 'steady unflinching determination'. There were other sides to him. He was apathetic, ignorant, desultory and forgetful. He was reputed to have yawned in the middle of his own maiden speech in the House of Commons. Lord Derby considered him 'constitutionally apt to be despondent'. A downright and taciturn man, who deplored garrulity in others, he loathed political pomposity, and hearing an orator in the House of Lords declare 'This is the proudest moment of my life,' murmured to his neighbour, 'The proudest moment of my life was when my pig won the first prize at Skipton Fair.' As his private secretary wrote, 'The witch, Imagination, had no power over him'; no last words were more surely expressive of their speaker's personality than those muttered in 1908 by the half-conscious Duke in his dying moments, 'Well, the game is over, and I am not sorry.'

His ignorance and forgetfulness were notorious, even when great issues of state were involved. It was to Devonshire that Queen Victoria first confided her scheme to pacify Ireland by a personal visit: she directed him to tell Salisbury and enlist his support. A few days later when the Queen met the Prime Minister, she asked what he thought of her plan. In mystification

Salisbury confessed that he knew nothing of any plan, which Devonshire had forgotten. Years later, in 1902, King Edward VII arrived for dinner at Devonshire House only to find that his host was absent. After thirty-five minutes' delay the Duke was traced to the Turf club, where he was playing cards, and returning home admitted that he had forgotten having invited the King to dine. On another occasion, after the future of Manchuria had been discussed at a series of Cabinet meetings, it emerged that he could not find Manchuria on a map of China. The Duke, so his Cabinet colleague Gerald Balfour decided, 'was a man of plain common sense and great character, but of limited education and information, with the slowest mind of anyone he knew'. As Esmé Wingfield-Stratford explained, 'the otherwise inexplicable trust reposed in the bovine, yawning Duke of Devonshire was due to the belief that so wealthy a nobleman could never be anything but disinterested'.

Harty-Tarty had his family's weakness for gambling and sexual irregularity. He was devoted to horse-racing and cards, subordinating important business to these passions, and engaged for thirty years in a marital intrigue with another duke's wife. His lover was the German-born Duchess of Manchester – 'not particularly well spoken of, an intriguing mischievous person, who has often been on the verge of losing her character, but has never quite lost it', as Lord Derby described her in 1888. From the 1870s onwards Harty-Tarty was a regular guest of the Manchesters at Kimbolton Castle, and in society the affair was well known. Her husband William Drogo, seventh Duke of Manchester, was a 'good-natured, simple-minded man, respectable, harmless & rather foolish', judged Derby. Manchester 'was a curious mixture of good nature and oddity; he was continually airing some extraordinary theory or complaining of some hitherto unknown ailment', Lord Huntley recalled. 'One day he asked me to examine his eye, as he felt sure there was "a small volcano" in it! I assured him I saw no eruption, but he went on to the next person he came across and made the same enquiry. He posed as an ardent soldier, was wont to attend the military manoeuvres, both in England and on the Continent, and held forth on tactics. He raised the Huntingdonshire Light Horse, and was a well-intentioned bore.'

Harty-Tarty and his Duchess eventually married in 1892, two years after she had been widowed and as her eldest son lay on his death-bed at the Manchesters' other castle, Tandaragee in Ireland. 'Always very décolletée in the evening with dresses that only a woman of thirty should wear,' wrote Princess Daisy of Pless of the Double Duchess in 1903, 'she generally has a wreath of green leaves in her hair (or rather wig!).' The gossip in Cannes that year was that the Duchess was shadowed by detectives through the gambling rooms at Monte Carlo and watched by the croupiers in case she tried to snatch money from the tables. At other times she was suspected of stock-exchange speculation on inside information and of card-sharping. This passion for gambling was a lethal family trait. It ruined her eldest son, who went bankrupt in 1889 owing £100,000 (the equivalent of over a million today). His son, the ninth Duke, turned in desperation to the United States for the family's financial rehabilitation, declaring that he must either marry an Astor or a Vanderbilt, or give up; his brazen pursuit of one New York heiress (who instead married the Duke of Roxburghe) led to an American newspaper headline, 'England's poorest duke after our richest heiress'. Although he ensnared in marriage the daughter of a Cincinnati railway mogul, this came too late to stop him from following his father into bankruptcy. As he was both addicted to gambling and the recurrent dupe of confidence tricksters, the Manchester fortunes never recovered, and at one time in his life he was reduced to working as a film promoter; 'sport has appealed to me more strongly than brain work', he admitted, 'which may be one of the reasons I have not succeeded in making money'.

By contrast Harty-Tarty's nephew and heir Victor Cavendish breathed the air of public service from childhood. On leaving Cambridge he worked for several months in an accountant's office and read law in the chambers of a judge. He was an active member of the board of such family companies as the

Barrow Hematite Steel Company and the Furness Railway. The youngest member of the House of Commons when elected in an unopposed contest at the age of twenty-three, he became a dedicated House of Commons man. He was first a Tory whip and then from 1903 until 1906 Financial Secretary to the Treasury, in which post he showed aptitude and grit in dealing with financial business. By ducal standards he was businesslike, and for a Cavendish he had an unusual degree of conjugal fidelity. As a young man in 1890 he took a fancy to Evie Fitzmaurice, the daughter of Lord Lansdowne; finding that his feelings had not changed two years later when she returned from India, where her father was Viceroy, he proposed and was accepted. 'I have never met him, but I know all his people well, and I believe he is a very good sort of lad,' wrote the Viceroy when friends congratulated him on such an auspicious engagement to Devonshire's heir. Lansdowne was pleased by the engagement but, faced with his friends' effusions about the brilliancy of the match, preferred to say nonchalantly that his new son-in-law was 'reasonably well provided for'. Victor Cavendish was a godson of Queen Victoria, who took a close but mournful interest in the engagement. 'They are both very young, but he is a very good and clever young man, and the Queen hopes they will be as happy as is possible in this uncertain world,' she wrote to Lansdowne, adding with the selfishness of someone who had loathed to let her own daughter go, 'Evie will be a terrible loss to her mother.'

His position as Harty-Tarty's heir was not always easy. A Tory whip in 1906 found him trembling after a stormy interview with his uncle, who had ended by kicking over the fender. Nor did his succession to the family estates and titles bring relief. 'Victor Cavendish came to the House of Commons the other afternoon and loafed about for four hours,' Lord Balniel recorded in his diary shortly after Harty-Tarty's death in 1908. 'Poor Victor is sadly lost in the Lords . . . the Duchess says he can't think what to do in the evenings and that he writes all sorts of needless letters to kill time. London is in fact so wearisome to him that he is to be sent to Chatsworth and Hardwick to supervise their obsolete system of drainage.' A month later Balniel dined at Devonshire House, and feared 'that the possession of much wealth and the care of many great houses' was upsetting the new Duchess. 'She is literally overwhelmed with projects, wants to do everything at once, and altogether is in a frame of mind almost *entêtée* and quite alien to her usual coolness and decision.' Despite increased taxation and the depression of agricultural prices the family held on to all but one of the great houses which Victor inherited in 1908. After the war, in 1920, their London home, Devonshire House in Piccadilly, was sold for £750,000 (the equivalent now of perhaps £8 million), inspiring Siegfried Sassoon to write his 'Monody on the Demolition of Devonshire House' commemorating:

> the low-built mansion, once so great,
> Ducal, demure, secure in its estate –
> Where Byron rang the bell and limped upstairs,
> And Lord knows what political affairs
> Got muddled and remodelled while Their Graces
> Manned unperturbed Elizabethan faces.

The building was replaced by a motorcar emporium erected for the tycoon Lord Rootes.

Devonshire sat in the Conservative Cabinets of 1922–4 as Colonial Secretary, prompting Sir Maurice Hankey, the Cabinet Secretary, to observe that he looked 'like an apoplectic idol and adds little counsel'. Hankey was a superbly efficient middle-class teetotaller who could be expected to discount a red-faced toping duke; but Devonshire's manner inspired confidence among those supporters of the Conservative Party who distrusted brilliance or originality and found security in his simplicity. 'What a solid person he is – uncouth in gesture, ponderous in appearance, slow in style – yet giving the impression of saying all that requires statement and doing so without any effort to score a success,' Lord Crawford reflected after Devonshire had intervened in a House of Lords debate in 1923. 'There is a massive imperturbability about him which gives confidence. He will never let one down, never play for his own advantage, never do anything brilliant, let us hope will never do anything wrong.' However in 1925, while still in his mid-fifties, the Duke justified Hankey's comment that he was apoplectic and was incapacitated by a stroke. He survived for another thirteen years, but changed from a patient, amiable man into an irascible ogre who turned against his family with an increasingly unpleasant fury. He passed his last years in morose seclusion at Chatsworth, where he died in 1938. 'By position, second to none in the peerage,' *The Times* declared in a massive obituary, 'he was a true Cavendish, with the strong nose and jaw, the ruddy complexion, the stolid absence of emotion, the sleepy air hiding a shrewd and vigilant faculty of observation, the sober, clear mind, and the entire freedom from any sort of ostentation or pretence.'

Victor Cavendish's wife and Dorothy Macmillan's mother Evie was a disagreeable woman in whom Nellie Macmillan met her match. King Edward VIII, meeting her when he visited Canada as Prince of Wales, thought her 'hopelessly pompous'. Her brother-in-law, the Duke of St Albans, considered her disagreeable and authoritarian. Always a cold and rigid woman, she came into greater ascendancy as her husband's mental condition deteriorated after 1925. Her entrenched habit of parsimony intensified with age. She treated her servants meanly, and imposed many economising fads. One of her crazes was the introduction of nettle soup to family menus to save expense: so many nettles were required for her needs that the Chatsworth gardener had to cultivate them in glasshouses. The Duchess was a barbarian who among other atrocities dynamited Paxton's great conservatory at Chatsworth and replanted his garden there with rhododendrons and bamboo. Oblivious of her surroundings, she vandalised the great houses of the Cavendishes and let their guests suffer with bad food and icy rooms.

Her lineage was remarkable not only for its length but for its diversity. The Fitzmaurices migrated to Ireland in the twelfth century, and her father the fifth Marquess of Lansdowne was the twenty-eighth Lord of Kerry in direct male succession. The earlier Fitzmaurices were an unruly race; several of them were killed by their heirs-at-law, and one murdered a judge on his bench. In Elizabethan times three successive Lords of Kerry rebelled against their sovereign, and their estates were temporarily forfeited to the Crown. The family was enriched not only in property but in mental endowments by the marriage of the twenty-first Lord Kerry in 1692 to the daughter and eventual heiress of Sir William Petty. This brilliantly original man was a clothier's son who had begun life as a common seaman, but his talents so excited the envy of his fellow seamen that they abandoned him on the French coast with a broken leg. He saved enough money to pay for his education in the Jesuit College at Caen, and then continued his studies in Paris, living in such poverty that he once survived for a week on a few pennies' worth of walnuts. Having studied medicine Petty gained fame for reviving the corpse of a woman hanged for infanticide and in 1648 moved to Oxford, where he became Professor of Anatomy. He later surveyed and made the first map of Ireland, amassed a fortune, invented new departures in ship design, designed a primitive version of the modern tank, was a founding fellow of the Royal Society, and developed what he called 'political arithmetic' (the use of statistics for political economy). In Paris he was the intimate of Thomas Hobbes, and later he was the 'singular friend' of John Aubrey, who celebrated his 'prodigious working wit' in his *Brief Lives*. His father-in-law was Sir Hardress Waller, one of the regicides responsible for the execution of King Charles I.

Petty's fortune, by the failure of his male heirs, devolved in 1751 upon his grandson John Fitzmaurice, who was created Earl of Shelburne. It was his son William (although best known as the Prime Minister Shelburne) who was the first of the Lansdownes. Brought up in Kerry, where he led a rough life and received little education, William succeeded to the great Petty estates and Shelburne title at the age of twenty-four and then emerged as a Whig politician of extreme libertarian principles who served as prime minister in 1782–3. Thereafter he accepted the marquessate of Lansdowne and became a disciple of Adam Smith; his largesse as a patron of artists and savants made his house acclaimed as an 'asylum of taste and science'. Burke called Lansdowne 'a serpent with two heads' and many others accused him of duplicity. 'I grow suspicious of him in every respect, the more I see every transaction of his,' wrote Sheridan in 1782. 'It is impossible not to see a reserve and disingenuous management in them.'

To all the hereditary distinctions and talents of the Pettys and Fitzmaurices another exotic strain of brilliance was added when in 1843 the fourth Marquess married Baroness Keith and Nairne, a Scottish heiress and peeress in her own right. Her father was a Frenchman, Count de Flahault de la Billardrie, a general who had been aide-de-camp to Napoleon Bonaparte; the Count had also been the lover of Bonaparte's stepdaughter Queen Hortense of Holland, by whom he fathered the Duke de Morny, half-brother and wisest adviser of Emperor Napoleon III. These were not the only irregularities in the family's inner history for Flahault himself was not the son of the French Count whose surname he bore, but the result of his mother's adultery with Charles-Maurice de Talleyrand-Périgord, some-time Bishop of Autun, the ruthless manipulator of French diplomatic destinies and wily survivor of all the horrors of the French revolution. Another child whose paternity Talleyrand acknowledged was the Romantic painter Eugène Delacroix, who was hence Flahault's half-brother. Flahault was intimately involved with the diplomatic policy of his father Talleyrand and was at different times French Ambassador to Berlin, Vienna and London. Dorothy Macmillan's mother Evie Devonshire was proud of her descent from Talleyrand, and there were some critical moments in Harold's career when he showed himself every bit as ruthless, and quite as much of an opportunist, as the wicked old man himself.

The eldest son of this Lansdowne and his Scottish–French

wife reached the highest power and distinction: Governor-General of Canada, Viceroy of India and finally Foreign Secretary from 1900 until 1905. 'He is very sensible, calm, prudent and industrious, has a charming wife and is a "grand seigneur", which is a very good thing for India,' wrote his predecessor as Viceroy, the Marquess of Dufferin and Ava, on the announcement of the appointment in 1888. 'He was possibly the greatest gentleman of his day,' his brother-in-law Lord Ernest Hamilton testified. 'In matters great and small, civic and domestic, his sense of duty and his meticulous observance of rectitude were quite remarkable.' Lansdowne was abstemious in eating and drinking, restrained in speech, with the fine manners of a French nobleman. His Frenchness did not extend to moral latitudinarism; he deplored modern French novels, and in 1889, as Viceroy of India, intervened to stop them from being sold at Indian railway bookstalls (agreeing with his correspondent Lord Northbrook 'as to the harm which the circulation of the Zola series must do to the young educated Indian').

This great Lord Lansdowne married an Ulsterwoman, the Duke of Abercorn's daughter, Lady Maud Hamilton ('nice', according to Asquith, 'but *au fond* quite a cat'). This marriage with the Hamiltons introduced a temperamental strain which it would be generous to call healthy stolidity and unkind to call ducal dullness. 'Known in his younger days chiefly as a fop, being remarkably handsome, and as vain of his looks as any woman,' as Lord Derby wrote, Abercorn had been 'an excellent and popular' Lord Lieutenant of Ireland; but many of his descendants were less bright. On the death of Lady Lansdowne's brother, the second Duke of Abercorn, in 1913, Lord Crawford and Balcarres noted in his diary: 'a droll little man, void of intellect, but endowed with an address and dignity which more than compensated for other shortcomings': his son and heir James Hamilton 'lacks these things, but I fancy will make a good outdoor Duke'.

Nellie was delighted by Harold's engagement. By any standards marriage with Dorothy Cavendish was a coup. Discussing suitable brides for the Prince of Wales in 1928, Princess Alice, Countess of Athlone, wrote to Queen Mary regretfully: 'Of course a Cavendish would have done but there are now none left.' Harold, among others, had pre-empted the King's son.

The marriage ceremony at St Margaret's, Westminster in April 1920 was performed by Alexander Macmillan's youngest son John (not yet a bishop) and a Cavendish connection, Canon William Temple, a future Archbishop of Canterbury. Evie Devonshire, who deespite being a duchess was also a crashing snob, not unreasonably invited rows of her family – Cavendishes, Cecils and Fitzmaurices – as well as Queen Alexandra, and two royal princes, the Dukes of Connaught and York. Nellie, who because she was not a duchess was even more socially competitive, filled her side of the church with great Macmillan authors. One such guest was Thomas Hardy, who sat with Lord Morley and signed as one of the witnesses. Morley, seeing Lord Bryce and the Duke of Devonshire near by, whispered the question, 'Which weighs most, three OMs or one duke?'

How did an earnest, diffident middle-class publisher fit into the supremely self-confident world of the Cavendishes? Awkwardly in many ways, but more because he was earnest and diffident than because of his social origins. The phrase 'middle-class' has never carried with it the pejorative associations of the French label *bourgeois*, nor did the British aristocracy always repulse outsiders with the furious defensiveness of Continental nobilities. After Harold's retirement as prime minister, in the 1960s, an Englishman walking in the streets of Paris was engulfed in a thunderstorm. As he dived into a taxi by one door, a thin, hawk-nosed and evidently blue-blooded Frenchman entered by the other door. The pair agreed in their common misfortune to share the taxi, and the Englishman politely voiced regret that the weather was likely to ruin the May Day celebrations on the following day. His companion replied caustically, 'C'est le bon Dieu qui crache sur le prolétariat' (God in his goodness craps on the proles). Class hatred like this would be thought a symptom of insanity in an English nobleman; but, although Harold was not the victim of any feeling of social exclusiveness on the part of the Devonshires, he was a social misfit at Chatsworth. The family passion for horse-racing bored him; his earnest, fussy, timorous manners grated with the Cavendishes. Among the British upper classes the quality which is most admired is fortitude: the solecism which they most scorn is ingratiation: yet until late in life it was Harold's truckling to the mighty, rather than his fortitude, that people noticed. James Stuart, an aristocratic Conservative MP who married Dorothy's sister Rachel in 1923, derided Harold's finickiness and made his life miserable. Stuart (later Churchill's wartime Chief Whip) was a laconic man, who talked out of the side of his mouth, rarely finished a sentence and like Harty-Tarty reputedly once yawned in the middle of one of his own speeches. He never fussed and never saw the point of burdening his listeners with gratuitous information. In all of this he differed greatly from Harold, although as colleagues in the Cabinet and Shadow Cabinet in the 1940s and 1950s the two men worked together cordially.

Despite his excessive eagerness to please, Harold's business sense impressed the Cavendish circle and was exploited by them. In 1934, after Evie Devonshire's nephew Lord Waterford died of gunshot wounds, Harold and his brother-in-law Hartington learnt that Waterford had named them as his executors. The new Marquess was a baby, 'and Macmillan, who is hard worked, is disturbed at the prospect of a long minority, and equally of the vile journey to County Waterford', Lord Crawford noted. Hartington had said, with doubtful generosity, that he would 'gladly leave all responsibility to his brother-in-law'.

The early years of Harold's marriage seemed to him blissful, although for Dorothy the rapture wore off. They lived in Chester Square, with Harold's nanny running the household and his mother a few minutes' walk away in Cadogan Place. Harold had little experience of women, and not surprisingly for someone whose childhood had been dominated by a termagant like Nellie, he felt threatened by them, although ease in their company came upon him as an octogenarian. For Dorothy herself Harold felt the passionate romantic infatuation to which only a shy, inexperienced man can succumb. In the early years of his marriage he idolised and idealised Dorothy, turning her into something unreal. 'The greater the love the more false to its object,' as Auden and MacNeice wrote in their *Letters from Iceland*. Romantic infatuation is fundamentally solitary and essentially impersonal: its objects are not seen plainly and accurately, or respected for their real character, but isolated inside a remote fantasy in which no one and nothing is real. There are no True Selves among the infatuated: only solitary dreamers. Yet Dorothy was warm, charming and humorous, a woman who lived by her instincts and was prone to sudden fits of temper; someone whose robustness balanced the nerviness with which Harold's mother had infected him. It must have been a bore for such a woman to find herself the object of such a woozy passion. Harold had learnt to practise compliance when trying to survive as a child under Nellie's suzerainty, and as a younger man he brought a touch of compliance to his adult relations too. The submissive tone in some of his dealings with important political figures seemed obsequious or even cringing, and his surviving letters to Dorothy too have a cloying, dutiful, placatory note that seems both anxious and immature.

Harold was not enthusiastic about the grapplings and gro-pings of the bed. His grandfather Daniel, who had adored his own mother Katherine, had warmed himself with the heats of desire; but Harold, though he did not dare know it, was hostile to his mother, distrusted women until late in life and was not sexually adamant with Dorothy. Like many other men whose lives have got too closely entangled with their mothers', Harold was frustrated: where he loved he did not sexually desire, and where he desired he could not love. The historian Ronald Hyam has included Harold Macmillan in a list of asexual people (dons like Jowett, explorers like Speke and Thesiger, soldiers like Gordon and Kitchener, even Winston Churchill) who were 'apathetic about sex' and created problems 'for others by their abstinence' as they lost 'touch with reality'. This over-intellectualised, under-sexed mentality of Harold's was the equivalent of pauperdom, and it was a depleting experience for someone like Dorothy who had to share it with him.

> The greatest poverty is not to live
> In a physical world, to feel that one's desire
> Is too difficult to tell from despair,

as Wallace Stevens declares in *Esthétique du Mal*.

Yet if Harold was not sexually adamant, nor was he impotent with Dorothy. Their first child and only son, Maurice, was born in 1921; followed by two daughters, Carol in 1923 and Catherine in 1926. Dorothy adored young children and gave more personal attention to hers than was usual at the time; but she preferred her daughters to her son and tended to lose interest in children as they grew older. Harold described himself as agitated by Maurice's birth, but either the early exultation wore off or the panic frightened him off; for, like his father before him, he was a remote and inaccessible parent. He was particularly awkward in approaching his only son: his occasional efforts to express affection were maladroit, and he was too exacting in his expectations of the boy, who grew up feeling inadequate.

From the outset the marriage was dogged by Nellie. She arranged a set of rooms for Harold and Dorothy at Birch Grove, and from 1920 until 1937 was a constant intruding shadow over the marriage. At Nellie's instigation the house at Birch Grove was rebuilt in 1926 into a large neo-Georgian building. The new house had an impressive reception hall, a drawing-room seventy-seven feet long, with other cold and gloomy rooms on a similar scale. This was costly work, all the more unusual at a time when most people (Evie Devonshire included) were obliged to retrench on their household expenditure. Although relations between Nellie and Dorothy were strained, the old woman preferred the notion of a duke's child as her daughter-in-law to an obscure Welshwoman or a Scottish divorcee. This prejudice was heightened because Dorothy was alone among her daughters-in-law in having children. Nellie's preference for Harold over Dan and Arthur became more pronounced after his Cavendish marriage, and resulted in Nellie instructing Maurice to bequeath the Birch Grove estate over the heads of his elder two sons to the youngest. Not satisfied with defying primogeniture in this way, Nellie also defied common sense: whereas in other families the widow would tactfully move out to a dower house on her husband's death, Maurice's testamentary arrangements stated that Nellie should be entitled to remain at Birch Grove, living with Harold and Dorothy, until her death. Dan as the eldest son would have been justified in resenting his loss of Birch Grove – Harold certainly felt guilty about it – but they continued as working partners. Dan was long inured to the wrongs done to him by his mother, and the causes of his sorrowing grumpiness were more universal than any grievances against Harold.

The layout of the reconstructed house was hard to compartmentalise. Nellie's domestic tyranny intruded everywhere. Harold was partly protected from her physical and emotional incursions, for he spent weekdays working in London and living in Chester Square; but Dorothy was exposed to the full onslaught of a tactless and meddlesome American woman who had never learnt to allow other people adequate living-space. She was once found by Carol sticking pins into an effigy of the unlovable old woman.

After his marriage Harold became a partner in the family firm and began his long career as a publisher. He was well suited to the job. 'Authors are actors, books are theatres,' wrote Wallace Stevens. 'Literature is the abnormal creating an illusion of the normal.' The histrionic quality of his False Self found satisfaction in publishing life, and his real power of literary discrimination made him a success at his work. His bookishness was also a way of warding off those imaginary scarecrows which seemed so ugly and threatening to him. The apprehensive, fatalistic little boy who had considered the world such an alarming place, and its human inhabitants so untrustworthy, grew into a man well suited to live and work as a bookman. There is some truth in Cyril Connolly's accusation that just 'as repressed sadists are said to become policemen or butchers, so those with an irrational fear of life become publishers'. Harold preferred books about men's minds, or inward investigations of people's thoughts, to books about outward reality or the striving of men of action.

Harold, as a publisher, suffered from some of the strains which had exhausted his great-uncle Alexander. In the period between the world wars, scientists advanced from discovery to discovery, while political and economic changes followed with bewildering rapidity. Educated men like Harold had to work so hard to 'keep up' that they seldom had time to read any author who thought and felt and wrote with style. 'In a rapidly changing age, there is a real danger that being well informed may prove incompatible with being cultivated,' as Aldous Huxley warned in 1932. 'To be well informed one must read quickly a great number of merely instructive books. To be cultivated, one must read slowly and with a lingering appreciation the comparatively few books that have been written by men who lived, thought and felt with style.' The results of having to plough through innumerable worthy, workmanlike but stylistically dull manuscripts as part of his publishing duties is evident in the turgidity of the books which Harold himself wrote in the 1930s. Significantly when he left active work in the family firm in the 1940s, at a time when he was working abroad with the leisure to read such impeccable stylists as Austen, Boswell, Dickens, Trollope or Rebecca West, he wrote the most effervescent prose of his life: his *War Diaries* not only brim with memorable phrases, but are sometimes written with the imagery of a novelist. The style is the man, and Harold's emancipation from the routine of publishing unstylish writing enriched his prose for a time.

Among the authors with whom he had dealings, Harold felt an affinity with the pessimism of Thomas Hardy. He enjoyed cordial relations with Yeats, and admired Rudyard Kipling, while pitying the way he was ensnared in the clutches of a bullying wife. His treatment of authors was usually exemplary. 'Went for first time to Macmillan's magnificent office in St. Martin's Street,' Vera Brittain recorded in her diary in 1939. 'Received with great courtesy – talked business for an hour with Harold Macmillan – who didn't keep me waiting at all.' His attitude contrasted with that of Dan Macmillan, who by middle age had become often ungracious to authors. The two brothers worked together, but there was an undercurrent of mutual resentment, which on Dan's side became obtrusive when Harold finally attained political power.

Although Harold treated his authors considerately, he was intimate with few of them. Sean O'Casey was one exception, and a significant one. O'Casey had been born in 1880, and was reared in the squalor of a Dublin tenement (a life powerfully evoked in his masterpiece, *Juno and the Paycock*). As a child he suffered from a painful eye disease which prevented any formal education, and he was put to work at a young age as a labourer. But against appalling odds he taught himself to read, nourished himself by reading the Bible and Shakespeare and developed a prose style of rich amplitude. He was still working as a labourer, mixing cement, when his first great play, *The Shadow of a Gunman*, was produced at the Abbey Theatre in Dublin in 1923. A man of shrewd but unsystematic political interests, his artistic creations were brilliantly original but too plainly disregarded contemporary taste to keep the permanent favour of theatrical audiences. O'Casey was a man who suffered long deprivations and repeated disappointments, but overcame his handicaps by magnificent efforts of tenacity and self-sufficiency. He was a brave man, in some ways a remote man, and someone who was usually certain that what he was doing was right. The circumstances of his life differed from Harold's, but they had a shared streak of indomitable self-discipline which it is impossible not to admire.

Another Macmillan author with whom Harold was specially intimate was the historian John Wheeler-Bennett, almost ten years his junior. Wheeler-Bennett was a rich, debonair, unflappable man, perfect in dress and manners, who in his younger days always sported a monocle and carnation. Appointed director of information at the Royal Institute of International Affairs at the age of twenty-eight, he made Germany the focus of his studies and in the early 1930s divided his time between a London flat in the Albany and a Berlin apartment in the Hotel Kaiserhof. He developed an exceptional range of contacts around the world and was a superb anecdotalist, whose books on German history, such as *Munich: Prologue to Tragedy* (1948) and *Nemesis of Power* (1953), were attuned to Harold's view of both Germany and appeasement. In a commemoration of Wheeler-Bennett Lord Bullock wrote that Harold Macmillan was 'the friend who in style and outlook perhaps came closest to him', and Wheeler-Bennett himself described Harold as his friend, mentor and father-confessor.

The firm's annual turnover in the years immediately after 1920 has been estimated at between £60,000 and £80,000. The Macmillans were not magnificently rich, but rich enough to have rebuilt Birch Grove, and with free time enough for Harold to enter politics. He had been interested in political issues since his Oxford days, had learnt the moral lesson of his grandfather Daniel's life that one had a duty to try to improve the world; his wish to ameliorate poverty and ignorance had been solidified by his experiences of trench warfare; his political ambitions were encouraged by late-night conversations with his father-in-law Devonshire, who never ceased to rue his own exclusion from a House of Commons career when he inherited his peerages.

Harold's party loyalties were loose. His family were traditionally radical Liberals who had lapsed into the quietude of Liberal Unionism; his undergraduate sympathies had been Liberal as much as anything; he adulated the social-reforming ideals of Lloyd George; and Devonshire, though he sat in Conservative Cabinets, was at bottom an old-fashioned Whig. But the Liberal Party was in unmistakable eclipse, and Devonshire's contacts were all with the hierarchy of the Conservative Party.

Indeed at the time of Harold's decision to stand for parliament, Devonshire was a Cabinet minister in the outgoing Conservative government. So it was to Conservative Central Office that Harold applied for a candidature.

He was given the chance to contest the traditionally Radical seat of Stockton for the Conservatives, and surprised everyone by coming within seventy-three votes of winning it in the general election of 1923. He was readopted after his defeat, and set about reorganising his local party association along more democratic lines. He contributed largely to his own election expenses, as was then customary; but he was unusual in getting his supporters to contribute more too. It is significant that from the outset of his political career he stood somewhat aloof from the official party apparatus. Thus, when the next general election was called for 1924, he campaigned without the assistance of speakers offered by Conservative Central Office, whose election literature he left in unopened parcels. Quietly and unprovocatively he marked his independence of official party machinery and ways of thinking; his decision was vindicated when he won by a margin of over 3,000 votes. It would be an exaggeration to say that he was no one's man but his own: in one way and another the launch of his political career owed a great deal to the Cavendish embrace. As late as 1936 he was still seen by some as a satellite of Chatsworth: 'the unprepossessing, bookish, eccentric member for Stockton-on-Tees (and incidentally the Duke of Devonshire's son-in-law)' was how Chips Channon introduced him in his diary that year.

Harold 'was just an ordinary man of business who felt it a duty to come forward at a time like the present', he was reported as declaring at his first adoption meeting in 1923. In the contest that followed, Harold described himself as having been 'brought up as a strict Free Trader' but as now convinced of the need to support the tariff-protection policy which Baldwin, on behalf of the Conservative Party, had recently announced – 'a bold, courageous and frank policy', Harold called it. In the next election, of 1924, he stressed his belief that the loans which Ramsay MacDonald's Labour government had recently proposed extending to Soviet Russia under a trade agreement would have been better spent on more direct measures to alleviate domestic unemployment.

In many ways Harold was a born politician. Politics is a struggle for existence; it is what a man does in order to conceal who he is; it is an ideal vocation for individuals who defend themselves by offering the façade of a False Self to the world. And Harold was a young man of hidden strength and tenacity, whose whole life had been a struggle to exist under Nellie's dominion, a man striving to show a false outer calm to disguise his strangulated nerves, a poseur who was slowly developing into one of the greatest showmen of British politics. Political life was peculiarly attractive to someone of his temperament, although for a fastidious, nervous, bookish man some of its demands were formidable. In 1884 Malcolm Macmillan had sneered at politics as 'stump-oratorising', electioneering as a 'petty sessions of loud philanthropic formula' and candidates as superior men humiliating themselves before the 'all-triumphant clod-hoppery' of the electorate. Harold was not fluent at stump-oratorising: indeed public speaking made him sick with nervousness; and he took his philanthropy beyond the stage of oratorical formula to practical action. He masterminded the conversion of a derelict shipyard at Stockton into a club and retraining centre where the unemployed could break the listless monotony of their lives; he provided charabanc outings for the elderly – both apparently with his own money.

Harold enjoyed trying to help his poorer constituents, and the way in which they came to him for advice reminded him agreeably of the way in which he had sometimes helped his men as an officer during the war. Though Harold was earnest and dutiful in his constituency work, it was Dorothy who came to the fore when constituents needed to be cajoled, flattered or mollified. 'Women's gatherings, inspired by Lady Dorothy Macmillan,' reported the *Stockton and Tees-side Herald* in 1923, 'are a feature of the Conservative campaign.' She treated her husband's constituents as if they were her father's tenants and felt genuine interest in their lives. Her success was based on her authenticity, just as Harold's shortcomings arose from his inauthenticity, the failure of his False Self to make him seem convincing or real as a person.

At Stockton and in the House of Commons Harold lacked the ready cordiality which can lubricate political existence. As a novice backbencher he stumbled over mouthing the half-truths which are the coinage of parliamentary life and was clumsy in those political artifices which lay easily on the consciences of other parliamentarians. His speeches to constituents were shy and stilted. As a younger man, his language was particular – 'too dry, too academic, and too precise', as he admitted in 1935 – and his political agenda never had the slipperiness requisite of an election manifesto. His knowledge of the world, to borrow Samuel Johnson's phrase, suffered from being strained through books. He was neither charming nor (with calamitously protruding rabbit teeth) physically prepossessing; he lacked those personal attractions which bring men easy social success.

He divided his working day between his publishing office and the House of Commons: the contribution of his literary life to his political career was crucial. Harold's traffic in books set his mind into an irredeemably literary mould. It was not just that his views were influenced by Macmillan authors like Keynes, but his earnest, laborious speeches and memoranda were the work of an introspective man who had only tenuous touch with other people. He developed some of the inelasticity of a man who lives mainly in a world of books. They provided too much of his sense of reality in these early years. 'I found ideas more real than things, because they were the first to give themselves to me and because they gave themselves like things' – so wrote Jean-Paul Sartre in *Words*. 'I met the universe in books: assimilated, classified, labelled and studied ... and I confused the chaos of my experience through books with the hazardous course of real events. Hence my idealism which it took me thirty years to undo.' Harold might have made similar admissions.

Yet he was not wholly untethered from reality. His insights into industrial policy were sharpened by his experiences as a director of the Great Western Railway from 1929 until his acceptance of government office in 1940. This company was the twentieth-largest employer in the country, with nearly 19,000 people on its payroll in 1935, and his non-executive responsibilities broadened his business knowledge. There was an unusual reason for his recruitment to the board of a railway company operating in counties with which he had no connections. The Great Western had in 1925 begun a concerted denunciation of the high level of municipal rates which were levied on its properties, its chairman Lord Churchill complaining that the company's annual rates bill exceeded £1.5 million. Harold, as we shall see, simultaneously took up the campaign for derating of industry, and his speeches persuaded the directors that he was the sort of man they needed as a colleague. The Great Western's network ran westward out of Paddington Station in London, reaching distant rural counties like Devon and Cornwall, the great commercial city of Bristol and the coalfields and steelworks of South Wales. The latter areas were as economically depressed as Harold's constituency at Stockton, and he likened the devastation in both places to the effects of trench warfare at Passchendaele. The falling production and rising unemployment in South Wales touched every aspect of the Great Western's operations: their freight traffic declined, and even their passenger traffic was affected. As the company explained to the Dowager Marchioness of Cambridge, when she complained that her luggage had been carried to Cardiff after she had alighted at Badminton to visit her daughter the Duchess of Beaufort, their calculations were 'entirely upset through the large number of ex-Welsh miners and dependants who had drifted to London and found employment wanting to travel back for the Christmas holidays'. Macmillan believed that transport policies offered one of the chief means of escape from the Depression of the 1930s, and in parliament in the 1930s urged 'a completely new conception of transport' involving the improvement of road and rail access to depressed areas, and the cheapening of haulage rates. But this is to anticipate the development of his thinking.

In 1927 he published a booklet entitled *Industry and the State*, which he had prepared jointly with three other younger Conservative MPs, Robert Boothby, John Loder and Oliver Stanley: 'He, poor fellow, is what is called a Tory Democrat,' Harold Laski had written of Stanley, 'which means you give blankets to the poor if they agree not to ask for eiderdowns.' Their principal themes were the deflationary impact of monetary policy upon domestic purchasing power and the need for larger scales of manufacturing to compete with industrial powers such as the United States. They proposed, among other ideas, that joint industrial councils should be vested with increased powers, that collective bargaining should enjoy statutory authority, and in general tried to point a middle way between the brutalities of unbridled capitalism and the waste of collectivism. Their opinions made a mark. 'Boothby ought to make a good man when he has outlived an appearance of precociousness,' judged one of the shrewdest members of Baldwin's Cabinet of 1924–9, William Bridgeman, 'and Harold Macmillan and Oliver Stanley can speak very well on industrial subjects.' Harold became associated with other MPs such as Lord Apsley and Noel Skelton in a group which was known by fellow members of the parliament of 1924 as the YMCA (an acronym denoting the Young Men's Christian Association, whose high-mindedness they were thought to resemble). The Conservative leader Baldwin described the YMCA as 'a band of keen and ardent young Conservatives, with a genuine desire to serve the public interest, rather than that of any particular class or faction of their own particular selfish interest'. His Labour counterpart, Ramsay MacDonald, having scorned Baldwin in 1925 as 'a pure Utopian' who 'believes that all our ills would be cured if we made an effort to live and let live', added: 'With him are a few young men who have incomes of their own and who are genuinely touched by the woes of humankind. They will not face historical & economic facts & sit and vote & help to keep in Parliament a crowd of "big business" agents who tolerate this sentimentality because they can use it for their own purposes.'

Harold was one such man, but he had few illusions about the calibre of industrialists or the integrity of their parliamentary mouthpieces. One of his greatest concerns was the rejuvenation of Britain's iron and steel sector. The ageing fuddy-duddies who controlled so many companies in the metallurgical sector opposed any restructuring which might reduce their independence, he told Baldwin. He supported the proposal that iron and steel output should be 'safeguarded' by tariffs, but warned that the implementation of full-scale tariff protection would be a distraction from the more vital task of rationalising industry: that is to say, the creation by mergers of streamlined, large-scale production units which would compete efficiently in world markets. Harold urged a corporatist scheme on the Prime Minister. He wanted the government to press the heavy steel manufacturers to form a centralised selling company. The sales of this company would be allocated among the various works, with a small amount of tonnage left over for competitive sales among members. Prices would be fixed centrally. Another course which he offered Baldwin was the forcible amalgamation of all steel companies to create for the metallurgical sector what the formation in 1926 of Imperial Chemical Industries (who were erecting a great plant near Stockton) had achieved for the chemical sector. Moderate-minded people, who predominated in the party and the nation, had no abstract dislike of governmental intervention in industry, he assured Baldwin. A few years later he supported the Confederation of Employers' Organisations idea of an immense national cartel to pull British industry out of its decline, a sort of Imperial Comecon.

In the late 1920s plans to rationalise British industry

preoccupied some of the best practical thinkers, but their hopes and plans were overwhelmed by the weight of inanition, crushed by the structural rigidities among manufacturers, financiers and trade unionists. The failure of rationalisation – despite the commitment of so much energy and the engagement of so much imagination – created a feeling of despair among politicians and business people about the capacity for renewal of modern economic systems. Their hesitancy and doubts resulted in bitter, meagre times in the 1930s. The prevailing fatalism was epitomised by the response to the Industrial Reorganisation Bill introduced by the younger Lord Melchett of ICI and Harold Macmillan in 1934–5. This bill was intended to facilitate rationalisation in fifteen specified industries (such as mining, shipbuilding and heavy metallurgy) and would have enabled recalcitrant minorities to be coerced into schemes of reorganisation; but Walter Runciman, then President of the Board of Trade, dismissed the Melchett/Macmillan proposals with bland and enervate generalities. It is eternally to Harold's credit that he did not yield to Runciman's counsel of despair, but worked ceaselessly and even magnificently to mitigate its consequences. A fatalist in his personal life, he could not bear the practical meaning of fatalism in public life.

Harold estimated that the unemployment rate in his constituency averaged over 25 per cent (occasionally half of all the men in the area were jobless) and never believed that rationalisation would prove the panacea for all Stockton's miseries. As early as 1925 he discussed with the Chancellor of the Exchequer, Churchill, the desirability of reducing the municipal rates levied by local authorities on industries. These rates were a heavy burden in depressed industrial areas, where local authorities had to provide more services, and Harold saw that they were an obstacle to reviving local business and hence in reducing the level of unemployment. After two years, in 1927, Churchill was sufficiently convinced to propose that factories and farms should be relieved of £30 million in rates; and in

December he consulted Harold about the details. The latter enthused about Churchill's proposal with the obsequiousness that riled some of his contemporaries. He hailed it as a bold stroke that offered the basis of a constructive Conservative policy. (*Constructive Conservatism* was the title of a tract published in 1924, written by Harold's ally in the YMCA, Noel Skelton, and prefaced by Harold's Great Western Railway colleague, Lord Horne of Slamannan, which set out a programme for establishing a property-owning democracy and deeply influenced Eden.)

Churchill invited Harold to visit the Treasury so that together with Boothby he might read and comment on the relevant official papers. Harold was assiduous in his contributions to the long parliamentary debates about the derating proposals, which were finally enacted in 1929. His consultations with Churchill earned him the great man's gratitude, and others too were impressed by the coherence of his programme. 'On the whole,' a shrewd political journalist and Oxford Union contemporary called J.G. Lockhart wrote at the time of Harold's derating speeches in 1928,

> if I had to 'spot' the future leader of the Tory Party from the ranks of the Young Conservatives, my choice would fall not on Duff Cooper but on Harold Macmillan. Up to a point there is a curious resemblance between them. They shared an early taste for the picturesque: while Duff Cooper was a cynical and disillusioned Tory, Harold Macmillan affected an eyeglass with a broad black band and a fairly aesthetic brand of Liberalism. Both joined the Brigade of Guards; both distinguished themselves rather unexpectedly in an uncongenial profession; and both have married Wives [dukes' daughters with powerful connections].

Yet whereas Cooper still seemed little 'more than a clever undergraduate', Lockhart judged that Macmillan had proved himself. 'In the House his reputation rests, not on a single effort, but on a sequence of thoughtful speeches, out of which emerges the germ of a constructive industrial policy. He knows his subjects.'

Yet he could be a remorseless bore in his pursuit of Constructive Conservatism. 'Recently Captain Macmillan spoke at Plymouth on such a thrill-less subject as derating for one and a quarter hours,' Lady Astor told a meeting at Stockton in 1929; she seemed surprised that she had not heard 'the slightest snore'. For a time Harold believed that derating provided the only hope for the Conservative Party's salvation. According to his analysis, the Baldwin government had been able to hide its lack of policies by a series of diversionary incidents – the 'providential' General Strike of 1926, the long dispute with the National Union of Mineworkers, the futile Trades Disputes Act of 1927 – but as he informed Churchill, 'we cannot go on indefinitely without a policy at all'. If the derating proposals went awry, he predicted 'the eventual, and perhaps early, dissolution of the Party', but if they succeeded, the party would be revivified.

Such views were ill received by many of his Conservative parliamentary colleagues. 'An Englishman not only has no ideas,' said a Macmillan author, Bishop Mandell Creighton, 'he hates an idea when he meets one.' This might have been the motto of the average English boarding-school boy of Harold's generation, particularly the sort of boy who had joined the Army as a youth, and it was Harold's misfortune that the House of Commons was full of such men sitting on the Conservative benches. In the three or four general elections after the First World War, Conservative constituency parties behaved as if men of military eminence were specially adapted for political power. Their election handbills emphasised the candidate's regiment and war record: military prefixes were the rage. Harold himself shared some of these prejudices. In the years of his early candidatures, he always described himself as 'Captain Macmillan', and he felt contempt for *embusqués*, those men who had not fought in the war. Yet his efforts to initiate a Constructive Conservative industrial policy suffered from the preponderance in the House of Commons of men who had been elected because they had fought in the war. These obedient, unimaginative MPs with their thick cortex of fixed ideas were well suited to command a platoon, giving orders and taking orders; but less fit to act as legislators and think for themselves. Perhaps significantly Harold abandoned his use of the title 'Captain' around 1931–2, just at the time when he was moving into his period of most strenuous opposition to political and economic orthodoxy.

The 1930s were a thin, sad, hectic time for Harold in both his public and private existence. He was defeated at Stockton in the general election of 1929, and wept at his loss; but, even more painfully, Dorothy began an affair with his friend and ally, Robert Boothby. He was six years younger than Harold, stylish, witty and zestful where Harold was cautious, dull and repressed. Elected as a member of parliament at the age of twenty-four, he was Churchill's parliamentary private secretary from 1926 until 1929, and had been tipped for high office. But eloquent and gifted though Boothby was, his vanity was fatal to his hopes. His personal indiscipline verged on the reckless and he had no sense of proper bounds. He habitually confused his business and political interests, until his ambitions were wrecked when he was caught in a financial impropriety in 1941. He also damaged his reputation by the openness of his affair with Dorothy. As Churchill told Lord Woolton in 1940, 'Boothby had much capacity but no virtue.'

It is striking how much Dorothy's two men had in common. In the public dimension they were both expansionists who venerated Lloyd George and advocated Keynesian economics. During the 1930s each of them was a man of thwarted ambition, pursuing power with almost self-destructive intensity; like other Tories with thwarted ambitions, such as Churchill, they became vehement opponents of Chamberlain's foreign policy, part of a gallimaufry of Conservatives who could find no way to coalesce except in opposing appeasement. Boothby and Harold revelled in the masculine company and conversations of London clubs, and in old age were both prone to elaborate, self-serving anecdotes. In other ways they had much in common. 'A fighter with delicate nerves' was Harold Nicolson's description of

Boothby, but the words were just as apt for Macmillan. They both admired courage, and chose men of valour as their heroes; they each had a histrionic streak, behaving stagily and enjoying applause. Yet they had at least one striking divergence. Except when his sexual desires were aroused, Boothby hated meanness or betrayal: his staunchness to friends was legendary. Conversely Harold struck some people as a man who 'specialises in disloyalties', as an unkind critic once told Woolton.

An over-regulated mind shall be its own punishment, as St Augustine ought to have written. Harold's earnest, intellectualised, withdrawn approach to life gave Dorothy little excitement or sympathy. Boothby gave her both. He was a heavy drinker and enthusiastic trencherman (whereas Harold was indifferent to food), and, with his dislike of unnecessary bounds, tended to pan-sexuality in contrast to Harold's asexuality. Boothby had the simple sense to be attracted to people who were attracted to him; he responded to the sexual desires of others, freely and generously, without worrying about labels. Though he preferred affairs with women, he had sexual contacts with other men; in attesting to the variety of his inclinations he had become a versatile and imaginative lover. All accounts of his affair with Dorothy in its early years make it sound like an overwhelming sexual obsession. Dorothy wanted Boothby badly, and he was the sort of man who was excited by such a need.

The biographers of Boothby and Harold have both been men, and neither has shown much sympathy for Dorothy. To Sir Robert Rhodes James she was 'exceptionally selfish . . . craved excitement and drama . . . highly sexed . . . and eager'. Alistair Horne recognises her contribution to Harold's career, but has quoted the comment of a member of the family who saw a photograph of Dorothy revealing a faint moustache: 'At last I know what it was that Bob saw in her.' It seems harsh to revile a woman as selfish for seeking satisfaction after a decade with a man whom she had married when she was simply a naive child. It is glib to blame her for enjoying the excitement of multiple sentiments; human love ought to be inexhaustible, rather than rationed or stinted.

Nevertheless there is no denying that the affair agonised all concerned. Dorothy herself was torn apart. 'Why did you ever wake me?' she reproached Boothby while on a Continental holiday with him in 1932. 'I never want to see any of my family again. . . . without you, life for me is going to be nothing but one big hurt.' Her conduct was a mixture of public propriety, private indulgence and that talent for self-deception which she shared with her two men. She abandoned sexual relations with Harold, and declared her fidelity to Boothby, who was the father of her last child Sarah, born in 1930. For Boothby the affair was 'misery (with glorious, but oh so transitory, reprieves)'. His life had 'no basis and no meaning', he wrote in 1932. 'Just an interminable series of agonising "goodbyes" . . . living always for the "next time". Work to hell. Nerves to hell.' Dorothy was, he wrote in the following year, 'the most formidable thing in the world – a possessive single-track woman. She wants me, completely, and she wants my children, and she wants practically nothing else. At every crucial moment she acts instinctively and overwhelmingly.' He was in the thrall of her sexual need. By contrast Harold as a cuckold was forlorn, pathetic and felt deeply humiliated. He adored Dorothy in his ethereal way, and suffered grievously from the fact that her adultery was so flagrant. The strength of his feelings was shown by an outburst at the time of the Abdication Crisis in 1936. As King Edward VIII was forced from his throne for his wish to marry a divorcee, Harold congratulated the Prime Minister, Baldwin, on his handling of the affair. He seldom admired Baldwin's words or deeds in the 1930s, but on this occasion applauded his party leader for upholding the sacredness of marriage vows. It was a calamity that Christian morals were collapsing, he told Baldwin, and they would be devastated if the government yielded to the king.

The Victorian veto on the exposure of society notorieties was as strong as ever in inter-war Britain. Nothing that could encourage social indiscipline was permissible. Broader-minded

aristocrats – contemporaries of Harty-Tarty and the Duchess
of Manchester, for example – had always sanctioned marital
infidelity so long as it was discreet. As Lord Dufferin wrote of
London society in 1887, 'Not only do half the ladies appear
to sleep with other women's husbands, but they announce the
fact without any compunction to half a dozen of their female
friends at five o'clock tea.' But marital sensations, particularly
when publicised for the multitude, were deplored. The divorce
of Lord and Lady Colin Campbell in 1886 was 'a disgusting
affair . . . doing infinite mischief', Sir William Gregory reported
to Lord Dufferin. 'In the Parks every Sunday, orators declaim
against the vices of the aristocracy, and there is not a kitchen
servant's hall in which the *Evening Standard* is not taken in
and the full details discussed. The consequence is that every ear
and eye of the domestic is on the watch and the most innocent
action of masters and mistresses are suspect.' Twenty years
later the journalistic moraliser John Snead-Cox complained
to the Parliamentary Committee on Stage Censorship of 1909
about dramatists who misled 'working men and women' into
believing that 'the principal occupation of the leisured classes
is . . . matrimonial intrigue'. The horror of this to Snead-Cox
was 'that it seems to lend to vice the prestige of fashion, and the
palliation of the example of the rich'. It was under the influence
of these conventions that Nellie urged Harold not to jeopardise
his political career by giving Dorothy the divorce which she
craved; under this influence too Boothby shied away from a
divorce that would bring him political ruin: 'The Power urge
and the Love urge [are] waging this terrific hellish battle within
me,' he wrote in 1933. Involvement in a divorce was considered
an inexcusable impropriety by official Britain long after the
1930s: Henry Hunloke, who had married Dorothy's sister Anne
Cavendish, resigned as an MP in 1944 after he had left her for
another woman; a decade later Anthony Eden's succession as
prime minister was denounced by his rival Rab Butler's wife on
the grounds that a divorced man should never hold the supreme
political office; and individuals who had undergone a divorce

were still barred by the Lord Chamberlain's Office from the Royal Enclosure at Ascot race-course at the time of Harold's premiership.

The effect of Dorothy's affair with Boothby on the Macmillan children was unhelpful. It brought Harold and his son Maurice together: in 1933 they cruised together in the eastern Mediterranean, temporarily breaking down some of the sad reserve which usually inhibited their dealings. (The regime of parental inattention to Maurice was all the stranger because he was their only son, destined to take over the publishing business, to the perpetuation of which there was absolute dedication in the family.) Maurice also reciprocated Boothby's protective affection for him, and as adults their relations remained warm. But overall the egocentricity of Dorothy's passion perhaps aggravated Maurice's feeling of being unwanted. One of her daughters, as an adult, was unforgiving of the pain and disruption which her mother's affair had caused. Others who may lack sympathy with the sexual independence of women have blamed the domestic turmoil for contributing to the alcoholism of her children, but this is an unacceptable attempt to fix guilt on her. The fact is that acute alcoholism was nicknamed 'the Cavendish disease', and some of her children had inherited a tragic disposition to it, for which her liaison can scarcely be blamed. Sarah's life, as will be described in the next chapter, was shaken by her discovery as a young woman that she was not Harold's daughter but Boothby's bastard; but it was ruined by a different trauma. Nevertheless the tension of family life at Birch Grove was strainful. Dorothy made little effort to hide the existence of her intrigue from the older children. The double family of the Macmillans had been superseded by a separated family: while Harold sat reading in one room at Birch Grove, Dorothy and the children amused themselves in another room at the far end of a corridor running the length of the great house. A family friend, Quentin Crewe, felt that Dorothy erected a barrier between Harold and their children, presenting him as a man too busy to give them attention. Harold in turn was unsure how to behave and, as in his later public life, 'assumed a persona which was unnatural and stilted and rather alarming to children'.

Some of Dorothy's sisters (perhaps the ones who competed not to sit next to Harold at Chatsworth meals) sympathised with her decision to take a lover. Her brother-in-law James Stuart developed a deep enmity against Boothby, whose political career he injured. Nellie was predictably condemnatory of Dorothy, but so, according to Harold, were others including Betty Cavendish, who had married Bobbety Cranborne. The opinion of other Macmillans was probably less important to Harold, but Dan did not show him sympathy on any score, and himself some years later began a long and unsecretive affair. Others in political society involved themselves in a way that nowadays seems ill-judged or meddlesome. A weekend party at Lympne was dominated by the sensation that Dorothy had 'absconded' with Boothby, and afterwards its host Sir Philip Sassoon made desperate attempts to interfere in the marital triangle. 'It was to be the scandal of the month, affecting everybody one way or another because we were so fond of them and didn't want anybody to get hurt,' recalled Lord Beaverbrook's daughter Janet. 'The reverberations of this social earthquake were felt far and wide, the tremors spreading out over the years to touch people who were nowhere near the epicentre when it happened.' The interference of people like Sassoon heightened the pain which Harold endured; all that can be said in mitigation is that his ordeal imbued him with a resilience and ruthlessness that contributed to his later political successes. He might have said, in the words of David Copperfield, 'As the endurance of my childish days had done its part to make me what I was, so greater calamities would nerve me on, to be yet better than I was.' But in the short term he was driven to a nervous breakdown in 1931. Once again Nellie intervened, despatching him to a sanatorium in Bavaria for several months of recuperation.

During these bad years of 1929–31 Harold continued hard at work as a publisher and contemplated his political future.

He tried to find a less marginal constituency than Stockton, nearer to London; but after coquetting with the Conservative constituency party at Hitchin, he was readopted as candidate at Stockton. His negotiations were complicated by his evident disaffection with the Conservative Party, and indeed with traditional party divisions. As early as 1927, in a debate on the Trades Disputes Bill, Harold warned that there were signs of 'the beginning of reactionary policy' which in turn would mean that both of the major parties would be 'captured by the extremists'. He felt that the Conservatives deserved their defeat in the general election of 1929 for their failure to reduce unemployment. His position became more controversial in 1930, when *The Times* published a letter from him commending Sir Oswald Mosley for having resigned as Chancellor of the Duchy of Lancaster in Ramsay MacDonald's Labour government in protest at its failure to implement promised measures to reduce unemployment. Some phrases of his letter caused deep offence and reveal the basis of his estrangement from orthodox party politics. 'The mere suggestion that election promises ought to be implemented seems to have . . . deeply shocked what are called "moderate men" of all parties,' he wrote. 'It is a novel and dangerous experiment, which might, if it were allowed to pass unchallenged, spread later on into a fantastic experiment, with serious and even devastating effects.' He felt that both party hierarchies had united to break Mosley and to condemn his proposals unheard, but many of his colleagues resented this sarcastic truth-telling about their necessary and institutionalised systems of mendacity.

'Mosley's advance is rather disquieting, and I think he will impose on young men of all parties,' the Conservative statesman Lord Bridgeman predicted in 1930 to the party chairman, J.C.C. Davidson: 'Harold Macmillan will probably join him ere long.' In the event, Harold was too wily to clamber aboard Mosley's careering political vehicle, the New Party, an extra-parliamentary group which soon veered towards fascism; but his association with Mosley in 1930–1 remained an important influence on his political thinking even after their paths had diverged. One tangible example of this influence was Macmillan's recruitment as his personal economic adviser of Allan Young, an ex-Marxist Clydesider who resigned as secretary of Mosley's New Party when it turned fascistic but whose ideas on regenerating the industrial economy seemed striking and constructive. It was Young who accompanied Macmillan on a visit to Russia in 1932.

In the general election of 1931 Harold was re-elected as Conservative MP for Stockton, the exigencies of the campaign forcing him to return from his Bavarian sanatorium and speeding his recovery from his breakdown. Dorothy campaigned energetically for him in the constituency, although she was in the depths of her thrall to Boothby. She made a feint of marital felicity, offered her public sacrifices to the idols of domestic conformity, and then returned to her lover. Her help for Harold at this time has since been presented as a marvellous example of loyalty, although it must have given a painfully complicated message to Harold, especially as the couple reverted to separate existences after the election. (Another tortuous decision was that of Boothby to marry Dorothy's cousin Diana Cavendish, although the marriage was dissolved after two years in 1937.)

The election of 1931 had been called after the Prime Minister, Ramsay MacDonald, had parted from most of his Labour colleagues and reconstructed the government as a Conservative-dominated coalition with some Liberal support. This revolution in parliamentary alignments was provoked by the unrelenting economic crisis, and especially by the need to restore financial confidence to save the pound sterling's tie to the Gold Standard. MacDonald expected this so-called national government to be a temporary expedient, but in the event he found himself trapped in a preponderantly Conservative coalition which continued in power until the outbreak of war. Despite failing to save the Gold Standard, the national government leaders presented themselves as national saviours; and by tricks of presentation this pretence was sustained for years. The coalition's two leaders, MacDonald and Baldwin, were consummate politicians who offered to the public the quintessence of False Selves. MacDonald was superbly confident on public platforms, charming and magnetic in his political dealings; but his diaries reveal a grieving, wounded and severely depressed inner man throughout the years of his greatest power. His mother never married, and he did not know his father. His childhood awareness of his illegitimacy was crucial to his adult character, as his biographer recognised. 'Lacking a secure identity, he made an identity for himself; belonging nowhere, he was determined to behave as if he could belong anywhere.' Baldwin too offered a false public personality to protect his tautly controlled bundle of conflicting tensions. To the world he posed as a bluff Worcestershire squire reflectively scratching the backs of his pigs and drawing on his pipe; yet behind the pose of a simple, homely, unexcitable countryman he was a passionate man who was strangulated by his nerves. His anxieties about his own stability were translated into anxieties about wider social disorder, and a fixation with subduing anything unsettling or unconventional, whether social, budgetary or political, under the blanket of his false calm. All political epochs are based on chimera and imposture; politicians not only habitually tell lies, but generally need to live lies; yet there is a sense in which (with leaders like MacDonald and Baldwin) the 1930s were supremely a time when, as A.J.P. Taylor concluded, 'façade became reality for a generation'.

In the distribution of government appointments that followed the election of 1931, Harold was one of the few of the younger intellectual Conservative MPs to be unrewarded. As colleagues like Rab Butler, Duff Cooper and Anthony Eden received their under secretaryships and climbed the slippery pole to political pre-eminence, he was left abject and discontented on the backbenches. He was hampered by his reputation as a pedestrian speaker and fretful theorist. A few years later Lord Crawford, an old friend of the Cavendishes, typically denigrated him as 'overprone to philander with the Socialists' and 'pontificat[ing] with greater gusto' than any other MP. Harold's nervousness remained excruciating. He was not one of those politicians like Ernest Bevin for whom public speaking was no harder than breathing. At the Jewellers Company Dinner in 1938 Elizabeth Pakenham (afterwards Countess of Longford) was seated beside Harold, who was due to make one of the evening's speeches. 'So tense was the future "unflappable" Prime Minister that he addressed not a word to either of his dinner partners but spent the whole time correcting and re-correcting his speech in different coloured inks.' Harold's failure to win political promotion was also due to the way in which his admiration for Lloyd George and Mosley gave the impression of a man who was too easily duped by political crooks. His admiration for these dubious characters led him into attacks on the national government's leaders which destroyed his chances of a government appointment. Baldwin and MacDonald 'have elevated inactivity into a principle and feebleness into a virtue', he wrote in an article of 1936, and his comments about Neville Chamberlain were scarcely less sardonic. The national leaders returned his antipathy, MacDonald in 1935 describing him as a 'conceited ass'.

The onslaught of unemployment at Stockton grew more terrible in 1932–3. Its growth made Harold more urgent in his pleadings that the national economy should be reinflated. In speeches, articles and pamphlets he recommended a house-building programme to restimulate the economy, the provision of cheap money for industrial borrowers, the institution of a corporatist investment and development board and other measures. In 1933 his book *Reconstruction*, the first to be published under his sole name, advocated cartelisation of industry, with each industrial sector self-governing through a national industrial council. He proposed that these industrial councils would be represented on a central economic council sitting under the chairmanship of a Cabinet minister. His somewhat bureaucratic proposals harked back to some of the corporatist structures favoured by his hero Lloyd George's wartime advisers, and resembled the proposals made by Dudley Docker, the founding president of the Federation of British Industries, as early as 1916. They were given a more sophisticated gloss by the influence of the writings of Keynes on Macmillan's thinking; but after reading *Reconstruction* Ramsay MacDonald judged that Macmillan's programme was 'Socialism with nothing new but the argument that it is not Socialism'. Other politicians looked equally askance, although literary folk were more impressed: 'I'm glad the young conservatives are waking up,' Aldous Huxley wrote to T.S. Eliot in 1934. 'There seemed to be a lot of sense in Harold Macmillan's contentions.'

Reconstruction was followed by the publication in 1938 of Harold's political testament, *The Middle Way*. This daunting and scarcely readable volume of 400 pages (packed with statistics collected by Allan Young) included many prescriptions for his country's economic ills which seemed revolutionary at the time: the nationalisation of the coalmines and of the Bank of England, for example (both measures implemented a decade later by Attlee's Labour government). He hoped to eliminate speculation by replacing the Stock Exchange with a national investment board; to improve diet and the efficiency of food distribution by the institution of a national nutrition board; and much else along these lines. The institutional innovations which he proposed foreshadowed some of the bodies inaugurated during his premiership, like the National Economic Development Council of government representatives, trade unionists and business people set up in 1961. His book had a respectful reception among economists, but was found less convincing by parliamentarians. The elaborateness of Macmillan's proposals had already provoked the objection that he had too much faith in 'Boards and then more Boards', to quote the Minister of Labour, Ernest Brown, 'to solve the great problems with which we are confronted'.

There was no love lost between Brown and Macmillan, as shown during a parliamentary debate of 1935 on regional unemployment. The government's case was put by Brown, and closed by another minister, Lord Eustace Percy. 'Both very bad, partly because the Government had nothing to say,' noted Harry Crookshank, by now a minister himself . 'Ernest shouted and yelled, and Eustace was sarcastic.' After Percy finished speaking, 'in the two minutes that remained Harold got up and in two sentences damned the Government, but the . . . debate closed at 11 and so the thing got talked out, amongst general hubbub.' In the moments allowed to him before the debate was guillotined, Harold likened Lord Eustace Percy to Pontius Pilate and denounced Brown for failing to answer any of the 'great questions of public policy' raised: Brown's speech had 'depressed the House to the lowest level of depression', Harold declared, 'since this Government came into office'. From 1933 onwards Harold was one of a bevy of political mavericks seeking a new consensus. They wanted to introduce to British politics some equivalent of the Popular Front in France, where in 1936 the Radicals led a broad-based left-wing coalition to an overwhelming election victory over increasingly violent and desperate right-wing parties. The French Popular Front offered a comprehensive programme of social and political reforms, including schemes of public works, a national grain board, state control of the Bank of France, the nationalisation of private armaments factories, more generous old-age pensions and unemployment relief, and a shorter working week. There were many similarities between the Popular Front's programmes and the ideas in *Reconstruction* and *The Middle Way*, although Harold wrote from the position of a proto-Keynesian who favoured the survival of capitalism rather than the triumph of socialism. He feared that the last hope of forestalling class warfare or social insurrection lay in some species of democratic radicalism. In most respects there was little difference of intention between the Conservative-based coalition national government and Macmillan's idea of a Popular Front. They both wished to ensure conditions in which – despite universal suffrage – a minority group (the Conservative Party) could

hold an electorate which was far more broadly based than
the Cavendishes and their sons-in-law. One of the latter was
John Cobbold, a Suffolk squire who was chairman of a small
family brewery, and some people thought that he was the target
of at least one of Harold's jibes, when he told a journalist in
1936 that 'a party dominated by second-class brewers and
company promoters – a Casino Capitalism – is not likely to
represent anybody but itself'. It was not surprising that when,
in the general election of the previous year, the Liberals put
up a spoiling candidate at Stockton against Harold, who was
consequently expected to lose to Labour, a junior member of
the national government, Lord De La Warr, commented, 'Tory
Head Office is delighted, and the Liberals as left-wingers are
simply cutting off their nose to spite their face.' In the event
Harold defeated his Labour challenger by about 4,000 votes.

Harold's estrangement from conventional party politics led
him into involvement with a succession of extra-parliamentary,
non-partisan groups. In 1933, for example, he called a meeting
of economists and businessmen at his house to discuss the
foundation of an economic institute to analyse the prevailing
economic crisis and 'to bring the pressure of an informed public
opinion to bear on our National Government'. Three years later
he was the only Conservative MP to attend a conference called
by the Fabian Society to press the need for union amalgamations
to strengthen collective bargaining. Among the audience was
a young trade unionist named James Callaghan, who served
his time well enough to become prime minister in the 1970s.
'I can still recall him,' Callaghan wrote half a century later:
'elegantly dressed, precise in speech, almost artificial in manner, but the delegates were ready to forgive his mannerisms
for it was a coup to have him with us.' Harold moved a
resolution urging the government to relieve unemployment by
a programme of public works, and in Callaghan's words, 'his
earnestness made us forget his manner and carried us along
with him'.

In the mid-1930s Harold gave great attention to the Next

Five Years Group, which formulated a radical industrial programme for Britain partly inspired by Roosevelt's New Deal, but
his behaviour was antagonistic. First he hijacked the Group's
newspaper, *New Outlook*, to propagate the case for a Popular
Front, based on a programme of collective security, abolition
of the means test, help for distressed areas, tariff reduction
and the extension of public control over industry. There were
further ructions when he tried to jockey the Group into an
alliance with Lloyd George's grandiloquently titled Council of
Action, which was a factious vehicle for the Welsh Wizard's
personal advancement. The chairman of the Group's executive,
Lord Allen of Hurtwood, warned that its influence would be
destroyed if it was submerged in a Popular Front working with
Lloyd George, and found Harold self-seeking and manipulative
in working to that end. As an increasingly 'ugly' mood developed in the Group, Allen told its executive bluntly 'that much
of the trouble has been due to one man, Mr Macmillan', trying
to arrogate all the power of the organisation; Alfred Barratt
Brown, the Group's secretary, condemned Harold's behaviour
as 'brutally pugnacious' and 'incredibly ungentlemanly'. After
the disagreements had become excessive, the Group wound
itself up in 1937.

As international relations deteriorated after 1935, Harold
became a dissentient from the national government's foreign
policy as well. The independence of his views had become
marked by December of that year, when the Foreign Secretary,
Sir Samuel Hoare, signed the infamous Hoare–Laval Pact,
which by allowing Mussolini to continue the Italian invasion of
Abyssinia with impunity signalled the destruction of the League
of Nations and the abandonment of the British commitment
to collective security. Ordinary opinion in the Conservative
Party favoured this emergent policy of appeasement. Walter
Buccleuch, the Scottish Duke whom Evie Devonshire had once
hoped that Dorothy would marry, wrote in commiseration to
Hoare after tumultuous protests at the provisions of the pact
had forced him to resign as Foreign Secretary: 'They were rather

too much for most people to swallow in a hurry, but the only possible and practical suggestions for a peaceful solution.' He regretted only 'that you were prevented from bringing off a really big thing, which would have helped our country so much in every way'. Buccleuch was typical of the Conservative majority which no longer believed that Britain had the will to enforce its commitments. Harold on the other hand indignantly derided the 'official and semi-official apologists' for what had happened. He recognised the Hoare–Laval Pact as a crisis in the survival of the League of Nations and was outraged that the government's recent general election commitment to maintain collective security should be reneged. It was unforgivable 'to undermine the very structure which a few weeks ago the nation authorised us to underpin'. Worse still, having failed to honour its pledges, the national government had no clear policy to offer instead.

When in 1936 the government abandoned the economic sanctions which had been imposed against Italy after the Abyssinian invasion, Harold was one of only two Conservative MPs to vote against the government. A few days later he resigned the whip, sitting as an Independent Conservative in the Commons until 1937, when he resumed the party whip after Neville Chamberlain had replaced Baldwin as prime minister. Yet his disruptions and dissent continued.

After Eden's resignation as foreign secretary in February 1938, Harold together with two other backbench dissidents, Ronald Cartland and Churchill's son-in-law Duncan Sandys, discussed with Labour leaders the possibility of a tripartite electoral alliance including some remnants of the Liberal Party. He was hoping to install a new, alternative coalition government composed of most of the parliamentary elements which were excluded from or opposed to the existing national government. Some limited procedural co-operation in the House of Commons was agreed as a result of these talks, but the three opposition groups did not work together at by-elections, until the great contest at Oxford. In September 1938, as Hitler's troops menaced Czechoslovakia, Chamberlain flew to Munich, and made an accord with the Nazis which marked the apotheosis of his appeasement policy. In response Liberals and some Conservatives worked with Labour sympathisers in the by-election which had been called for October in Oxford; this coalition of forces supported A.D. Lindsay, the Master of Balliol, who stood as an Independent anti-appeasement candidate against the official Conservative, the young and bumptious Quintin Hogg. Harold saw in Lindsay's candidature the long-awaited opportunity of creating a Popular Front against the national government; courageously, he endorsed Lindsay's candidature both in speech and in writing. Opponents of the Munich agreement rallied to the support of Lindsay, with his campaign slogan 'A vote for Hogg is a vote for Hitler'. 'So . . . Oxford went to the polls,' Louis MacNeice wrote afterwards, 'and made its coward vote and the streets resounded / to the triumphant cheers of the lost souls – the profiteers, the dunderheads, the smarties.' When Hogg was elected with an ignominiously reduced majority, Harold was heaped with opprobrium by fellow Conservatives for his disloyalty to the party. 'At Grillions Eden was fussing and fidgeting . . . vain as a peacock with all the mannerisms of the petit maître,' Lord Crawford recorded shortly afterwards: 'Macmillan M.P., who has just distinguished himself by supporting the Master of Balliol in the Oxford by-election, kept pumping sedition into his ear.'

Animosities grew and resignations continued. To Harold's delight and admiration, Duff Cooper resigned in October 1938 as First Lord of the Admiralty in protest at the Munich agreement. On Guy Fawkes Day in November the Macmillans built a bonfire at Birch Grove and burnt a guy dressed to resemble Neville Chamberlain, provoking the wrath of other members of the family (perhaps including Dorothy's brothers-in-law Stuart and Cobbold, who both behaved with vindictive rage towards a former Conservative MP, the Duchess of Atholl, who stood as an anti-appeasement candidate in a by-election at this time). In December three junior members of the government – the

Marquess of Dufferin and Ava, Robert Hudson and Lord Strathcona and Mountroyal – ominously joined in complaint to Chamberlain that four Cabinet mediocrities, Hore-Belisha, Inskip, Runciman and Winterton were dangerously incompetent and that national defence was hopelessly unprepared. Other members of the government, Lord Feversham, Kenneth Lindsay and Harold's friend Crookshank, were also concerned in the rebellion. In March 1939 when, six months after the Munich agreement, German troops marched into Prague, the last justification of appeasement was ruined; none but the most desperate appeasers could feel sure of Chamberlain's policy. The Chamberlainites waited helplessly on events or feverishly denied that anything more would happen, although the Italian invasion of Albania belied their hopes. Cabinet ministers vied with one another in optimistic assurances to the country, and one of them coined the soubriquet 'Jitterbugs' for those like Harold who still sounded notes of warning.

Harold was enraged that Chamberlain remained in power and railed against the Edenites for lacking the ruthlessness to overturn him. He was sickened by the obsequious stupidity of the appeasers. 'If Chamberlain says that black is white, the Tories applaud his brilliance,' Harold told a new political ally, Harold Nicolson, in April 1939. 'If a week later he says that black is after all black, they applaud his realism. Never has there been such servility.' Towards the end of that tense and miserable summer, Harold left for a cruise with one of his Great Western Railway colleagues, Lord Portal, a lavish host of gargantuan appetites who had added to his porcine reputation by becoming an expert in pig marketing. When Portal's yacht docked at Poole on 23 August, Harold first heard confirmation of the Molotov–Ribbentrop Pact between Soviet Russia and Nazi Germany, and knew that the outbreak of war was imminent.

It was a measure of Harold's isolation under the Chamberlainite regime that he obtained no war work until January 1940. In that month the Cabinet approved the formation of a semi-official committee to organise aid to Finland, which had been invaded by Soviet troops, and to recruit a volunteer international force to fight alongside the Finns. Harold joined the committee and in February visited Finland with his colleague Lord Davies (a fellow director of the Great Western). British and French support for the Finns was half-hearted, arguably for good strategic reasons, and a few days after Harold's return to London in March the Finns capitulated to the Russians. The British government's efforts to distance themselves from this débâcle outraged Harold and, rather than accept their disclaimer as propaganda to cover a reverse, he interpreted official statements as another instance of Chamberlainite duplicity. In a speech to the House of Commons on 19 March, he indicted British involvement in the Finnish campaign and went far in convicting Chamberlain of misstating the facts; it was a speech which was still remembered two months later, when the House debated the fiasco of the Norwegian campaign. It was this debate in May which tore away the last vestiges of Chamberlain's authority and resulted in his replacement as prime minister by Churchill. Harold and a Labour MP excitedly sang 'Rule Britannia', to the resentment of Chamberlain, 'who rose looking old and white-haired', Rab Butler recounted, 'and marched out realising, as he did, that he could not go on'.

In forming his administration, Churchill offered an indemnity to his opponents and oblivion for his friends. Typically while Chamberlain's Chief Whip, David Margesson, was promoted to be Secretary of State for War, Harold (despite his talents, admirable record and long vigil on the backbenches) was merely appointed parliamentary secretary to the newly instituted Ministry of Supply. There was amusement in the House of Commons at his blatant delight in his new job – 'he rushed frenziedly about', Chips Channon recorded – but it was tempered with respect, for Harold had persistently urged upon reluctant Chamberlainites the formation of a separate ministry of politicians, business people, economists and officers to co-ordinate the war economy.

A retrospect in 1940 of Harold's backbench career would have been an inglorious story. If he had been killed when returning from Finland, or like colleagues in the parliamentary YMCA such as Noel Skelton and Terence O'Connor he had not survived beyond 1940, then like them he would not now provide even a footnote to British political history; he would be remembered only in a few society memoirs as the irredeemably dull first husband of that redoubtable political hostess of the 1940s and 1950s, Lady Dorothy Boothby. But he was a great survivor, and his career now can be seen in a longer perspective. In 1857 his grandfather had published *Tom Brown's Schooldays*, in which good old squire Brown said of his son, 'If he'll only turn out a brave, helpful, truth-telling Englishman, and a gentleman, and a good Christian, that's all I want.' This was the ideal that Harold met in the 1930s. Of course he was priggish, fretful, neutered, boring and fawning; but he was also exceptionally brave, surviving blows and hurts that would sunder most people, always indomitable when rejected and courageous when dejected. At Stockton and in other concentrations of mass unemployment he tried to be helpful; in politics, with all the inflexibility of a bookish man, he was insistently and reiteratively truth-telling. Long after it had ceased to be discreet or effective he nagged away with his version of the truth about the national government's empty policies. One of the impressions that emerges most strongly of Harold in the 1930s is the naive sincerity of his indignation when election pledges were broken or lies were told. Veracity was highly valued by him. He had a profound belief in the truth, and incomprehension of deceit. In the years of his political ascent, and in the glory of his political apogee, many of these virtues would be corrupted. The trappings of office, after all, usually prove to be the shackles of integrity.

CHAPTER 8

The Servant of Fame

Men in *Great Place* are thrice *Servants*: Servants of the Sovereign or State; Servants of Fame; and Servants of Business. So as they have no Freedom; neither in their Persons; nor in their Actions; nor in their Times. It is a strange desire, to seek Power, and to lose Liberty; or to seek Power over others, and to lose Power over a Man's Self. The Rising unto *Place* is Laborious; And by Pains Men come to greater Pains; And it is sometimes base; and by Indignities, Men come to Dignities.

Francis Bacon, 'Of Great Place'

He is thought to have been a hypocrite for the sake of power; whereas, in fact, he was sincere until power by degrees made him a hypocrite.

Walter Savage Landor, 'William Penn'

The 1940s were the decade of Harold's enlargement and liberation. He was promoted to high political office: as the British Minister Resident in the Mediterranean in the last years of the war his power was more absolute than at any other time in his life. He found at last a great arena for his False Self: in his preoccupation with public affairs he found some quiescence for private anxieties; in power politics he escaped from the dismal insistence of daily living. For years he had been in that state described by Matthew Arnold as wandering between two worlds, one dead, the other powerless to be born. The war years finally brought his rebirth. He had always had great capacities, but only now did he learn how to use them. The rejections which he had suffered during the 1930s at home and in parliament had raised a huge charge of resentment in him. Let loose in the 1940s this resentment took the form of an urge for power that was hard, irrefragable and shameless. He came to present the paradox of a literary-minded intellectual with some old Christian Socialist ideals whose sympathies nevertheless sometimes narrowed to those of a caged rat. He had dwelt so long in his own thoughts that they had taken him prisoner; but, when his duties as Minister Resident forced him into the outer world, he became instead the captive of power. He experienced reality as a system of power, and felt better when exercising power than he had ever felt before. 'He has grown in stature during the war more than anyone,' Sir Robert Bruce Lockhart observed in 1946. 'He was always clever, but shy and diffident, had a clammy handshake and was more like a wet fish than a man. Now he is full of confidence and . . . speaks brilliantly.' In the adversities of war Harold finally proved his mettle and found his opportunity.

The great changes in Harold were inseparable from the great changes in public life. At the time the coalition government which took office in 1940 under Churchill's leadership seemed to be only an improvisation arising from the political alliances which had developed to oppose Chamberlain since 1938. In fact the coalition was the beginning of a new regime, for it brought to office a host of new servants of State, Fame and Business, among whom were several theorists of social equality and national regeneration like Harold. The Labour Party was an almost equal partner in the coalition, and even at the height of wartime mobilisation it spread a new reforming zeal in government circles. By the spring of 1943 preparations were under way to introduce not only universal social security, family allowances, educational reforms, a state-funded health service and town and country planning, but also the full employment policies and greater state intervention in industry which Harold had urged. The adoption of Keynesian budgetary techniques was imminent. Fatalists like Ernest Brown and Walter Runciman who had exasperated Harold in the 1930s by their despairing, hidebound, do-nothing policies were ousted. By 1944 one young man could tell the journalist J.L. Hodson, 'We've virtually exploded the arguments of old fogies and Better-Notters who said we can't afford this and mustn't do that.'

Yet the beginnings of Harold's power were not magnificent. An under secretaryship, as Lord Hugh Cecil once told Winston Churchill, was 'only a stipendiary echo'. As Under Secretary at the Ministry of Supply Harold had to answer questions for the Minister in the House of Commons on mundane subjects such as salvage work or the collection of scrap-metal for use in munitions production. He found parliamentary question-time a nerve-racking ordeal, and continued to irritate some MPs by the manner of his replies. As an administrator he was more effective. The thought and energy which in the 1930s he had given to designing the great interlocking machinery of a corporatist state – the cartels, industrial and regional boards, consultative committees – proved valuable in building the structure of a wartime economy geared to maximum productive output.

The first Minister of Supply under whom he worked was Herbert Morrison, Labour leader of the London County Council in peacetime. Five years earlier Morrison had been a favoured candidate of Harold and others for leadership of a Popular Front in Britain, although Morrison had dismissed such notions as 'romantic nonsense'. At the Ministry of Supply the two men worked hard together; Harold found little difficulty in collaborating with a socialist, and facetiously told the Commons in 1940 that but for the resistance of the Labour Party he would be introducing state socialism to Britain. The German invasion of Russia in 1941 resulted in new demands on the Ministry to provide tanks and munitions for Stalin's embattled troops. Churchill chose the Canadian press lord, Beaverbrook, to take charge as Minister. Beaverbrook was among the most malign influences to corrupt public life in his generation; but, despite his deceits, treacheries, bullying and self-promotion, he advanced the war effort, not only galvanising the efforts of the Ministry of Supply, but also cheering Churchill when he was beset by melancholia. Again Harold worked well with his Minister, although neither man trusted the other. Harold thought Beaverbrook 'half mad and half genius', so he told Harold Nicolson in 1941.

It is not enough to succeed, as Gore Vidal says; others must fail. As Harold's star rose, Boothby's fell. The latter in 1940 undermined his standing with Churchill by sending him a frantic expostulation that 'the War Cabinet should be replaced by a Committee of Public Safety' (of all preposterously Jacobinical phrases) holding 'absolute and omnipotent powers' with parliament virtually suspended. In the following year Boothby was forced from office after being detected in a business indiscretion, and languished for the rest of his career on the backbenches. With some of that defiance of moral conformity which had characterised his affair with Dorothy, Boothby in 1953 initiated the long parliamentary struggle for the decriminalisation of homosexual acts which culminated in the Sexual Offences Act of 1967. Given his bisexual sympathies, this required moral courage at a time when more committedly homosexual parliamentarians were intimidated into silence: his robust speeches about sexual prejudice and ridicule of homophobia drew the grubby interest of the *Sunday Mirror*, which in 1964 paid him huge damages after implying that he was the lover of the East End gangster Ronald Kray. Boothby's public commitment to sexual liberty was admirable; but otherwise he degenerated into a braggart and parliamentary buffoon about whom derisive stories circulated. Simon Raven regaled many with his account of the Bumper Bob Boothby Disaster of 1951. Raven, who was exuberantly bisexual, joined Dadie Rylands (the quintessence of a lovable Cambridge bachelor don) and Maurice Bowra (an uninhibitedly bisexual Oxford classicist) in Boothby's spanking new Rolls-Royce to visit the Festival of Britain in Lambeth.

> At first we were denied admission to the site – but then the gatekeeper recognised Bob Boothby and bowed us through. When we drove up near the buildings some late workers also recognised him and raised quite a satisfying 'Hoorah for Bob Boothby'. As we departed the gate-keeper threw up a smart military salute – to Bob Boothby. As we drove towards the Athenaeum Bob himself took up the topic – of Bob Boothby: how he had been cheered and saluted, how he was dressed in his new and splendid suit and was driving in his new and peerless car, and how privileged we were to be driving with him . . . until, as Bob reached a crescendo of self-applause, there was suddenly that well-known choking noise and one of us in the back (never ask me who) was sick all over Boothby's new suit and Boothby's new car and Boothby's quacking head, as neat an instance of hubris and nemesis as ever I heard of.

Others too were unsure whether Boothby's bombast was risible or sick-making.

Although most of Harold's duties at the Ministry of Supply were monochromatic, some colourful people came his way. Foremost among these was his young private secretary, John Wyndham, a key figure in the Macmillan story, whose deceptively flippant manner was a cover for a character as sensitive and highly strung as Harold's. As nephew and heir not only to Lord Leconfield but to 70,000 acres and the two great houses of Petworth in Sussex and Cockermouth in Cumberland, Wyndham was as superb a grandee as any Cavendish. One anecdote among many conveys the grandeur of his family. After Wyndham's marriage in 1947, he took his wife to meet his uncle Charles at Petworth. Looking out on a summer's day over the park laid out by Capability Brown with a stretch of water about the size of the Serpentine in the foreground, wishing to please as well as being entranced by the view, she exclaimed at the beauty of the 'lake'. An ominous silence followed, broken by Lord Leconfield replying in his most crushing manner: 'My dear young lady, one day your husband will inherit from me not only all this, but also, among other things in Cumberland, half Derwentwater, the whole of Bassenthwaite Lake and the whole of Wastwater, comprising in all about thirty-five square miles of lake. That which you see there is not a lake. It is a *pond*.' Wyndham's limitless fund of anecdotes about life in the grand manner at Petworth captivated the older man. Hitherto Harold had been disdained at Chatsworth and never tried to ape the manners of the Cavendishes. A colourless man himself, after he met Wyndham he came to crave identification with a colourful hierarchy; the vivacity and affection of their relations brought him a new fascination with the English patrician mystique. His assumption of the airs of an Edwardian grandee dated from the early days of his friendship with Wyndham. So too did his new conversational manner. Harold had always enjoyed the company of anecdotalists, but in the 1940s, under the studiously relaxed tutelage of Wyndham, he began to practise his own virtuosity as a story-teller. In the twenty years before his death he was recognised as a master of the art.

It was said of the American statesman Charles Sumner that he took for granted the rule that, just as arsenic poisoned, a friend in power was a friend lost. Harold certainly was a doubtful friend to colleagues in power, but he needed friendship at least as much as other men, and was trustworthy to people who were not his equals or rivals. It was the certainty of Wyndham's position as heir to Petworth that enabled him to be uniquely disinterested, offering a friendship that power could not poison; combined with his sensitivity and worldliness, this made him an ideal private secretary. Harold, during his years of power, depended not only on his secretary's contacts but on his peculiar sense of fun. He once recounted how he had complained to Wyndham that he had not been invited to a great party at Petworth. 'But you *were* invited,' replied Wyndham. 'I sent off the cards myself. Then, of course, as your secretary, I received the invitation, and knowing that you wouldn't want to be bothered with things like that, I wrote back and refused on your behalf.' Wyndham was 'dark, bespectacled, like a wise young owl; not demonstrative, but cynical and extremely bright': so James Lees-Milne described him in 1945, catching some of the characteristics which Harold valued most in this uncommon man. With his jokes, love of literature and artistic taste Wyndham was of a similar pattern to Harold's other friends: Sumner, Willink, Crookshank, Wheeler-Bennett, even Madan, all intelligent, literate raconteurs, complex men whose early hurts left them hurting without rest. Each of them – Wyndham not least – had a talent for apt quotations which delighted Harold. 'In the dying world I come from quotation is a national vice,' said an Englishman in Evelyn Waugh's *The Loved One* published in 1948; and, like Waugh, Harold repined at the victories of barbarism that darkened the 1940s. His friends' habits of literary allusion and wide, discriminate reading for pleasure were part of a rich amplitude in life which was vanishing in that stern, unrelenting decade. It was closing time in the gardens of the west.

Another young man confirmed Harold's new romantic fascination with patrician eccentricity. In 1940 Harold met the Earl of Suffolk and Berkshire, who by the age of thirty-five had been a Guards officer, merchant seaman, Australian farmhand and scientist. His scientific work was so accomplished that he had worked for Lord Nuffield's Foundation at Oxford, but he was in Paris when the Nazis invaded. Soon afterwards he arrived at the Ministry of Supply announcing that he had escaped from France on a coal-boat together with £4 million of industrial diamonds, sundry distinguished French scientists and a quantity of heavy water (which, although Harold did not yet know it, would prove essential in developing atomic weaponry). Later Suffolk formed his own Unexploded Bomb Squad comprising himself, his woman secretary and his elderly chauffeur, known as the Holy Trinity. 'Thirty-four unexploded bombs did they tackle with urbane and smiling efficiency,' as Winston Churchill wrote, 'but the thirty-fifth claimed its forfeit.' Such was the

feeling for him that the Poet Laureate, Masefield, was inspired
to commemorate Suffolk's memory:

> He loved the bright ship with the lifting wing,
> He felt the anguish of the hunted thing,
> He dared the danger which besets the guides
> Who lead men to the knowledge Nature hides;
> Probing and playing with the lightning thus
> He and his faithful friends met death for us.
> The beauty of a splendid man abides.

For Harold this young Earl, with his pointed beard and
swaggering clothes, was the one romantic hero of the war,
a latter day buccaneer whose aristocratic valour was enhanced
by the practical spirit and ingenuity of his maternal grandfather,
Levi Ziegler Leiter, the Chicago wheat tycoon. As he recalled
later, Suffolk's character was a unique mixture of dash,
originality, guts and scientific gifts.

Bombs nearly claimed Harold too. In October 1940 he was
drinking sherry with David Margesson, the Chief Whip, in the
Carlton club when it received a direct hit. 'They heard the bomb
screaming down and ducked instinctively,' as Harold Nicolson
recounted. 'There was a loud crash, the main lights went out
and the whole place was filled with the smell of cordite and the
dust of rubble. The side-lights on the tables remained alight,
glimmering murkily in the thick fog which settled down on
everything, plastering their hair and eye-brows with thick dust.'
The members of the Carlton, which was not bombed again until
Irish terrorists struck in 1990, showed aplomb under attack,
although club-land stories abound of imperturbability during
air-raids. In the midst of one committee meeting at Pratt's in
1944, there was crash from a bomb, the lights went out and the
building shook. 'Well, gentlemen,' said Harold's brother-in-law
Eddy Devonshire when the lights came on again, 'I am not quite
clear whether we elected that fellow or not.'

When Beaverbrook left the government in 1942, Harold was
promoted by Churchill to the post of Under Secretary at the
Colonial Office. Harold was depressed by the contrast between

the hectic pressure and noisy propaganda of the Ministry of Supply, which had been pokily housed in a brutally ugly office block, and the sedate traditions of the Colonial Office, which was situated in a building of cavernous elegance in Downing Street. As he knew little of colonial policy, his relations with some of his officials would have been awkward but for the emollience of John Wyndham, who was translated from the Ministry of Supply and remained his private secretary. For almost all of Harold's time as Under Secretary, his Minister was Bobbety Cranborne, an Oxford contemporary and Cavendish connection. Cranborne delegated responsibility for all trade and economic questions arising at the Office to Harold, who applied his experience from the Ministry of Supply to establishing a department to increase colonial production for war purposes of every type of commodity from rubber and tin to food. Harold was involved in implementing import controls and in devising a shipping programme for each colonial territory.

All this occurred against a darkening background of military reverses. Eighty-five thousand British troops in Singapore capitulated to the Japanese only days after Harold's appointment to the Colonial Office. A few months later 30,000 British troops surrendered at Tobruk. Politicians meanwhile pursued their twisted courses. 'How I *hate* Members of Parliament,' wrote Sir Alexander Cadogan of the Foreign Office. 'They embody everything that my training has taught me to eschew – ambition, prejudice, dishonesty, self-seeking, light-hearted irresponsibility, black-hearted mendacity.' Later in 1942, after a particularly disruptive outbreak of personal antipathies and ambitions in the Cabinet, Churchill was forced to reconstruct his government: by now Harold was aggrieved with his low status as an under secretary and making his dissatisfaction known. In November the Prime Minister discussed with Leo Amery the appointment of Harold as Viceroy of India; but the idea was abandoned on the grounds of the mental instability of the Macmillans, which had been notorious to Downing Street advisers since John Macmillan's time as Bishop of Dover.

Eventually, in December, Harold accepted a post which had just been declined by his friend Crookshank: that of Minister Resident at Allied Forces Headquarters in North Africa. The Colonial Office under secretaryship however remained in the family, for Harold's brother-in-law Devonshire held the post until 1945.

Harold installed himself with a small staff (including Wyndham) at Algiers in January 1943. The British and Americans had recently invaded French North Africa, an area which the USA claimed as a sphere of special influence. His arrival was suspect to American officers and officials in Algiers, but Harold dispelled their doubts and was soon co-operating with conspicuous success with Dwight Eisenhower, the American General who was in command of the Allied Forces in North Africa. It was an attraction of opposites: an outburst of Eisenhower's, following a spate of press criticism that he was co-operating with collaborationist French leaders, particularly delighted Harold. 'I can't understand why all those long-haired, starry-eyed boys keep gunning for me,' Ike told him. 'I ain't a cynic. Christ on the mountain, I'm as idealistic as hell.' Eisenhower was the type of decisive man of action whom Harold had admired in the Guards; he liked the soldier's unjealous and unpretentious character. A key moment in their relationship occurred in January 1943, when Harold attended the Casablanca Conference between Churchill, Roosevelt and their entourages. This was Harold's first enthralling experience of the summit diplomacy of which, in the late 1950s, he became the world's principal exponent. After arriving at Casablanca, Harold was ushered to a room where Roosevelt lay in bed with Churchill sitting by his side and Eisenhower standing to attention nearby. Roosevelt greeted him warmly, saying 'Hello, Harold, I'm glad to see you.' Eisenhower was impressed, and asked Harold afterwards why he had not mentioned that he was on forename terms with the President. In fact Harold had met Roosevelt only once before and had thought the presidential effusion insincere; more discreetly he said to Eisenhower that they had some mutual friends. 'You're funny people, you English people,' Eisenhower replied. 'If you'd been an American you would have told me this before.' Their relations relaxed after this incident, when Eisenhower began to recognise the idiosyncratic merits of the British.

Harold detected in Roosevelt a streak of anti-colonialism that he had long observed was strongest in the oldest American families. 'All my Boston friends never seem to be able to forget that trouble there was about the tea chests,' he told Sir Ian Trethowan in 1967. Roosevelt in Harold's opinion 'disliked the British Empire and did a great deal to injure it', and exploited a devious and facile charm with deplorable consequences. 'He thought he could handle Stalin better than anybody else, and that proved later at Yalta to be a great disaster.'

Much of Harold's tact and ingenuity was devoted to handling the irreconcilable French leaders in Algeria. As a fluent French speaker, Harold was more adroit than the Americans in dealings with the French, although even his resources were taxed by the difficulties of keeping the peace between Charles de Gaulle, the haughty and exasperating leader of the Free French, and some of his fellow countrymen. When de Gaulle visited London in 1943, Anthony Eden, the Foreign Secretary, said to him that the French had caused more trouble to the British than all the other allies put together. 'I don't doubt it,' de Gaulle replied with a smile, 'France is a great power.' Nevertheless the leader of the Free French was not completely unbending: later that year, when Harold asked de Gaulle's opinion of the Allies, the Frenchman replied, 'You British are so annoying, the Americans are so tiring and the Russians are so disturbing: I prefer to be annoyed rather than tired or disturbed.' As it proved, Algiers in 1943 was a forcing ground of world leaders: sixteen years later Eisenhower was President of the USA, de Gaulle was President of France and Harold was Prime Minister in Britain.

Richard Crossman, who was sent to Algiers as an expert in Psychological Warfare, has left an excellent assessmennt of the Minister Resident. 'I worked under Macmillan when he was at his peak – a dashing man of action, self-confidently poised in his behaviour, gambling on his hunches and, when we lost, as we sometimes did, loyal to his subordinates,' Crossman recalled in 1964.

> Not even the Prime Minister in Britain enjoyed quite such unquestioned prestige as Harold Macmillan had earned for himself both in his own British staff and in Ike's entourage. As a Conservative politician he had had to conceal for years the fact that he is not merely a supremely intelligent man but an intellectual who was prepared to stake everything on an idea. Among the soldiers in A.F.H.Q. these qualities brought him not suspicion but admiration, and the more he dazzled the Americans, the more fertile his mind became.

In retrospect Crossman believed that 'it was in Algiers, where he could do all the thinking and take all the decisions while Ike took all the credit, that Harold Macmillan first realised his own capacity for supreme leadership, and developed that streak of intellectual recklessness which was to be the cause both of his success and of his failure when he finally reached No 10.'

But these triumphs were nearly aborted in February 1943, when Harold came close to death in a flying accident. He was travelling from Algiers to Cairo and felt a premonition of danger from the outset. He was put in the cockpit next to the pilot during take-off, but within moments the plane careered off the runway and burst into flames. One of Harold's first thoughts was relief that the accident had happened immediately. He felt so certain of disaster that he was glad to face it immediately. His account to Dorothy of his escape is a characteristic setpiece. The pilot and navigator quickly scrambled out, but he was not as young, agile or thin, and found his way to the exit obstructed by a tangle of broken machinery. He described with studied detachment the horror of the flames creeping towards him, and his success in getting out through a small hole in the wrecked cabin just as he was despairing of his chances.

This was Harold's account of his escape, although an American official who was present claimed that he saw Harold re-enter the burning aircraft to rescue a Frenchman. Whatever the truth of this story of selfless gallantry, Harold was burnt about the face and concussed. In hospital he seems to have thought he was back at the Somme, and his first words were a message to his dead mother. During his recuperation he diverted himself reading Gibbon's *History of the Decline and Fall of the Roman Empire*, the great themes of which were capturing his imagination as he lived in the Mediterranean.

In this context Crossman's account of his first interview with Harold in Algiers in 1943 is vivid and revealing. 'Remember,' Harold told him,

> when you go to the Hotel St George, you will regularly enter a room and see an American colonel, his cigar in his mouth and his feet on the table. When your eyes get used to the darkness, you will see in a corner an English captain, his feet down, his shoulders hunched, writing like mad, with a full in-tray and a full out-tray, and no cigar. Mr Crossman, you will never call attention to this discrepancy. When you install a similar arrangement in your own office, you will always permit your American colleague not only to have a superior rank to yourself and much higher pay, but also the feeling that he is running the show. This will enable you to run it yourself. We, my dear Crossman, are Greeks in this American empire. You will find the Americans much as the Greeks found the Romans – great big, vulgar, bustling people, more vigorous than we are and also more idle, with more unspoiled virtues but also more corrupt. We must run A.F.H.Q. as the Greek slaves ran the operations of the Emperor Claudius.

Harold's relations with American leaders encouraged him to fancy himself as having special insight into American politics. He told Leo Amery in 1944 that he wanted to be appointed British Ambassador in Washington, explaining that other British misunderstood the Americans: US statecraft in the 1940s resembled that of King Charles II in the 1660s, with similar distrust of the elegant and measured clarity of memoranda and a preference for taking quick decisions after informal conversations.

Much though Harold liked Eisenhower, his hero in Mediterranean operations was the American's Irish deputy, General Sir Harold Alexander. He considered Alexander to be the greatest British commander since Marlborough. 'He had an extraordinary power of making people do what he wanted without exactly giving orders,' Harold explained to Sir Ian Trethowan. 'I saw him in many terrible conditions ... but he remained extraordinarily calm and quiet – made almost a fetish of it. In his mess, where I often went to stay, you were never allowed to discuss the war ... politics, books, sport, anything, but not that.' A hero is someone to be emulated, and significantly it was Alexander's exceptional self-control that drew Harold's supreme admiration. 'Many people who seem calm are highly strung, nervous, artistic temperaments who have won self-control over themselves,' as he said. Alexander responded to this admiration, and during the war years, when they worked closely together, found Harold 'a delightful companion who was both wise in advice and always amusing; a man of great intellect, morally and physically brave, but far too reserved to show these admirable qualities outwardly'. Following the Casablanca Conference, Alexander set to work on the strategy of his Tunisian campaign. After an elaborate plan of deception, his troops broke the enemy's defensive front with a devastating offensive, and within two days captured a quarter of a million enemy troops. On 13 May Alexander signalled to Churchill, 'We are masters of the North African shores.'

A few days later Harold attended a big Victory Parade which deeply moved him. First came the brave French native troops who had fought with old muskets, dressed in tatters with their boots falling off. The Americans followed, gloriously clad with helmets and rubber-soled shoes, marching in silence and resembling robots in Harold's fancy. Then after a slight and dramatic pause, the sound of Scottish pipers came across the North African sand, eerily echoing through the streets of the desert town. The pipes reduced most of the older British men to tears. Then the British Army marched by in drill order, sunburnt and in wonderful condition. They reminded Harold of the troops who had fought with him at the Somme: he thought, 'at that moment they were masters of the world'.

The description of the parade which Harold sent back to Britain was circulated through the Macmillan and Cavendish families. As the Duchess of Devonshire recounted to a friend, the generals who were in high-powered cars could not be seen as they were hurried to the saluting point, but Harold, with the showmanship of his new-found public confidence, followed behind with the American diplomat Robert Murphy in a humble jeep, bedecked with the Stars and Stripes and the Union Jack, cheering and waving and blowing kisses to the women on the roofs and streets of Tunis. He was rewarded with a shout of 'Good Old Mac', and joked afterwards that if he was ever exiled from Britain, he would stand as a municipal candidate in Tunis.

The Casablanca Conference had settled that Sicily would be the next Allied objective after the conquest of North Africa, and within months Alexander's armies occupied Sicily and southern Italy. Mussolini was toppled in July, and an Italian armistice was signed in September. Shortly afterwards Harold was appointed British High Commissioner in Italy, while remaining Resident Minister at Allied Headquarters, which later moved to Naples.

Harold's dealings with the outer world were changing. His rise to political power gave him a feeling of greater immunity from the assaults of ordinary life. Part of the change in Harold was the result of his maturing out of Nellie's influence. As a child and as a younger man, he had been anxious to propitiate her powerful, looming personality; it was always in his mind how to anticipate and thus avert her painful interference in his life. As a result he seemed to many people fawningly deferential. He showed the more despicable traits of an obsequious underling in his behaviour as Under Secretary to successive Ministers of Supply. 'His advice for my advancement', Herbert Morrison recalled, 'tended to occupy his mind to such an extent that I had to remind him that we had a war job to do and that personal careers were not important.' A similar tendency is discernible in Harold's correspondence with Beaverbrook in 1941–2. Michael Foot distrusted Harold's unctuousness and remembered him at this time eulogising Beaverbrook with a view to his flattery being repeated to its subject. Similarly John Colville, Churchill's private secretary, having met Harold at Tunis in 1943, found him 'finicky and probably a little insincere', and two years later still mistrusted him: 'I don't like the would-be ingratiating way in which Macmillan bares his teeth.' There was a world of significance in Colville's observation that Macmillan bared his teeth when he was being nauseatingly obsequious. Animals bare their teeth to show hostility; it is what they do when they are warning that they will attack, or want to attack. Harold in this respect was little different. He was a highly aggressive man who had put much complex ingenuity into hiding the fact. His resentment of the way his mother treated her children was so intolerably strong that – unlike his brothers – he spent a lifetime insisting on their mutual devotion and denying that he felt any rage against her. He never admitted to the hostility towards her which others expressed; whereas they spoke of her with dislike, his False Self always insisted on his gratitude and devotion. Compliance to her authority was one of the earliest habits he learnt. He grew up with a much remarked obsequiousness which was the reverse side of almost uncontainable hostility. When he fawned to someone, it was his False Self at work; what he really wished to do was crush them. Yet he betrayed himself, for when he tried to be ingratiating he bared his teeth. The profoundest lessons are not lessons of reason but come from the strains that permanently warp the mind. The split between Harold's behaviour and his wishes was warped by the pain of his cuckolding by Boothby, an ordeal which several of his friends recognised had made him increasingly assertive.'I won't be put upon,' he often insisted to his first parliamentary private secretary, Reginald Bevins, to whom he would reiterate 'that if you allowed yourself to be "put upon" people would end up by trampling on you'.

Harold continued to have critics as well as admirers. There were inevitable misunderstandings with diplomats in London, and Harold had to bear the hostility of Eden, whose jealousy of him was remarked by several observers. Harold's influence over Alexander was resented in the military hierarchy, and late in 1943 Sir Alan Brooke, the Chief of Imperial General Staff in London, warned Alexander 'that some of us had doubts as to whether Macmillan or Alexander was Supreme Commander of the Mediterranean . . . he was being too much influenced by his very able political partner, the Resident Minister of State'. These reservations about Harold were partly evidence of the patronising incomprehension with which London principals often view their men-on-the-spot overseas, but they also suggest that Harold's desire for power was becoming more obvious to others, and more obnoxious.

Harold believed that Mussolini's fascist regime had been a symptom rather than the cause of Italian ills, and feared that a simple restoration of the old political crowd would end in either fascist revival or communist victory. Like Churchill he wanted to ensure the survival of the Italian throne, but Roosevelt's need of the votes of anti-monarchical Italians in New York, and American republicanism generally, resulted first in the abdication of King Victor Emmanuel III and later in the fall of the House of Savoy. Harold was involved in long, laborious and intricate constitutional manoeuvres, as well as in the strategic planning of the campaign which resulted in the Allied Liberation of Rome in June 1944. All this ocurred in a country dispirited by starvation, homeless-ness, epidemic disease, civil disorder and monetary inflation. For the most part he revelled in his absolute powers, and savoured the great changes in his life; when he was received by Pope Pius XII, he was distracted from remembering their conversation by thoughts of the strange contingencies that had brought his family from a crofter's cottage on Arran to its eminence in London publishing, and on his own rise to power.

Italy was only part of Harold's fief. By the end of his time as Minister Resident, the British Ambassadors to Bulgaria, France, Greece, Italy, Roumania and Yugoslavia were answering to Harold. He was involved in the bloody conflict in Yugoslavia between German forces, Tito's partisans and the Chetnik guerrilla movement which was loyal to King Peter II (although ostensibly resisting the Germans, some Chetniks collaborated with them). When Greece was liberated in 1944, Harold was not merely involved in its economic and constitutional reconstruction, but was hurled into the midst of a civil war. In December at Athens he could only reach the besieged British Embassy in a tank, peering through its periscope as he was driven along shelled roads. When the Embassy was strafed by sniper fire, Harold affected to be stimulated by the dangers and discomforts. Together with Churchill and Eden, he and Alexander attended the Athens conference at Christmas of 1944: 'the new Wise Men travelling to find peace on Earth or rather to make it if they can,' Edith Olivier called the assembled peace-makers. Brecht however made this the occasion for his indignant poem 'On the News of the Tory Blood Baths in Greece'. The conference produced a settlement which saved Greece from communist tyranny, to the regret of some British left-wingers. When in January 1945 six MPs visited Italy, they were given 'an unsuitably sumptuous' dinner by Harold, as one of their number, a Labour MP called Fred Bellenger, later told Cecil King of the *Daily Mirror* priggishly: 'Macmillan afterwards spoke very prosily for an hour or more on Greece.' When Bellenger challenged British policy, suggesting that it was up to the Greeks if they wanted to kill each other, and that Allied interests were limited to keeping the harbours and airfields needed to defeat the Germans, Harold gave the 'very lame answer' that 'saving civilisation' was 'worth some sacrifices'. Bellenger later told Stuart Campbell of the *Sunday Pictorial* that 'Macmillan made no attempt to justify our foreign policy in the Mediterranean area, and said specifically he couldn't.' Harold by contrast thought the evening had been a success, while noting Bellenger as a clever-boots.

The exigencies of Mediterranean politics involved Harold in an episode which became the most controversial passage of his career, and led him to be heaped in obloquy in the 1980s. From Austria northwards to the Baltic a demarcation line between the Western Allies and the Red Army had been agreed in 1944, but south of the Austrian province of Carinthia, where the frontiers of pre-war Austria and Italy met Yugoslavia, no demarcation had been settled between the Anglo-American forces moving from Italy and Tito's partisans pushing up from Dalmatia. By May 1945 British soldiers and administrators faced immense problems in the region. Tito was greedy to grab all the territory he could, and guerilla warfare by his partisans against the British seemed imminent. The risk of fighting sent Harold hurrying to Klagenfurt on 13 May to confer with the local British commander, Lieutenant-General Charles Keightley. This crisis would not have arisen if the politicians had settled the southern demarcation lines, but first the British and Americans, and later the Titoists with their Soviet backers, had decided that they might maximise their advantages if the position was left vague.

Among nearly 400,000 German troops who had surrendered to Keightley's forces in Carinthia were about 45,000 Russians, including not only soldiers who had fought with the Nazis, but also about 11,000 women and children. Perhaps as many as one-quarter of the 45,000 were not Soviet citizens, but White Russians who had escaped after the Bolshevik revolution and were not liable to repatriation under the terms of the Yalta Agreement. But as a sequel to Harold's conference with Keightley, in May and June 1945, they were nevertheless handed over by the British with the rest to Soviet troops. Their transfer was disgraced by the breaking of promises of asylum, cruel subterfuge, brutality and treachery; many of the repatriated were summarily executed, others killed themselves, still more were condemned to labour camps where they died. This miserable transaction was followed by the forced repatriation from Carinthia of up to 26,000 Yugoslav men, women and children, opponents of Tito who were handed over to his partisans, by whom they were killed, tortured or imprisoned. The fate of these Serbs, Croats, Montenegrins and Slovenes – called Chetniks or 'anti-partisans' – had not been settled at Yalta. Many of those handed over were civilians, in flat contradiction of orders; and military plans to repatriate over 6,000 Slovenian civilians (mainly women and children) were foiled only by the intervention of British Red Cross workers. The despatch of soldiers in German uniform to death or ill-treatment breached international conventions on the treatment of prisoners of war; indeed about a thousand of those handed over were not Russians at all, but German officers and NCOs in uniform, while thousands of others sent to their deaths held French, German and Yugoslav passports, or Nansen certificates issued to stateless persons by the League of Nations.

This was far from the greatest sacrifice of eastern Europeans to Russian hegemony. Evelyn Waugh recalled staying with Harold at Naples in 1944 when the news arrived that the Western Allies had agreed to the Russian occupation of the independent Baltic republic of Lithuania. Harold shocked Waugh by saying, 'Well, that's one problem the less'; years later, remembering the incident, the novelist concluded that the politician had 'grown a carapace of cynicism to protect a tender conscience'. A similar dismissive cynicism was evident when on 13 May 1945 Harold flew to Klagenfurt in Austria to discuss with Keightley the fate of the Cossacks, White Russians and their dependants. As Harold summarised the problem in his diary (quoted by Richard Rampton QC in open court during Lord Aldington's libel action against Count Tolstoy):

To hand them over to the Russians is condemning them to slavery, torture and probably death. To refuse, is deeply to offend the Russians, and incidentally break the Yalta agreement. We have decided to hand them over ... but I suggested that the Russians should at the same time give us any British prisoners or wounded who may be in [their] area ... To add to the confusion, thousands of so-called Ustashi or Chetniks, mostly with wives and children, are fleeing in panic into this area in front of the advancing Yugoslavs. These expressions, Ustashi and Chetnik, cover anything from guerrilla forces raised by the Germans from Slovenes and Croats and Serbs to fight Tito, and armed and maintained by the Germans – to people who, either because they are Roman Catholics or Conservative in politics or for whatever cause, are out of sympathy with revolutionary Communism and therefore labelled as Fascists or Nazis.

Keightley – an ambitious officer who was not very bright – signalled on 14 May, 'Cannot see any point in keeping this large number of Soviet nationals who are clearly great source contention between Soviets and ourselves.' This message involved either inexcusable carelessness or deliberate deception, for Keightley knew that many of those to be repatriated (especially the most prominent) were not 'Soviet nationals'. He then set to work implementing the repatriations which he had agreed with Harold.

Harold's later apologists have rested a great deal on the fact that he had no formal authority to issue orders to Keightley, but the reality at the time is conveyed by a message sent on 23 May from V Corps to the Eighth Army:

As a result of verbal directive from Macmillan to Corps Comd at recent meeting we have undertaken to return all Soviet nationals in Corps area to Soviet forces. Macmillan mentioned no proviso about use of force and we have issued instructions that use of force may be used if absolutely necessary. Consider quite impossible to guarantee to return Cossacks and so honour our verbal agreement with Soviet forces unless we are allowed free hand in this matter. Cossacks will view any move with suspicion as to destination.

The difference between an order and a 'verbal directive' is negligible. It made no difference either to the fate of those concerned or to the attribution of responsibility.

Few British soldiers regarded the ensuing operations with anything but distaste. Two of the three divisional commanders objected forcibly (the reaction of the third is unknown). Colonel Robin Rose Price of the Welsh Guards was typical at the time in describing the repatriations order as 'sinister duplicity'. Anthony Crosland, the future Foreign Secretary who was then an Intelligence officer with 6th Armoured Division, which handed over most of the Yugoslavs, wrote on 18 May 1945, 'The problem of the anti-Tito Croats & Slovenes is almost causing a civil war within the British Army . . . Among officers here, there is gt. revolt & resentment against the deception and dishonesty involved, & many of the Guardsmen particularly have worked themselves into a rather hysterical state of protest about it.' This was how it seemed at the time to almost everyone involved.

Harold knew what would happen to the White Russians and others in Stalinist hands for he had recently been upset by reading an account of the Soviet penal system. His published war diaries faithfully record his reading of the classics and nineteenth-century novels; he preferred to retreat from the asperities and realism of modern literature. But, exceptionally, shortly before the repatriations in March 1945, he noted that in addition to enjoying Thackeray's *Book of Snobs*, he had read and disliked Arthur Koestler's *Darkness at Noon*. With an epigraph from Saint-Just ('nobody can rule guiltlessly'), this gritty novel described the imprisonment, interrogation and execution of Rubashov, a pitiless communist leader, and concluded that 'whoever becomes too cunning loses all decency'. It is not surprising that Harold was disturbed by *Darkness at Noon*, for in the 1940s he had come to fancy himself as a neo-Machiavellian and it is the story of the destruction of such a man; but his reading should have inspired more care about the fate of the Cossacks, for the only attractive character in the book is an imprisoned Tsarist cavalryman who has fallen into the grip of Stalin's henchmen. Instead Harold remained involved in what was happening or even abetted it: on his return to AFHQ, he seems to have discussed the covert handover of the Yugoslavs with General Sir Brian Robertson, and he personally received a copy of the extract from Keightley's message referring to the Cossacks.

Some apologists have protested that the British and their rulers had been demoralised and brutalised by six years of total war: that it is unfair to bring the moral sensibilities of peacetime to bear on people who had just suffered the miseries and squalor of protracted conflict. Yet Churchill and Eden, who initiated the policy of repatriation at Yalta, had been exceptionally insulated from the squalors and miseries of war, swaddled by the comforts and conveniences of supreme command. For them (like Harold) the war years were exciting and uplifting: a wonderful purpose had been given to their lives. As an armistice in Europe had been signed on 7 May, the repatriations are far more an example of the instantly brutalising corruptions of peace: although some of the British failings also arose from misplaced national pride. As General Robertson said at the time, he could not be bothered to distinguish between the nationalities of the displaced people in Carinthia; the crucial decision to classify all Cossack formations as Soviet nationals was the result of the British sense of their own cultural or even racial superiority.

Altogether the fate of defeated troops was miserable after the Nazi capitulation. James Bacque's investigation into the mass deaths of German prisoners after the Second World War estimates that 576,000 died in US camps, and another 210,000 died after release as a result of their maltreatment. His figures and arguments have been contested, but it is clear that many hundreds of thousands died, partly because of intractable administrative difficulties, but also as a result of attitudes among the victors which ranged from weary indifference to the vindictiveness which had prompted the Morgenthau plan for deindustrialising Germany. Up to 400,000 German prisoners of war were held in Britain as forced labour for up to three years after the defeat of the Hitlerites. The story of the repatriations was revealed in the 1970s and 1980s in books by Lord Bethell and Count Nikolai Tolstoy. As part of the sequel, Lord Aldington (who had been Keightley's senior staff officer in Carinthia) was awarded libel damages of £1.5 million against Tolstoy in 1989.

Harold's behaviour after the publication of the Bethell and Tolstoy books can be characterised, according to taste, as either dignified and sensible or cunning and evasive. It was perhaps a mixture of all. He said very little in public, and his reported private remarks were contradictory. He certainly conceded that the results of the decision reached with Keightley were objectionable: that the British went beyond the Yalta Repatriation Agreement by handing over White Russians, Chetniks, their dependants and others who were vilely abused by their new captors. It is idle to pretend that his advice was not ruthlessly negligent or that at the time he was concerned about its consequences. Brigadier Cowgill, Lord Brimelow and Christopher Booker in their investigation of the repatriations 'conclude without reservation that Harold Macmillan in no sense knowingly or personally participated in any decision specifically directed to the handing back against their will of the dissident Yugoslavs' – but this is legalistic quibbling which Harold, to his credit, disdained. The course which resulted in injustice and deceits being perpetrated by the British Army on the Yugoslavs was set in train by Harold's Klagenfurt conference with Keightley. If evil is done it is a weak defence to claim that evil was not intended; indeed old Daniel and Alexander Macmillan would have regarded it as a low and amoral defence.

On later occasions too Harold seemed indifferent to the maltreatment or killing of prisoners and discarded humanitarian considerations for parliamentary advantage. His behaviour at Klagenfurt, and its sequel, can be seen in the context of his behaviour fifteen years later. When, during his premiership, eleven Kenyans who had been detained following the Mau Mau uprising died of 'multiple bruising' in the camp at Hola, Harold recognised that wrongs had been done; but his chief concern was to protect his administration from parliamentary discomfiture. When the matter was debated, he was content that the Labour opposition muddled its timing, so that their criticisms did not get fully covered in the next day's newspapers. Later in 1959, a British judge, the future Lord Devlin, in an official report on disturbances in Africa, wrote that 'Nyasaland is – no doubt temporarily – a police state' where opposition supporters were 'not safe', and generally indicted the colonial administration: Harold was outraged, abusing Devlin as a vindictive lying Irish Fenian, whose word could not be trusted because his brother was a Jesuit and his sister a nun. The Governor of Nyasaland was asked to submit an alternative report, which was written at Chequers in two days and whitewashed the administration. This deeply compromised document was published simultaneously with Devlin's report, Harold's chief concern being to fix a friendly press and isolate his few parliamentary critics like Lord Lambton and Enoch Powell.

Nevertheless it is easier to sympathise with Harold's predicament over the repatriations in the years before his death than with the casuistry of some of his posthumous defenders, who insist that the verdict of the jury for Aldington covered everyone in a blanket exculpation. If such people are to be believed, although British conduct was brutal, deceitful and treacherous (with scores of defenceless people killed and hundreds savagely manhandled by British troops), every Britisher involved is exonerated. The responsibility for the massacres lay with the Soviets and the Titoists absolutely; not a trace of it can attach to anyone else. This is palpable nonsense. Harold, after his only discussion on the subject with Keightley, recognised that many of the repatriates would be condemned to slavery, torture and death. There is abundant evidence that officers knew what was happening, and hated it: some prisoners were allowed to escape by men like General Horatius Murray, who forewarned his captives that he would enforce his orders on the following morning and enabled them to escape, or Nigel

Nicolson, who turned his back to let a man escape (and was called 'wet' by the judge in the Aldington case). Some British soldiers charged with this dirty business almost mutinied. But Harold's part in the Klagenfurt conference and its sequel were (as his wartime admirer Richard Crossman wrote in a different context in 1963) 'another example of Macmillan not knowing because he didn't want to know'.

While Harold had been experiencing the pleasures and strains of proconsular power overseas, there had been many domestic changes. At the start of his foreign exile, he began sending letters to Dorothy just as in the First World War he had sent a regular letter diary from the trenches to his mother. The letter format was dropped within months, but he continued to keep a daily journal which was returned to England for filing. It was written, if not for posterity, for a wider readership than Dorothy, and gave him a chance to show the witty and more frivolous False Self which he was developing under the stimuli of political acclaim and John Wyndham. He missed Dorothy acutely, and his worst bouts of depression were related to their separation; but, paradoxically, her chief significance in this period was her absence. Separated from her, Harold at last found the confidence to act as a leader. Their separation relieved the strains between them, Dorothy found herself able to treat him more kindly, and the pain and bitterness of the 1930s receded.

The younger Cavendishes and Macmillans were also growing up, falling in love and marrying. One of these engagements connected Harold to a rising American political dynasty, with important consequences when twenty years later he was Prime Minister of the United Kingdom and Jack Kennedy became President of the United States. Dorothy's handsome nephew, Billy Hartington, the Devonshire heir, became involved with Kathleen Kennedy in the late 1930s. She was the vivacious daughter of the US Ambassador to the Court of St James's, Joseph Kennedy, who had fought and tricked his way from the Irish slums of East Boston to a Wall Street fortune, eminence in Hollywood and high influence in the Democratic Party. Kennedy was a coarse, destructive man who initially opposed his daughter marrying out of the Roman Catholic faith into such a die-hard Protestant family as the Cavendishes. The latter equally disliked the threat of an alliance with the Kennedys. 'I am a black Protestant and proud of it,' Eddie Devonshire declared at a party of Lady Cunard's in 1944 before telling several anti-papal stories and recalling that his own marriage to a daughter of Lord Salisbury had been deprecated by his father because Hatfield was 'a Tory High Church household'.

The Duke sometimes roused himself to other acts of magnificent high-handedness which were ill suited to the temper of the times. The West Derbyshire constituency, near Chatsworth, had been represented for two centuries by successive members of the Cavendish family, with the exception of five years after 1918. When Henry Hunloke, who had married Dorothy's youngest sister Anne, resigned the seat in 1943, his brother-in-law Devonshire ensured that the local party association invited Billy Hartington to become the new candidate. Churchill, who three years earlier had agreed to recommend Devonshire for a Garter because 'he was not bad as Dukes go', supported Hartington with a public letter extolling the 'constancy and fidelity' of the Cavendishes to Derbyshire and the nation; but the young man was defeated all the same. 'The way the Duke of Devonshire managed the Unionist Association at the adoption meeting was the main cause of the Govt difficulties,' the Labour politician James Chuter-Ede told Rab Butler a few days later. 'The reason Hunloke had retired was that, having married the sister of the Duke, he had run away with another married woman.' This had 'convinced the electorate that the Cavendish idea is that if you drop out of the Cavendish family you must surrender the family seat'. As Loelia, Duchess of Westminster commented (recalling the way Georgiana, Duchess of Devonshire had helped Charles James Fox in the famous Westminster election of 1784), 'Duchess's kisses are not what they used to be.' So strong were memories of this fiasco that when, in 1962, Aidan Crawley

successfully contested West Derbyshire for the Conservatives
at a by-election when Harold was Prime Minister, Ann Fleming
claimed to Evelyn Waugh that during 'a jolly weekend at
Chatsworth' the tactless Conservative hostess Lady Pamela
Berry had lectured the Duchess of Devonshire 'on Derbyshire,
the unpopularity of the Cavendishes, and the orders from
Central Office that they were to play no part in the election'.

After much family unhappiness, in which the Kennedys
proved more recalcitrant than the Cavendishes, Hartington
married Kik Kennedy in May 1944; but he was killed by
a German sniper in France a few months later. His widow
remained in England, grieving for her husband, but eventually
became the lover of Lord Fitzwilliam, with whom she was killed
in an air-smash in France in 1948. 'They were a glamorous
couple – gay, dashing, attractive, carefree, colossally rich –
and very much in love,' Chips Channon recorded when the
news reached London. Channon was a snobbish adventurer
from Chicago who on the strength of his marriage to a
Guinness heiress had been elected to the British parliament,
and remained an MP even after he had transferred his affection
to an equally snobbish young garden designer, Peter Coats.
Channon considered himself, with perhaps slender entitlement,
an expert observer of the Cavendishes; but he gave a shrewd
enough summary when Dorothy's brother died in 1950. 'He
was a frustrated man, hated being a Duke and was really a bit
bored by all his possessions and palaces . . . but he was gay at
heart and loved life, ladies – and, above all, port,' Channon
wrote. Evelyn Waugh was less kind about the dead Duke: 'that
testy alcoholic', he called him.

The sight of Eddy Devonshire 'lit up', as recorded by James
Lees-Milne at the Turf club in 1947, was such a familiar
one that when, at a reception at Buckingham Palace before
Princess Elizabeth's marriage to Prince Philip in 1947, the Duke
was assaulted by a drunk Indian rajah, her private secretary
John Colville noted emphatically that Devonshire was sober.
(After his more temperate son, the eleventh Duke, gave up

drinking, Ann Fleming reported to Patrick Leigh Fermor that at a dreary dinner for Lord Carrington in 1972 the 'only comedy was Andrew proudly sober'.) His younger brother Charles Cavendish was an endearing alcoholic who earned the soubriquet 'Lord Useless' while working for Pierpont Morgan in New York. He was eventually sacked by the great financier, and then found that they were sailing to Britain on the same liner. In revenge he exasperated Morgan by inciting their fellow passengers to make ghostly sounds outside Morgan's cabin at night. Charles Cavendish married Fred Astaire's sister Adele, a musical comedy actress, of whom Alastair Forbes recalled that as a young woman she 'hadn't cared who knew she wore no knickers and why'. Charles and Adele Cavendish settled at his family's Irish home, Lismore Castle; but his drinking never abated. In the early 1930s, staying as the guest at Clandeboye of the beautiful, charming but hard-drinking Marquess of Dufferin and Ava, he announced that he would soon be back at Lismore, 'dispensing justice to peasants and rebels – between drinks of course'. He proved unstoppable in dispensing drinks to himself, and his addiction killed him at the age of thirty-nine in 1944. The Cavendish vulnerability to alcoholism was transmitted to some of Dorothy's descendants (see page 331); but whereas the Cavendishes were endowed with robust nerves, the Macmillans for generations had been highly strung. This conjunction was to prove excruciating.

Harold himself suffered a bout of nervous prostration and depression in 1943, and further illnesses of apparently nervous origin in 1944. Wyndham was also prone to depression, and proved more adept at bringing Harold out of the clutches of his blue devils of melancholia than any member of the Macmillan family. Their dependence persisted in the years of peace. His comrade John Wyndham was accompanying him, Harold wrote to Sir Orme Sargent about his imminent trip to Persia and India in 1946–7, because at the age of fifty-two he needed support. He was already posing as an exaggeratedly old man in the late 1940s: Humphry Berkeley in 1948 saw

him tottering along a railway platform until he realised that
he was going to miss a train, whereupon he showed the agility
of an Olympic athlete in leaping aboard as it left the station.
Just as Randolph Churchill was hurt when his father Winston
took a surrogate son in the unprepossessing form of Brendan
Bracken, so Maurice felt rejected by his father's preference for
Wyndham, not least on the occasion of the Indian trip, for
which the pretext was publishing business in which Maurice
could suitably have been involved.

Maurice had matured into an uncommunicative, almost
mysterious young man who appropriately finished the Second
World War serving in a special unit called the Phantom Signals.
At the age of twenty-four he contested the rock-solid Labour
parliamentary seat of Seaham as a Conservative in the general
election of 1945, and was duly defeated. He then toured Europe
and Asia as military assistant to the Adjutant-General and,
after demobilisation, fulfilled his long-foreshadowed destiny
by working as a learner in the MacLehose printing works in
Scotland, and then starting life as a publisher.

In 1942 he had married Katharine Ormsby-Gore. Her father
Lord Harlech had been Colonial Secretary in the national
government and at the time of his daughter's marriage was High
Commissioner in South Africa. A generation earlier 'young Billy
Gore' had been talked of in the Conservative Party as 'one of our
rising young men', but his political career had been handicapped
by a cocksure manner. He gave the impression of thinking he
knew everything, and of knowing that he was always right. His
superior manner was accentuated by his physical appearance:
a long, pointed nose, habitual drawl and provocative smile led
people to conclude that he was supercilious. Yet Billy Gore did
not climb to political power on the reputation or connections of
his family. His father was an obscure Shropshire peer, and Billy
Gore was brought up in the most inward-looking county society
anywhere in England. His ability and intellectual capacity were
of his own making; he developed exceptional self-dependence;
one contemporary was reminded by him of Kipling's 'Cat Who

Walked by Himself'. Personally he was industrious, kind, loyal and generous; in politics, although impetuous, he was unusually receptive to new ideas, and on several occasions he showed moral courage in striking out on his own. He opposed the Hoare–Laval Pact of 1935 (more effectively than Harold, from a senior position inside the government), and his hostility to Nazi Germany made him an uncomfortable member of a Cabinet of appeasers: when, on inheriting his father's barony in 1938, he offered his resignation as Colonial Secretary to Chamberlain, it was accepted with alacrity.

His wife Beatrice was a Cecil: her sister had married Dorothy's brother Eddy Devonshire, and her brother was Harold's political colleague Bobbety Cranborne, afterwards fifth Marquess of Salisbury. Like other Cecils she was best known by a nickname, Mima (her sister the Duchess of Devonshire was Mowcher). She was a 'clever, amusing and charming' woman who 'combined the traditional humour and independence of the Cecils with high spirits and a fearless outspokenness', according to one contemporary in the 1920s; 'Mima Harlech is delightful and always was,' George Lyttelton wrote to Rupert Hart-Davis in 1957. Many of her gifts were inherited by her daughter Katie Macmillan, who soon needed every resource in her difficult marriage. By the late 1940s it was clear that young Maurice Macmillan was an alcoholic, a disease which each of Dorothy's four children suffered 'at one time or another', according to Alistair Horne, 'to lesser or greater degree'. Katie was always critical of the way in which Maurice had been treated by his parents, and became especially antagonistic to Dorothy, who always seemed to treat her son with indifference or worse. Within a few years of Maurice's marriage, Dorothy had come to regard Katie with loathing and, with the younger woman living in a small house in the grounds of Birch Grove, there were many rows. Maurice's addiction dismayed his father, who was impatient of his son's failure of self-control and frustrated by the way it threatened the family's prospects as a publishing and political dynasty. Maurice reached his nadir in the mid-1950s (although he was nevertheless elected as Conservative MP for Halifax in 1955); by the time he finally stopped drinking at the end of the decade, his health had been permanently damaged.

The early generations of Macmillans had been tormented by over-sensitive consciences or scoured by guilt. They had dedicated themselves to their God and to their work as a way of fighting their sense of their own badness. They saw themselves as people of corrupt and destructive impulses, wrongdoers who had to train themselves to do right. Byron in his Monody on the death of Sheridan wrote of:

> The secret enemy whose sleepless eye
> Stands sentinel – accuser – judge – and spy.

The secret enemy of the early Macmillans was guilt, and so too of some of their descendants. They judged too harshly of themselves, found themselves wanting and reality too forbidding. The domestic tensions at Birch Grove, like Harold's implacable attitude to Maurice and Dorothy's hostility, had left Maurice with a sense of fault; if he was treated as a reprobate, there must be a reason for which he was culpable. The bodily alchemy of the Cavendishes did the rest.

Harold's impatience with Maurice's 'weakness' contrasted with his toleration of John Wyndham's drinking, which grew increasingly heavy through the years. Ann Fleming has left a glimpse of a dinner at the Swedish Embassy in 1963 at which 'only too soon' Wyndham and the alcoholic Lord Arran 'held the table with noisy private English jokes' leaving their foreign neighbours 'in bewildered isolation'. Harold perhaps treated Maurice's excesses as less pardonable than Wyndham's because he was distressed by some of the scenes; nevertheless in his own eyes (if not everyone else's) he tried to help his son at critical moments, and was proud when Maurice mastered his dependency at the end of the 1950s. The trouble was that Harold recoiled from signs of weakness in himself or others. He hated to admit to physical pain or weariness: the fortitude with which his grandfather Daniel had faced slow, agonising

Dorothy and Harold in the
1950s. In reality they were sitting
with some distance between them
on the bench, but for publicity
purposes the middle of this
photograph was cut out, so that
they were presented to the world
as a close and united couple.

Harold the Showman
revelling in the applause
of the crowd.

Harold with his son
Maurice. There was 'a
tough wall of failed
contact' between them.

Sarah Macmillan,
Dorothy's unhappy
daughter by Bob
Boothby.

Catherine in the 1950s.

Catherine some
twenty years later.

Catherine Amery and her sister Carol Faber at Birch Grove.

The Prime Minister on the moors with the Duchess of Devonshire and her son Lord Hartington.

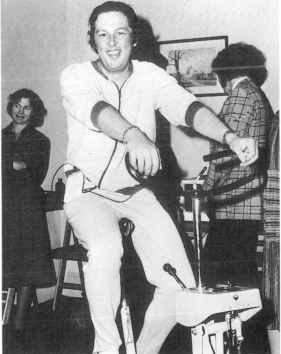

Harold with his beloved
friends Pamela and John
Wyndham.

Alexander recovering
from his early heart
attack.

Joshua dancing.

Debo, the Duchess of
Devonshire, outside
Chatsworth. In old
age Harold treasured
his visits to the
house. Her husband
Andrew has been a
crucial figure in
running the
Macmillan Trust.

Rachael Macmillan with
a band of pop
musicians.

Her brother Adam, a
popular and admired
member of the family.

Alexander, now Earl of Stockton,
before the finish at Birch Grove.

death from tuberculosis was a model for Harold. His admiration of valorous men and hawkish vigilance for signs of cowardice in others showed in even casual conversation. Chatting at the Turf club with Bobbety Salisbury and James Stuart in 1953, Harold was 'contemptuous of Tito who he says has no courage', telling stories of the Croatian leader 'being afraid to sleep in a tent and frightened in a rowing boat', Evelyn Shuckburgh recorded.

Harold retained a hardened attitude to alcoholism. In 1980 he was a guest at the British Embassy in Vienna when the Foreign Secretary Lord Carrington mentioned that he was breakfasting next day with Edmund Muskie, the US Secretary of State. In his stagey, sly, quavering voice, Harold asked if Muskie was the senator who had wept in public because someone had denounced his wife as an alcoholic. The British Ambassador bridled at the old man's malice. 'That's not a very agreeable remark, Mr Macmillan,' he countered: 'how would you like it if you were at a meeting in your constituency and someone from the back of the hall yelled out, "Lady Dorothy Macmillan is an old drunk"?' 'Ah,' replied Macmillan, raising his voice and rousing his manner, 'I would shout back, "You should have seen her mother!"'

Quentin Crewe, who became Sarah Macmillan's lover, first encountered the family in the late 1940s. They struck him as delightful but histrionic, at once divided and self-sufficient, full of shifting alliances and short-lived feuds. Family life was dominated by Dorothy, whose vitality, ardour, strong will and appetite for melodrama were felt everywhere at Birch Grove. 'Lady Dorothy's furies were dramatic, though seldom directed overtly at Harold himself,' Crewe recalled. 'In her determination to do what pleased her and do little that displeased her, she allowed her liking and disliking of people too free a rein, especially within her own family.' Even in the early 1950s it felt to Crewe as if Boothby overshadowed the household. He wrote almost daily to Dorothy, who 'was always the first down to breakfast to snatch up the letter, lest Harold should see it'. She still adored him, and on her visits to London would stay not with Harold but at the Dorchester Hotel or occasionally in Boothby's flat. Sometimes they travelled together to Italy. In time Dorothy and Crewe formed a close relationship, in which she treated him as a mixture 'between a favourite son and a fellow conspirator or perhaps confessor', he wrote. 'She would in the mornings come and sit on the end of my bath and chat. She loved sleeping out on the terrace and sometimes dragged another bed out for me to sleep on, and she would talk long into the night – often about Bob and about Harold.'

The Macmillans' eldest daughter Carol in 1944 married Julian Faber, then an officer in the Welsh Guards, who afterwards worked in the family firm of insurance brokers, Willis Faber, of which he was chairman in the 1970s. He kept a dignified reserve during the more dramatic scenes thrown by the Macmillans; of all the children Carol most resembled her mother, according to Crewe, 'though lacking the full measure of her warmth and having a capacity for irritable boredom'.

Harold saw many similarities between his son Maurice and his second daughter Catherine: the two children who most resembled him in character and appearance, and not coincidentally the two children whom Dorothy showed that she liked least. Harold thought that Catherine, like Maurice, was cursed with the Macmillan tendency to introspective morbidity and the Cavendish disposition to alcoholism. In 1950 she married Julian Amery, the son of Harold's friend Leo and a man whose solemn dedication to politics was unappealing to Dorothy. Like his father-in-law, Julian Amery was the product of Summerfields, Eton and Balliol. He had been a war correspondent during the Spanish Civil War, a diplomatic attaché in the Balkans, liaison officer with Albanian guerrillas and Churchill's personal representative to the Chinese Generalissimo Chiang Kai-shek. From 1950 he sat in the House of Commons, where in a voice of unforgettably gravelly hardness he enunciated the views of the more imperial-minded Conservatives. Reflecting his interests he held parliamentary under secretaryships at the War Office and Colonial Office in the 1950s, before being appointed by his father-in-law as Secretary of State for Air in 1960 and Minister of Aviation in 1962.

The guilt of the innocent is hardest to bear. At the age of seventeen Sarah discovered with brutal suddenness that Boothby was her father. She was dancing in a nightclub with Colin Tennant (afterwards Lord Glenconner), when a girl who had come with him and was drunk broke in jealously. 'What do you think you're doing with Colin?' she demanded. 'You're only illegitimate anyhow, you're Boothby's daughter.' This revelation devastated her. On a later occasion, when she was dancing with an awkward young man who apologised for his clumsiness with some reference to Harold's political importance, she exclaimed with furious misery: 'You're dancing with the most famous bastard in England. Everyone knows I'm Bob Boothby's daughter.' No ceremony of words could patch the havoc. She visited Boothby in pathetic and touching efforts to construct a daughter's relationship with him, and grew more distant for a time in her relations with Harold.

While staying one weekend with a family named Mostyn-Owen she met Quentin Crewe, a seductive young man who had been stricken with the progressively disabling disease of muscular dystrophy. 'She was not especially pretty,' he recalled. 'Her eyes were too small and her lips thin, but when she smiled her eyes crinkled in a way that was for years to make my heart turn over. She had a beautiful figure, which she spoilt much of the time by moving, when she was nervous, with a diffident crouch. There was a vulnerability about her which I found touching, but also, even at the very beginning, there was a waywardness that was challenging and an enigmatic quality that gave me no peace.' Crewe became informally engaged to her in 1950, but the pattern of her life was disturbed. She had 'a desperate need to be liked, to be reassured that her illegitimacy, as she thought of it, did not matter'; like other people with low self-esteem and little sense of identity, she practised 'a compulsive infidelity, not attributable to any kind of nymphomania, but more to an emotional nomadism'.

She feared stability, became wilder in her ways, fell in love with another young man called Andrew Heath. Then, in July 1951, she announced that she was pregnant. Although the father might have been either Crewe or Heath, she preferred to insist that it was the latter.

Dorothy treated the pregnancy as primarily a threat to Harold's political ambitions. A general election was imminent (it was announced in September for the following month), and Dorothy would not have his chances of promotion marred by stories of Sarah's pregnancy. According to Crewe, she coerced Sarah into an abortion, but was so determined to keep the facts from Harold that she went to Scotland with him for a holiday as if nothing was happening. Others have suggested that Harold knew of the pregnancy, but went away to Scotland, not wishing to be involved in its termination. Either way Sarah's happiness was sacrificed. She had the abortion, but never recovered from her grief at it. She was left with an obliterating sense of infirmity: that she had failed her mother, and her lovers, but supremely that she had failed her child, killed though she had been desperate to keep it. Two years later, in 1953, she married Heath, but, when the abortion then proved to have sterilised her, began a headlong descent into alcoholism. Her marriage failed, although the Heaths adopted two sons; but curiously, though Sarah was not Harold's child, by the 1960s he was closer to her than to Dorothy's other children.

One of the great themes of Harold's life is concealment. Both his political and his personal life rested on his talent as a concealer. The exercise of political power, for Harold no less than for other parliamentarians, depended upon the control of information and the concealment of motives. The rhetoric of public service and proud formulae about the national interest are routinely deployed to conceal the ambushes, plots, ambitions, jealousies, feuds, alliances and urge to dominate that constitute the main part of a parliamentarian's life. Harold was no different from most of his colleagues. He was ruthlessly ambitious (as Churchill warned Eden as early as 1954), full of suppressed animosities and secret schemes which had to be at least partly concealed. The suppression of truth and facts were necessary and habitual to him: early in his premiership, in 1957, he had no hesitation in suppressing a damning report by Sir William Penney on what had been the world's worse nuclear power accident to date, at Windscale (whose name was subsequently sanitised into Sellafield). Not only were all prints of Penney's report destroyed, but so also was the type used by the printers. Ostensibly Penney's revelations of incompetence were suppressed in order not to jeopardise Anglo-American exchanges of nuclear information: in practice Harold was also concerned to avoid parliamentary embarrassments at home, or the discrediting of the technology and personnel employed at Windscale/Sellafield by informed public discussion. The public as well as the Americans could not be trusted with the truth.

The reticences, evasions, expedients and palliations of parliamentary life had long been reflected in Harold's domestic life. There too facts and feelings were hidden for the 'protection' of others; although nobody was truly protected, for we do not require words to see and hear the truth. Concealment increases pain, and pain makes many people feel culpable. Each of the four Macmillan children suffered from the tense mixture of concealment and ambition that had underlain life at Birch Grove. The pressure on Sarah to abort her child was the apotheosis of this. 'When ambition comes, it puts an end to natural feeling,' Honoré de Balzac wrote in *Lost Illusions*; all the suppressions and concealments of the years festered.

The general election of July 1945 gave the Labour Party its first overall majority in the House of Commons. Harold was defeated at Stockton, but in November was re-elected in a by-election at Bromley, a safe Conservative constituency in the southern suburbs of London. He returned to a scene of political transformation. While he had been in the Mediterranean, the foundations of the welfare state had been laid, and Labour's plans for the nationalisation of various industries and services had been settled. In opposition Harold was appointed by

Churchill as a frontbench spokesman, principally on industrial and economic affairs; but he remained unpopular. His own party distrusted his sympathies with nationalisation. 'Many of the Tories are becoming restive about the industrial policy which is being sedulously advocated by Macmillan,' Bracken informed Beaverbrook in 1946. 'Speaking for the Party in the Debate on the King's Speech, Macmillan said that the State should have greater powers to intervene and to manage industry. He also said that discipline in factories should be left to workers' – a view which Bracken thought communistic. Having been a dull and earnest backbench speaker, Harold now reverted to the Oxford Union manner which he had cultivated in imitation of Ronald Knox. He also showed unexpected bitterness against his opponents: in 1947, for example, he reviled the Minister of Transport as 'guilty of blackmail of the worst and most filthy kind'. Harold 'became the Tory Front Bench spokesman who could most easily raise the temperature of the House', wrote the Labour MP Emrys Hughes. As 'the political actor and poseur, the cynic, the knock-about artiste of the Parliamentary stage', he infuriated his opponents. His tricks of voice and gesture were histrionic: 'his polished phrases reeked of midnight oil. He delighted in jibes at the benches opposite and the taunts that invited retort.'

In conversation with Harold Nicolson and the Duke of Norfolk in 1942, Harold had declared that the British were 'supremely prosperous and happy', their lives marred only by their dread of German bombs and the inevitability of 'extreme Socialism' in the future. During the war he had even viewed with equanimity the defeat of the Conservatives at the next general election: they would return marvellously reinvigorated by a few years in opposition, he told Leo Amery. But once the Labour government triumphed in 1945, he was less sanguine. He developed a morbid fascination with European dereliction. His feeling that Britain was losing out on every count matched his perpetual apprehension of calamity and engulfment by hostile forces. Power had tethered him to reality during the war, but in 1945–51 he was excluded from the power that had meant so much to him. As an exile in parliamentary opposition he might have reverted to his remote and ineffectual pre-war type; yet, so long as he could continue perceiving the world as hostile, he could remain linked to it. Throughout the late 1940s (a period of economic austerity when the British people were hang-dog, discontented and truculent) he indulged in doom-laden historical analogies: part of his new resemblance to Machiavelli, who had also thought about statecraft in terms of historical parallels, and drew his precepts from the rise and fall of principalities. Dining with Leo Amery and Harold Nicolson in 1946, he elaborated on the theme that, like Greece in 350 BC, Western European civilisation was powerless to unite against the barbarians. The massacre of young officers at the Battle of the Somme in 1916 had 'drained off what should have been the leadership, and now the country is in irreparable decline – under your gang', he said bitterly to the socialist Richard Crossman a few years later. 'I think Europe is finished,' he told Hugh Dalton in 1950 while under the influence of rereading Thucydides: its desperate state resembled 'Greece after the second Peloponnesian war'.

Such fatalism was not unique to Harold. There is 'a type, unknown in the New World but quite common in Europe, which is fascinated by obscurity and failure', as Evelyn Waugh depicted it in his novel about post-war disarray, *Scott-King's Modern Europe* (1947), and this outlook grew even more prevalent in the early 1950s. 'The temper of international opinion is all set against the things which made us a great nation,' Evelyn Shuckburgh of the Foreign Office reflected in 1952. 'Bit by bit we shall be driven back into our island where we shall starve.' Seven years after the war ended, the country was still beset by shortages of raw materials, high taxation and centralised controls. The gravity of British weakness was hidden by a façade of full employment, record output and manufacturing profits, but the truth was that Britain relied on US charity to avoid bankruptcy.

Of twentieth-century prime ministers Harold most resembled Arthur Balfour in temperament: both of them were intellectuals, capable of both charm and callousness; Sir Colin Coote (who knew each of them) described them with the same words, 'tall, willowy, languid, never at a loss, seldom at a height, ready at any time to make a defence of philosophical doubt'. In a typical show of Edwardian pessimism, Balfour had spoken in 1908 of the 'ruined fragments of our civilisation' and had predicted that the Western world would 'be buried under a barbaric flood ... like that which in Asia submerged forever the last traces of Hellenic culture'. Such images were almost congenial to Harold. Oppressed, or perhaps excited, by the destitution of culture and depletion of power in Europe, he became a pioneer of Continental unity, attending the Congress of Europe in 1948 and the inauguration of the Council of Europe next year, and supporting Robert Schuman's proposal for a European iron and steel community in 1950. Recent experiences had roused in him a fear of Marxist dominion in Europe. Without British help the Continent would succumb to 'economic sickness and the perpetual ceaseless moral disintegration to which communist agitation and infiltration subject her', he declared in 1949. He was reminded of the Goths' destruction of the Roman Empire in the fifth century AD, when civilisation had been saved only by 'the conversion of the conquerors to Christianity'. Yet overall he blew hot and cold on European unity. 'The Empire must always have first preference: Europe must come second,' he told the Sunday Despatch at a time when he was privately reiterating his belief that the future lay with the United States. The stubborn idealist of the 1930s had become a master of equivocation.

When Churchill formed his first peacetime government in 1951, Harold at first seemed stinted in the division of the spoils of office. He was offered the newly formed Ministry of Housing and Local Government, which ranked as the third most junior office in a Cabinet of sixteen. He accepted on the advice of Crookshank, who had himself been tipped for a senior economic post but was relegated to the Ministry of Health. The truth was that although Harold in his memoirs tried to present himself as a Churchillian, neither the Prime Minister nor his entourage liked or trusted him. They thought his affectionate respect for Churchill was counterfeit; they condemned his manner as fawning and his conversation as stilted. Even Harold's long opposition to appeasement was undervalued by the Churchillians: it is notable that Churchill makes no reference to him in his account of the prelude to war, *The Gathering Storm*.

Harold soon recovered from his disappointment. 'We shall have a great party,' he told Reginald Bevins a few days later when inviting him to become his parliamentary private secretary. He was determined to make a success of his job, and roused himself in imitation of Beaverbrook at the Ministry of Supply ten years earlier. He set the Ministry of Housing almost on a wartime footing: with the help of a hand-picked staff, he started work with sly and ruthless skill. Initially he behaved as if his Ministry was a production department, rather than a supervisory body which had to approve local authorities' plans to build council houses and provide them with finance and raw-materials allocations at a time of continuing shortages. 'As Minister of Materials, I had to find him the sinews of war,' wrote Lord Swinton in a revealingly martial phrase. 'Because he was realistic and practical and did not try to over-bid or over-insure I always gave him what he wanted, though there were plenty of rival claimants baying like hounds at feeding time.' Harold's socialist predecessor, Dalton, had left behind some 216,000 unfinished houses; although the Conservatives' target in 1951 of building 300,000 new houses annually was thought impossible by many, that target was surpassed by 1953, when 318,779 new houses were built.

'Ministers are the kings against the civil servants who are the modern barons,' Harold told Bevins at Housing; but he could not execute the barons who obstructed him. Instead he developed his own version of exile for them. Sir Thomas

Sheepshanks, the permanent secretary of the Ministry, seemed
hopelessly enervate to Harold, who by-passed him by recruiting
Sir Percy Mills as special adviser to the Ministry. Mills was a
Birmingham businessman whom Harold had first met when he
was temporarily working at the Ministry of Supply. 'It's like a
man who doesn't get on with his wife,' Harold explained to
Bevins of his treatment of Sheepshanks. 'He leaves her alone
and takes a mistress.' Mills was well rewarded: Harold as
Prime Minister appointed him to three successive ministerial
posts and recommended him for a viscountcy. As his junior
minister Harold appointed Ernie Marples, a Conservative
backbencher and building tycoon who had once worked as
a booker's dodger. A bumptious self-publicist, he might have
taken as his credo a remark of Harold to Bevins that it was
'better to be laughed at than to be ignored'.

With his familiar self-serving romanticism, Harold invoked
memories of the crofters' hovels on Arran in his new job.
'His pride of ancestry is very great,' Sir George Mallaby of
the Cabinet Office remembered, 'and the first time I ever spoke
to him – in his room when he was Minister of Housing – he
took up most of our official time in showing me a picture of
the lowly dwelling' on Arran from which his family began
their ascent to affluence. 'Life for him was an adventure,'
Bevins wrote of Harold at this time. 'He exuded enthusiasm
– his zeal was infectious. . . . Macmillan was really superb in
handling people, tactful, courteous, never giving much away.'
He learnt all the Whitehall tricks in his new department. 'If
you want to get anything done in government,' he once told
Wyndham and Nicholas Henderson, 'it's no good going to
the top. You have to know someone who knows someone
who really does the job.' As Mallaby recounted, Harold 'was
cunning enough to see that he might use me and the Cabinet
Office to help him get round some of the difficulties he was
encountering. He did it very well and very charmingly. . . . He
liked the oblique approach. He sent for you because he wanted
to see you, he liked your company, he wanted to talk about his

ancestry and yours, his Oxford days, and so on; and, as a sort of incidental offhand suggestion muttered out not very clearly as he shuffled about the room, perhaps you would be so good as to think up some way of overcoming the obstruction being erected against him by some Minister.' Such charm was like the surface of a shield.

Harold's tendency to psychosomatic illness receded in the early 1950s, and he shed the last vestiges of the compliance which he had learnt as Nellie's child. Bevins found him prone 'to extremes of temper, not nervily or petulantly like Eden but with great gusto and abandon'. When he was irate he showed it healthily; on one occasion, he broke into fisticuffs in the House of Commons. After a clash at parliamentary question-time, Harold had been chased to his room by a Tory backbencher, Sir Waldron Smithers. When Bevins arrived, 'the two of them were lashing out at each other. The language was marvellously lower deck. After getting a clout myself I managed to separate them.'

Altogether Harold and Walter Monckton (the Minister of Labour charged by the Cabinet with avoiding friction with the trades unions at almost any cost) were probably the most popular ministers. Together with derationing, the housebuilding programme was acclaimed as the great domestic success of Churchill's government. Harold fed journalists with a regular pabulum of rising official statistics of housebuilding and enlisted the Conservative Party's propagandists to publicise his success. In a speech to the party conference of 1952, he took as his catchphrase the words of a popular song, 'Ours is a nice house, ours is'. It was an inspired piece of huckstering which captured the headlines and ensured the party's gratitude. 'Housing is the greatest of all social needs', he told the conference. 'Even the best of schools, clinics, hospitals, playing fields and libraries are something of a mockery to those thousands of families who have no home of their own. For the home is the basis of the family, just as the family is the basis of the nation. A nation – at any rate a Christian nation – is not just a jungle of warring individuals; it is a community of families.' He depicted housebuilding as 'a great national crusade' and ended with the resounding peroration: 'The buildings are going up and so are the figures: houses completed, houses building, houses started – all are going up.' Even his opponents recognised the power of this speech. 'It had everything, the crusading spirit, the moral and family appeal, the high note mixed up with a popular sentimental appeal with a music-hall touch,' Emrys Hughes conceded begrudgingly. (It is worth adding that the momentum of the housing crusade was slipping by the time Harold left the Ministry in 1954, and by the time of his premiership Britain's housebuilding programme was one of the most retarded in Western Europe.)

In other ways Harold was astute in his dealings with the public. Small touches, such as visiting the scene of floods in Devonshire in 1952, were applauded. 'Although his sense of history and an innate taste inclined him to an earlier era, he was extraordinarily modern in mastering the current idiom and images of politics,' judged one of his shrewdest Cabinet colleagues Lord Swinton. It was for this reason that Harold was selected to give the first Conservative Party political broadcast on television in 1953. On the occasion of Churchill's last Cabinet meeting in 1955, Harold posed in Downing Street before joining Lord Woolton in their car, and then waved to the crowds as they drove away. Woolton reflected afterwards 'that a public man has to be something of an actor', but doubted if it was 'really necessary to be a showman as well. Winston, of course, has always done it; Eden does it in a very gentlemanly way, bringing his hand up to the semi-salute. But there's nothing semi about Harold; he sort of says, "Give them a cheer" and waves to them although they are not waving to him.'

For most of his life Harold was many things – a frightened man, an earnest man, a brave man and ruthless. 'He has all the characteristics, good and bad, of those who seek and achieve power,' Malcolm Muggeridge wrote in 1957. 'He can be cold, unforgiving or excitable, of the left or the right or the centre, according to the exigencies of the moment.' He was also vain. His estrangement from his party in the 1930s had been chiefly the result of honest indignation at the ineptitude of its leaders, but it had also satisfied his vanity to think that only he was clever enough to be right, and that the dunces were in confederacy against him. Now in the 1950s his vanity was stimulated by more outward signs. He became the Servant of Fame who needed the cheers of the multitude. Driving down Whitehall with Woolton he waved at the public out of self-love: the self-love that does not hide a man's faults from himself, but wants to be assured that other people have not noticed them.

He still struck some people as a crashing bore. Lunching with Lady Colefax in 1949, James Lees-Milne found his fellow guest 'H. Macmillan a pompous, inflated man full of self-importance', and was downcast by 'the silly talk of politicians' at a good meal. At other moments during the 1940s Harold struck the diplomats Oliver Harvey as 'a bore', William Strang as 'a wet' and Orme Sargent as 'a cold fish'. He remained riven by inconsistencies which led people to see him as a man playing a double game. 'Success has turned Harold into a healthy heretic & he has shed his defensive armour of respectability,' Bracken wrote in 1953 from Chequers, where he was staying with Macmillan as Churchill's guest. 'He is now chock-full of fun and is looking for new fields to conquer.' Yet his heretical pose was only one in his repertoire. When it suited him, he could act as a die-hard reactionary who loved all the old ways. 'Harold Macmillan is a splendid Tory,' Evelyn Shuckburgh wrote in 1954 after meeting him at a lunch for John Foster Dulles, where he 'spoke well in favour of stopping "progress" wherever possible'.

After his success at Housing, 'Macmillan moved rapidly like a leading actor through a sequence of senior ministries, Defence, Foreign Affairs, Exchequer', in Lord Swinton's words. Such rapid changes were bad for departments, but they gave him a diversity of experience which was useful as Prime Minister. First, in October 1954, Harold accepted from Churchill the post of Minister of Defence, but six months later, following Churchill's retirement in April 1955, he was transferred to the Foreign Office, a post to which he had aspired since 1944 at least. Then, in December 1955, the new Prime Minister, Eden, who had been watching Harold mistrustfully, moved him to the chancellorship of the Exchequer. 'Now Macmillan is there, with the most profound suspicion of the Treasury advisers and their intellectual arrogance,' Woolton reflected, 'we may get a new view, because Macmillan cannot bear to follow in anybody's footsteps.' His doubts about Treasury officials were reciprocated. Meeting him at dinner with Edwin Plowden in 1953, ostensibly to talk about European economic affairs, the government's economic adviser, Sir Robert Hall, had recorded, 'He has a restless and not very orderly mind and it could hardly be called a reasoned conversation, in fact it was largely a monologue.' Now Hall saw much more of Harold. 'The Chancellor was quite good,' he recorded of a briefing to financial journalists in 1956. 'However the meeting went on too long and the Chancellor really got a little drunk which surprised and somewhat horrified me as I thought a man of his experience would not run any risks. He was a bit indiscreet about his plans to end rent control, and also went in for a humanitarian outburst on the horrors of unemployment which was a bit against the picture of the Iron Man he had started to build up.' Overall, by the end of Harold's chancellorship, Hall judged him 'a man of courage'.

Having neither the time nor perhaps the energy to scrutinise every issue, Harold accepted the conventional wisdom on matters which did not interest him. He found political strength in indifference, and personal relief in the masquerade of indifference. What Sir George Mallaby admired about Harold in the 1950s was his 'outwardly imperturbable temperament' and 'civilised unconcern'. So many things, Harold seemed to imply, did not matter. So often the correct action was no action at all. His nonchalance seemed vindicated in cases great and small. When, after the floods of 1953, there was a plague of flies, Harold ignored all the outlandish remedies which were suggested, and (as he wrote) 'fortunately like so many other troubles, the flies in due course disappeared'. Just as happily, so it seemed to him, Britain's economic troubles in 1954 vanished like the flies: 'Nobody could explain how this happened, and some of the critics seemed rather mortified.'

He revelled in the disorder of politics and rejoiced at the mortification of his critics. Secure behind the inanimate elegance of his False Self he had put behind him his dark dives of depression. Discussing in 1955 his wish for Churchill to retire as Prime Minister, Harold bewailed to Lord Moran that Winston 'missed so many curtains, when he could have gone with everyone applauding, that it won't be as easy now'. Harold, too, now that he was at the centre of the political stage, rejoiced in the public attention, and wanted everyone applauding.

CHAPTER 9

The Prime Minister

A false calm is the best calm.
Robert Lowell, 'Suburban Surf'

All rising to great place is by a winding stair.
Francis Bacon, 'Of Great Place'

A man's public life degrades his personal life. Fame is
hard on anyone who wants to *be himself*.

Paul Valéry, *Analects*

Politics are rough, but judgment of politicians should be
rougher. Political decisions, which involve the lives, liberties
and happiness of millions of ordinary, rather helpless citizens,
are taken by people with a generous ratio of human vices. 'The
permanent and valid interest of politics', Henry Fairlie wrote
in 1957, 'is precisely that it shows human beings like you or
me, possessed of avarice, lust, wrath, envy, slothfulness, pride
and greed, wrestling with problems of more than ordinary
importance on a more than life-size scale. For this reason,
it is both inevitable and desirable that the men who take
to politics should find their actions and their motives are
constantly tested, doubted and derided in what at times seems
to be no more than a rat race.' Parliamentarians may profess
patriotism, or wish to protect the poor, or yearn to reform

inefficiencies, or itch to remedy injustices; but 'politics, as a practice, whatever its professions', to quote *The Education of Henry Adams*, has 'always been the systematic organization of hatreds'. It is the curse of politics that what one man gains, another must lose. There are no friends at the top, only adherents or rivals. Parliamentarians must become expert in laying delicately planned schemes with indelicate ends. Their promises like pie-crust are easily broken, and though people of integrity can survive in the lower altitudes of politics, one seldom survives higher up without the instincts and habits of a racketeer.

Harold was a fastidious man of literary tastes; but he had abandoned many of his earlier rules of life. Human beings deteriorate under the temptations and strains of power, and Harold had been duly corrupted. In the last years of Churchill's government and throughout Eden's administration he showed himself not only as an earnest and industrious departmental minister but also a keen and masterly intriguer – his protests of sated ambition notwithstanding. 'You know, being Anthony's Foreign Secretary is a wonderful thing,' he told Anthony Nutting. 'Of course, if I were younger I might be tempted to intrigue! But at my age I could never succeed him – so my ambitions are satisfied.' It was an unconvincing disavowal.

Relations between the three senior commoners in Eden's Cabinet were not unstintingly generous. What Harold admired most – in a man like Alexander – was self-control and steady nerves. He was impatient of physical weakness, prided himself on conquering illness and fought a daily battle against his fears and nerves: not surprisingly Eden's volatile, fretful, peevish character distracted him. He was contemptuous too of Eden's infirmities. Other colleagues commented on the jealousy in Eden's nature, which they called effeminate, a judgment that showed how little they understood women, for no type is more jealous than Cabinet ministers. 'Mr Harold Macmillan I rather think doesn't like women fussing about,' the explorer Freya Stark had told Lady Wavell in 1944 – and Clarissa Eden was one of the objects of his misogyny. 'Harold Macmillan told me he didn't like the woman,' Lord Woolton recorded in 1955. His intrigues were all the more cold and remorseless because of his antagonism towards the Prime Minister's young wife.

Eden was perhaps no more jealous a man than his Cabinet colleague Butler. Rab was vain and shy, with a weakness for indiscretions and an egocentricity which was possibly his compensation for his physical disfigurement. He had a reputation for intellectuality and an authentic streak of altruism, but there was something false and repellent in his character; after meeting him in 1956, Evelyn Waugh described him with a novelist's acuity as 'squinny-eyed, awkward, given to horrible bursts of "Yo ho ho"'. Whereas Harold's urge for power showed itself in steely ruthlessness, Butler's unrelenting ambition took the form of an exasperating sleekness. He seemed to feel that he would achieve supreme office if he acted as all things to all men; he was never abrupt, abhorring dispute; he never rebelled or defied anyone, he trimmed to his party line and preferred to conciliate his opponents. As junior minister at the Foreign Office in 1938–9, he had been an arch-appeaser, and Harold, who as Chips Channon noticed was 'obsessed' by the memory of the Munich agreement, never forgave Butler for this: in turn more than twenty years later, in 1962, Butler remembered feeling 'offended' by Harold singing 'Rule Britannia' from the Conservative benches 'at the time of Chamberlain's downfall'. Harold was always hostile to Butler, though the hostility was sometimes masked; inwardly he disdained him. 'Rab is one of those men who cannot cook without meat,' he told Bevins. 'I can cook with bread and water.' To Cabinet colleagues too he denigrated Rab – 'round the bend' was the phrase he used to Selwyn Lloyd.

Against this ominous but hardly unusual background of personal hostility Eden's Cabinet had to react to the decision in July 1956 by the Egyptian Prime Minister, Gamal Abdel Nasser, to nationalise the British and French controlling shareholdings in the Suez Canal Company. The course of the Suez crisis is incomprehensible without recognising the unease of Conservative supporters that Britain's world status and the reputation of

Eden's administration at home were being eroded by weak leadership. The government's handling of trades unions, the constant increases in prices, controversy over capital punishment, the tumult between British soldiers and Cypriot nationalists: all these seemed evidence of weakness. Party members had been momentarily heartened when the insurrectionist Archbishop Makarios was deported from Cyprus in March 1956; but when the moment of confrontation with the Egyptians hit the Cabinet, 'like all weak men they had recourse to what they called strong measures' (to quote Disraeli in *Coningsby*). 'I was torn and distressed and could not get my mind straight about it, and so was useless,' one Cabinet member, Buchan-Hepburn, wrote later to Eden while stressing 'my admiration for your courage throughout that dreadful time'. For men embarking upon an aggressive policy they were too tremulous. As one Tory backbencher from the pro-interventionist Suez Group, Fitzroy Maclean, complained to Denis Healey at the time, 'You can't make war with church mice.'

After settling a secret compact, British, French and Israeli forces attacked Egypt at the end of October 1956. In the prelude to this operation, Harold had been the leading Cabinet belligerent, warning that unless action was taken Britain would be reduced to the status in Europe of the Netherlands and speaking emotively of his wish to keep 'the lawns of England green' for his grandchildren. 'He relished the atmosphere of crisis, realised he could keep his nerve in it more easily perhaps than any other Minister, and enjoyed some of the cloak-and-dagger side of preparations,' Hugh Thomas has explained. 'He hated with all his soul the decline of Britain as a great power,' and was burning to prove 'there was life in the old lion still . . . that Churchill's successors were worthy of their immortal predecessor'. He urged on Eden a grand design in which Britain settled all the frontiers of the Middle East, in imitation of the Cairo Conference which Churchill had convened in 1921, and, in a revealing fantasy, likened his proposals to Napoleon's efforts at the unification of Italy. His description in August of military

operations against Egypt as a certain success provoked the
Minister of Defence, Monckton, into a furious outburst in
Cabinet Committee – all the more shocking for those present
because Monckton was usually so equable. Yet Harold abruptly
turned from being a roaring lion into a bleating sheep. The
Cabinet's policy was supported by British public opinion, and
by Conservative loyalists who were in a jingo frenzy, but a
large and perhaps preponderating number of ministers were
dubious about using force against Egypt. Sir Edward Boyle, a
talented young MP who was working with Harold as Financial
Secretary to the Treasury, resigned in protest at Eden's policy
and further resignations by ministers and senior civil servants
seemed imminent. The Cabinet was more shaken though by the
objections of the Eisenhower administration to their military
adventure (especially the threat of oil sanctions) and by a run
on the pound sterling which Harold as Chancellor reported in
alarm to the Cabinet. In the space of hours his counsel in Cabinet
underwent a complete reversal and decisively changed the direction of British policy. When the Egyptians and Israelis ceased fire
on 6 November, Eden ordered British troops to halt.

During these months of crisis Harold reread all the novels
of George Eliot, together with Thackeray's *Vanity Fair* and
studies of Machiavelli by Macaulay and the Italian nationalist
Pasquale Villari. But for the distraction of this reading, 'I'd
have gone barmy,' he told Alistair Horne. The influence on
Harold's excited and suggestive mind of this bout of literary
Machiavellianism can only be imagined. One passage in Villari's
book will strike anyone who considers Macmillan's behaviour
as Eden's Suez policy disintegrated. 'He saw clearly that statecraft has ways and means of its own, which are not the ways and
means of private morality . . . and that it is mainly vacillation
. . . that leads to the downfall of States,' Villari wrote. 'There
must be no vacillation . . . but a daring adoption of the measures
demanded by the nature of events. Such measures will always
be justified when the measure is obtained. And the end in view
must be the welfare of the State. He who achieves this, even if

a wicked man, may be condemned for his wickedness, but will deserve, as a prince, everlasting glory.'

'Diplomatists', wrote Henry Adams, 'have no right to complain of mere lies; it is their own fault, if, educated as they are, the lies deceive them, but they complain bitterly of traps.' Harold (in common with others like Eden and the Foreign Secretary, Selwyn Lloyd) lied about the Suez adventure, but more significantly he also set a series of traps which caught Eden. Despite visiting Washington he inexplicably misread American opinion and misled the Cabinet over the intentions of Eisenhower's administration ('I know Ike,' he promised in September, 'Ike will lie doggo'); he incited the Cabinet into collusion with the French and Israelis; he ignored or suppressed the warnings of civil servants, and Eisenhower's emissaries, that Britain's economy could not stand the inevitable disruption of oil supplies or the certain withdrawal of American financial support; he did not take the obvious precaution as Chancellor of reducing the gold tranche from the International Monetary Fund or of extending Treasury controls over capital movements; and, as grievously as anything, he exaggerated to colleagues the run on sterling. He told the Cabinet that £100 million of the sterling area's currency reserves ($280 million, or one-eighth of the total) had been withdrawn in the first week of November alone, when the correct figure was £31.7 million. This discrepancy is so huge that he must either have been off his head with panic or misleading his colleagues for some purpose of his own, such as obtaining an immediate ceasefire which would placate the Americans.

Certainly he was in frequent, secret contact with the US Ambassador in London, Winthrop Aldrich. As the latter wrote later, from the date of the attack on Egypt until Eden's retirement he was 'enormously helped' by a senior Cabinet minister speaking to him 'with great frankness', and permitting the transmission of his 'views and ideas directly to Washington, without passing through the Foreign Office'. Apart from discussing diplomatic dilemmas, and especially ways for the British Cabinet to placate the Eisenhower administration, the two men delicately but recurrently skirted the possibilities that would arise if Eden was displaced as prime minister. On the day before Eden publicly announced his breakdown in health after the crisis, Harold was at Aldrich's home proposing that he might visit Washington as 'Eden's deputy', and melodramatically promising the Ambassador to be available to him 'at any minute of the day or night'. He was playing ruthlessly for the succession and trying to develop his secret intimacies with the Americans as one of his aces. Aldrich was convinced at this time that, if Eden resigned, 'the Queen would summon Harold Macmillan, since Salisbury – in whom I knew the Queen had great confidence, and who I felt sure would be consulted – had come to the conclusion that Macmillan was the person best fitted to deal with President Eisenhower, because of the close association they had in Africa during the war'. But, if Harold was his informant, it means that he began conspiring – with the Americans and against Eden – as soon as Egypt was attacked. Certainly he had much to hide, for he destroyed his diary for this period (supposedly at Eden's request).

Harold's part in the Suez affair has been likened by Michael Foot to those of the villains of Shakespearean tragedy: to Iago, tricking the jealous Othello towards self-destruction, or to the remorseless schemer in *King Lear*, Edmund the Bastard. Certainly he was the demon king of Suez. There was no humbug about his patriotism: his pride in the Grenadiers was one of the truest emotions he felt. He would have done nothing immediately detrimental to his country or hazardous to its soldiers. But he saw Eden's policy faltering, felt the Prime Minister was 'playing ducks and drakes' with the country and thought the government was disintegrating under the strain; it was in his power to break Eden on a wheel of his own devising, and that is what he did. Harold was three years older than Eden and knew that if the latter's premiership survived the current parliament, he would be too old for consideration as successor. If his conduct during the Suez crisis was contradictory, his course afterwards was devious but consistent.

He was unremittingly self-seeking. In mid-November he heard that Anthony Nutting, a promising young MP who had resigned as Minister of State for Foreign Affairs in protest at the Anglo-French collusion with Israel's attack on Egypt, was planning to make a personal statement in parliament explaining his resignation. He asked Nutting to show him the text of his intended remarks.

> When he had finished reading it, he shook his head and in solemn and almost funereal tones, he said, 'This is very damaging. It could easily bring down the Government, and for you, dear boy, it will do irreparable harm.' Then, after pausing for dramatic effect, he went on, 'Why say anything at all? You have already been proved right and we have been proved wrong. You have also done the right thing by resigning and, if you keep silent now, you will be revered and rewarded. You will lead the Party one day.'

Nutting's response to this advice was revulsion. 'At that moment I wanted to be quit of politics and all the hypocrisy that seemed to go with it. I did not even stop to argue and, picking up my speech, walked silently from the room. Outside in the street, I tore my notes up and stuffed them down a drain. It seemed a fitting gesture.' (Far from being revered, Nutting was ostracised. 'One should never, of course, trust Britons who call one dear boy,' commented Russell Braddon: 'Macmillan, while waving a flag of truce, shot his enemy dead.')

On 23 November Eden flew to Jamaica for a month's convalescence. 'I shall always remember the anger with which Harold Macmillan greeted this news and his strongly expressed judgment that this was suicide for Eden,' Butler noted afterwards. When Eden returned, he faced a demoralised and aggrieved Conservative Party. 'My confidence in, and respect for, the man have evaporated totally,' wrote Dorothy Macmillan's brother-in-law James Stuart, the Secretary of State for Scotland, on 13 December. 'I couldn't shake hands with him and don't want to be in the same room with him.' Harold showed his divergence from the Prime Minister discreetly but unmistakably.

Lord Tonypandy remembers him on one occasion at the end of 1956, 'standing at the Bar of the House, looking round, and instead of going to his place on the front bench next to the Prime Minister, walking to a seat on a bench below the gangway to chat to Tory backbenchers, making it plain that he was distancing himself from Eden'. Harold had a weakness for inapt analogies, and while jockeying for power exploited the grotesque feeling among Tory MPs that Nasser was another Hitler and that the Suez crisis had been another Munich. He saw here an advantage and made the most of it. On 12 November, for example, he told the Commons why he had not supported 'a policy of appeasement' of Nasser. 'I will tell the House frankly and sincerely,' he said, with studiedly ominous meaning, 'it is because I have seen it all happen before.' His words were not only a reminder of his courage in opposing Munich, but a sly dig at his rival for the party succession, Butler, who had been a principal exponent of appeasement. Although Harold tried to fox journalists by hinting that he intended to retire from politics, Bracken recognised 'his real intentions are to push his boss out of No. 10', and by 7 December Harold's old mentor Beaverbrook was predicting that unless he failed 'in his conspiracies . . . Britain will have further terrible failures if he becomes Prime Minister'. Rumours abounded; yet it came as a bombshell when, on the afternoon of 9 January, Eden told Harold of his decision to resign.

Two hours later Eden stunned a meeting of the full Cabinet by repeating his announcement to them. The Lord Chancellor, Kilmuir, and Salisbury, the senior Cabinet Minister, then saw each member of the Cabinet in turn, Salisbury lisping the same question to them all: 'Well, which is it, Wab or Hawold?' All but one of the Cabinet favoured Macmillan. Their choice was affected by several considerations: they thought him more decisive than Butler; knowing his wartime association with Eisenhower they felt he would have a personal advantage in repairing Anglo-American relations; some of the Tory old guard thought that he was one of them; a few of the more astute realised that Harold would have the brazenness and moral agility to turn around and move away as fast as possible from Suez and Eden's humiliation. The feeling of the Cabinet was clear, but further soundings were taken. Eden was consulted by the Queen, and commended Butler; but the preference of the 1922 Committee of Tory backbenchers was for Harold. To the delight of the irreverent he and Butler had both addressed it on 22 November. Butler, it was felt, had kept 'his head well down beneath the parapet during the parliamentary crisis when the shot and shell were at their fiercest', so Peter Rawlinson recounted; and if, by contrast, Macmillan like the Grand Old Duke of York had 'marched his men to the top of the hill and then very smartly . . . marched them down again . . . it was also felt that he had at least been in action'. Perhaps responding to such feelings, Rab gave a dull performance which disheartened the meeting, but was followed by Harold on his liveliest form, with histrionic pauses and revealingly savage baring of his teeth. He spoke with insolent defiance about Suez, and teased his audience by musing about the evening of his political days and the viscountcy with which he would soon retire from the Cabinet; but for most of his half-hour oration he was rousingly exuberant about the future, revelling in the 'long adventure of politics, full of hard knocks but still a game more worth playing than any other'. A few MPs, including Enoch Powell, were disgusted by his crafty act; but the overwhelming majority were heartened and took cruel relish in Butler's discomfiture as he was outspoken and outsmarted. The contrast between the two men on that night was remembered by everyone as soundings were taken on 9 January. Harold half-jokingly told Reginald Maudling on the evening of Eden's resignation that his son Maurice had assured him that he would be the most successful candidate 'because the Party think I am too old and too sick to last for very long'. The reality was different.

On the evening of the 9th, the Chancellor left Downing Street with Dorothy and walked down Whitehall followed by a troop of journalists and photographers. Reaching Whitehall Court he asked with deliberate audibility, 'Which is Lord Woolton's flat?' This was a device to indicate that he was dining with a former chairman of the Conservative Party, for he must have known the answer well enough; then he went upstairs. Despite Harold's cool showmanship outside, Woolton found him 'distrait and wanting to talk about going back to the publishing business': so much so that when Harold was called away to the telephone, Woolton told Dorothy 'that he must be stopped talking like that and she told me that it was all right, he would go on. He obviously required urging to do so.' At the crucial hour, Harold needed Dorothy to impel him and to restrain his nerves.

On the following morning he calmed himself by reading *Pride and Prejudice* until summoned to Buckingham Palace to kiss hands with the Queen. Many felt he had become Prime Minister as the reward for his somersault over Suez. An MP called Kenneth Younger summarised this view by adapting a refrain from W.S. Gilbert:

> I sounded the charge while I beat the retreat
> So now I am Prime Minister in Downing Street.

A few days later when the Edens left by sea for New Zealand, Harold went to bid them farewell and wept at the dockside. 'Mind you, Harold cries frightfully easily,' Clarissa Eden said later.

His first task was to reconstruct the government. 'I am appointing my ministers,' he told the Under Secretary of State for Foreign Affairs, Douglas Dodds-Parker, who had been intimately involved in Suez. 'We cannot all play. I must ask you to go and sit in the pavilion.' An awkward moment in his Cabinet-making came when Boothby wrote asking for a Cabinet post and a peerage: Wyndham was so shocked by the letter that he kept it from Harold for several days and was astonished that, when he finally presented it to the Prime Minister, the latter said emphatically, 'Of course he must have it' (meaning the peerage but not Cabinet office). With the agonies of the 1930s long over, if not forgotten, Harold and Boothby shared some of the affection and mutual understanding which one would expect from two civilised men who had known and adored the same woman for so long. But when in 1958 Boothby was gazetted as the first of the barons under the new Life Peerage Act, there was some dismay among the cognoscenti. 'What about the peerage for Bob Boothby!' Salisbury exclaimed to Eden. 'I may be out of date; but I don't like these things.' Otherwise the government was smoothly reconstructed, although as Harold confided to Butler in October 1957, he wished his colleagues were more ruthless: 'he regretted' that 'there were no tough guys like Swinton or Oliver Lyttelton'. He did not want 'great oratorical brilliance in the House of Commons, or great administrative ability in your departments', he told a meeting of new ministers in 1962. 'All I ask of you is sheer physical endurance.'

In the early days he fumbled. On 29 January Maurice Collis went to see Harold appear at Prime Minister's question-time in the House of Commons – an ordeal before which he often vomited through nervousness. 'He wears his hair rather long and has an anxious peering expression,' Collis described. 'He moved down the front bench till opposite the despatch box and clutching a large book containing questions and answers hurriedly turned the pages to find the right place, giving the impression of an old woman scrattling in her bag. He lacked dignity and presence and did not in any way dominate the House.' Collis agreed with a Tory backbencher, Sir John Smyth VC, that Harold seemed 'afraid of the Commons'. At other times he overplayed his hand. Six months later in the Commons he had 'a jolly spat' with the socialist Aneurin Bevan about the hydrogen bomb. When Bevan lost his temper and accused his opponents of being 'bloodthirsty', the Prime Minister 'rose and did his soft-shoe shuffle to the table', Bernard Levin recorded in the *Spectator*. 'Striking an attitude which would have got him thrown out of the Wigan Pier Fol-de-Rols for hamming it up too much, he puffed up his moustache and declared that he deeply resented Mr Bevan's interpretation. This was patently nonsense, and many worthy folk showed clearly that they knew it.'

Initially the outlook seemed desperate, beyond retrieving or contesting. At home the Conservative Party was split and shaken; the economic situation was precarious; Britain had fallen in stature and repute abroad; and, most calamitously of all, Anglo-American relations seemed wrecked. Harold warned the Queen that his administration might not last six weeks, and others doubted that the government would survive the year. A series of adverse by-elections seemed to confirm this. Salisbury, who with Kilmuir had canvassed party opinion before Harold's appointment to succeed Eden, resigned in March 1957, ostensibly over the liberation of Archbishop Makarios from exile and his return to Cyprus, but also, as he confided to Eden, because he found Macmillan 'very uncongenial' in Cabinet. As recently as November Churchill had regarded Salisbury as Harold's chief rival for the premiership, and the Foreign Secretary Selwyn Lloyd felt that Harold welcomed Salisbury's departure 'because it removed the only member of the Cabinet who was a contemporary and his equal in experience and authority'; as a result the Cabinet became more malleable to his will. Once excluded from power, Salisbury became a spasmodic but vexatious critic of the Macmillan government, especially its policy of African decolonisation. 'He had not liked parting with Lord Salisbury whom he had known since school days,' Butler recorded the Prime Minister as telling him in 1962. 'But his parting on such a silly pretext as Makarios' release had reconciled Harold,' who persuaded Butler that 'the real trouble' was a longstanding family antipathy. Salisbury was married to Dorothy Macmillan's cousin Betty Cavendish ('fascinating, funny, unexpected and fatally attractive', in David Herbert's description): her younger sister Diana had been briefly and unhappily married to Boothby in the 1930s. There had been, so Harold told Butler, a 'very old difficulty for Betty and Dorothy to get on together'. Moreover, 'Bobbety had always had his eye on the Foreign Secretaryship', and after Harold's appointment of Lord Home to the post in 1960, his disappointment became 'even more painful when he could see how successful a Peer could be as Foreign Secretary'. So, at least, it suited Harold to tell Butler.

Salisbury's version was different. 'Oh dear! Oh dear! I don't think that I am meant for politics, especially Harold's kind,' he wrote to Eden in May 1957. 'He is too clever by half for me.' He compared Harold to Neville Chamberlain ('the same lack of any proper moral standard; the same unblushing opportunism') and likened the last year of Harold's premiership to the corrupt last months in 1922 of the coalition government under Lloyd George ('the man leading the Conserv: Party but yet not really part of it'). He thought Harold 'a very able man' with 'immense powers of self-deception' who 'killed the British Colonial Empire stone dead', as he told Eden in a series of letters which form a powerful if jaundiced commentary on the Macmillan years.

'The commonest error in politics is sticking to the carcasses of dead policies; when a mast falls overboard you do not try to save a rope here, and a spar there, in memory of their former utility; you cut away the hamper altogether. And it should be the same with a policy.' So Salisbury's grandfather, the Victorian Prime Minister, had written to Lord Lytton seventy years before. The discarding of dead carcasses, their prompt and hygienic jettisoning overboard, became one of the hallmarks of the Macmillan premiership.

When Harold became Prime Minister, the Labour Party was thirteen points ahead in opinion polls. 'Our first objective', he told Swinton, 'must be to keep the Party together, at all costs united. It's like keeping five balls in the air simultaneously, knowing that we are doomed if we drop one.' He set himself the task of reviving confidence by a show of cool resolution and a pose of serene confidence. As his office motto, he adopted a phrase from Gilbert and Sullivan's *Gondoliers*, 'Quiet calm deliberation disentangles every knot.' From the outset he caricatured himself: 'the Edwardian mask, the drooping moustache, the old-world gestures and mannerisms, the fruity voice, the hooded eyes, the manners, the studied cadences', in Swinton's description, flummoxed opponents by temporarily masking the fact that they were dealing with 'the shrewdest party boss for generations'. Not everyone was as enthusiastic as Swinton about the mimicries of Harold's False Self. Lord Altrincham (who later renounced his peerage and as John Grigg was the sharpest political observer of his generation) caught Harold's measure exactly. 'He is a pawky Scottish business man trying to convince himself and others that he is an English aristocrat of the old school,' Grigg wrote as early as February 1957.

> That does not mean that he is ashamed of his Scottish ancestry; on the contrary, he is proud of it. . . . But at the same time he seeks, maybe unconsciously, to project a patrician, Anglo-Saxon, Churchillian *persona*. Like Sir Winston at the Other Club, Mr Macmillan holds forth in the grand manner at Pratts – only with this vital difference, that neither the manner nor the setting is his own. As a practical man he is genuine and acceptable; as an imitation grandee he is nauseating.

Surveying Harold's post-war record of 'cold-blooded opportunism', Grigg predicted that, before long, 'we shall find ourselves in the same state as France, where it is accepted that politicians have a code of their own, and most people have an instinctive repugnance to the idea of entering politics.'

Dorothy, as the Duke's earthy daughter in tweeds and sensible shoes, was an integral part of Harold's patrician image. 'Here again appearances are apt to be deceptive,' Grigg wrote in a profile of 1958 which was unique in hinting at the Macmillans' domestic irregularities. 'Like her husband, Lady Dorothy is not quite all that she seems in some respects, and a great deal more than she seems in others. To the casual observer she is just a typical English upper-class cup of tea; but on closer inspection he would find that it was laced with liquid of a more stimulating kind.'

Most prime ministers are pretenders and dissemblers. The cases of Lloyd George and Wilson are too notorious to need comment; the discrepancies between the public personalities and private anxieties of Baldwin and MacDonald were described in a previous chapter. But other prime ministers acted or played false: men as varied as Balfour, who radiated an impersonal geniality to disguise his indifference to everyone and everything, or Winston Churchill, likened by Harold Laski to 'a great actor playing a part'. Similarly Ronald Higgins, who was Heath's private secretary for two and a half years during the European Community negotiations of the early 1960s, told Tony Benn in 1969 that 'he had known Ted Heath as well as anyone could and that Ted Heath's real nature and character had been so suppressed that there was nothing real underneath any more. He had just got a concrete shell round his real self and this is why he never appeared to be sincere.' Harold took a pose of marmoreal perfection: cold, hard and immobile. He strove to achieve a false air of imperturbability, but there were few politicians with the astuteness or self-knowledge to recognise that, in a phrase of Lord Strauss, 'Harold Macmillan concealed his terror behind an air of sublime self-confidence.'

As earlier chapters have shown, concealment was one of the themes of his life. He liked to hide things. His character was hidden from his mother behind a False Self; his broken marriage was hidden from the electors of Stockton by displays of marital unity on public platforms; Sarah's pregnancy was hidden by an abortion. As a Cabinet minister, he had always preferred the oblique approach: Sir George Mallaby's account of his halting, indirect manoeuvres at the Ministry of Housing has already been quoted. As Prime Minister too he hid things – like the Thor missile agreement with the Americans – or was stealthy. He could hardly hide the abandonment of Empire, for example, but all his instincts were to do such a thing by stealth. Harold himself once said that power was like a Dead Sea Fruit, that one fought for it and then, when one got it, found there was nothing there. The hardest thing to hide is something that does not exist: our greatest pretences are made to hide not the evil or the ugly in us, but our emptiness.

He often gave the impression that 'spiritually he had never left the Edwardian era', a Tory backbencher, C.M. Woodhouse, wrote in 1966; but it was the mantle of Edwardian materialism that enveloped him, not the gloom of Edwardian pessimism. Though his own upbringing had not been epicurean, the spirit of the times had been. Even during the first war, when Harold was invalided back from the Front, there had been endless talk about the 'good times' to come. There was something Edwardian about his wish for a nation whose people had 'never had it so good'. Edwardians too had been chauvinists, and there were many chauvinist assumptions underlying Harold's policies: at heart he wanted Europe to be the super-continent and Great Britain the super-country. It was in this spirit that he committed the country to prestige projects like the heavily subsidised Cunard passenger liner, *Queen Elizabeth II*, the Magnox nuclear power stations and the exorbitantly costly Concorde supersonic airliner.

Among his earliest resolves was to take foreign affairs into his own hands as best he could. He was perhaps mindful of the judgment in the 1930s of the Tory theorist F.S. Oliver that there had been only two great foreign secretaries, Palmerston and Salisbury, the latter for most of the time in the 1880s and 1890s holding office as Foreign Secretary and Prime Minister simultaneously. Like Salisbury he was a Tory in the true sense, a practitioner of the politics of depression; both men exulted that, in Salisbury's phrase, politics was an inexact science; they were dull orators, who were occasionally enlivened into catchy vulgar phrases before popular audiences; they were prolific but dreary authors, whose few memorable phrases were chiefly caustic asides; they both professed a deep Christianity but were regarded as incorrigible cynics. Harold, like Salisbury, was a good delegator, with a taste for racy sporting metaphors: 'even if I had fancied I saw flaws in it I should have scrupled to say so, on the principle that you do not address advice to a billiard player at the moment he is about to strike,' Salisbury had written to the author of an important diplomatic missive in 1876. In their leadership of the nation too they shared a common basis. For Salisbury the object of Conservatism was not to stop change, but to stop the nation 'splitting . . . into a bundle of unfriendly and distrustful fragments' – a sentiment similar to Harold's animating principles throughout his political career.

Harold founded his government's policy on Britain's relations with his mother's native land. He began repairing Anglo-American relations by meeting Eisenhower at Bermuda in March 1957. 'We are', he ruminated privately at this time, 'the Greeks of the Hellenistic age: the power has passed from us to Rome's equivalent, the United States of America, and we can at most aspire to civilise and occasionally to influence them.' In his first major speech after taking office, he asserted that Britain would never be a satellite state, but a month later, at Bermuda, he perfected his country's final and total dependence on the USA for survival in a big war. Within three months he had restored Anglo-American relations to their pre-Suez equilibrium, and he put a huge effort into reaching an agreement on the exchange of nuclear technological information. To Butler in 1957 'he spoke of his ambition to merge US and UK policy', especially on defence, and of his feeling that the two nations had a 'special relationship'; by December Eden was writing privately that Harold's policy was 'making us the 49th state', and Butler warned him in the same sense. He wanted a trans-Atlantic conservative coalition in which the Americans supplied the money and the might, while the British offered guile and classiness. He deliberately appealed to the snobbery of American Anglophiles, and duped many people with a pose of weary, unworldly superiority. 'Mr Macmillan gives the impression of a civilized man who has risen above what he considers some of the brutalities of the modern age,' the *Indianapolis Star* reported in 1957.

He hated Soviet totalitarianism and, when it suited his purposes, imagined the Russians as barbarians before the gates of Rome. In the early years of his premiership there were bitter and furious confrontations with Khrushchev, but after the Cuban missile crisis of 1962 both sides moderated their tone and took more conciliatory postures. 'I pin my faith on them gradually getting more like other people, more and more wanting the same things, so that over generations the differences between us and them will narrow,' he said of the Russians in 1962. 'Meanwhile, do not yield to them, but avoid picking quarrels.'

To trace the pattern of Harold's diplomacy, to follow his long and patient negotiations with the two super-powers, to relive his clashes with Khrushchev or his friendship with Jack Kennedy took Harold himself several volumes – worthy of his Victorian forefathers in their massive, earnest, indigestible way. The issues were momentous, Harold's commitment was superb and his courage was magnificent. Every move was made with steadfast high intent to prevent the 'extinction of civilisation'. There were appalling setbacks to his strategy of diplomatic summitry – reversals like the ruin of the Paris summit of 1960 by the shooting down over Russia of a US spy aeroplane – which would have crushed or disillusioned another man. But he tried again and again. Whatever the turpitude he showed on other occasions, whatever the inauthenticity of the man, his tenacity was real enough.

His only great success after the 1959 election was the Test Ban Treaty of 1963. From 1961 his whole stock of energy and ingenuity were dedicated to obtaining this treaty: it is hard to realise today how imminent international catastrophe seemed or how huge the obstacles loomed. For Harold it was a great effort and great work. It was 'a true Macmillan achievement', his aide Harold Evans recorded. 'It was he – with his sense of history – who read the signs aright in Russia and saw the opportunities: who coaxed and prodded the Americans: who argued the case with Khrushchev: and finally took the initiative.' At the time he even impressed Butler as 'an elder statesman deeply moved by a sense of duty to save the world from destruction'. Yet at some moments of the negotiations the strain overwhelmed him, and he retreated into theatrical mystification. On one occasion in 1963 Zuckerman, the Ministry of Defence's chief scientific adviser, was called to Birch Grove where Harold was discussing the treaty with Kennedy. Shortly before midnight Harold left his conference with the President and beckoned Zuckerman into his study, saying that he needed help to find a book. The two men moved to the corner furthest from the door, where the Prime Minister started fiddling with books on a high shelf. 'Stand closer,' he said, 'stand closer still.' He then slipped into Zuckerman's pocket a paper that Kennedy had given him, summarising the objections of the American Joint Chiefs of Staff. There was nothing hush-hush about Kennedy's paper or novel about its arguments; but at times of strain Harold felt persecuted and behaved stealthily.

Super-power summitry provided one theme for his premiership. The dismemberment of Empire was another. At the outset in 1957 he instructed the Cabinet Secretary, Sir Norman Brook, to superintend Whitehall's first cost-benefit analysis of British colonialism, an investigation which concluded that there was no economic benefit in colonialism. Although the precision of this analysis was new, Harold's sentiments had been tending in the same direction since the war. 'This is the age of Diocletian – the end of Empire,' he had in 1955 told Sir Robin Turton, who thought the remark was based on a misreading of Diocletian's reign. Nevertheless one of his earliest priorities as Prime Minister was to restore confidence and cohesion in the wake of Suez: tasks which he fulfilled at the Commonwealth Prime Ministers Conference in 1957 and during his Commonwealth tour of 1958. He turned his attention to the future of British Africa only after the general election of 1959, when his victory freed him from the need to court the jingo wing of his party. In the following year he made a much publicised tour of Africa, visiting Ghana, Nigeria and the Federation of Rhodesia and Nyasaland, before culminating in South Africa, where at Pretoria he made his famous 'Winds of Change' speech.

His greatest tests in Africa concerned the Federation of Rhodesia and Nyasaland. This had been created in 1953 with high hopes of a multiracial society embracing three African colonies (now Zimbabwe, Zambia and Malawi); but from the outset the wishes of blacks and whites were irreconcilable. When trouble arose in Nyasaland in 1959, Harold behaved, in Anthony Sampson's words, 'as he had after Suez, as if nothing had happened: it was the lowpoint of his political morality'. In their conduct towards Sir Roy Welensky, the Prime Minister of the Federation, he and his ministers were evasive, postponing confrontation, blurring issues and professing support to those they were moving against. 'He was always one of the most accomplished actors in public life, and in the three hours I spent with him he put on a truly magnificent performance,' Welensky wrote of a dinner in London with Harold in 1961.

> As he spoke of his deep sympathy and understanding of us in Africa, his eyes were moist and shining and his voice vibrated with emotion. Paddling out into this tide of words, I mentioned recent happenings in North Rhodesia. The tears rolled down Macmillan's cheeks. 'Roy, do you really believe that I, who have seen the horror of two world wars, would have tolerated a situation in which Britishers would have been shooting down Britishers, their brothers, alongside whom they had fought on many a battlefield?'

If Harold seemed hypocritical to Welensky, it is not surprising given his negotiating technique, as described by a journalist who attended a conference of the two men in 1961. 'At unpredictable moments during the talks, especially if they were reaching an awkward point, he would suddenly appear to become preoccupied with any question except the one under discussion; with no warning, and with no suggestion of relevance, he would embark upon a gentle dissertation about the smaller pleasantries of life or, for it was just as likely, sweep his bemused listeners through the sad but instructive history of some remote and ancient civilisation; suddenly, and again with no warning, he would pounce and bring those whose minds he had been leading away abruptly face to face with the point which ten minutes before he had seemed to be avoiding': so Henry Fairlie reported. 'He had bided his own time; he had watched and calculated; he had disarmed; and the important effect of all this careful stagecraft was that he consistently forced those with whom he was dealing to consider the question at issue in the terms in which *he* chose to present it.' These unappealing manipulations seemed unavoidable though. When, in 1961, Harold offered Cub Alport the post of High Commissioner to the Federation, he dilated for some time on great proconsuls of the past like Cromer and Milner. His prolixity was often remembered ruefully by Alport once he was installed at Salisbury. Cromer and Milner had 'possessed *power* – the ultimate power of Britain's financial, diplomatic and in the last resort military strength in the heyday of its world leadership', Alport reflected. 'But in the 1960s a British representative abroad had to rely mainly on his own ingenuity and personal influence, knowing that in the last resort there was precious little support at all to sustain his authority.' It was from a sense of hopeless weakness that the British were so devious.

Both Harold's policies towards the super-powers and the colonies were intimately enmeshed with his policy towards the European mainland. Competition from industrial powers across the North Sea was pressing increasingly hard on the economy. Britain's economic position was now tedious, he told Eden in 1957, because of its misplaced leniency to Germany in the post-war settlement. (The German leader Adenauer in 1958 compared Britain to 'a rich man who has lost all his property but does not realise it.') In 1959 he arranged for Sir Patrick Dean, a diplomat whom he admired for his lion-hearted resolve, to superintend a confidential Whitehall enquiry into Britain's power and world role in the following decade. During the election campaign of that year, many Conservatives, including some ministers, opposed any British attempt to join the EEC. Harold, professedly a fervent European, allowed the relics of the Empire Crusaders to give an anti-European aspect to Conservative policy during the election campaign. The Cabinet was not told of Dean's remit, which is unmentioned in Harold's exhaustive autobiography; moreover, though a paper which summarised the findings of Dean's review was circulated to the Cabinet in February 1960, it was not released after thirty years to the Public Record Office and reference to it has been expunged from the record office catalogue. Harold's stealthiness lived on after his retirement. Nevertheless the civil servant's conclusions were a critical influence on the later strategies of Macmillan's premiership. Dean envisaged the European Community becoming an economic and political unit 'overshadowing' Britain by the early 1970s; and the burden of Dean's report was encapsulated in some later small-talk of Harold's: 'If we do not join the Common Market, do you imagine that in twenty years' time there will be any question of the President of the United States going to the trouble, as today, of consulting the Prime Minister of Great Britain about anything? Why should he do so? We should have dwindled into a small, unimportant island. Europe with its tens of millions would go on without us.'

Harold initially hoped for a mass junction with the EEC of the European Free Trade Association, to which seven of the smaller nations, including Britain, belonged; and during a visit to the USA in 1960 the *Washington Post* leaked an account of his remarks at the State Department which had a devastating effect in Europe. Among other sweeping remarks, Harold reportedly said that he feared a Nazi recrudescence in Germany and that Britain must thwart Napoleonic ambitions for French domination of Europe. The leak, though officially contradicted, had the smack of verisimilitude. Meanwhile Harold surreptitiously edged his party and public opinion towards accepting a British application for membership of the Community. He was in a tight spot – talking to Richard Crossman in 1961, his daughter Catherine Amery was frank 'about the crisis in the Tory Party on the Common Market and the danger that all the agricultural constituencies would get upset and the party be split' – but his speech to the Commons on 2 August justifying the application was an ominous mixture of rhetorical assertions and inner contradictions: 'full of double-talk', according to an anti-marketeer Tory MP, who dubbed him 'a national disaster'. His off-the-record briefing to the parliamentary lobby correspondents in the same week showed his state of mind. 'He had lunched at Buck's (on top of pills), and though he got through the statement effectively, its success, coupled with a post-prandial afterglow, had induced a too light-hearted mood by the time he reached the Lobby,' Harold Evans recorded. There he began by attacking recent stories in the *Daily Express* and *Daily Mail*, then 'swung the chairman's gavel perilously back and forwards, talked about the trenches and how they enabled you to appear calm when you felt terrified, said that he could still do the eighteenth in four and that he was now going away to let off three or four hundred cartridges'.

Not surprisingly de Gaulle could not be conciliated. There was much ambivalence, and long, taxing negotiations with the Community. When in December 1962 Harold and Kennedy agreed that Britain would acquire the Americans' Polaris missile, de Gaulle saw this as proof of a pre-eminent pro-American bias in British policy. Harold tried to repeat his success with Kennedy over Polaris by making a similarly sentimental appeal to de Gaulle over Community membership, but his act flopped. 'The poor old fellow looked so woebegone, I felt like singing to him like Edith Piaf, "Ne Pleurez Pas, Milord",' de Gaulle reputedly said. In January 1963, a month after the Polaris agreement, the French vetoed British membership of the Community. Although the pretext for de Gaulle's veto seems dubious with hindsight, his instincts about Harold were sound enough. The latter had always blown hot and cold over Europe, and his commitment to 'inter-dependence' with the Americans had no limit; like the British people themselves, he would have been an ambivalent, perhaps retarding influence in European development. 'Macmillan and de Gaulle had been going different ways for some time, especially with regard to the Americans in Europe,' Butler said in February, 'I always thought those shooting parties at Château Rambouillet were a mistake, especially getting Lady Dorothy out of mothballs for the trip. No truths were ever exchanged.'

The European negotiations were perhaps bound to fail under

his leadership. 'He was the great exponent of doing good by stealth,' according to the Liberal Mark Bonham-Carter, 'which meant he was successful with his negative policies and hopeless with his positive policies. That's why he won the 1959 election on an *anti* Common Market platform but two years later failed with his positive plan to finesse his way into Europe.'

Others have dwelt upon Harold's mastery of foreign affairs, but it is his actions as party leader which show his character clearest. Politics was a gamble, its issues could turn out well or ill, he told Butler in 1959, but the essential point was to take one's chips when the play went well. Asked by Henry Fairlie that year which British peacetime prime minister he admired most, Harold played momentarily with the names of Baldwin and Disraeli before nominating Walpole, and indeed he had much of Walpole's guile in handling men and evaluating their motives. In his memoirs Harold seldom mentioned his leadership of the Conservative Party or his management of parliament, yet he was constant in his attention to them. He once said that leadership in Britain could only be given by the House of Commons, and he courted the House much as Walpole had bribed it. In some ways MPs of the 1950s were more servile than their eighteenth-century predecessors, whose votes were purchasable. Traditionally few politicians had depended on their membership of parliament for their living, and the expenses of the life had not necessarily been great. Boothby had been able before the war to live comfortably on an annual income of £400, but inflation and the ebb of social privileges made this impossible in post-war conditions. The salary of MPs was raised to £1,500 in 1954, because many members (including Conservatives) needed it; MPs of the Macmillan era more than at any previous time depended on their seats not only for advancement but for their livelihoods. They tended to follow their leader knowing that he controlled the party organisation and the supply of peerages, baronetcies, knighthoods and lesser accolades. More than ever they were coaxed or cajoled to vote with their leader, even when they spoke against his policies. Recalling the way he had traipsed through the division lobbies at the whips' command in the 1950s, the Tory backbencher Christopher Hollis quoted the words of Lecky, himself once a member: 'Most of the duties of a Member of Parliament could be better performed by a fairly intelligent poodle dog.'

From his experience of backbench dissidence and bitter exclusion from power in the 1930s, Harold knew that the man who controlled the party machine was irresistible and that the MPs were the cogs of that machinery. Chamberlain's whips like David Margesson and James Stuart had been indispensable: Harold from the outset of his premiership cultivated his Chief Whip, Edward Heath. The first words which he uttered in public as Prime Minister were indicative. 'Where's the Chief Whip?' he cried in Downing Street on the evening of 11 January 1957. 'We're off to the Turf to celebrate.' (Characteristically he professed surprise when, leaving the Turf club later, he found the pavement outside thronged with journalists.) His reliance on Heath was so pronounced that by July 1958 Butler was reporting 'intense personal rivalries' between Heath and Ian Macleod, another younger minister. 'They are the same age and look anxiously to the throne. The Chief Whip's status has been raised to God Almighty by the PM asking him to every meeting on every subject at every hour of the day and night. This is unfair since it has strained a first-class man to the utmost.'

Harold always fretted about the support of his parliamentary party. As Enoch Powell wrote after his death, 'Though destined to lift the Conservative Party to an electoral high-water mark, he had no use for the conservative loyalties and affections: they interfered too much with the Whig's true vocation of detecting trends in events and riding them skilfully so as to preserve the privileges, property and interests of his class.' For all his sententiousness, Harold had little hope that people and nations could be 'led by reason or fired by sincerity: success and the surmounting of difficulties and dangers were the reward of dexterity and illusionism'. Powell never forgot Harold saying to him in 1958, after settling an interim agreement on Cyprus, 'I think we have tricked the Greeks.' In a real sense, too, he tricked the Conservative Party. His succession as Prime Minister was an unparalleled hoodwinking of its right wing, which initially hailed him as a fellow jingo – 'at heart', as one parliamentarian diagnosed him in 1957, 'a white supremacy man'. Not until 1990, when John Major became Prime Minister after Thatcher was forced from office, were right-wing power-brokers so utterly confounded in their calculations: for Major was elected as the preferred candidate of his predecessor, reputedly a stalwart torchbearer of Thatcherite policies, but within months he abandoned many of her brutal dogmas and embraced a new creed of social-market 'One Nation' Conservatism.

In the aftermath of the con-trick of January 1957 Harold faced a tetchy, puzzled and divided parliamentary party. When he addressed the 1922 Committee he would betray his anxiety by the way he fingered his Brigade tie. Whenever he sensed that his support was ebbing, he would visit the Carlton club to be seen sharing a bottle of port with some such dissident as Sir Victor Raikes or appear in the Smoking Room of the House of Commons. 'He would just come in and sit down next to you and start talking', recalled one junior backbencher, Humphry Berkeley. 'He never gave any indication that he knew who I actually was.' Once he told Berkeley of a recent visit to Oxford, where he had been elected Chancellor of the University in 1960. The number of women undergraduates had startled him. 'In my day you had chaps' sisters and cousins in eights week, and then there were Gaiety Girls', he said, leaving Berkeley wondering 'if he mistook me for somebody else, or whether perhaps he was deliberately caricaturing himself to watch my reaction'. Berkeley often watched Harold, after the party had suffered a reverse, flitting among dejected Conservative MPs in the Smoking Room. 'So-and-so's son had been commissioned in the Coldstream Guards had he, how splendid! X had become Lord Lieutenant of Leicestershire, how well deserved! They say that grouse are plentiful at Swinton this year, admirable. The

Conservative MPs would go home to dinner in the comfortable knowledge that their world had not really been disturbed.'

The Conservative parliamentary party ran on class feeling, combined with a compelling desire for place and power. Few Tory MPs had many strong opinions of their own, so they were torn between an instinctive obedience to their leader and an instinctive fear of their constituency supporters. Members regarded power as their natural right: their exclusion from it (then as now) was treated with incredulity. This unifying belief is their great advantage over the Labour and Liberal parties, some of whose members prefer protest to power and are never content unless in adolescent defiance of authority or puerile acts of petulance. In the Macmillan era, as again in the 1980s, some Labour leaders seemed frightened of power. The party was vitiated by a righteous, imbecile spirit of exclusiveness, and by the influence of trade unionists whose idea of strong leadership was to oppose whatever management had said or done. These men had built their careers on rejecting other people's ideas, and could not lead or take initiatives themselves. They were epitomised by Frank Cousins, a trade union leader who proved one of Wilson's feeblest appointments (as Minister of Technology), declaring during Harold's premiership that the Labour Party did not want to win Tory votes in the country.

The Conservative parliamentary party contained remarkable extremes of shrewdness and dullness; but members were united by their respect for authority and their glorification of mediocrity – or to put it more generously, in a phrase of Harold's Lord Chancellor, Kilmuir, loyalty was the Tories' secret weapon. A year after Harold's succession his sway was so complete that one Tory MP told the *Spectator*'s political columnist that, if the government introduced a bill to hang the Queen in Trafalgar Square, at least 300 Tories would troop through the lobbies to support it. 'Young man,' said Charles Hill in 1959 to Julian Critchley whom he saw reading a book in the Smoking Room, 'it does not do to appear clever: advancement in this man's party is due entirely to alcoholic stupidity.' A description in the radical Tory *National Review* of Derick Heathcoat-Amory, who replaced Thorneycroft as Chancellor of the Exchequer in the crisis of 1958, catches the tone of the Conservative Party in this period. 'He is often described as "sound", an adjective which in this specialized usage connotes a decently concealed intelligence, more than average efficiency, a willingness to take pains (for instance, in not hurting the feelings of moronic colleagues), a belief in good relations between management and the (not so easily) managed, a fine war record and a squirearchical background.' Amory was distrusted by the party for opposing capital punishment; but his friends pleaded in mitigation that he was a zealous huntsman. 'He is the sort of man who makes up for not being first-class by pretending to be third-class, and so receives a quite disproportionate amount of credit for being top second-class.'

The House of Commons is a theatre in which every MP is required to be an actor, or *hypocrites*, in the original Greek sense, but the level of debate had fallen to an abysmal level by the 1950s. It was a dire punishment to have to listen to more than a few minutes of the windy eloquence, sanctimonious perfidies, platitudes, recriminations and mendacities of parliament. The idealists were often tedious, the fanatics always bores and the constant duty of sitting among the great mass of fat-gilled, wind-bellied hypocrites was simply corrupting. Harold was sometimes deft and witty at the despatch box – signalling the success of a well-turned phrase with a triumphant little kick of his right foot – but as often irretrievably dull.

He was adept at abandoning attitudes which his more gullible adherents had regarded as fixed and sacred while continuing to make the sounds which were needed to maintain their support. He stressed to Sir Robert Menzies in 1957 'the importance of representing what had happened in Egypt as a success', and took a resolutely positive tone on Suez, a tone rightly described by Salisbury in 1958 as 'absolute bosh'. A good example was the speech with which he concluded a parliamentary debate on the financial settlement with Egypt in 1959. 'A more scrupulous man would have found it impossible to speak as he did on this occasion, and a less infatuated audience would have either walked out on him or heard him in stony silence,' commented the *National Review*. 'As it was, Macmillan's effrontery was just what Tory MPs needed. They cheered him as though he were a hero and laughed savagely when Gaitskell suggested that those responsible for Suez should be brought to trial.'

'He modelled himself upon an American President, with subordinates, not colleagues,' Selwyn Lloyd judged. Although a few men were treated as friends, he talked about most of his ministers 'as though they were junior officers in a unit he commanded'. His generation of political leaders were free in their resort to sedatives. Before Cabinet meetings at which he expected awkwardness, Harold would arrange for a packet of 'relaxtabs' to be left on the blotter of each minister. It gives an unexpected insight into the burdens of office that Butler was carrying Valium at one Cabinet meeting (in October 1963) and gave a tablet to Harold. In Cabinet, he treated stubborn or indecisive colleagues patiently, and his determination and subtlety usually triumphed. For example, when he wanted the Cabinet to approve the Anglo-French Concorde supersonic air-liner project (negotiated by his son-in-law Amery), he diverted them with his stories of his ideal form of transport, the great sluggish Daimler motorcars of the 1920s, perfect for funerals and old ladies from South Kensington in large hats, driven by uniformed chauffeurs slowly in the middle of the road emitting a haze of oily smoke from their Silent Knight engines; but, alas, he sighed, the world had moved on, people wanted to hurtle about the heavens, and Britain must participate in these new profitable crazes. The Cabinet, perhaps unwisely, was duped and the project approved: its cost, estimated to parliament by Amery in 1962 at a maximum of £160 million had surpassed £730 million by 1970 and was still rising.

He braved the simultaneous resignation of his Chancellor of the Exchequer, Thorneycroft, and two Treasury ministers, Nigel Birch and Enoch Powell, in 1958, with an outward show of cheery aplomb which enhanced his standing in his party and the country. Inwardly he was exceedingly irritated and spent a night fretting about what to say before concocting a phrase which had the right tone of nonchalance: 'I thought the best thing to do was to settle up with these little local difficulties and then turn to the wider vision of the Commonwealth' (characteristically he pretended that this carefully polished remark was casual and spontaneous). Once abroad he maintained an outward show of 'false calm' while sending nervous telegrams to Heath at the Whips' Office to check the repercussions in the parliamentary party. Although he took great care with his public image, he was not always as adept or manipulative as people thought. In a series of newspaper articles in 1957–8, and in a book of 1959, Randolph Churchill wrote about Suez in terms which were savagely critical of Eden.'He has been entirely nobbled by Harold, and everything he writes is done to build him up,' Salisbury assured Eden. It was not intrinsically objectionable for prime ministers to be boosted by their supporters, but intolerable 'on a basis that has no vestige of truth'. Though Harold's critics thought Churchill was slavish in his tone about the new Prime Minister, Harold and his adherents equally resented Churchill's revelations, particularly the suggestion that Suez had been abandoned because of economic miscalculation (implicitly by Harold at the Treasury). Moreover the fidelity of journalists is short-lived. 'Unlike Lord Boothby, I don't get on and off band-wagons once a week,' Churchill wrote to Wyndham after the Government Information Service was mobilised against him in 1958. 'I was among the first to mount Harold's band-wagon and I don't mean to get off unless I am pushed.' He had taken 'pains . . . to deflect criticisms from Harold; but if he is going to use civil servants . . . and bottlewashers . . . to attack me I am bound to retaliate'. News management was never easy.

Harold was by turns obtuse and aware, sensitive and callous: similarly his speeches swung between studied witticisms and dreary sententious platitudes. 'A collection of Macmillan's speeches as Prime Minister would be unbearable,' as Emrys Hughes wrote: 'not even Macmillans would publish it.' For the most part he would utter with apparent conviction those commonplaces that most politicians use as the small change of their dealings with the public, never betraying an original thought or real feeling. The vagueness of his remarks allowed his hearers to imagine whatever suited them or what they already thought in any case. The former Labour Prime Minister Attlee thought him 'terribly insincere', and Harold's tribute on the death of Gaitskell in 1963 seemed 'revolting' to Tony Benn since notoriously 'he and Gaitskell hated each other' ('the trouble with Gaitskell', Harold said privately with characteristic contempt, 'is that he has never seen troops under fire').

'The PM is a master of acquiring ideas – this is a good thing,' Lloyd noted in 1959: 'he persuades himself they are his own – also a good thing.' He was receptive to the suggestions of others: the Oxford economist Sir Roy Harrod was regularly consulted by him, and he valued the opinions of civil servants like Sir Patrick Dean of the Foreign Office, Sir Frank Lee at the Treasury, Sir Richard Powell at the Board of Trade and Sir Laurence Helsby at the Ministry of Labour. He was indifferent to most domestic issues, which he left to Butler. As befitted the man who as Chancellor of the Exchequer had introduced the con of Premium Bonds (which he gloatingly described later as leading the financially credulous to develop 'an extreme desire to lend money to the Government free of interest'), his most notable piece of domestic legislation as premier was the Betting and Gaming Act.

'We have a good many old men at the top living in the past,' that supremely shrewd observer Lord Franks mused in 1957. Macmillan haunted by his memories of mass unemployment and a Labour leader permanently embittered because for ten years his father 'tramped up and down the Great North Road, looking for a job' were part of the same problem: 'we need younger men who are not obsessed with the past'. Harold at times seemed to plumb the lowest depth of outmoded futility, scorned by the irreverent as Mr MacMothballs. Like an old general he fought the war of the economy by applying obsolete lessons from previous conflicts. Britain was beset by consumer shortages: its economic problems were inflation and an adverse balance of payments at a time of escalating demand; yet the Prime Minister behaved as if the chief problem were still unemployment. On one occasion he even asked shipbuilding employers to raise their pay offer to workers despite the sector being among the least efficient in the country. A generation later Thatcherites reviled the Macmillan government's surrender to inflationary pay settlements. They attributed to him a sentimental attitude to the poor learnt at Stockton in the 1930s, and complained that his Cabinet had been bluffed by the trade unions, although in fact productivity during his premiership grew at 2.5 per cent annually against 2 per cent in the first decade of Thatcher's rule. The trouble was that few of the Macmillan Cabinet were hurt by inflation, or cared about it. They were too rich. Its impact did not touch them. 'I once had hopes of this Government,' a senior civil servant was quoted as saying in 1957, 'but now I know that at root they're so many rich men.'

Harold revelled in his successes. Just before Christmas in 1958 he and Dorothy accompanied the US Ambassador to a production of the musical *West Side Story*. 'When the PM came back to his seat after the interval, the whole house cheered him,' wrote Rupert Hart-Davis, who was sitting near by. 'He was clearly delighted.' He reorganised Conservative Central Office, and in the autumn of 1959 the party was returned at the general election with an overall majority of precisely 100 seats. It would have seemed inconceivable eighteen months earlier that the Conservatives could wrest their third consecutive election victory. While others had despaired, his courage had been unquenchable and his tact was unfaltering. Yet the trend of his second administration was 'one of slow and irresistible decay, coupled with a number of personal scandals for the extent and mismanagement of which Harold himself was at least partly responsible', as Lord Hailsham summarised it. Harold himself rightly said that he was called MacWonder at one moment and MacBlunder at the next: contradictory epithets were pitched at him because he seemed such a contradictory character.

He envied Gladstone for never spending less than five months of the year at Hawarden during the period of his premierships. 'I haven't time to read new books, but I like taking up a book I know well,' he told Moran in 1959. He liked political biographies. 'Of course, we all read them when we were young . . . but it is quite different reading them when you know the machine.' On the sixth anniversary of becoming prime minister, he gossiped with Butler. 'We had a short talk on the awfulness of going into business and that politics despite its dangers was the greatest game in the world,' Butler recorded. 'He said, "As PM sometimes the strain is awful, you have to resort to Jane Austen. Latterly I have been reading Roman history and I am going back to Mommsen."' Theodor Mommsen had been the greatest Roman historian of the nineteenth century, combining minute research with a powerful faculty for bold generalisation: he taught, so Henry Adams had written, 'what, as a rule, needed no teaching, the lessons of a rather cheap imagination and cheaper politics. Rome was a bewildering complex of ideas, experiments, ambitions, energies; without her, the Western world was pointless and fragmentary; she gave heart and unity to it all; yet . . . perhaps it meant nothing.' A novelist who gave Harold special solace was Trollope, who shared his disbelief in anything but the power of work to keep pessimism and doubts at bay; Trollope, who 'grew worldliness like a second skin over the raw wounds of his youth', according to V.S. Pritchett, and 'longed merely for the normal'. Harold turned often to Disraeli's novels. 'Every page of him', he told Fairlie, 'is worth reading and rereading.' He was, supremely, a publisher who had entered politics. He got both distraction and perspective from his reading, and was kept human by it – in contrast, say, to Thatcher, whose publicity agents liked to portray her as a super-human surviving on a few hours' sleep, as if such compulsive behaviour should inspire respect or trust.

Hearing a long list of her speaking engagements and activities during a parliamentary recess, Harold commented, 'She would be much better to stay at home in her garden – has she got a garden? – and read Monypenny and Buckle's life of Disraeli.'

For those in supreme office self-restraint among friends requires more effort than discretion before enemies. Churchill and Eden had both enjoyed talking unguardedly to their entourages, and so did Harold. 'I dined at Petworth where John Wyndham was entertaining the Prime Minister,' Ann Fleming reported to Evelyn Waugh in 1961.

> Mrs Wyndham was away, Lady Dorothy was absent, so the PM, John, Mr and Mrs Robin McEwen and myself sat down to dinner at a table ornamented with gold candelabra, supped soup from golden plates while the Japanese deer stared through the windows. It was a splendid occasion to observe Mr Macmillan, he was suave with impersonal eyes, he ate and drank with extreme moderation and he talked from eight o'clock to one a.m., the only pause at midnight when he advanced to the door and we humbly followed expecting the great man's bedtime – but no, it was for a natural purpose – and in a trice he returned to us and was at it again.

Ann Fleming disliked his 'weakness for anecdotes about the peerage' and indeed under the Petworth influence his snobbery became persistent and inexcusable. Early in the 1945 parliament he had confided to Woodrow Wyatt 'that he minded the fact of the Labour government less than seeing the common people who ran it'. He disdained the men without family, substance or tradition who grappled with the problems of post-war reconstruction. Thereafter his snobbery (though often treated as a joke) was ugly and conspicuous. After a Cabinet meeting in 1957, he confided to Butler his regret that their colleagues were too 'brash'. 'What a pity', he said to Sir Victor Raikes in 1957 when Lord Lambton resigned as parliamentary private secretary to Selwyn Lloyd, 'that we should have had to sacrifice an aristocrat for a middle-class lawyer from Liverpool.'

Thereafter he often referred to his Foreign Secretary by this cheap, belittling soubriquet. Told on one occasion that Lloyd came from the Wirral, he gestured contemptuously, then muttered, 'Funny place to come from.' In conversation with Lloyd himself, he dismissed their colleague Maudling as a man of 'no background', and in 1963, urging Lord Home as his successor, assured Lloyd that 'the British liked a real aristocrat who could talk to ordinary people – people like the Duke of Devonshire, his father-in-law' ('there is only one Minister who could displace me now, and that is Alec Home', Harold had told Butler after the Cuban missile crisis in 1962, adding with a characteristic piece of genealogical mumbo-jumbo that 'he thought Alec had some special genius, probably from his Lambton mother'). Older Tory grandees like Salisbury might find Harold's pretensions contemptible, but the aura of power can be dazzling. Dorothy's brother-in-law James Stuart, who had mocked Harold in the 1920s, became a steadfast admirer (and received a viscountcy at Harold's recommendation in 1959). Some younger grandees were equally impressed: several members of the Chatsworth circle were brought into the government. Dorothy's nephew was appointed Under Secretary for Commonwealth Relations in 1960, and promoted to the rank of Minister of State at the Commonwealth Relations Office in 1962. 'Andrew Devonshire is awfully good with natives,' Harold said by way of commendation to Humphry Berkeley. 'The Devonshires have always been good with natives.' He was especially prone to snobbery about his wife's relations. After offering Nigel Fisher an under secretaryship at the Colonial Office in 1962, he barked out, 'Do you know George Lansdowne?', referring to Dorothy's cousin whom he had appointed as a lord in waiting as soon as he became Prime Minister and had promoted by stages to the height of Minister of State at the Colonial Office. 'George will never set the Thames on fire, but he is very good, and they like him in the Lords, because of course he is a *real* marquess, none of your jumped-up stuff.'

These symptoms of class exclusiveness were all the sadder

because Harold, as a reformer in the 1930s, had stood out against such human waste. In his writings he had recognised that the divisions between state and private schools, with the latter monopolising the best resources, perpetuated social injustice and poisoned the country with class feeling. Before 1939 he had advocated measures to equalise educational opportunities, and to democratise the public school system; but after the war, in common with other politicians, he shirked the educational reforms which might have given Britain more nearly the semblance of a classless community, without depriving it of dynamism or variety. Instead, as Harold retreated more and more into the snobbery of his False Self, he seemed to revitalise the spirit of class exclusion. At an election in the 1950s Bobbety Salisbury's wife Betty had been shouted at by a heckler, 'You think you're better than us, don't you?' and to the delight of her friend David Herbert, an ageing Bright Young Thing, had replied, 'No, just different!' It was gratifying to feel different, and Harold's party, for all his protective rhetoric about the disadvantaged, was determined to preserve those differences. The remoteness of the patricians is well conveyed by the minutes of a board meeting at the *Financial Times* in 1968. The print unions were disrupting production and blackmailing management into paying endless bonuses. When one director, Lord Robbins, asked whether everything possible was being done 'to foster good relations on the production side', the chairman Lord Drogheda 'said he would not object to further cocktail parties being arranged but he did not think this sort of event should take place too often'. Too many national leaders dwelt in a higher stratosphere where it seemed that cocktail parties were the way to pacify truculent print-workers.

Harold was always a fearful man, and behind his patronising attitudes there lay fear of the unsettlement which equal educational opportunities might bring, fear of what would happen if privileged children had to compete on equal terms with the less privileged. He was as alarmed as the characters in Evelyn Waugh's war trilogy by the ubiquity and ambitions of the lower-middle classes, with their objectionable accents and disastrous haircuts. For all his ostentatious ancestor-worship, he forgot that his grandfather Daniel and great-uncle Alexander would have remained behind the counter, their descendants condemned as unremembered scriveners, if the Hares had cared about their accents, inflexion of voice, gestures and posture, or had believed that social marks should be indelible: but in this respect early Victorian England compared favourably with Britain in the 1950s. Harold's aristocratic pantomime, like the morbid attention paid to minor nuances of social distinction, were shameful nonsense and especially incongruous given Dorothy's total lack of class consciousness. The excitement over Nancy Mitford's pronouncements on U and non-U were a symptom of the British weakness of believing only in oneself and one's own conventions. By 1960 Harold cared solely for the spacious conventions of Birch Grove, Balliol and Pratt's, and rejected all the rich talents, imagination, generosity and humour which might lie unrecognised in a meanly proportioned semi-detached house on a new estate at Harpenden.

'Believe me,' Butler once cried to an ordinary Conservative audience, 'believe me, your problems are my problems,' and perhaps he believed it. But in fact Butler and Macmillan distanced themselves forcibly from the middle class into which they had both been born, and on which Conservative support was based. 'One may be pardoned for wondering sometimes', a right-winger wrote in the *Spectator* ten months into Macmillan's premiership, 'what Minister would bat an eyelid – or even notice – if the whole middle class suddenly dropped through a hole in the ground.'

The old Harrovian Baldwin when forming his first Cabinet had been preoccupied with ensuring that it contained at least as many men who had been at Harrow as at Eton. Early in his premiership, too, Harold liked to boast that he was the first King's Scholar from Eton to be Prime Minister since Walpole, and he filled his government with Etonians. Some such as John Hare and Lord Home were aristocrats, but many

others like Sandys, Soames, Thorneycroft and even Hailsham
were not. 'The Government backbenches are crowded with
Members of Parliament who are Old Etonians only because
their fathers could afford to send them to that school,' wrote
a Tory backbencher, Henry Kerby, at the time when Harold
was making his first government appointments. They were
'representatives of a money-bags plutocracy, however much
many of them may try to disguise their origins. The House is
crammed with first-generation descendants of hard-faced men
who have done well for themselves in trade of every sort.'
Typical of the Old Etonian MPs indicated by Kerby was John
Morrison, the chairman of the 1922 Committee throughout
the Macmillan premiership, a big, benign man, apparently an
archetypal squire from Wiltshire, living on an estate which had
in fact been inherited from a merchant-banking great-uncle who
had left £10 million in 1909. Kerby blamed the snobbery of
constituency selection committees: mesmerised by the sight of a
prospective candidate in an OE tie, they felt that men with three
feet of dark cloth with a blue stripe round their necks would be
swiftly elevated to positions of power and patronage.

The Etonian hegemony was ultimately fatal. During a Lords
debate on Africa, Hailsham rose to defend the Colonial Secretary, Macleod, from attacks by Salisbury and the Duke of
Montrose, who was later a minister in the rebel Rhodesian
government of Ian Smith. By way of rebuttal, Hailsham recalled
being bitten by Montrose at Eton while playing the Wall Game:
the future of much of central Africa was at stake, yet the allusions were to Eton rites. According to taste, these caste-marks
were delightful, silly, irritating or outrageous. In practice this
flaunted exclusiveness helped to power the Wilson government
of 1964, with its meritocratic cant and illusory promise of a
white-hot technological revolution.

Typically Harold's most memorable intervention as prime
minister in educational policy involved Eton. The Old Etonian
philosopher A.J. Ayer discovered that the Eton authorities
had passed a statute barring boys whose fathers were not

British-born from being elected as Collegers. This was intended
to exclude the sons of Jewish refugees, boys whom the Provost
Sir Claude Elliot told Ayer were 'too clever', or rather 'not
clever in the right way', before protesting that 'you couldn't
expect them to play the Wall Game'. When Ayer countered
that his own father was Swiss, his mother Jewish and that
he had been in the College Wall eleven for two years, Elliot
replied, 'You can't regard yourself as a typical case.' Ayer
had no success in lobbying against this anti-semitic statute
until he told his story to Harold's former coadjutor at the
Treasury, Sir Edward Boyle, who promised to raise it with
the Prime Minister. To Harold's credit, within a fortnight
of hearing Boyle's account he drew a public statement from
the Provost and Fellows of Eton that the statute would be
rescinded; but to the fate of less advantaged young men he
was indifferent. 'We can do with Education what we did with
Housing,' he minuted to ministers in 1959, but was crushing
when at the end of the year Sir David Eccles, the Minister of
Education, advocated an ambitious state-funded programme 'to
give everybody better opportunities, from school to old age, for
a richer and more satisfying life outside work'. Eccles proposed
the appointment of a minister to be responsible for Arts, Sports
and Youth Service to meet the increasing leisure demands 'in
our Affluent Age', but Harold killed the proposal stone-dead
by minuting sarcastically, 'Yes, indeed. I am all for tempting
the Teddy Boys into the Geological Museum.' His insouciance
would have seemed wicked to his grandfather Daniel.

Yet the Prime Minister's leisure was priceless to him. The smell
and taste of grouse may resemble, as Daudet told Zola, an old
whore's flesh marinaded in a bidet, but for Harold the sporting
rites of killing game birds were staunching and immutable in a
world that otherwise seemed perplexing and impermanent. The
sites of old civilisations, like the great cities of Italy which earlier
Macmillans had visited for holidays, were ruined by the detritus
of modern tourism, with ill-dressed human detritus the most
obnoxious of all. But the great territorial magnates of Yorkshire

or Scotland had kept their moors sacrosanct. They were exclusive and secure. The beaters were deferential, local farmers knew their place. The moors gave succour which Venice could not. Nothing seemed to have changed much when he shot with the Swintons in Yorkshire. All was right with the world, and everyone in their place, when he shot at Hever as the guest of George Lansdowne's stepfather, the proprietor of *The Times*, John Jacob Astor, 'a name which', as he might have thought in the words of a character of Herman Melville's, 'I love to repeat; for it hath a rounded and orbicular sound to it, and rings like unto bullion'.

Unlike Eden, Harold did not pester his ministers with trivial departmental enquiries, and encouraged their initiative. He was generous in praising ministers who had no hopes to succeed him, sending notes of encouragement or congratulations, especially when they had braved the Commons in a testing debate. Yet Harold, for all his much vaunted tact, worldliness and discretion, was often clumsy, foolish or seemingly vindictive in his handling of people. At moments his judgment deserted him oddly: his dealings with Cabinet colleagues were sometimes vexed. Lord Hailsham, for example, despite his contribution to the Conservative victory in the general election of 1959, forfeited Harold's confidence for several years. The fallen favourite was at first mystified by Harold's hostility, and then outraged when he learnt the explanation. The Prime Minister had misunderstood Hailsham's role in a matrimonial case in which he had been called as a witness. 'It was thoroughly unjust, wholly unfounded, and to have been influenced by it was very discreditable to him,' Hailsham judged. 'What to me was intolerable was his almost Borgia-like behaviour in his use of his public position to pursue what he made into a private vendetta.' Harold made amends later; but on other occasions he cultivated a younger man, only to undermine him later as he emerged as a contender for the party leadership. Ian Macleod, Edward Heath and Reginald Maudling all suffered this treatment at different times and in different ways.

In other incidents Harold showed bad judgment. Before the 1959 general election, he sent a series of handwritten letters to Eden beseeching him for a personal endorsement in the campaign. Eden offered to issue a statement supporting the Conservative Party, but recoiled from giving his imprimatur to Harold personally. Harold showed poor judgment and worse taste in this tussle; in his next dealings with Eden, he showed himself at worst embittered and at best negligent. When in 1961 the retired Prime Minister indicated to his successor that he would like a peerage, Harold replied offering to recommend him for a viscountcy. As earldoms were customary for retired prime ministers (the last to be fobbed off with a mere viscountcy was Addington in 1805) Eden was mortally offended and sent a tart rejoinder, which elicited the proper offer of an earldom (he took the title of Avon). Eden's final judgment of his successor was partial but pertinent: 'he should have been a cardinal in the middle ages, under a strong Pope'.

Harold was double-faced in his dealings with Butler, who eagerly aspired to the succession. Butler was gullible and too easily flattered by Harold. He knew that the Prime Minister was untrustworthy, yet he was fascinated by the man's charisma and seemed an almost willing dupe. He understood Harold well and sympathised with him. 'Under his very determined and worldly exterior, he conceals considerable anxiety,' Butler wrote in 1960. 'He gets very nervous before speaking . . . but he follows the first rule of public life never to show such things.' A man with few intimates himself, Butler approved Harold's need to escape from 'the lonely isolation' of his job with discursive and flippant monologues: 'as Winston proved to us . . . problems are resolved by long and unrushed conversations'.

The most notorious occasion of Harold's clumsiness, poor judgment and infidelity to colleagues arose from his appointment in 1960 of Selwyn Lloyd as Chancellor of the Exchequer. This itself was a mistake, although worse errors were to follow. Lloyd had been a loyal and accommodating Foreign Secretary, who had acquiesced in Harold's involvement in foreign affairs; but he had little aptitude for Treasury work, and it was impossible for Harold to exercise the close supervision over economic policy which was required. Lloyd's budgets and mini-budgets seemed maladroit improvised reactions to trends and pressures which had been perceived too late. His introduction of a pay-pause had been particularly inept, since it was first imposed on some of the most deserving and popular employees in the country, hospital nurses. With unemployment reaching 800,000 in 1962, many Tory MPs were demanding reflation in order to restore the popularity of the government, but Lloyd was reluctant to accede to these demands at a time when the balance of payments was deteriorating. On 21 June Harold lunched with Butler, who agreed that the government's economic policy was ill-presented and that Lloyd should be replaced as chancellor. This was the first move in a sequence of events in which Harold showed almost suicidal misjudgment: the Night of the Long Knives, a fiasco which was more responsible for the decline in Conservative fortunes than any other incident of his premiership. Over the next fortnight Harold decided to sack Lloyd, braced himself for a painful interview and considered the extent of a possible restructuring of the Cabinet; but on 11 July Butler lunched with the lobby correspondent of the *Daily Mail*, which the following day published a scoop predicting Lloyd's dismissal and the promotion of Butler. Harold panicked.

On the evening of the 12th, he abruptly dismissed Lloyd, telling him 'that the situation was desperate and something had to be done quickly', especially as he suspected 'a conspiracy against him'. In the judgment of Lloyd's biographer, the Chancellor was treated in a shameful manner which could not be justified by political expedience or urgent necessity. He had been a loyal and generous Cabinet supporter, whom Harold tried to hasten into political oblivion. On Friday the 13th a reporter telephoned Birch Grove to ask if Lloyd was staying there for the weekend. 'You must be out of your mind,' replied Dorothy, who had answered the call. The idea of a rapprochement between the two men was madness; yet, astonishingly, a fortnight later, Lloyd was summoned to a confidential meeting with the man who had knifed him. He was met at the entrance by one of Harold's private secretaries, who uttered the absurd remark, 'He is spending all his time thinking of how to bring you back.' As Lloyd recorded his subsequent talk with Macmillan,

> He said that he had made a mistake. He had been rushed. One day he would tell me the conspiracy against him which had forced his hand. . . . Butler had been plotting to divide the party on the Common Market and bring him down. . . . my conclusion after the interview was one of his utter ruthlessness, and his determination to retain power by the sacrifice of even his closest friends. He was now concerned to conciliate me, because I had become a possible danger.

At his wildest moments on the Night of the Long Knives Harold seems to have thought that Lloyd and Lord Chancellor Kilmuir constituted a Liverpudlian Mafia. Evans, the Downing Street adviser on public relations, had known as early as 7 July that Kilmuir's removal was contemplated, but it came as a furious shock to the Lord Chancellor when he was sacked on the morning of the 13th: indeed it was a death-blow to him, for he became depressed and died prematurely. At the time he complained that his cook would have had more notice of dismissal: to which Harold countered that it was easier to get Lord Chancellors than cooks. Nevertheless on Sunday the 15th Harold sent Kilmuir a long, handwritten, grotesquely misjudged letter, sentimental, undignified and propitiatory in tone: he gushed that the deposed Lord Chancellor had been his most trustworthy political friend and Cabinet colleague. It seemed unbalanced for Harold to turn in a moment's spasm from praise to dismissal to praise, especially as only a few months earlier he had lamented to Butler 'how few there were now apart from David Kilmuir with old-fashioned experience of politics' in the Cabinet. More incongruously still, Kilmuir's successor was Lord Dilhorne: previously called Sir Reginald Manningham-Buller, he was nicknamed Sir Reginald Bullying-Manner and was described by one colleague as 'impartially truculent'. He did not obviously strengthen either the Cabinet or the government's public reputation.

Other colleagues were removed (as one bitterly remarked) 'with no more notice than you would give to an office boy caught robbing the till'. Hill, the Minister of Housing; Lord Mills, Minister without Portfolio; Watkinson, the Minister of Defence; Maclay, the Secretary for Scotland; and Eccles, the Minister of Education, were all dismissed. Butler was moved from the Home Office to the nebulous post of First Secretary of State. Harold had dismissed one-third of his Cabinet at a stroke: an act without precedent in political history, although a generation later Thatcher removed a greater number of her Cabinet in a gradual process intended to eliminate Tory grandees or others who might contradict her in Cabinet. The closest parallel is the clumsy, frantic dismissals of five Cabinet members and many White House staff which had such lethal effect on American perceptions of President Carter in 1979.

Harold spent the weekend in the country in nervous misery, but was back in London on Monday to complete his ministerial reconstruction. Summoning the barrister-politician Peter Rawlinson, he first pretended that Kilmuir had wished to retire, then offered the solicitor-generalship. Before Rawlinson could reply, Harold raised his hand and began a long monologue, full of measured periphrasis, on the unique position of law officers as the last public servants of the Crown to have seats in the House of Commons. Rawlinson sat in silence as the Prime Minister honoured him with a review of medieval office holders, discussed appointments and patronage in the sixteenth and seventeenth centuries before dilating on the official career of Samuel Pepys, and concluded with admonitions on the duties and loyalties of a contemporary law officer. With such performances Harold sought to steady his own nerves as well as his party's.

What was behind his knife attack? In his dismissal interview with Kilmuir, he had tried to justify what he was doing with the remark, 'the government is breaking up': this was his fear, which swelled out of proportion. 'Underneath the surface he was a very, very apprehensive man,' his grandson Alexander Stockton told the *Evening Standard* in 1989. 'I've seen him quivering and sick because he has had to go and deliver prizes at a prep school. And of course my grandfather used to get depressed. He could have been in one of his depressive cycles during the Night of the Long Knives. That is enough to drive anyone to make panicky decisions.' The effect on Harold's standing was disastrous. His fright and avidity for power were too blatant. His reactions had been too obviously unbalanced for the pose of imperturbability to seem convincing again. The mask of his False Self had slipped, and people had distrusted what they saw. He stood revealed as a frightened, panicky man, an odd mixture of bigness and pettiness, prudence and impetuosity.

Nothing recedes like success; and from the summer of 1962 critics (especially on the right of his party) inflicted increasing damage on his parliamentary standing. The political hostess Lady Pamela Berry outraged Lady Elizabeth Cavendish shortly afterwards, 'telling her that her uncle the PM was a wicked senile old man'. He was hurt by sustained criticism in the *Daily Express* from its columnist Lord Lambton, an imperialist back-bencher who believed that the Anglo-American relationship was a trick. He was injured too by the barbed wit of Nigel Birch, once described by Roy Jenkins as presenting 'his normal false front of arrogant irascibility'.

Politics is the science of surprises, said Disraeli, and in 1963 the Macmillan administration had to learn new lessons in that science. Early on the French vetoed Britain's application to join the European Community. The collapse of these negotiations left Harold looking 'tired and disappointed that all his castles in the air have crumbled away', the Tory anti-marketeer Robin Turton told Eden in February. Then followed other parliamentary commotions. A month later Harold was humiliated in the Commons defending his government's intention to repatriate a Nigerian, Chief Enahoro, to face trial for subversion. Confronted by a Nigerian threat to leave the Commonwealth unless Enahoro was deported, the government was pusillanimous and evasive. A debate in March ended in 'a most incredible scene',

a young Conservative backbencher (and future member of the
Thatcher Cabinet) called Paul Channon complained to Butler.
'The feeling among our members was immensely high – that
the PM, Home Secretary and Attorney-General had behaved
with gross incompetence. At one moment our own benches
were almost telling the PM to sit down – so lamentable was
his performance.'

'For the first time there was a really substantial movement
to push him out, but it died pretty soon because nobody could
decide who was going to succeed him,' Lambton reported
to Eden on 2 March. With his usual instinct for survival,
Harold suddenly became enthusiastic about legislation to enable
members of the House of Lords to renounce their peerages and
stand as candidates for the House of Commons. This confused
the succession further, for while many people favoured Lord
Hailsham as next prime minister, John Morrison, chairman
of the 1922 Committee, and others in the centre of the party,
favoured Lord Home. The only unanimity was 'discontent and
disenchantment with Harold', concluded Lambton, 'but one
really cannot tell anything as he is so slippery, and luck seems
to play so well into his hands'.

It was at this time that his administration was caught in
an essentially trivial sexual imbroglio. His first instinct when
confronted by scandal was to run away. 'Why on earth did
not the wretched fellow flee the country like poor old Willie
Beauchamp did so many years ago?' he asked in 1962 on the
eve of the trial on a homosexual charge of a Tory politician,
Sir Ian Horobin. (Lord Beauchamp, a Knight of the Garter and
former Cabinet minister, had been hounded out of the country
for homosexuality in 1931.) His troubles began with John
Vassall, unmasked in 1962 as a Russian spy in the Admiralty.
The Director of Public Prosecutions, Toby Mathew, 'looking
decidedly pleased with himself', had announced the affair to
the Solicitor-General, Rawlinson, with the words, 'We have
arrested a spy who is a bugger, and a minister is involved.'
Mathew was a vicious homophobe with a peculiar need of

his own to hunt homosexuality. In this case Tam Galbraith, the Civil Lord at the Admiralty, had sent some letters about office furniture and travel arrangements, addressed 'My dear Vassall', to the spy, who had for a time been assistant to his private secretary. The letters were innocuous, and if Mathew had been a man of ordinary sense he would have kept them out of the case. Instead, they were publicised and made the excuse for filthy-minded press speculation, which it is doubtful if the journalists believed in their most convivial moments. After the Labour MP George Brown had exploited the case in parliament, Harold reluctantly accepted Galbraith's resignation from the government in November, remarking, 'Very well, we shall retire, but we shall retire to the thunder of the guns.' An investigatory tribunal under Lord Radcliffe was appointed, but, although its report exonerated Galbraith, his career was broken and his family life spoiled. It was a disgusting business, in which a good man had been ruined by prurient liars.

The journalists who refused to co-operate with Radcliffe were deservedly gaoled for contempt in March 1963. The response to this was ominously vindictive. 'I wonder if Mr Macmillan understands what he has let himself in for?' demanded Paul Johnson in the *New Statesman*. 'Any Tory Minister or MP . . . who gets involved in a scandal during the next year or so must expect . . . the full treatment,' he threatened; 'between now and polling day . . . the slanting of news will be heavily pro-Labour.' Then, on 21 March, during a debate on the fate of the journalists, a Labour MP, George Wigg, referred to stories that had been circulating for some time involving the Secretary for War, John Profumo, with whores, pimps, a West Indian drugs dealer and a Soviet attaché. Wigg was a violent-minded bully with a dirty imagination and nastier manners. His behaviour throughout the Profumo affair was 'evil' (Hailsham's word): dishonest and mixed with twisted motives of his own (earlier in 1963, standing next to Julian Critchley in a Commons urinal, he had denounced Profumo as 'a massive homosexual'). The first law of sexual ethics is:

always distrust the accuser; so few can have been surprised when Wigg was charged with kerb-crawling in 1976.

Profumo was hastened into making a personal statement in the Commons denying that he had had a sexual relationship with Christine Keeler, one of the women mentioned by Wigg; Harold, who regretted Galbraith's premature resignation and deplored press witch-hunts, supported him, although privately he (and others) had heard stories about Profumo for months and did not find them unbelievable. However Wigg's foul conspiracy flourished until June, when Profumo resigned, admitting that he had lied to the Commons. A sensation ensued. Though in reality the worst damage to Harold's parliamentary standing had been inflicted a year earlier, on the Night of the Long Knives, the Profumo affair (far less important to understanding Harold than his role at Suez) humiliated him. He had posed as a man of the world, whom nothing could startle or fluster; but, by cruel paradox, in the Profumo affair he had to defend himself as an unworldly man, protesting that he was an old, easily deceived ignoramus ('I do not move among young people fairly widely'). He was made to look absurd: caught, not like Profumo with his trousers down, but like an old fool with his teeth out. Harold's position was exposed because he was so squeamish sexually. His cuckolding by Boothby made him recoil from sexual gossip and, perhaps for the same reason, others who knew of Profumo's adultery hesitated to tell him. His son Maurice (whose head, it was whispered, communists had superimposed on a compromising photograph) tried on several occasions to forewarn him, but there was a tough wall of failed contact between the two men, and a family discussion of adultery would have been too tense.

Some saw Harold as the personification of national degeneracy. Thus on 12 June a Conservative peer, Caldecote, wrote to Butler urging the need for a change of leadership. 'I have been tremendously struck by the opinion of so many of my friends, all staunch Conservatives, who are utterly sick of the standard of integrity, of the lack of moral courage and the politics of expediency' epitomised by the Prime Minister. 'We would suffer both personally and nationally from a Socialist government, but if this is the only way of clearing up the mess . . . so be it.' From others there were more licentious accusations or grotesque humbug.

Supposedly a personal statement to the Commons is an occasion for exceptional truthfulness, because the MP making it cannot be questioned: many Conservatives professed to be outraged by Profumo's lie, not least Hailsham speaking on television on 13 June. 'A great party is not to be brought down because of a scandal by a woman of easy virtue and a proved liar,' he fulminated. 'If I had any reason to suppose he had been going with this young woman I would not have stayed in the government five minutes – or I would have seen he was out.' It was Hailsham's delusion that 'people expect decent, moral, clean, truth-telling lives' from their political leaders; what he professed to find most unforgivable and most exceptional was that Profumo 'should have lied, and lied and lied – lied to his friends, lied to his solicitor and lied to the House of Commons'. Hailsham was roused to this grim moral fervour by mendacity, and particularly by the revelation that lies are told in public life.

Yet the truth is always too slippery to hold in parliament, where lies lose their simple function of misrepresenting reality. Nobody believes anybody, everyone is in the know. Lies are told to convey to someone that one has no need of him or his good opinion: they become a technique of insolence. That was what affronted Conservative leaders about Profumo's deception. 'A terrible thing has happened,' Harold bewailed in the Commons. 'A minister has deceived his colleagues, both in the government and in the House of Commons.' To Lord Annan, Macmillan's surprise that Profumo had lied in the Commons was 'odious' hypocrisy given that 'he and Selwyn Lloyd had lied like troopers' denying the meetings with the French and Israelis before Suez: Harold's lies about Suez were a technique of insolence too, and admired as such by the Conservative parliamentary party.

It seemed as if Macmillan were being pelted with every missile at hand. His enemy Sir William Haley, editor of *The Times*, penned an obituary of him beginning with the words, 'This man has been a national disaster.' Even his admirers conceded 'that he was slipping, while to his enemies in both camps the old actor–manager was coming apart before their eyes, the seedy grandeur lurching into a sad or squalid knockabout', the lobby journalist Norman Shrapnel wrote of 1963. Yet, as the night of 11 July proved, he was not yet finished. 'The one-man repertory still had a hit up its sleeve. With the stage props falling about his ears, the scenery supported with his own two hands, the audience walking out on him and some of the backers openly rebellious, the Great Macmillan could still give us one more gaudy night.' He came in triumphant mood to the Commons to announce the Test Ban Treaty, giving a brilliant speech ending with the words, 'This success is deeply moving to us all.' All the Tories, and some Opposition MPs, rose to their feet and cheered, the ultimate parliamentary accolade, equivalent to a dozen curtain-calls. 'Mac made the most of every heady moment. He walked slowly along the Treasury bench, past his cheering ministerial colleagues . . . reaching the Speaker's Chair, he did an unheard of thing. Instead of disappearing from view behind the Chair in the conventional way, he turned and bowed to his ecstatic audience. He bowed again, and the cheers re-echoed.' The applause continued after he had gone, leaving people wondering whether he would return for another curtain. 'But enough was enough: this master of the grandiloquent gesture knew when to stop.'

He was steeled by this success, and in the autumn was encouraged to continue as prime minister by his son Maurice, his son-in-law Amery and Dorothy's brother-in-law James Stuart. But on the night of 7 October, shortly before the start of the annual party conference, at which he intended to announce that he would lead the party into the next election, he found himself unable to urinate and gripped by excruciating spasms. A physician arrived at Downing Street at 4 a.m. on the 8th and drained his bladder; with customary courage he presided over a three-hour Cabinet meeting later that morning. It was obvious that he was ill, and according to John Boyd-Carpenter, 'several of those present were thinking hard and quickly about the possible effect of this sudden shaking of the political kaleidoscope on their own prospects'. After the Cabinet, Harold was examined by a leading urological surgeon, who diagnosed inflammation of the prostate gland, by either benign or malignant tumour. It was at this moment that his premiership moved into extremis.

He had been decisive in the resignations of his two predecessors, Churchill and Eden; but the deliverer of the *coup de grâce* to him is strangely unaccredited. It was his successor, Home. On 9 October, lying in a hospital bed, drugged and suffering, privately convinced that his tumour was malignant, Harold wrote to the Queen intimating that he must resign and drafted a letter for Home to read to the party conference at Blackpool explaining that he was too weak to lead the Conservatives into the election. This decision was premature. To make such an announcement at the conference would disrupt, if not ruin, the proceedings. There was no need for haste. Within a day Harold knew that he did not have cancer and was regretting his decision to step down. Maurice Macmillan was urging his father to persevere, and Harold himself realised that he could have soldiered on. Any disinterested friend would have urged Harold to postpone his decision, taken impulsively, after minimal consultation, while he was suffering great physical pain and mental perturbation. Home however took an opposite course. According to him when he arrived to discuss the situation, Harold surprised him by urging that he should disclaim his peerage and contest the leadership; but, according to Harold, he had already twice mooted this possibility to Home in the previous few days. On the evidence Home's recollection is less plausible: certainly he did not act as a disinterested friend. Presented with a hint about the succession from the Prime Minister himself, he took the statement, hastened to Blackpool and on 10 October, before Harold could have second thoughts, wrecked the conference by reading out the resignation message. The conference instantly broke into a scrimmage. Ambitious men, and their avid, excitable supporters, fought for power. Harold had been a master of dropping misleading hints about the succession to aspirants like Butler, sometimes through the medium of his private secretaries. Home alone knew that he was the incumbent's preferred successor.

It was a time of intrigue, bustle, vanity and crawling meanness; it did great harm to the party; and the outcome defeated the surmises of the editors. Television viewers saw the 'odious' sight of 'Hailsham trying to control himself, and looking like a man in the grip of suppressed hysteria, smirking and protesting loyalty to Macmillan', Tony Benn noted in his diary. The deportment of Hailsham, after his announcement that he was renouncing his peerage and would revert to being Quintin Hogg, 'surrounded by hysterical and weeping women', reminded Butler 'of a Hitler campaign' and Harold's adviser Harold Evans of a 'Nuremberg rally'. Yet at this moment Hailsham felt as apprehensive as Harold on the day of Eden's resignation. 'A very distinctive step has just been taken by a very frightened old Hogg', he was heard to mutter by Anthony Howard.

As Harold wished, the honours went to Home. Like de Gaulle Harold believed in the existence of some priceless but intangible quality called national character. They had some similar instinct that social or political change could be made less disruptive or dangerous if a country was led by someone who embodied its national genius. De Gaulle convinced himself that he personified French genius; Harold persuaded himself that Home came from a tradition of upright public service and aristocratic self-confidence that represented the strongest and best in British public life: he even told Butler that Home had 'special genius'. Perhaps he was right, for Home's short premiership saved his party from a landslide defeat in 1964. Nevertheless to many people 'this last cruel blow brought about by Nigel Birch and Macmillan relations', as Paul Channon wrote to Butler on 18 October, proved 'how decadent the Tory government and party had become in 1963 and how extraordinary Mr Macmillan's decisions had become in his last few months of office'.

Certainly he seemed overwhelmingly decadent at the end, and was brilliantly satirised as such. The False Self which made him mimic George Lansdowne or Simon Dalhousie or Philip Swinton shooting birds in the north had brought him political advantages in the late 1950s, as he sought to steady flurried nerves and emphasise the possibility of continuity; but after the Night of the Long Knives his pretences never seemed very believable. Without the protection of a convincing False Self he seemed much less of a man and was far more vulnerable.

Bernard Berenson divided humanity into two classes, the life-enhancers and the life-diminishers: it is a distinction which ought to be used in every human evaluation. Harold Macmillan as Prime Minister was overwhelmingly a life-enhancer. There was a terrible complexity about his means of doing so, for in the course of his premiership there was a convergence of hereditary influences and family forces. The earnest, steadfast statesman driving himself at almost inconceivable pressure in the cause of world peace was Daniel's grandson: the manipulative party leader was his mother's frightened son. Overall he was just a consummate politician. Throughout his seven years of leadership he was prone to opportunism, prevarication, over-elaboration and stealthiness. He was an out-and-out neo-Machiavellian. Time and again he followed his instincts to play people along and to play them off against one another. But these are all traits which occur in most political leaders: Harold's vices were no more incorrigible than those of many other prime ministers. If, at times, he lacked moral courage, he made up for this with heroic self-control, mastering appallingly vulnerable nerves, fighting down fears, living at a pitch of anxiety that would have broken or killed most people, holding himself together with a False Self which some found contemptible and others endearing. He was bogus, but so are most great parliamentarians. In a relaxed moment in old age he once described himself as 'a shit', and everyone who aspires to be Prime Minister has an element of shittiness. Not all of them, however, had such audacity and courage.

CHAPTER 10

End-Games

Greatnesse of name, in the father, oft-times helpes
not forth, but o'rewhelmes the Sonne: they stand
too neere one another. The shadow kills the growth;
so much, that wee see the Grand-child come more,
and oftner, to be the heire of the *first*, than doth
the *second*: He dies betweene; the Possession is
the *thirds*

Ben Jonson, *Discoveries*

The Macmillans were supremely a publishing family. Books
were where they got their ideas from, and their money. The
publishing office of Macmillan and Company was where they
worked. To Harold the business was a great family property, as important to them as the Chatsworth estate was to
the Cavendishes: predictably it was to publishing that Harold
turned after his political death in 1963. For all the years of
his ascendancy his eldest brother Dan had been chairman and
managing director; but after Harold's political retirement, the
managing directorship was transferred to him, although Dan
remained chairman until his death in 1965.

If the new responsibilities handed to Harold were not a
poisoned chalice, they at least contained some bitter dregs. Dan
(who had joined the business as early as 1911) was described by
one of his employees in the 1960s as a man with 'tunnel vision'.
He cared passionately about the firm's educational books and
those on classical history, but had neglected other sides of the

business. Socially, outside the office, he could be charming and generous, with a pleasant habit of minor gallantries to young women; but at work he was cantankerous, perhaps especially after his wife mysteriously drowned in her bath in 1957 and he was diagnosed in 1960 as having cancer. He felt the despair and repugnance of an ailing man. 'I'm worth three million pounds,' he said to one young woman a little time after his diagnosis, 'what use is it to me?' But even before the onset of illness, he left some authors with the impression that he despised them as a breed. Under his stewardship since 1945, there had been a reversion to the earlier pattern set under the dead hand of Mowbray Morris. The new generation of innovative writers was missing from Macmillan's general lists, though the commitment to their longer-established authors was magnificent. In the late 1940s, for example, when paper and printing were still rationed, the company declined the offer of Winston Churchill's war memoirs (whose success was certain), because they preferred to use their allotment of paper and binding-cloth in reissuing hundreds of school-books and university texts which had gone out of print during the war, as well as the works of authors who depended on Macmillan for their livelihood – like Charles Morgan, James Hilton, Sean O'Casey, Eric Linklater or Storm Jameson – or those like Hardy, Kipling and Yeats whose literary properties they felt a duty to protect.

The firm was class-bound. It was divided, said one old hand, between 'the family directors and the yardmen'. Even some senior directors were treated contemptuously unless they served the family interest. Nevertheless many older employees were proud of the firm and spoke with pathetic gratitude of the way they had been treated by the family. The casualness with which men and women who had given their working lives to the Macmillans were treated when they came to retire, and the neglect of little attentions at their retirement parties, shocked younger employees, who were above all saddened by the sentimental way in which old employees accepted their cold-hearted treatment with deferential thanks. Working conditions in their office in St Martin's Street were almost as uncongenial as those of the Edwardian scriveners whom Nellie Macmillan had recruited to the firm when a school visitor in Pimlico. The company employed too many lazy, second-rate editors, who resembled squabbling archdeacons reporting to a haughty bishop. In preparing books for publication, they were prone suddenly to 'go all dreamy', complained one of their authors, Eric Linklater, in 1963 – though every publishing house gets such sniping from its writers. Dan's style of management was so demoralising that some editors had almost a wish to fail. Their talents were wasted: many brighter spirits left or grew embittered. On some occasions an editor would summon some vestigial enthusiasm for his job and advocate buying a book by a new author who was judged to have talent: only for Dan to crush the suggestion in a couple of devastatingly well-chosen sentences. He could be cruelly snubbing.

Dan was openly disparaging about Harold. He never let anyone forget that he was the elder brother (the epileptic middle brother Arthur, being outside the family business, was always discounted). Like other family publishing houses at the time, the senior member was always called by his surname and the others by their forenames prefixed with 'Mr': a practice which to younger people emphasised the company's similarity to a traditional estate like Chatsworth. In a typical incident, on a momentous day in January 1957, a secretary rushed into Dan's office and announced excitedly, 'Mr Macmillan has just been made Prime Minister,' only to be snubbed with a reply delivered with adamant contempt, 'No, "Mr Macmillan" has not been made Prime Minister, "Mr Harold" has.' A hundred years earlier the loyalty between the original Daniel Macmillan and his brother Alexander had been one of the lovelier features of London publishing, but fraternity was one of the virtues that the family had lost. Despite some effort by Harold to give a polished overglaze of decorum to his brotherly relations, there was an underlying resentment. Dan in particular showed little loyalty in front of outsiders, and his dismissiveness of Harold's

talents as a publisher was unmistakable. To one young editor
he said, in almost so many words, 'Ignore what Harold says: he's
only a politician, and you can't believe what he says.' He treated
Harold as a second-rate mind who could never have won a first
at Oxford; it was doubted that Harold would have dared, if Dan
had still been alive, to describe (in *Winds of Change*, published
in 1966) reading Greek texts to divert himself from the horrors
of trench warfare: Dan's scorn at Harold posing as a classicist
would have been too harsh.

Ownership of the company had long since been transferred
to the Macmillan Trust, which at the time of Harold's political
retirement owned all but 505 of the 370,000 shares in the
company. Profits had been ploughed back, so that by the
early 1960s there was not only issued capital of £740,000, but
accumulated reserves of £1.3 million. Dan in 1951 had sold their
controlling interest in the Macmillan Company of New York for
£25 million, and much of this cash was apparently transferred
to the Trust. (When Boothby telephoned Dorothy to tease her
about this increase in the family fortune, she was so angry that
she ripped the telephone from the wall; beyond this tantrum,
the sale prevented the London firm from using their trade name
in the United States, a matter of increasing inconvenience in
the decades that followed.) A company called Birch Grove
Estates Ltd – with two directors, Dorothy and Maurice –
owned not only the house and estate in Sussex, but £94,000
in preference shares in the firm, and was in turn owned by the
Trust. The previous generation had all left sizeable fortunes in
1936: George left the most with £343,401, then Frederick with
£193,171 and Maurice's £112,304. Having made provisions to
avoid death duties, Harold in 1987 left an estate worth only
£42,000, but overall the size of the family fortune increased
greatly (Maurice junior left £832,881 in 1984). Indeed Harold's
eldest grandson Alexander Stockton regularly features in lists
of the few hundred richest people in Britain compiled by the
Sunday Times, although the computation seems inexact and
apparently includes assets held in trust for his brothers and

their descendants. The workings of the Macmillan Trust have always been secretive, and have been operated single-mindedly in the interests of the family.

When Harold took the managing directorship in 1963, the portents for the business were ominous, although Macmillan journals and periodicals, of which *Nature* was the most famous, were lucrative and provided the foundation of future profits. But the business was out of date and making poor returns. Harold responded with his habitual ruthlessness. He cut a swathe of dismissals through the senior levels of the firm; for the most part, the firings made good business sense, but their manner did not make him loved. As a compensation for losing power, he became a great deal more interested in money. On behalf of the company, he made magnificent overseas marketing tours, in which he used his prestige and guile to develop business. The sales of Macmillan school textbooks in Commonwealth countries were particularly stimulated by the effects of his visits. His foreign successes provoked many hard, suspicious words, and much outright envy, from marketing people of other publishers. Indeed some of the deals reached in Africa, and the negotiating techniques used to achieve them, were distinctive at the time. Harold's prestige and guile were similarly enlisted to lure authors into contracts with Macmillan. When, in 1969, it became known that the novelist Patrick White (a few years away from a Nobel Laureate) was defecting from Eyre & Spottiswoode, Harold (who was in Australia) visited him in Sydney and, briefed that he had a passion for Greece and its men, spent an hour talking about Mount Athos, in a typically oblique but bewitching attempt to win him over to Macmillan. Some editors considered Harold's intervention a masterstroke: another more wearily concluded that Harold was more interested in 'showing off' to potential authors than in acquiring them for the company. In the event Cape offered a better deal and won White. (Personal approaches by Harold would not have seduced all authors: the name of Harold Macmillan was anathema to John Osborne for one. 'There is murder in my brain, and I carry a knife in my heart for every one of you,' cried Jimmy Porter in *Look Back in Anger*. 'Macmillan, and you, Gaitskell, you particularly.')

In 1965, following an offer from property developers, the old office in St Martin's Street was vacated, and the company moved to a new building in Little Essex Street, near the west end of Fleet Street. It is an ugly modern office, not generously appointed, but with plenty of natural light and was an improvement on the previous Dickensian accommodation. Another office, for employees such as accountants involved in the less literary side of the business, together with warehousing, was built at Basingstoke. Subsequently the whole group structure was reorganised. A holding company called Macmillan Ltd was formed, with a sub-holding company named Macmillan Publishers, and a range of operating companies such as Macmillan Press (academic publishing), Macmillan Educational (for schoolbook publishing) and Macmillan Journals, each with a different speciality. Though the credit for these changes was given to Harold by his admirers, in truth both the details and the implementation of these reforms rested on various executives and salaried managers. The expansions and restructuring of the late 1960s and early 1970s did not alter the ownership of the company, but both decision-taking and implementation shifted away from family members. Harold recognised the inevitability of this shift and accepted it more gracefully than some other members of his family.

Harold was more flexible and responsive to new proposals than Dan, although some of the rough and hurrying currents of modern publishing passed him by. The fiction list became brighter as younger novelists like Muriel Spark were promoted. Biographers and historians whose subjects interested the old man were honoured with detailed comments from him at manuscript or proof stage. Under the stimulus of the new policies initiated under Harold's chairmanship and implemented by executives like Frank Whitehead and Maurice's boon companion Alan Maclean, the firm's UK profits rose from £2.5 million in 1963 to reach £40 million in 1985.

Part of the increased profits was due to paperback sales. As early as 1952, when Dan and Maurice were the only members of the family active in the business, Macmillan had joined a consortium with Cape, Chatto & Windus, Collins, Heinemann and Hodder & Stoughton owning Pan Books, a new company which issued paperback editions of books previously published in hardback by the participating owners. Known originally at Macmillan as Project X, Pan soon became the second paperback publisher in Britain, after Penguin, specialising in middle-brow entertainment. Later, in 1957, and seventy-five years after Macmillan's successful People's Edition series, they resumed their own paperback publishing with the St Martin's Library series, inaugurated with an abridged version of Frazer's *Golden Bough*, two Hardy novels and part of Sir Osbert Sitwell's autobiography. This diversification was timely, for paperback sales took off in the 1960s, and showed the possibility of reaching a mass market dreamt of by Victorian meliorists like Daniel and Alexander Macmillan, George Routledge or George Cassell. Though most publishers in the 1950s and 1960s viewed the advent of paperbacks with mingled regret, distaste and fear, Macmillan's approach was more eager, astute and prescient than most of its competitors. When in 1961 the New American Library offered to buy Pan outright, only Macmillan of the six companies in the consortium refused to sell. For all his commitment to 'special relationships' with the United States, John St John of Heinemann recalled, 'Harold Macmillan argued that it would be folly to allow an American company to control the second-largest UK paperback concern and he persuaded William Collins to support him, and so Collins ended up sharing Pan with Macmillan owning 51 per cent of the equity.' Harold continued to intervene in the development of Pan, in which Heinemann bought a one-third interest for £415,000 in 1969. Pan's turnover grew from £4.9 million in 1973 to £15.9 million in 1982. A year after Harold's death turnover reached £26.5 million.

Maurice, with the help of his wife Katie, had finally conquered his alcoholism (encouraged, among others, by Boothby, with whom his relations were affectionate). 'I am going to do something about my life,' he told a parliamentary colleague shortly after being elected as MP for Halifax in 1955; and he made the sustained effort of will to conquer what had become his governing habit. There was no secret about his alcoholism, and his friends cited his recovery as an example of his endurance. Even Harold was wont to talk about Maurice's alcoholism with political colleagues. Lunching with Butler at Brooks's in 1962, and putting on his usual pose of extreme antiquity, 'Harold said that he felt those of middle age today did not know what it is to go through trouble.' As Butler recorded, 'He spoke movingly and with tears in his eyes of the triumph in which he had shared with his son Maurice on his inherited tendency to succumb to alcohol. He spoke of calling for his son and attending early communion service and of their strength through prayer. He spoke of other domestic difficulties in his family which he had similarly overcome.'

To Katie's regret, Maurice was excluded from office during his father's premiership, despite the promotion of his brother-in-law Amery and others from the Chatsworth circle. 'Lack of confidence on the part of a parent is the one unforgivable sin,' as Paul Bowles has written in *Pages from Cold Point*; it was a sin which Dorothy and Harold committed venially and chillingly throughout Maurice's life. Katie's sense that he was still being ungenerously served in the early 1960s worsened her relations with Dorothy, which were already strained. Certainly to most people Maurice seemed a marginal figure during the Macmillan premiership. In 1960, for example, he produced some proposals to help exports, such as the discouragement of the appointment of sole agents abroad and fiscal change so that wives could be charged as deductible expenses for businessmen travelling abroad (a measure intended to discourage adultery and reduce marital breakdown among foreign salesmen). Downing Street forwarded these proposals to the Treasury for comment, which were returned in such dismissive style that even Harold was vexed on his son's behalf. 'This is a *very* bad Treasury reply,' he minuted. As Harold's premiership became more embattled, and his distrust of his colleagues more acute, he turned increasingly to his domestic circle for advice. He had always drawn on Dorothy's sound sense, but by 1963 he was relying on Maurice for reports on party feelings, and his son was an important new influence in the last ten months of his premiership. One of the first appointments of the new Prime Minister, Home, was Maurice as Economic Secretary to the Treasury.

The economic secretaryship was a job which suited him. It gave no chance for public self-promotion, which was as well, for he was a dull public speaker and shied away from attention. Though most observers judged him a success in his first government post, he thought its importance was nugatory. 'He is a very self-critical man,' as one friend said. 'You have to be to conclude that the job you are doing doesn't matter.' As a young man he had shrunk with revulsion when complimented cheerfully on his good looks by a woman of about the same age, and he continued to have a streak which outreached typical Macmillan self-criticism into moments of outright self-abnegation. In other ways he was an opaque character, except in his choice of brightly defiant shirts and quirky ties, worn as if to compensate for lacking his father's histrionic power. His redoubtable wife Katie was also keenly interested in politics and served as a vice-chairman of the Conservative Party in 1968–71.

With the defeat of the Conservatives in the general election of 1964, Maurice went into opposition and returned to publishing, becoming chairman of Macmillan in 1967, with his father taking the ornamental title of company President. 'Mr Maurice', as he long continued to be known in the firm, was well attuned to the intellectual trends of the times. As a result of his political connections he often introduced manuscripts on political or economic themes to his editors, and many rising writers on these subjects were signed up early in their careers as Macmillan authors. Like his father and grandfather he was a canny Scottish businessman, of whom one acquaintance said, 'You won't find him giving any pennies away.' But Maurice was handicapped by looking as if he did not believe in himself. He was tall, with a crinkly face which betrayed signs of his tension and past suffering; he seemed effaced, bleached and indistinct; although reticent about himself, his low self-esteem was manifest. His manner all but invited junior employees to dismiss him as a dried-out alcoholic. He was attentive to other people, but the 'emotional blockage' between Harold and Maurice was obvious, and depressing.

Maurice was sensitive, kind and compassionate with a sardonic humour. Whereas his father's feelings for the poor and disadvantage were essentially sentimental, Maurice's generosity was practical and unswerving. It was not until late in life that Harold showed much warmth towards him, and in turn he showed a certain estrangement of feeling at times from his own eldest son, but he is remembered with affection by those who knew him well: commemorated, for example, by Woodrow Wyatt as 'gentle, clever . . . Maurice, who made up songs about mussels, and poems, for my daughter Petronella, when he stayed with us in Italy'. Similarly Maurice's fellow Tory, Sir Robert Rhodes James, treasured memories of him: 'That slow smile, that sharp look, that diffidently given, but always wise, advice; that rare but jaylike laugh; and that spasm of pain when anything dishonourable or intellectually shallow was proposed or done'. In the late 1960s Maurice was the Conservative frontbench spokesman on health, so there was surprise when he was appointed Financial Secretary to the Treasury in the Heath government of 1970. He was chairman of the Wider Share-Ownership Council, and it was part of Conservative economic strategy to raise the level of personal savings so as to facilitate cuts in direct taxation; he was supposed to give attention to this, though not much was achieved in the event.

He finally reached the Cabinet in 1972, when Heath promoted him to be Secretary of State for Employment. 'He might well have got there much earlier, had he not been his father's son and suffered in consequence (much as did Randolph Churchill) and had he not (also like Randolph) gone through a spell during which he drank a lot,' commented the *Spectator*. His long years of sobriety had proved 'his strength of character, for the circles in which he enjoys moving are not noted for their aversion to alcohol'. Maurice's success pleased his father, of course; but at the time of his elevation to Cabinet rank Harold reportedly told one of his family that Maurice would never get to the top 'because unlike you or me he's not a shit at heart'.

He went to the Department of Employment with high hopes. To one shrewd observer in 1972 he seemed 'probably the most underrated man in public life': within a week of taking on the job he was pitchforked into a furious confrontation with the railway trades unions. This was the first test of the Industrial Relations Act, which was central to the strategy of the Heath administration and had been enacted despite fierce opposition from the Trades Union Congress and the Labour Party. The railway unions had instructed their members to work to rule from midnight on 16 April, following the collapse of pay negotiations. Maurice's task was to avert disruption of transport services and to vindicate the new legislation. At first the railwaymen's leaders got on well with him, but then there was a disastrous meeting at which he lost all chance of a quick settlement. 'He barked at us and showed typical signs of arrogance, like a Scottish laird turning a crofter out of his home,' said a trade unionist who was present. 'He didn't even say good morning or good evening. He just got up and the civil servants also rose and they walked out without saying a word. He was obviously in a furious temper.' Maurice then applied to the Industrial Relations Court for a cooling-off period of a fortnight, and used the provisions of the new act to enforce a ballot to elicit whether rail workers wanted industrial action. The result went against him, endorsing the recommendations of the union leaders, and the dispute was settled on terms which gratified the railwaymen. Labour leaders hailed this outcome as proof that attempts to impose statutory controls on union activity were otiose. In retrospect the incident was an early warning that the Heath government's economic and employment strategy was going awry.

Henceforth Maurice was seldom considered a success as

Secretary for Employment. The basic trouble was not personal to him. The Industrial Relations Act was a failure, based on the false belief that trade union members were obedient to their leaders, whereas in fact the leaders responded to their membership. The act had been conceived and framed by men steeped by their schooling or war service in the tradition of subordination, and they were confounded when their assumptions proved irrelevant to the way trade unionists behaved. The act not only failed to reduce the number of strikes, but made them more likely by politicising industrial disputes and making compromise harder. Moreover the act was sponsored by a Cabinet which lacked the will to confront the recalcitrance of trade union opposition: a confrontation accepted with gusto a decade later by the Thatcherites. The failures at the Department of Employment in 1972–3 were therefore mainly the result of circumstances rather than personalities; nevertheless to some observers Maurice epitomised the weakness of Heath's men. He seemed 'a ridiculous choice' for the job to the newspaper publisher Cecil King, who assiduously collected other adverse opinions. The only reason that Vic Feather, General Secretary of the Trades Union Congress, could imagine for Maurice's selection was 'that he must know something about the north' as he had been MP for Halifax and his father had sat for Stockton. The industrialist Lord Weinstock judged 'that Macmillan could not be worse', Lord Shawcross 'thought nothing' of him and the Labour MP Brian Walden told King: 'Macmillan is quite incompetent, and his appointment can only be explained by a desire to please old Harold.' Part of the trouble was public presentation. Maurice in private was a charming, shrewd man, but in official dealings he could appear aloof and unconvincing. One of the crises which confronted Maurice at the Department of Employment was the threat of a dock strike. In an attempt to avoid this, Jack Jones (General Secretary of the Transport and General Workers' Union) conferred with John Peyton, the Minister of Transport, and Maurice. 'Peyton was very much a Tory of the old school, a "man of the world" with a twinkle in his eye; Macmillan, sallow in complexion, appeared dour and somewhat shy,' Jones wrote. This was a typical response. By the time the government's second, and fatal, clash with the coalminers began in 1973, the Prime Minister was paying more attention to the Cabinet Secretary, Sir William Armstrong, than to Maurice on industrial relations. Shortly afterwards the latter was demoted to the post of Postmaster-General – the upshot of his failures at self-presentation and his politically fatal lack of a False Self.

Following the fall of the Conservative government in 1974, Katie's contribution to the party and her husband's career was recognised when she was made a Dame of the British Empire in Heath's dissolution honours. Maurice meanwhile returned to the backbenches and set himself apart from future trends in the party by supporting calls for a government of national unity (which his father had ambitions to head). He also resumed the chairmanship of Macmillan, although his most effective days in business were past. In 1978 a financial investigator, who had been hired by a rival conglomerate to scrutinise the possibility of a takeover and had confidentially interviewed past and present Macmillan employees, penned the following assessment of Maurice.

> Despite wide experience in both business and government now has a reputation of being weak, vacillating and indecisive. Does not seem to have accepted that his family have lost control to professional managers, who in fact have saved the company from bankruptcy. Rather than thanking them for this resents their presence and frequently hankers after the days when the company was managed by members of the family. Health considered to be very poor and life expectancy not great. However an informed and formidable opponent to change, unless he can be persuaded that the family (i.e. he and his younger sons) would benefit directly. Much affected by the views of his wife Dame Katherine Macmillan, a shrewd, ruthless and energetic woman who displays a traditional aristocratic disdain and distrust for 'trade'

This was a harsh assessment, which personal acquaintance might have tempered, but it was fundamentally true.

Partly as a result of his earlier heavy drinking, Maurice's health deteriorated steadily in the late 1970s. He nearly died in 1980 of a collapsed lung, and never recovered his strength. In 1984 a lung infection recurred, and after a heart operation from which he seemed to be recovering, he died in his sleep on 10 March, aged sixty-three. Harold was downcast by Maurice's death, which was the last of four family bereavements that shadowed the last decades of his life.

He had first been distressed by the death in 1965 of Maurice's second son, Joshua, then an Oxford undergraduate of twenty. Joshua was a boy of great gaiety with an adolescent taste for sleaze and an intrepid turn when it came to exploring badlands. Having begun smoking hemp on a visit to Morocco, he progressed to cocaine and heroin, and became an amateurish junkie, which is the most dangerous kind. A few months before his death he was treated for heroin addiction in Switzerland, and on his return to Oxford took to mixing alcohol and sedatives 'to forget his anxiety'. On the last night of his life he went in a depressed mood to the Victoria Arms in Walton Street, where he drank heavily with his friends Andy Mowatt of Wadham and Howard Marks. He kept playing 'Cast Your Fate to the Winds' on the jukebox, returned to college in a befuddled and despondent mood, took about twenty tablets of Valium, passed out and died of respiratory obstruction caused by the position in which he was lying. Joshua's friend Marks was a revealing companion to choose: a working-class Welsh youth, by the standards of Oxford in those days he enjoyed exceptional sexual successes with women, was later recruited by the British secret service and then became a major dealer in cannabis until he was arrested in 1988 in an operation involving drug-enforcement agencies from fourteen countries. On the morning after he and Joshua had played 'Cast Your Fate to the Winds', he came out of his room in Balliol to see Joshua's corpse, still in corduroy jacket and drainpipe trousers, being carried downstairs from his college rooms and across the Balliol quadrangle.

The death in these circumstances of the ex-Prime Minister's grandson caused an eruption of repellent press comment. Joshua had hung out in coffee bars, grown long hair, worn rock-and-rollers' suede shoes, visited Mexico and Morocco, known beatniks and jazz musicians and black men in Notting Hill. He was the sort of dashing, privileged young man who appeals to the snobbery of newspaper gossip columnists; worse still, the circumstances of his death excited the lip-smacking moralists who feel a twisted pleasure when tragedy overwhelms a young member of a rich and powerful family. His death was essentially a private tragedy: the loss of a particularly attractive and original young man in circumstances which were to become less unfamiliar in the next twenty years. The intrusions of the press on Dorothy and Harold made their grief more painful and showed how unfair can be the burdens on the families of the famous and mighty.

The next death was Dorothy's. Their marriage seemed stronger after Harold reached supreme office. She continued to see Boothby regularly as a loving friend, but she responded to the strains of power put on Harold by becoming exceptionally supportive. It was as if she felt that his special position deserved a special effort: this she gave unstintingly. She was a sound and sensible adviser throughout his premiership, and kept him tethered at some of the moments when he might have floated off into the more pompous unrealities of public life. Her joviality and zest were a great help to Harold in the years after 1957. The posthumous tribute to her by Lord Hailsham was not just a polite convention: 'one of the most gracious of the ladies who occupied 10 Downing Street', he called her, 'a wonderful help and inspiration to her husband, a charming hostess and a tireless worker'. Yet the stories of a late blossoming in their marriage can be exaggerated: their interests were very different, and they continued to live somewhat separated lives, with a glacial inner core to the new-found outer warmth. This discrepancy, it seemed to one of those who knew and worked with their descendants, was 'a key in understanding the whole subsequent tribe'. The outward cheeriness was belied: as Virginia Woolf wrote in *Mrs Dalloway*, 'the secret signal which one generation passes under disguise to the next generation is loathing, hatred, despair'.

One morning in May 1966 Dorothy was putting on her boots in the hall at Birch Grove before taking some grandchildren to a point-to-point when she complained to a parlour-maid of back-ache. She next went upstairs to discuss plans for dinner with Harold and then returned to the hall, where she fell dead of a heart-attack. The grandchildren who were waiting for her had to be ushered away to save their feelings; then, because her corpse was so heavy, a door was taken off its hinges to carry her upstairs. Instantly Dorothy became the subject of encomia covered in all the smugness and half-truths of official life. 'Wherever she was, whether at home with the family, or in the garden she loved, or in the bustle of political gatherings, or presiding over the public life at Downing Street, she radiated happiness and confidence,' declared Alec Douglas-Home. 'All who knew and loved her feel a deep sense of personal loss, which will be shared by millions who did not know her but who recognised her simple and homely goodness.' Dorothy was often happy and confident; but never as simple as she looked, and hardly a straightforward case of homely goodness.

Harold was desolated by Dorothy's loss and was past consoling, except by work: a little time after her death he began the formidable working regime under which he wrote six volumes of autobiography. Dorothy and Maurice's wife Katie had often clashed, with the former absurdly telling staff at Birch Grove to lock the house at night to stop her daughter-in-law making off with the furniture, but Harold now passed the main house to Maurice, and moved to a bachelor apartment which had last been used by the family when the big rooms were filled with evacuees during the war. His little flat was in fact the butler's quarters, accessible only through kitchens and up a steep staircase. There was one reception room, two bedrooms and a bathroom: a frugal arrangement, which pleasantly reminded him of his undergraduate rooms at Oxford. A cook and chauffeur who attended him lived out. Birch Grove became, according to a regular visitor, an 'eery' place, which Harold loved precisely because it was 'devoid of people', except when other members of the family came down at weekends. Although he was urged by family and friends to take a flat in London or stay overnight at one of his clubs, he insisted on returning to Birch Grove for the night whenever he could.

Boothby too was badly hit by Dorothy's death and drank heavily for a time. He and Harold corresponded with some intimacy almost to the end of their lives and met occasionally: two old men sharing poignant memories. Boothby burnt Dorothy's letters and, giving Harold as his source, told how the old statesman found a large cache of Boothby's letters to his wife in her bedroom at Birch Grove and tried to burn them in a garden incinerator. But the wind blew up and caught the half-charred letters, which fluttered away, chased by the myopic old man through the grounds. It is a good story, which either man might have invented; but it is spoiled by the fact that Dorothy's daughter, Carol Faber, burnt a lot of the letters herself. 'I doubt my grandfather knew where the incinerator was, let alone how to light it,' Carol's daughter Anne Cockerell commented after this anecdote had been published by Sir Robert Rhodes James.

The other premature death was Sarah's. Following her abortion and sterilisation, she descended into acute alcoholism, for which she sought cures in Switzerland and at home. Her marriage to Andrew Heath was dissolved in 1966, and in March 1970 she died from bleeding on the brain at the age of thirty-nine. The coroner suggested that the bleeding had been started by her accidentally knocking her head against a door, but the basic cause of death was alcoholism. Some of the factors which make blood clot (and would prevent a knock on the head from being fatal) are produced in the liver from Vitamin K and, if the liver is damaged by alcohol, the clotting process is deranged. In Sarah's case she had been a chronic alcoholic for years, and at the time of her death had the high level of 283 milligrams of alcohol per 100 millilitres of blood.

Sarah's sister Catherine Amery was also cursed with the Cavendish disease. She has been described by Alastair Forbes as 'by far the most delightful, amusing and beautiful' of the three Macmillan sisters, and in her prime was one of the brightest and shrewdest of political wives. Sadly she was stricken for years by her dependency on alcohol, which weakened her frame and ravaged her beauty. She survived only until her mid-sixties, dying in 1991. Her husband Julian Amery, though he received the Ministry of Housing when the Heath government was formed in 1970, did not reach the top of the slippery pole. In the Commons his oratorical periods seemed to caricature earlier generations of parliamentarians: his tortured vowels alienated his listeners. He speaks, wrote Colin Welch, 'as if from the bottom of a deep well into which a very old Etonian has fallen after a decent dinner.' Some friends felt that his wartime escapades in the secret service had left him with the attitudes of a character in a Bulldog Drummond novel or hankering after the life of Richard Hannay in a story by John Buchan. 'His trouble is that he's never known the difference between nostalgia and reality,' Lord Carrington said of him. Lost in an imperial reverie inspired by his father Leo, he opposed economic sanctions against the Rhodesian rebels in the 1960s and campaigned for a strong British military presence in the Far East. As the victor at an important by-election in 1969, he decried laisser-faire as leading 'to anarchy', socialism 'to slavery', and advocated his father-in-law's Middle Way. Denounced by one of the other candidates as 'one of the backward dreamers who feels he has a divine right to rule', he loathed the state of Britain in the 1960s and 1970s. For a time his opinions seemed increasingly like political aberrations, but he held to them resolutely and eventually some returned to fashion.

For an outsider to pry into the causes of an individual's addictions is stupid, and to judge them is futile. The fact is that Catherine Amery, her sister Sarah, her brother Maurice and three of his children (Alexander, Joshua and Rachel) have been troubled by chemical dependencies, and the conjecture is that some inherited kink in the alchemy of the Cavendishes was the preponderant cause of this. But no one can doubt the emotional sacrifices that were made in the pursuit of political power who recalls Sarah's suffering when she was coerced into her abortion in 1951 or the agonies that were endured because Boothby and Harold would not jeopardise their political careers by getting involved in divorce in the 1930s. Political families sacrifice feelings to action; they defend themselves behind deep retrenchments of hypocrisy; ambition can freeze their hearts; power becomes a dangerous, destructive master. A lot of hurtful decisions were taken in the family, and hurt needs to be assuaged, as drugs of one kind or another can seem to do. It was not just that earlier Cavendishes were physically predisposed to alcoholism; but earlier generations of the Macmillans were harried by feelings of guilt, judged themselves too harshly, found reality sometimes too forbidding and retreated from it. At their most constructive they fled into a world of books, Malcolm perhaps became a fugitive in the wilds of Asia Minor, his kin found sanctuary in Christianity; but some among the later generations, who could not control themselves with the discipline of piety, sought their refuge in bottles or chemicals. Even then they showed some of the family courage and confronted or mastered their problems with the tenacity and fortitude of Harold himself.

For almost a lifetime Harold treated women as if they were a strange, undescribed new species. Gradually, though, his attitude relaxed. Even during his premiership he had taken one woman confidante, Ava, Viscountess Waverley, a somewhat affected and self-dramatising political widow. She had 'cultivated an unerring gift of flattering men who like her' which explained 'why women hate her', Lord Ivor Churchill told a dinner party of Lady Lamington's in 1949; 'she has a caressing, insinuating voice like the serpent of Old Nile', James Lees-Milne added. His other close women friends included John Wyndham's widow, Pamela Egremont, and Eileen O'Casey, the playwright's scintillating, warm-hearted widow. After Dorothy's death Mrs O'Casey was often invited to stay at Birch Grove or to lunch with Harold at the Ritz; their pleasure in one another's company was shining and clear. To Eileen O'Casey he seemed a shy man, who found it hard to show his affections and felt uneasy in discussing intimacies; but he was blessed with delicious humour, a spirited sense of fun, and she found him lovable in his way. Harold responded to her good feelings for him, and one weekend at Birch Grove, when other members of the family were lunching with them, he asked her to sit in the chair at the other end of the table from him, which no one had used since Dorothy's death. For a time marriage between them seemed possible, but in the end they remained devoted friends. In the family circle Harold was close to some of his granddaughters, and was fond of his grandson Alexander's wife, Bitta, a generous and supportive woman who bought much gaiety into the house.

Harold's granddaughter Anne Cockerell found it incomprehensible that anyone who knew him 'could possibly call him boring and tedious', and it is pleasant to think that he captivated and delighted younger members of his family; but the fact is that many people, outside the immediate domestic circle on which he increasingly relied, continued to think of him as a dreary bore whose manner, in the slang of the 1920s, was just 'too bogus'. Middle-class male dons sat rapt listening to his recitals, and journalists delighted in stories about him, but some others from the upper classes (especially worldly and intelligent women) found him tedious, snobbish, frightened or unreal. Harold spent a weekend at Petworth, for example, when the Wyndhams' other guests included Isaiah Berlin, Peter Quennell, Ann Fleming and three bus-loads of Bolshoi ballet dancers. 'I concluded he was a crashing bore; it's not uncommon to love lords but it's rare to be besotted about dukes,' Ann Fleming reported to Evelyn Waugh. 'Isaiah cheered the PM one evening, and Quennell didn't do too badly, but otherwise the PM was glum unless anecdoting on 1914, 15 16 or merry tales of dukes in clubs, at home, on grouse moors etc.' She thought Harold should be psychoanalysed, diagnosing his problems as 'sense of humour limited and facetious, terror of women, worship of the aristocracy'.

The old man's favourite duke was Dorothy's nephew Andrew Devonshire, a man of singularity and special attractions, about whom many enticing stories circulate. He and his Duchess, Debo, were fiercely protective of the old man, although never too solemn about his achievements. 'We had a noisy evening with Avons and Devonshires,' Ann Fleming wrote to Waugh. 'Nigel Birch came to tell Anthony the gossip, and Andrew was very loyal to his uncle; it was civilised until Lord Avon's bedtime, then there was a great uproar between Andrew and Nigel and lots of four-letter words; Debo said to Roy Jenkins, "Can't you stop them by saying something Labour?", but this is something Roy has never been able to do.' As a trustee of the Macmillan Trust, Andrew Devonshire has been a crucial figure. The Devonshires have always been one of those ducal families that is interested in money; they have had none of the forlorn weakness or petulant extravagance that ruined dukes like the Manchesters or Leinsters. Under Devonshire's influence the Macmillan trustees have been the strictest of stewards working for the family's interests.

One source of enrichment were the six volumes of memoirs which Harold began writing in 1965, the last of which was published in 1973. They were a commercial success, although their critical reception was mixed. Most of his fellow politicians disliked them. 'They lack the style, the light and shade, much of the humour and, inevitably, the pauses and the perfect timing which made him such a brilliant conversationalist and such a fascinating performer,' conceded his admirer Sir Nigel Fisher. 'As the autobiographer has drawn on through the years, the style has become more wooden, cliché-ridden and pedestrian than ever, until in this last volume the reader has a recurrent sensation akin to that of chewing cardboard,' Enoch Powell wrote in 1973. Powell concluded that 'for all his finesse and subtlety as a political operator, and his acutely observed experience' Macmillan saw politics and life in a set of clichés. The diary extracts interpolated into Harold's text were identical in style to the surrounding narrative: 'when you find that someone, in the privacy of his diary and the midst of events, talks to himself in the same platitudes and phrases as he uses in a party speech or a press communiqué, you have to believe it is the genuine article'.

High political office is like malaria, bringing a fever for power which can never be shaken off. The chronic and absolute egotism of politicians means that many of them spend their retirements harkening for the summons back. Harold did. He refused an earldom after his political retirement in 1963, partly to avoid marring Maurice's hopes of high Cabinet rank, partly because (as he told Cub Alport) 'a peerage makes people think you are so old', but mainly because he still hoped to be called back to the Commons to save his country (he had relinquished his seat in 1964). Alec Douglas-Home more than once tried to persuade him to accept a peerage and looked vexed when Eileen O'Casey in her forthright way backed Harold's determination to remain a commoner when the three were at luncheon together. Eventually he indicated that he would accept an earldom, and this was gazetted on his ninetieth birthday in February 1984. His reasons for this were mixed. Maurice was in failing health and had no hopes of preferment from Thatcher; his career was past being damaged by inheriting a peerage. Ennoblement was also urged on him by his eldest grandson Alexander, who wanted to sit in the Lords; but, equally important, his eyesight was too dim for reading, he was bored and he wanted to raise a stir again.

Heath and Thatcher both found it unbearable to accept that they had lost supreme power and never forgave those responsible. Avon too was haunted by the memory of the last months of his premiership. Harold was less distracted by his loss than some others, but for at least twenty years after his retirement he had hopes of returning to play the great game. He called his years of enforced political retirement 'life after death' and still in the 1970s awaited the call to head a coalition government to rescue the country from economic collapse and social disarray. He spoke of this to politicians as varied as Callaghan and Carrington and, on one occasion, showed his ambitions so nakedly to a television interviewer that Lord Egremont interrupted and insisted that the cameras be stilled. He thought that the Heath government's two confrontations with the National Union of Mineworkers were 'bungling': as he told Cecil King in 1972, 'he had fought with miners in the trenches – and they never gave in'. After Heath's government had been defeated by the coalminers in 1974 and replaced by a supine minority Labour government, the millionaire Arnold Weinstock told him that the nation had only three alternatives: an extremist government, either of the far left or hard right, or else a coalition national government. 'Macmillan thought the last much the most likely,' Weinstock reported: not only because it might revive his own ideas for a Popular Front in the 1930s, but also because, like de Gaulle's emergence from retirement at Colombey-les-Deux-Eglises to reunite a divided nation, Harold was hoping to return from Birch Grove as national saviour. He talked of standing again for the House of Commons as a national candidate in the second general election of 1974, and visited Lord Avon to discuss the possibility of forming a coalition government. In 1976, too, he broadcast an appeal for 'a government of national unity' of which, no doubt, he hoped to be more than a figurehead. (His television broadcasts were always consummate pieces of acting, made more effective by the interventions of his grandson Alexander, who was usually present at these brilliant self-promotions.)

Still he was not taken altogether seriously by many of those contemporaries who had known him longest. Watching him shuffle down the aisle at a memorial service, leaning on his stick with one hand and resting on a grandson's arm with

the other, Rab Butler exclaimed in a stage whisper intended
to be heard by half the church, 'It's all put on, you know.'
'He can be very amusing, but he should really have been a
Cardinal Archbishop in the Middle Ages, where absolution
from irregularity over the facts could always be obtained by
a short visit to the Vatican,' Harold's old colleague from the
Churchill Cabinet Lord Chandos wrote to Avon in 1971. As
far as men like Chandos were concerned, Boothby was part of
the Macmillan joke. The bumptious life-peer had recently been
'unspeakable' in his self-promotions: 'If I get a chance of kicking
him I will, but he is so discredited that I believe it would be a
waste of shoe leather,' Chandos continued, but 'if Harold had
been a Cardinal we could have got him excommunicated'. Some
of the younger generation were sceptical about his performances
too. In 1972 he spoke at a dinner in London to honour Lester
Pearson, the former Canadian Prime Minister. 'He had an
affectation of senility even when he was younger but he has
grown into the part, he was just a bit more florid and a bit
more shaky,' Tony Benn noted in his diary. 'He began by
saying how Britain had never been a big country when it was
the most powerful in the Middle Ages, and therefore influence
didn't depend on size; he saw a great future for England.'
He dismissed 'little differences' in the Commons as trivial
compared with the momentous challenges of membership of
the European Community. 'It was Mac the politician speaking
with great emphasis; his mind is as bright as can be. It was
impressive and I enjoyed it, but what he was saying simply had
no bearing on the problems of our times.' He made a brilliant
if mannered impression on other occasions. At David Bruce's
memorial service in Westminster Abbey in 1978, he indulged
in 'a spectacular piece of ham acting and show-stealing, but
very well done', according to Roy Jenkins, who was there.
As a speaker, whether in public or private, his most effective
ploy was to pause: once, in a television tribute to Kennedy, he
held his pause for as long as thirteen seconds. It captivated his
audience.

He liked the rattle of political gossip in the clubs. During his life he was a member of the Carlton, Beefsteak, Buck's, the Athenaeum, Turf, Pratt's and the Guards. This signified one great difference between him and Avon. The latter, who was possibly the only man to have resigned from Grillions, detested club life for exposing him 'to all the greatest bores in the country'. For Avon membership of the Carlton had been 'a most painful duty', a hell-hole where he had endured hours of humbug, but Harold, who could charge commonplaces with poignant meaning, revelled in such places. His clubland monologues were the mark of an incorrigible politician, for few political leaders talk to anyone else. They berate, or lecture, or canvass, or try to disarm – Thatcher, Crossman, Major and Baldwin are examples of the four conversational modes – but they have little capacity for ordinary human dialogues. 'Went to the Beefsteak club and was richly rewarded as Harold Macmillan was there in wonderful form; witty, wise, wide-ranging talk,' the diplomat Charles Ritchie noted in his diary in 1969. The past, Carlyle once wrote, is attractive because it is drained of fear, and Harold's talk was usually about the past and drained of his fears. He perfected what Peter Rawlinson has called the Great Speech.

> Those who heard it never tired of its repetition, for it was a work of art. It began in a stately manner with the funeral procession of Queen Victoria led by Captain Ames, the tallest man in the British Army. This solemn introduction was followed by a somewhat quizzical reverie upon the number of domestic servants then in service in Edwardian English homes. That done, the orator – apparently emotionally overcome during the next passage but happily only temporarily – led his audiences through the mud of Flanders in one war and the sands of the Western Desert in another. Rallying after these plaintive memories of 'old, unhappy, far-off things and battles long ago', the tone sharpened and the speech trotted along, gathering pace as it reflected on the role of the British as Greeks and the Americans as Romans and concluding in fine scorn over the sale of the family silver.

In 1981 Frank Longford attended a party given by Lord
Gage, the father of the House of Lords, who had married
Boothby's ex-wife Diana Cavendish. 'The guest of honour
was Harold Macmillan,' wrote Longford. 'As he totters along
on his stick he creates an impression of infinite dignity and
a sort of mischievous benignity.' To Elizabeth Longford (the
biographer of Queen Victoria) Harold lamented the threat to
the royal family of hired assassins and murderous lunatics and
urged that royalty should not cluster together at the Trooping
of the Colour 'like a covey of partridges'. Longford asked his
opinion of Thatcherite monetarism. 'It is the greatest mistake',
he replied, 'to lay down a principle. You must have principles
of course. But to proclaim them is a sure means of producing
an ugly confrontation.' It was a classic opinion of his: and it
was followed by a classic piece of snobbery. When the guests
were called to luncheon, Longford stood aside to let the older
man pass first; but he was an earl and a Knight of the Garter;
and Harold, still a commoner, insisted on giving way to what
he called 'the nobility'.

As the years drew on he became increasingly frail but at times
superbly venerated. In June 1986 Harold, who was by then aged
ninety-two, was staying at Chatsworth when Major-General
Peter Cavendish used the house for a party to mark his year
as High Sheriff of Derbyshire. Harold sat in a room, while
the General's guests 'queued like children at a hoop-la stall
to talk to him', Debo Devonshire recounted. When the guests
left, a sixteen-strong band from the General's old regiment
marched from the hall, where they had been playing, through the
dining-room and drawing-room to the old school-room where
Harold and the Devonshires were sitting. The noise of trumpets,
drums and big brass was so tremendous that the windows were
almost blown out. When, in Harold's honour, they struck up
'The British Grenadiers', the old Grenadier officer, survivor of
the Somme, struggled to his feet, leaning on two sticks as near
to attention as he could. 'It was', the Duchess wrote, 'one of
the most moving sights I ever saw.' By the end of the year he

was visibly failing, and his surviving children, grandchildren and great-grandchildren gathered at Birch Grove for the Christmas holiday. He had always tended to seasonal gloom at Christmas, and he faded out, dying at 6.20 on the evening of 29 December. Though his memory had weakened, his mind was clear to the end, and his last words were fittingly calm. 'I think I will go to sleep now.'

The new head of the family was Maurice's eldest child, Alexander, who had been born in 1943 at Oswestry in Shropshire, where his mother's family, the Ormsby-Gores, had a home. Alexander was educated at Eton, proceeding to university in Paris and later taking a course at the University of Strathclyde. He became a sub-editor on the *Glasgow Herald* in 1963, and it was in Scotland that he began drinking seven pints of beer with chasers each night. Two years later he joined the staff of the *Daily Telegraph*, and by the time he started work as a foreign correspondent of the *Telegraph* newspapers he was consuming half a bottle of whisky daily. By the late 1960s he was drinking himself to death: two glasses of beer in the morning, four gins before luncheon, a bottle and a half of wine with the meal followed by two brandies, two afternoon beers, four whiskies before dinner, another bottle and a half of wine, with four brandies after dinner. One night in Paris he went to sleep with both his legs in the same leg of his pyjamas and, when he woke, was terrified that he was paralysed from the waist down. Yet with all this ignominy he could still file his copy faultlessly. The *Telegraph* management considered him a good operator, but, given his alcoholic consumption, it was not to be expected that he was energetic.

A crisis was averted because in 1970 he took one of the best decisions of his life and married Bitta Hamilton (they were divorced in 1991); around the same time he abandoned journalism to become a director of Macmillan. His drinking continued unabated, however, and some passages in those years are blank. Bitta Stockton is admired and liked by all who know her, and her attitude of 'tough love', coupled with the inspiration of his father Maurice's example in overcoming alcoholism, helped Alexander to cease drinking after two years of marriage. 'Whenever you want a drink you have to think of the reality of getting drunk, being sick, lying on the floor unable to move, and the look of contempt and pity in people's eyes,' he has said. 'Think of that and it's very easy to say no.' His alcoholism had already taken its toll physically. At the age of thirty-two he had a coronary thrombosis, and he has always considered his greatest achievement was to come to terms with his alcoholism. 'People ... think that I'm a drunk who cannot be trusted,' he declared. 'They don't realize that having been down there, looked over the edge of hell and come back,' had been an experience which made him 'a stronger person, not a weaker one', he told a journalist, although his grandfather's denials of inner weakness, with their accompanying self-punishing and self-deceiving insistence on his strength, might be a warning of the painful cost of such an insistent belief.

In his early period with Macmillan in the 1970s an attempt was made to use his journalistic experience in the magazine division, but he was then moved sideways to experiment with a diversification into film and audio-visual business. Comparably his younger brother Adam was later involved in an experimental diversification into computer games, Macmillan Piranha. Salaried executives with their own prospects to promote were not averse to Alexander or Adam pursuing these distractions, which left little time for involvement in other aspects of management. Alexander became deputy chairman of Macmillan in 1976, and liked to be seen by outsiders as one of the owners, with both hereditary commitment and aptitude for publishing. Harold believed in primogeniture and was a consistent protector of the interests of Alexander, whose relations with some other members of his family were variable.

Stockton is a thickly bearded man, with a piratical appearance. He is talkative, forceful and bustling. He can be charming when he wishes and has something of his grandfather's talent at public presentation, though less intelligence. He is short-tempered, particularly when frustrated, impatient of fools and easily bored. Some women find him attractive and his conversation fascinating; for others he is less compelling. He has few physical inhibitions and can startle people by his general candour. Indeed he enjoys talking about himself and is flattered by the interest of others; perceptive, and outspoken, about some of his weaknesses, he has some blind-spots in his self-knowledge. There is nothing small or timid about his imagination or his accounts of his doings; he can talk magnificently in a way which provides journalists with good copy; he has the capacity to impress some authors and talks with wonderful fluency (when well briefed) about the great world of publishing.

He had more influence with his grandfather than many other members of the family, including Maurice, and his position in the company in the 1970s and 1980s owed much to Harold. He speaks with understanding of the old man's character and motives, although he is less convincing when he claims his grandfather as a great influence on his own character and outlook. 'He taught me not to take things too seriously,' he told an interviewer in 1990. 'Whatever you do should be fun, or it's not worth doing. The best jokes are the ones against yourself. He wasn't a worrier.'

Alexander made his first speech at the age of eight at his school's debating society (opposing compulsory games) and remains prolix. He has ambitions in the House of Lords, where he has been a constant attender since inheriting the peerage which he encouraged his grandfather to accept. In the early days he tried not to be awed by his grandfather's reputation in the chamber and made a contentious maiden speech advocating higher pay for schoolteachers. His legs shook so badly that he had to wedge himself against the bench in front; throughout he was conscious (he said afterwards) that, if he succeeded, peers might say, 'You know who taught him to do that,' and that, if he flopped, they would mutter, 'He's not as good as the old man.'

He has since been prominent in debates on the Broadcasting Bill of 1990, when he led efforts to prevent Rupert Murdoch's Sky satellite company being exempt from rules on cross-media ownership applied to other television companies. He speaks on such issues as education and cultural diplomacy; in imitation of his grandfather he has taken a protective interest in the north-east of England. Issues special to the area around Stockton, whether the building of a barrage across the River Tees or allegations of the sexual abuse of children in Cleveland, often bring him to his feet. He has hopes of a minor post in a Conservative government (being more attuned to the politics of Major than Thatcher), but despite his regular attendance and interventions, and the paucity of younger peers suitable for promotion, he has remained on the backbenches. It is not only Alexander Stockton who has inherited the family's political interest. Another grandson, Mark Faber, made a persuasive appeal in *The Times* a few months before his premature death in 1991 to Margaret Thatcher to stop complaining about the Tory leadership system which had been used to oust her and to cease degrading herself as Heath had done by cavilling at his successor's leadership. His younger brother David Faber is the conservative prospective parliamentary candidate for Westbury.

Alexander Stockton has been involved in many good causes: the Book Trade Benevolent Society, the Book Rest Appeal, the Lindemann Fellowship, the Chemical Dependency Centre, the English Speaking Union, the Royal Society for Nature Conservation and many others. He has been a school governor and for a time was vice-chairman of the Carlton Club Political Committee. Like his grandfather, he is a devoted clubman, and in addition to the Carlton is a member of the Beefsteak, Buck's, Pratt's, White's and the more *déclassé* Groucho. He has expressed scant sympathy for the young indigents who slept at night in boxes and bags outside Macmillan's London office in the late 1980s and 1990s; nevertheless he is chairman of the Central London Training and Enterprise Council set up by the government to involve local business leaders in administering youth-training schemes. Speaking at a community centre at

White City in 1990, he warned that current redevelopment plans for Paddington, Kings Cross and Hammersmith might 'be a recipe for social disaster if the chromium palaces of capitalism, immediately adjacent to some of the areas of worst social deprivation in the country, do not provide jobs for kids who . . . face the prospect of, at best, dead-end jobs or, at worst, long-term unemployment'.

Maurice and Katie had four other children: Joshua, born in 1945, who died at Balliol; Adam, born in 1948; Rachel, born in 1955; and David, born in 1957. For the most part these and Harold's other grandchildren enjoyed having a prime minister in the family. The younger Macmillans have not been blighted by power politics as, say, some of the Kennedys' lives have been ruined in the United States. Dorothy made her grandchildren welcome at 10 Downing Street, the hall of which was cluttered with bikes and scooters (except on Cabinet days, when they were banished). In the great days of the late 1950s the younger generation were instructed that, if they played draughts in the hall with policemen, they must not obstruct diplomats or Cabinet ministers who might arrive; games of dominoes were confined to the police room. It was a pleasure to the office staff to work in a building which was also a family home; though the feelings of Sarah and Maurice, at least, had been sacrificed to the exigencies of political ambition, the Macmillan premiership was fun for the young of the family.

'Great names debase rather than exalt those who cannot live up to them,' wrote La Rochefoucauld, and Maurice and his sons 'were placed in false and hopeless positions', as one publishing colleague thought, by the business expectations of them. For Alexander, it has been particularly difficult. Overall since 1963 it has been not the urge to power that has dominated the family, but the urge of acquisition. It has been bank balances, not ballot boxes, that have preoccupied them; their thoughts have been on Little Essex Street, not Downing Street. The Macmillans have been playing an end-game. They own a great and historic business which no family could still control: the difficulties have been surpassing.

Of Alexander's surviving brothers Adam was educated at Eton and Strasbourg University, and managed the family's agricultural properties in Sussex for a time. He was also a successful small-time racing driver. At intervals he has worked at Little Essex Street, where he was regarded as a likeable but scarcely dynamic man upon whom unfair expectations were rested by those who hoped that the family would remain a strong executive force in the company. He inspires affection, but was never admired for first-class business acumen. He married in 1982, and his only son and Alexander's only son are co-heirs of their great-grandfather's settlements, and hence of the house of Macmillan. Adam is the family trustee of the Harold Macmillan Trust, set up by his grandfather, which among other tasks is working to develop classroom materials and teacher training in Africa and Latin America.

The youngest and most determined of the family is David. He left Harrow School in 1975 with a poor educational record and, like his father before him, began his work for the family business with a training tour of ancillary operations such as printers, binders and bookshops. Like Maurice he did not always make a strong impression and could look haggard at meetings or conferences; but like his father too he inspires affection and sympathy among a wide range of people. Already in his early twenties, he caught the attention of senior executives, although a jaundiced spirit might say that it was impossible for them to ignore him anyway. Several key figures had early hopes that he was the family member of his generation with the best capacity to maintain a genuine role in management, but for a time the distractions of life outside the office retarded his progress. When he arrived at Little Essex Street in the late 1970s he seemed to feel that family members were being fended off with spurious responsibilities. One observer at that time sensed his resentment of the way that his father and elder brothers had 'handed the family fortune and birthright over to a lot of middle-class intellectuals and managers'. Certainly he is too honest a man to respect some of the pretensions of his family about publishing, and too much of a realist to resist the inevitable.

Other great family publishing concerns have moved necessarily and irreversibly into the control of professional managers. Sir Newman Flower was succeeded in 1958 as chairman of Cassell by his son Desmond, who presided over the company's sale to an American group which brusquely removed him from the chairmanship in 1971. Sir Stanley Unwin was succeeded at Allen & Unwin on his death in 1968 by his son Rayner, who in the 1980s resorted to various intricate but unsuccessful devices to secure the succession for his son Merlin and nephew Corydon. The two sons of Sir William Collins took over his business after his death in 1976, the elder son as chairman and the younger as managing director of the publishing division; but their dedication was not matched by their acumen as managers, and there were dramatic disagreements within the family, whose influence was supplanted. In both cases the company eventually lost its independence: Collins went into the maw of Rupert Murdoch in 1989, and Allen & Unwin were bought by HarperCollins in 1990.

The Cavendish disease has continued to afflict the Macmillan family. They were all hurt by the press coverage of the death at the age of thirty-one in 1987 of Rachel Macmillan: 'a vivacious, enthusiastic, amusing, entertaining girl who adored all of us and who we all adored', as Alexander described her. She was the manager of a rock group, divorced after a brief marriage to an Australian record producer, Leith Corbett. She had been involved with drugs and alcohol for most of her adult life, but had been clean for some time before she died. The night before her death was a disaster. She began by getting drunk on champagne and vodka. Then, at 4.15 in the morning, in central London, she accepted a lift from three men in a car which they claimed was a mini-cab and was driven to a rough area, where a knife was produced and she was robbed of her handbag and jewellery. Collected from a police station by her brother Adam, she went home in an 'angry, bitter and upset' mood, determined to get a good night's sleep, and took five times the recommended dose of her prescribed anti-depressant drug, dying some hours later. 'She rarely behaved particularly well when drunk,' Adam Macmillan told the coroner's inquest of his journey with her from the police station. 'She would make terrible scenes. She changed moods two or three times in the car on the way back, from being extremely angry to being very remorseful.' 'Losing your only sister is a ghastly thing,' Alexander told *The Times*. 'It was particularly ghastly because I thought she'd kicked it. Her death was tragic in the proper sense of the word. She had a slip and did all the things she had sworn she would never do again. In a state of rage and disappointment, she wanted to go to sleep and start all over again in the morning.' Some newspaper reports seemed to Alexander to gloat over his sister's death. Journalists stereotype the alcoholic as 'either a bundle of rags, shuffling along the Embankment, or a free-living, free-spending, irresponsible toff', he complained. 'The truth is, there are more of us catching the 8.30 to work every morning than there are under the arches at Charing Cross.'

Among other properties Alexander took over the Birch Grove estate after Harold's death, and asserted his rights over it. Later, in 1988, he put up the house at Birch Grove together with 1,234 acres for sale at £5 million, explaining that he was 'a publisher first and foremost, and most of my business is in London'. Indeed, he was as committed to the family firm as his father or grandfather and was proud of his chairmanship in the five years after 1985. During that time Macmillan spent about £30 million on expansion. They bought from Lord Forte's Trust House group the publishing firm of Sidgwick & Jackson in 1986. During earlier crises at Collins, that company had sold its interest in Pan Books to its partners Heinemann and Macmillan. In 1987, Reed International merged with the Octopus Group (which owned Heinemann) and hoped to take over Pan, but were aghast to find that with the change of ownership Heinemann's Pan holding had to be offered first to Macmillan. The latter exercised their right, paying £22 million to take control of Pan and thus forcing Octopus into a big outlay to develop their Mandarin paperback business. The total acquisition of Pan was a coup for Macmillan, of far-reaching importance for the group's future, as are their ties with two American companies, the paperback imprint Tor and St Martin's Press. Tor is a company associated with publishing stories about fighting men or desperate Amazonians, full of ritualised violence and under-stated eroticism, such as appeal to over-heated juveniles. St Martin's Press is a fast-growing company which originally specialised in academic books published at a high price with short print runs but which has more recently moved into the market for books about rock musicians. Tom McCormack, an energetic American who runs St Martin's with a distinctive personal style, is on the board of Macmillan in London, where his contribution has been crucial, not least because he is neither awed by family mystique nor sentimental about old loyalties.

Alexander revelled in his involvement in the deals and alliances of the late 1980s and drew part of his sense of himself from being chairman of a great family publishers. It therefore cannot have been pleasant from him to be replaced as chairman in 1990 by Nicky Byam Shaw, who had joined the company as a sales manager in 1964 and had been a managing director since 1969. Byam Shaw is a formidable man who, as one colleague says, 'can make figures sound like iambic pentameters'. Opinions about him vary from the eulogistic to the unprintably defamatory. He is an urbane but hard man with an intuitive sense, in every transaction, of the necessary amount of force to be used to get his way. He has seemed, perhaps unconsciously, to model himself on Harold Macmillan, and there are resemblances between the two men. Their admiration was mutual, possibly based on recognition of their common determination to get what they want. Byam Shaw, like Harold, is canny about other people's motives and practises Lloyd George's adage about colleagues: 'If you can't square 'em, squash 'em.' Just as Harold was a man of many poses so Byam Shaw is a man who wears several different suits. He makes much of his naval background (his father was killed in action in 1941, and as a young man he too served in the Royal Navy); other members of the family have had a high artistic reputation, and he can don the mantle of a cultivated bohemian; he likes to be recognised as a creative publisher, and for a long time there was a feeling that his achievements deserved greater recognition from the book trade. Like Harold he has his insecurities: his relations with some of the Macmillan editors most admired by other people have not always been easy.

At the time when Byam Shaw took over, Alexander was promoted to the honorific heights of President of Macmillan (vowing meanwhile to write a novel of his own). His youngest brother David fulfilled a long ambition to represent the family on the board, becoming Sales Director. It is the first time that the group has not had a member of the family as chairman and marks the apotheosis of executives in the management of Macmillan. Alexander's deposition as chairman has meant more than the cancelling of his claims to publishing glory. The Macmillans will keep their money, and help administer their trusts, and battle with their family demons, but after 150 years their days are closing as a publishing dynasty whose members live in the grip of prodigious traditions and have their lives defined by books. The traditions and mentality of Arran, which so directly inspired Harold's working life and indirectly influenced Maurice's character, have ceased to matter. That combination of earnestness, guilt, self-criticism and hard work is irrelevant to men whose outlook and ethics are essentially those of late-twentieth-century Belgravians. 'All happy families', as Tolstoy wrote, 'are more or less like one another; every unhappy family is unhappy in its own particular way.' For a long time the Macmillans were distinctive, not least in their unhappiness; now they resemble other rich men, buttressed by family trusts, but without the humiliating pressure to prove they have some hereditary instinctual superiority as publishers.

For a quarter of a century, until 1990, they were playing an end-game. The future for them was the giving over of a game that must be lost.

Sources

A NOTE ON SOURCES

The place of publication of books listed in these notes is London unless otherwise specified. Books are listed in the sources for the chapter in which they have been first used, and are not cited again in the source notes for later chapters.

Chapter 1: The Family Silver

The chief Stockton quotations come from House of Lords Debates, volume 475, 13 November 1984 (columns 234–41 on Economic and Industrial Affairs) and volume 470, 21 January 1986 (columns 158–60 on Shops Bill). His remark to Lord Longford is quoted in the latter's *Diary of a Year* (1982). The quotations from Lord Hailsham of St Marylebone are taken from his obituary, 'Maurice Harold Macmillan, First Earl of Stockton' in *Biographical Memoirs of Fellows of the Royal Society*, volume 33 (1987). The quotation from Norman Tebbit is taken from Sarah Baxter's interview with him published in *New Statesman and Society* of 10 May 1991. Other sources include Peter Hennessy's article on Macmillan in the *Economist* of 20 April 1991.

Chapter 2: Duncan

On Arran I have followed William Lytteil, *Landmarks of Scottish Life and Language* (Edinburgh, 1877), the Rev. David Landsborough's *Arran,*

*a poem, and Excursions to Arran, with reference to the Natural History
of the Island* (1847), Thomas Pennant's *Tour in Scotland and Voyage
to the Hebrides, 1772* (1776), and James Bryce's *Geology of Clydesdale
and Arran; embracing also the Marine Zoology and the Flora of Arran*
(1859). On Scottish customs I have used John Graham Dalyell's *The
Darker Superstitions of Scotland Illustrated from History and Practice*
(Edinburgh, 1834); Henry Grey Graham's *Social Life of Scotland in the
Eighteenth Century* (1899); Mrs Ann Grant of Laggan's *Superstitions of
the Highlanders* (1811); and Colonel David Stewart of Garth's *Sketches of
the Character, Manners and Present State of the Highlanders of Scotland*
(Edinburgh, 1822). Alexander Haldane's *Memoirs of the Lives of Robert
Haldane of Airthrey and of his Brother James Alexander Haldane* (1852)
is indispensable for the Arran revival meetings.

Chapter 3: Daniel

The chief source for this chapter are Daniel Macmillan's letters in the British
Library supplemented by the biography of him by Thomas Hughes, *Memoir
of Daniel Macmillan* (1882).

My account of tuberculosis follows F.B. Smith's excellent book *The
Retreat of Tuberculosis 1850–1950* (1988), together with Linda Bryder's
*Below the Magic Mountain: A Social History of Tuberculosis in the
Twentieth Century* (Oxford, 1988). Other major influences have been
Walter Houghton's excellent *The Victorian Frame of Mind 1830–1870*
(1957), and David Vincent's masterly *Literacy and Popular Culture:
England 1750–1914* (Cambridge, 1989). The history of childhood and
of attitudes to children has been unduly influenced by the writings of the
French dogmatist Philippe Aries, but in this and subsequent chapters I
have followed Linda Pollock's revisionist *Forgotten Children: Parent–Child
Relations from 1500 to 1900* (1983): an excellent book, despite its author's
affectation of referring to Queen Victoria as 'Victoria Hanover' or (more
often and sillier) 'Hanover'. I owe some ideas to Peter Gay's *The Bourgeois
Experience: Victoria to Freud*, 2 volumes (Oxford, 1984–6) and to David
Kynaston's sprightly *King Labour* (1977). For Victorian literary life see
Simon Nowell–Smith, *The House of Cassell 1848–1958* (1958).

Various quotations and other information are taken from biographies of
Daniel Macmillan's literary acquaintances, notably Sir Frederick Maurice's
Life of Frederick Denison Maurice (1884) and Lady Chitty's *The Beast and
the Monk: A Life of Charles Kingsley* (1975). My description of Glasgow
takes phrases from *Letters from High Latitudes* (1857), that delightful
travel book by Lord Dufferin and Clandeboye (afterwards Marquess of
Dufferin and Ava). Other quotations or ideas are taken from George
Curtis's two-volume edition of *The Correspondence of John Lothrop
Motley* (1889).

Chapter 4: Alexander

The main sources for this chapter are the Macmillan papers in the British Museum supplemented by Charles Graves's *Life and Letters of Alexander Macmillan* (1910), by Sir George Macmillan's exercise in filial celebration, *Letters of Alexander Macmillan* (1908) and by Alfred Ainger's commemoration in *Macmillan's Magazine*, vol. 73 (1896).

Apart from the Macmillan correspondence at the British Library, I have used and quoted from the Gladstone papers in the same archive, especially Add. 44107, 44246 and 44786, and from Charles Kingsley's papers, especially Add. 41299. Other archival material consulted includes the papers of Archibald Campbell Tait, Archbishop of Canterbury, at Lambeth Palace Library, especially volumes 99, 100, 238 and 268.

There are a multitude of books by or about Macmillan authors on which I have drawn. These include in alphabetical order of subject Edith Sichel's *The Life and Letters of Alfred Ainger* (1906); G.W.E. Russell's two-volume edition of the *Letters of Matthew Arnold 1848–1888* (1895); Morton Cohen and Anita Gandolfo's *Lewis Carroll and the House of Macmillan* (Cambridge, 1987); the seven volumes of Gordon Haight's Yale edition of *The George Eliot Letters* (1956); Sir Leslie Stephen's *Life of Henry Fawcett* (1886); John Spencer Clark's *The Life and Letters of John Fiske* (New York, 1917); W.R.W. Stephens's *Life and Letters of Edward Augustus Freeman* (1895); Herbert Gilchrist's biography of his mother, *Ann Gilchrist* (1887); Sir Leslie Stephen's *Letters of John Richard Green* (1901); Florence Hardy, *The Early Life of Thomas Hardy 1840–1891* (1928); Robert Gittings, *The Older Hardy* (1978); Arthur Fenton Hort, *Life and Letters of Fenton Hort* (1896); Leon Edel's edition of *Henry James Letters 1883–1895* (1981); Rayburn Moore's edition of the *Selected Letters of Henry James to Edmund Gosse 1882–1915* (1988); S.M. Ellis, *Henry Kingsley: Towards a Vindication* (1931); Ronald Bayne's edition of *Sermons and Lectures by the late Rev. Brooke Lambert, with a Memoir by J.E.G. De Montmorency* (1902); Viscount Morley of Blackburn's *Recollections* (1917); Jane Grey Perkins, *The Life of Mrs Norton* (1909); George Birkbeck Hill, *Letters of Dante Gabriel Rossetti to William Allingham 1854–1870* (1897); Georgina Battiscombe, *Christina Rossetti: A Divided Life* (1981); Lona Mosk Packer, *Christina Rossetti* (Cambridge, 1963); Lona Mosk Packer, *The Rossetti–Macmillan Letters* (Berkeley and Los Angeles, 1963); Cecil Lang and Edgar Shannon (eds), *The Letters of Alfred, Lord Tennyson*, volume 2 (Oxford 1987).

Special incidents have required particular sources. My reliance on the text of Henry Jebb's novel *Out of the Depths: The Story of a Woman's Life* (1859) will be obvious enough. There is a hostile review of it in *Universal Review*, volume 2 (1859), pages 90–110. The story bears comparison with the account of a Magdalen in Samuel Warren's *Diary of a Late Physician* (1838 onwards). Less obvious will be my reliance in the references to Byron on Louis Crompton's great book *Byron and Greek Love* (1985) and on the account of Byron given by Vicary Gibbs in *Complete Peerage*, volume 2 (1912). The account of Alexander's discussion with Lord Stanley of the prospects of electoral reform is taken from the diary of the fifteenth Earl of Derby, dated 19 June 1864, in Liverpool Record Office. The value of the foreign policy articles in *Macmillan's Magazine* is attested in Lord Cowley's letter of 4 January 1861 to Lord John Russell, in the Russell papers at the Public Record Office (PRO 30/22/56).

On Victorian literary life I have been guided by Frederick Harrison, *The Choice of Books* (1887) and John Gross's *The Rise and Fall of the Man of Letters* (1969).

Chapter 5: The Double Family

The Selected Letters of Malcolm Kingsley Macmillan (1893) are the chief guide to his personality. A detailed account of his disappearance and of subsequent searches is given by Arthur Hardinge's letter to Sir William White dated 13 July 1889 and forwarded to Lord Salisbury, in the Public Record Office, FO 78/4204. References to the Albanian shepherds are contained in a letter to Sir William White from Maurice Macmillan and Norman MacLehose dated 5 August 1889, and in George Macmillan's letters to Sir Thomas Sanderson of 15 August 1889 and to Sir Francis Hyde Villiers of 18 September 1889, in FO 78/4224, which also contains Salisbury's minute and Sanderson's letter of 28 September 1889 to George Macmillan, both quoted in the text. There are other references to the affair in FO 78/4200, 4206 and 4209. Lord Dufferin's assessment of Sultan Abdul Hamid is in his despatch 679 of 14 December 1883 in FO 78/3514.

There are many references to John Macmillan, or correspondence with him, in the papers of successive Archbishops of Canterbury deposited in Lambeth Palace Library. Randall Davidson's letter of 22 May 1916 quoted in the text is in volume 9 of his papers. I have drawn heavily on volumes 120 and 126 of Cosmo Lang's papers, and on volume 33 of William Temple's. Bishop Mandell Creighton's accusation about a Romanist compositor imposing on Macmillan is contained in a letter of 1894 in the papers of Edward White Benson, Archbishop of Canterbury, volume 129 (also in Lambeth Palace Library).

On Victorian schooling the Dowager Marchioness of Dufferin and Ava's memoir *My Russian and Turkish Journals* (1916) has been consulted, together with Lord Ernle's *Whippingham to Westminster* (1938), A.G. Bradley, A.C. Champneys and J.W. Baines's *History of Marlborough College* (1893), Arthur Hugh Mead's history of St Paul's School, *A Miraculous Draught of Fishes* (1990) and Richard Usborne's disjointed *A Century of Summerfields* (1964).

On literary life in the epoch covered by this chapter I have consulted, among others, Sir Newman Flower's edition of the *Journals of Arnold Bennett* (1932); Royal Gettmann's study of George Bentley, *A Victorian*

Publisher (Cambridge, 1960); the unpublished diary of Maurice Hewlett (Add. ms 41075); Samuel Hynes, *The Edwardian Turn of Mind* (1968) and *Edwardian Occasions* (1972); Charles Morgan's *The House of Macmillan* (1942); Simon Nowell–Smith's *Letters to Macmillan* (1967); John St John's *William Heinemann: A Century of Publishing 1890–1990* (1990); and the obituaries of Mowbray Morris and Charles Whibley in *Blackwood's Magazine*, volumes 190 (1911) and 227 (1930). Some revealing letters of 1893–6 from Morris are in volume 58 of the papers of H.A.L. Fisher at the Bodleian Library, Oxford, where the catalogue misidentifies them as from Maurice Macmillan.

Among biographies and autobiographies of Macmillan associates which I have consulted are Maud Howe Elliott's *My Cousin F. Marion Crawford* (1934); Lovat Dickson's memoirs *The House of Words* (1963), Joan Evans's biography of her half-brother Sir Arthur Evans, *Time and Chance* (1943); the second and third volumes of Leon Edel's edition of the *Letters of Henry James* (1978–81); Stephen Gwynn's *Experiences of a Literary Man* (1926); the first two volumes of Herbert Hensley Henson's *Retrospect of an Unimportant Life* (1942–3); Garry O'Connor's *Sean O'Casey* (1988); Sir Rupert Hart–Davis's masterly *Hugh Walpole: A Biography* (1952); Norman and Jeanne Mackenzie's biography of H.G. Wells, *The Time Traveller* (1973) together with David C. Smith's *H.G. Wells, Desperately Mortal* (1986); and Richard Ellman's *Oscar Wilde* (1987).

A commercial perspective on censorship in this period is given by two excellent sources: the chapter entitled 'Taste, Morality and the Law: The Distributor's Lot' in the history of W.H. Smith, Charles Wilson's *First with the News* (1985); and the chapter entitled 'The Problem of "Evil Literature"' in L.M. Cullen's *Eason & Son: A History* (Dublin, 1989).

Other sources include Caroline Jebb, *Life and Letters of Sir Richard Claverhouse Jebb* (1907); Lord Kinross's *Society Racket* (1933); Sir John Squire's tribute to Sir Frederick Macmillan reprinted in the *Bookseller* of 4 June 1936; and *The Society of Dilettanti, its Regalia and Pictures*, described by Sir Cecil Harcourt–Smith and George Macmillan (1932).

Chapter 6: Nellie and Harold

Two major sources for this chapter are the first volume of Harold Macmillan's autobiography, *Winds of Change* (1966), and the first volume of Alistair Horne's official biography, *Macmillan 1894–1956* (1988). I have also drawn on the text of Harold Macmillan's conversation with Nigel Lawson and others published in the *Listener* of 8 September 1966. A little-known account of Edwardian England by Harold is his foreword to John Goodall's *An Edwardian Summer* (1976).

On Maurice's education, see Add. MS 55171 and George Parkin's *Edward Thring, Headmaster of Uppingham School: Life, Diary and Letters*, published in two volumes by Macmillan in 1898. Sources on Nellie's early years include contemporary newspapers from southern Indiana, Charles Blanchard's *History of Owen County* (Owen County, 1884), Dixie Klein's *Fact and Folklore of Owen County* (Bloomington, 1982) and Gayle Thornbrough's edition of *The Diary of Calvin Fletcher*, 9 volumes (Indianapolis, 1972–83).

Cosmo Lang's memorandum of December 1939 entitled 'Mr Arthur Macmillan', together with accompanying correspondence about Arthur's marriage and wish for ordination, is in volume 178 of the Lang papers at Lambeth Palace Library. William Temple's correspondence of 1944 with and about Arthur is in volume 33 of his papers deposited in the same collection.

For accounts of Lord and Lady Arthur Russell, see the diary of Lord Derby for 4 April 1892 and 9 March 1893 (at Liverpool Record Office); *The Times*, 6 April 1892 and 2 March 1910; and the first volume of Quentin Bell's biography *Virginia Woolf* (1972).

My development of ideas about Harold Macmillan's False Self is a personal interpretation of the writings of Donald Winnicott, which are most accessibly summarised in Adam Phillips's *Winnicott* (1988). Jonathan Gathorne–Hardy's *The Rise and Fall of the British Nanny* (1972) is the source for my quotation from Ellen Stevens and for other ideas. Paul Fussell's *The Great War and Modern Memory* (Oxford, 1975) and Samuel Hynes's cultural history *A War Imagined* (1990) are further influences.

Other sources include A.C. Benson's *Edwardian Excursions* (1981); Lord Boyd–Carpenter's *Way of Life* (1980); Lord Butler of Saffron Walden's *The Art of the Possible* (1971); Kenneth Rose, *The Later Cecils* (1975); William Purcell's *Fisher of Lambeth* (1969); Viscount Chandos, *Memoirs* (1962); Sir Mountstuart Grant–Duff, *Notes from a Diary 1896–1901* (1905); the Dowager Countess of Jersey's memoirs *Fifty One Years of Victorian Life* (1923) and her tribute to Nellie Macmillan in *The Times* of 29 October 1937; Sir Lawrence Jones's memoir of *A Victorian Boyhood* (1955); Robert Skidelsky's exemplary *John Maynard Keynes: Hopes Betrayed 1883–1920* (1983); Cecil King's *Diary 1970–1974* (1975); Duff Hart–Davis, *End of an Era: Letters and Journals of Sir Alan Lascelles 1887–1920* (1986); Sir Rupert Hart–Davis, *The Lyttleton Hart–Davis Letters*, volumes 1 (1978) and 4 (1982); J.A. Gere and John Sparrow's edition of *Geoffrey Madan's Notebooks* (1981), with a foreword by Harold Macmillan; Bernard Crick's biography of *George Orwell* (1980); Noel Stock's *Life of Ezra Pound* (1970); Owen Chadwick's *Michael Ramsay* (Oxford, 1990); Edith Sitwell's *Selected Letters* (1970), edited by John Lehmann and Derek Parker; the article 'Lord Stockton Remembered' by Lord Charteris of Amisfield printed in the *Eton College Chronicle* of 9 February 1987; Sir Charles Webster's obituary of Humphrey Sumner in *Proceedings of the British Academy*, volume 37 (1951); and Ronald Hyam's memoir of Sir Henry Willink in *Magdalene College Magazine and Record*, new series, volume 17 (1973).

I have consulted *Isis* and the *Oxford Magazine* for Harold's undergraduate years and have quoted from the diary of Lord Crookshank deposited in the Bodleian Library at Oxford.

Chapter 7: Dorothy and Harold

John Pearson's *Stags and Serpents: The House of Cavendish and the Dukes of Devonshire* (1983) is an amusing guide to the family history. On the character of Harty-Tarty see Lord Stalbridge to Lord Dufferin, 6 September 1887, in the Dufferin and Ava papers at the India Office Library, MSS Eur F 130/27B. Lord Derby's descriptions of the character of the Double Duchess and her husband Manchester are taken from Derby's diary, 16 September 1888 (the Duke) and 12 October 1888 (the Duchess) at Liverpool Record Office. Other similar references to the Duke are in the same diary, 11 August 1888 and 23 March 1890.

I have drawn on Lord Newton's *Lord Lansdowne* (1929) for my account of his lineage and character, together with Lord Dufferin's letter to Sir William Gregory, dated 19 February 1888, in the Dufferin and Ava papers already cited, MSS Eur F 130/29B. On the suppression of Zola's novels see Lord Northbrook to Lansdowne, 30 November 1888, and Lansdowne to Northbrook, 13 January 1889, India Office Library, MSS Eur D 558/11. Queen Victoria's letter of 2 June 1892 on the engagement of Evie Fitzmaurice and Victor Cavendish is in Eur D 558/1. For Lansdowne's reactions to the engagement see his letters to Sir Hubert Jerningham (3 June 1892), to Lord Reay (8 July 1892), to Moreton Frewen (11 July 1892) and to Sir James Lyall (9 August 1892) in D 558/14.

Other unpublished sources used in this chapter include the diaries of Harry Crookshank and of Lord Woolton (for 17 October 1940 and 30 March 1955), both deposited in the Bodleian Library, Oxford; the papers of Stanley Baldwin, of Lord Templewood and of Sir Charles Craven in the Vickers microfilm collection, all deposited in Cambridge University Library; the papers of the Great Western Railway and of Ramsay MacDonald in the Public Record Office; the papers of Sir Arthur Steel–Maitland in the Scottish Record Office at Edinburgh.

The three quotations from the diaries of Ramsay MacDonald (PRO 30/69/1753) are dated 18 May 1925, 8 January 1934 and 15 March 1935. As a condition of quoting them I am obliged to state that the diaries' contents were, in Ramsay MacDonald's words, 'meant as notes to guide and revive memory as regards happenings and must on no account be published as they are'.

Two volumes of diaries splendidly edited by Professor John Vincent have provided quotations and information for this chapter: *The Later Derby Diaries, Home Rule, Liberal Unionism and Aristocratic Life in Late Victorian England* (Bristol, 1981); and *The Crawford Papers: The*

Journals of David Lindsay, twenty-seventh Earl of Crawford and tenth Earl of Balcarres (Manchester, 1984).

Other quotations or information come from Martin Gilbert's biography of Lord Allen of Hurtwood, *Plough My Own Furrow* (1965); Michael and Eleanor Brock's invaluable edition of *H.H. Asquith: Letters to Venetia Stanley* (Oxford, 1982); W.H. Auden's *A Certain World* (1971); John Ramsden's edition of the political diaries of Lord Bayford, *Real Old Tory Politics* (1984); Sir Robert Rhodes James's *Bob Boothby* (1991); the diaries and letters of Lord Bridgeman edited by Philip Williamson as *The Modernisation of Conservative Politics* (1988); Lord Callaghan's memoirs, *Time and Chance* (1987); the edition by Sir Robert Rhodes James entitled *Chips: The Diaries of Sir Henry Channon* (1967); Martin Gilbert's three documentary volumes covering 1922–39 in the life of *Winston S. Churchill* (1979–82); Quentin Crewe's *Well, I Forget the Rest* (1991); the edition of Lord Davidson's papers compiled by Sir Robert Rhodes James entitled *Memoirs of a Conservative* (1969); Philip Ziegler's superb biography of *King Edward VIII* (1990); the second volume of Stephen Roskill's great biography of Lord Hankey, *Man of Secrets* (1972); Florence Hardy's *The Later Years of Thomas Hardy* (1930); the Marquess of Huntley's *Milestones* (1926); Grover Smith's edition of the *Letters of Aldous Huxley* (1969); Janet Aitken Kidd's *The Beaverbrook Girl* (1987); *The Feet of the Young Men, by 'Janitor'* (1928), a pseudonymous book written by J.G. Lockhart and Mary Lyttelton (Lady Craik); Tom Jones, *A Diary with Letters 1931–50* (1954) and *Whitehall Diary*, volume 2 (1969); the Countess of Longford's memoirs, *The Pebbled Shore* (1986); David Marquand's biography of *Ramsay MacDonald* (1977); Lord Mersey, *A Picture of Life 1872–1940* (1941); Daisy Princess of Pless, *From My Private Diary* (1931); Cecil Price's edition of *The Letters of Richard Brinsley Sheridan* (Oxford, 1966); Sir John Wheeler–Bennett's *Knaves, Fools and Heroes* (1974); Lord Bullock's obituary of Sir John Wheeler–Bennett in *Proceedings of the British Academy*, volume 65 (1979); and Esmé Wingfield–Stratford's *The Victorian Sunset* (1932).

Some ideas are drawn from the dossier 'Harold Macmillan' in *National Review*, volume 150 (1958); David Cannadine's *The Decline and Fall of the British Aristocracy* (1990); Maurice Cowling's brilliantly provocative account of British politics in the 1930s, *The Impact of Hitler* (Cambridge, 1975); Ronald Hyam's excellent *Empire and Sexuality* (Manchester, 1990); several of the essays in Richard Davenport-Hines (ed.), *Business in the Age of Depression and War* (1990); Keith Middlemas's *Politics in Industrial Society* (1979); and Oswald Nock's *History of the Great Western Railway 1923–1947* (1967).

An excellent impression of the life and responsibilities of a governor-general of Canada (albeit of an earlier epoch) is given in the wonderfully vivid collection of letters, *Dufferin–Carnarvon Correspondence 1874–1878* (Toronto, 1955), edited by C.W. de Kiewiet and F.H. Underhill.

Chapter 8: The Servant of Fame

The main sources for this chapter are Harold Macmillan's *The Blast of War 1939–45* (1967), his *War Diaries: Politics and War in the Mediterranean, January 1943 to May 1945* (1984) and two further volumes in his autobiography, *Tides of Fortune* (1969) and *Riding the Storm* (1971). Both volumes of Alistair Horne's biography have been consulted, together with other biographies by Sir Nigel Fisher, Emrys Hughes, George Hutchinson and Anthony Sampson. In addition the text of Sir Ian Trethowan's interview with Harold Macmillan, published in the *Listener* of 21 September 1967, has been quoted.

Harold Macmillan's letter of 29 November 1946 to Sir Orme Sargent is in PRO FO 371/52746. The quotations from the diary of Lord Woolton at the Bodleian Library, Oxford are from the entries dated 5 April and 22 December 1955.

I have also used Sir Arthur Bryant's version of Lord Alanbrooke's war diaries, *The Turn of the Tide* (1957); Leo Amery's diaries, *The Empire at Bay 1929–45* (1988) with a foreword by the first Lord Stockton; Hugo Vickers's *Cecil Beaton* (1985); A.J.P. Taylor's *Beaverbrook* (1972); Richard Cockett's edition of the letters of Lord Bracken to Lord Beaverbrook entitled *My Dear Max* (1990); the memoirs of Reginald Bevins, *The Greasy Pole* (1965); the edition by David Dilks of *The Diaries of Sir Alexander Cadogan 1938–1945* (1971); Lord Carrington's *Reflect on Things Past* (1988); Kevin Jefferys's edition of Lord Chuter-Ede's diaries, *Labour and the Wartime Coalition* (1987); Sir John Colville's diaries, *The Fringes of Power* (1985); Sir Colin Coote's *Editorial* (1965); Richard Crossman's article in the *Sunday Telegraph* of 9 February 1964; Janet Morgan's edition of *The Backbench Diaries of Richard Crossman* (1981); Ben Pimlott's edition of *The Political Diary of Hugh Dalton* (1986); the account of Basil, Marquess of Dufferin and Ava in Bevis Hillier's *Young Betjeman* (1988) together with the tributes by Frank Pakenham (afterwards Long Longford), Sir Cosmo Parkinson and Lord Birkenhead in *The Times* of 5, 6 and 10 April 1945; Lord Egremont's article 'My Uncle Charles: Memories of Life in the Grand Manner at Petworth' in the *Spectator* of 24 December 1965, and his memoir, *Wyndham and Children First* (1968); the two volumes of Sir Alec Cairncross's edition of *The Robert Hall Diaries* (1989–91); Peter Collier and David Horowitz's *The Kennedys: An American Drama* (New York, 1984); Cecil King's war diary, *With Malice Toward None* (1970); the incandescent diaries of the 1940s written by James Lees-Milne and published as *Prophesying Peace* (1977), *Caves of Ice* (1983) and *Midway on the Waves* (1985); the second volume of Kenneth Young's edition of *The Diaries of Sir Robert Bruce Lockhart* (1980); Sir George Mallaby's memoir, *From My Level* (1965); Lord Donoughue and G.W. Jones's *Herbert Morrison* (1973); Robert Murphy's *Diplomat among Warriors* (1964); Sir Harold Nicolson's *Diaries and Letters 1939–45* (1967); Edith Olivier's *Journals 1924–48* (1989); Simon Raven's memoir, *Shadows on*

the Grass (1982); Baroness Ravensdale's *In Many Rhythms* (1953); Sir
Evelyn Shuckburgh's diaries of 1951–56, *Descent to Suez* (1986); Lord
Swinton's *Sixty Years of Power* (1966); and Mark Amory's edition of *The
Letters of Evelyn Waugh* (1980).

Among more general sources I have used Angus McLaren's *History
of Contraception* (1990); Roland Barthes' *A Lover's Discourse* (1978);
Anthony Seldon's *Churchill's Indian Summer* (1981); and Jean-Charles
Sournia's *History of Alcoholism* (1990).

Among many sources on the repatriations of 1945 I have drawn on
the BBC2 television programme *A British Betrayal* broadcast in January
1991; Lord Bethell's *The Last Secret* (1974); Anthony Cowgill, Lord
Brimelow and C.J.P. Booker's *The Repatriations from Austria in 1945*
(1990); Matthew Barry Sullivan's account of German prisoners of war in
Britain, *Thresholds of Peace* (1979); Count Nikolai Tolstoy's *Victims of
Yalta* (1974), *Stalin's Secret War* (1981), his article 'The Klagenfurt
Conspiracy' printed in *Encounter* of May 1983, and *The Minister and
the Massacres* (1986, but suppressed). I have also quoted from the chapter
entitled 'The Most Nauseating Act' in Susan Crosland's biography *Tony
Crosland* (1982).

Chapter 9: The Prime Minister

Harold's bulky prime ministerial memoirs are a chief source for this chapter:
Riding the Storm 1956–1959 (1971); *Pointing the Way 1959–61* (1972);
and *At the End of the Day 1961–1963* (1973). These are supplemented by
Sir Harold Evans, *Downing Street Diary: The Macmillan Years 1957–1963*
(1981).

Unpublished sources include the diary entries of Lord Woolton for 6
April 1955 and 9 January 1957 (Bodleian Library, Oxford). I have culled
the Cabinet and Premier categories at the Public Record Office; the paper
'Leisure in Our Affluent Age', dated 23 December 1959, submitted by Lord
Eccles to Macmillan is in Prem 11/2950; Randolph Churchill's letter of 6
December 1958 to John Wyndham (quoted in the text) is in Prem 11/2293.
I have drawn upon the papers of Lord Butler of Saffron Walden deposited
at Trinity College, Cambridge. I have used particularly the following of
Butler's memoranda or *aide-mémoires*: undated (G32/98); 22 October
1957 (G31); 12 July 1958 (G32); 9 March 1960 (G35); 7 September
1960 (G36); 24 January, 1 November and 18 November 1962 (G38);
8 January and 7 March 1963 (G40); 23 September 1971 (G46). Among
letters to Butler I have quoted those of James Stuart, 13 December 1956
(G46); Paul Channon, 28 March 1963 (G46) and 18 October 1963 (G40);
and Lord Caldecote, 12 June 1963 (G46).

From Lord Avon's papers deposited at Birmingham University Library I have drawn on Anthony Eden to the Marquess of Salisbury, 28 December 1957, AP 23/60/14A; Lord Salisbury's letters to Eden dated 21 May 1957 (AP23/60/2), 7 September 1957 (AP23/60/9), 20 July 1958 (AP23/60/26A), 23 September 1959 (AP23/60/40B) and 18 March 1963 (AP23/60/102); the letter of Lord Hailes to Lord Avon of 14 February 1962; Viscount Lambton's letter of 2 March 1963 to Avon (AP 23/43/38); and the letter of Sir Robin Turton (now Lord Tranmire) to Avon dated 13 February 1963 (AP23/64/16).

Secondary biographical sources include Lord Alport's *The Sudden Assignment* (1965); Sir A.J. Ayer's memoirs, *More of My Life* (1984); Tony Benn's *Out of the Wilderness* (1987) and *Office without Power* (1988); Humphry Berkeley's *Crossing the Floor* (1972); Ann Gold's *Edward Boyle* (1991); Anthony Howard's biography of Lord Butler of Saffron Walden, *Rab* (1987); Maurice Collis's *Diaries 1949–1969* (1977); Julian Critchley's *Westminster Blues* (1985); Lord Cudlipp's *Walking on the Water* (1976); the accounts of Lord Dilhorne and Lord Kilmuir in R.F.V. Heuston's *Lives of the Lord Chancellors 1940–1970* (Oxford, 1987); Mark Amory's edition of *The Letters of Ann Fleming* (1985); Sir Douglas Dodds-Parker's *Political Eunuch* (1986); the biography of Lord Avon by Sir Robert Rhodes James, *Anthony Eden* (1986); Sir Nigel Fisher's *Iain Macleod* (1973); Denis Healey's *The Time of My Life* (1989); Sir Nicholas Henderson's *The Private Office* (1984); Sir David Hunt's *On the Spot* (1975); Lord Hailsham of St Marylebone's *A Sparrow's Flight* (1990); Christopher Hollis's *The Seven Ages* (1974); D.R. Thorpe's *Selwyn Lloyd* (1989); Lord Longford's *Five Lives* (1964); the six volumes (1978–84) of published correspondence between George Lyttelton and Sir Rupert Hart-Davis; Reginald Maudling's *Memoirs* (1978); Charles Ritchie's *Storm Signals* (1983); Norman Shrapnel's *The Performers* (1978); the fifth volume of Lucy Moorehead's edition of the *Freya Stark Letters* (1978); Lord Stewart of Fulham's memoirs, *Life and Labour* (1980); Lord Swinton's *Sixty Years of Power* (1966); Viscount Tonypandy's *George Thomas, Mr Speaker* (1985); Sir Roy Welensky's *4000 Days* (1964); Lord Wyatt of Weeford's *Confessions of an Optimist* (1985); and Lord Zuckerman's *Monkeys, Men and Missiles* (1988).

I have also used Lord Annan's *Our Age* (1990); Vernon Bogdanor and Lord Skidelsky's *The Age of Affluence 1951–1964* (1970); Russell Braddon's *Suez* (1973); Keith Kyle's *Suez* (1991); Sir Anthony Nutting's *No End of a Lesson: The Story of Suez* (1967); Lord Thomas of Swynnerton's *The Suez Affair* (1967); Henry Fairlie, 'On Resignation', *National Review*, volume 148 (1957) and 'From Walpole to Macmillan', *Encounter* (February 1961); Peter Hennessy's 'Harold Macmillan' in the *Economist* of 20 April 1991; R.K. Middlemas's *Power, Competition and the State* (1990); and sundry articles published in the *National Review* under the editorship of Lord Altrincham (John Grigg), including 'Organised Hypocrisy' in volume 148 (February 1957), and others attributable to Sir Edward Boyle.

Chapter 10: End-Games

Far more than in any other chapter my chief sources have been confidential interviews or other forms of private information. There are references to Maurice Macmillan in Rab Butler's *aide-mémoires* of 24 January 1962 and 7 March 1963 in the Butler papers, G38 and G40 (Trinity College Library, Cambridge), and in PRO Prem 11/2957 and Prem 11/3120. I have also quoted from the letter of Lord Chandos to Lord Avon of 14 October 1971, in the Avon papers, AP 23/17/172A (Birmingham University Library). From published records, I have drawn on an edited version of the text of Harold's interview with Sir Robin Day, which was printed in the *Listener* of 21 October 1976. Other secondary sources include the Duchess of Devonshire's diary in the *Spectator* of 5 July 1986; Martin Holme's *Political Pressure and Economic Policy in British Government 1970–1974* (1982); Anthony Howard and Richard West's *The Making of the Prime Minister* (1965); Jack Jones's *Union Man* (1986); Lord Jenkins of Hillhead's *European Diary 1977–1981* (1989); Celia Goodman's *Living with Koestler* (1985); Cecil King's *Diary 1970–74* (1975); Michael Parnell's *Eric Linklater* (1984); Lord Longford's *Diary of a Year* (1982); Ivan Rowan's profile of Maurice Macmillan in *Sunday Telegraph* of 23 April 1972; David Leigh's biography of Howard Marks, *High Times* (1984); interviews with Alexander Stockton by Ruth Gledhill in *The Times* of 25 May 1987 and by Nick Smurthwaite in *London Portrait* of May 1990; and David Marr's *Patrick White* (1991).

Photograph Acknowledgements

2, 3, 5, 6, 7, 9, 10, 11, 12, 13, 14, 15, 16, 17, 18, 19, 20, 21, 22, 23, 24, 25, 26, 27, 28 & 29: Hulton Picture Library
8: The Society of Dilettanti; photograph Courtauld Institute of Art
30: Times Newspapers

Index